WEBSPINNER

WEBSPINNER

*Songs, Stories, and Reflections of
Duncan Williamson, Scottish Traveller*

JOHN D. NILES

Line drawings by Helen Beccard Niles
Musical transcriptions by Alan Niles in consultation with Linda Williamson
Photographs by Leonard Yarensky and others

UNIVERSITY PRESS OF MISSISSIPPI / JACKSON

The University Press of Mississippi is the scholarly publishing agency of
the Mississippi Institutions of Higher Learning: Alcorn State University,
Delta State University, Jackson State University, Mississippi State University,
Mississippi University for Women, Mississippi Valley State University,
University of Mississippi, and University of Southern Mississippi.

www.upress.state.ms.us

The University Press of Mississippi is a member
of the Association of University Presses.

Library of Congress Cataloging-in-Publication Data

Names: Niles, John D., author. | Niles, Helen Louise Beccard, 1903–1994,
illustrator. | Niles, Alan, transcriber. | Williamson, Linda, 1949–
consultant. | Yarensky, Leonard, photographer.
Title: Webspinner : songs, stories, and reflections of Duncan Williamson,
Scottish Traveller / John D. Niles; line drawings by Helen Beccard
Niles, musical transcriptions by Alan Niles in consultation with Linda
Williamson, photographs by Leonard Yarensky and others.
Description: Jackson : University Press of Mississippi, 2022. | Includes
lists of songs, stories, and transcriptions, and a glossary of Scots
words and travellers' cant. | Includes bibliographical references and
index.
Identifiers: LCCN 2022025498 (print) | LCCN 2022025499 (ebook) | ISBN
9781496841575 (hardback) | ISBN 9781496841582 (trade paperback) | ISBN
9781496841599 (epub) | ISBN 9781496841605 (epub) | ISBN 9781496841612
(pdf) | ISBN 9781496841629 (pdf)
Subjects: LCSH: Williamson, Duncan, 1928–2007. | Scottish Travellers
(Nomadic people)—Folklore. | Storytellers—Scotland. |
Folklore—Scotland.
Classification: LCC GR144 .N56 2022 (print) | LCC GR144 (ebook) | DDC
398.209411—dc23/eng/20220624
LC record available at https://lccn.loc.gov/2022025498
LC ebook record available at https://lccn.loc.gov/2022025499

British Library Cataloging-in-Publication Data available

CONTENTS

ACKNOWLEDGMENTS

I wish to express my deep gratitude both to the institutions that advanced the research underlying the present book and to the many individuals who gave generously of their time to assist my fieldwork and its subsequent processing.

The initial task of mastering my Scottish field tapes was undertaken by the Sound Archives of the University of California, Berkeley. The recordings were subsequently digitized at the Digital Media Center of the University of Wisconsin–Madison. The bulk of my field collection, including notes, logs, and transcriptions as well as audio and video recordings, is housed at the Archive of Folk Culture of the American Folklife Center at the Library of Congress, Washington, DC. My thanks go to Joseph Hickerson and Michael Taft, former directors of the Archive of Folk Culture, and to the Archive's other staff for hosting me in Washington and for working to ensure that the collection is preserved under optimal conditions where it will be available to the public in futurity.

Extensive selections from my fieldwork as a whole, including both color and black-and-white photographs and documentation of festivals, games, landscapes, and the ecosystem within which cultural practices take place, are now available to the public via the searchable Scottish Voices website of the University of Wisconsin Digital Collections Center. I am grateful to members of the University Library's staff, including Peter C. Gorman, Vicki L. Tobias, Jesse Henderson, and Karen Rattende, for having embraced this multimedia project and for guiding it to its present state of completion. Kaitlin Fife, lecturer in film at Central Washington University, was my skilled project assistant. The Scottish Voices database both complements and extends the portrait of Duncan Williamson that is offered in the present book, presenting many recordings and photographs that could not be included here for lack of space.

I have a longstanding debt to the School of Scottish Studies, Edinburgh, now subsumed into the subject area of Celtic and Scottish Studies of the University of Edinburgh, for its encouragement of my fieldwork. Dr. Alan Bruford, the School's former archivist, pointed me in the direction of my research during a conference of the International Society for Folk Narrative Research held in Edinburgh in 1979. And I will not forget the warm welcome that Hamish Henderson—accompanied by his dog Sandy—offered me in 1984 in his fourth-floor walk-up office at 27 George Square. This was among other courtesies that have been offered to me over the years by the school's staff, including Professor John MacQueen, its former director, and Dr. Cathlin Macaulay, the current curator of the School of Scottish Studies Archive.

The Committee on Research of the University of California, Berkeley, provided financial support for the purchase of equipment and supplies and for the hiring of both graduate and undergraduate students to help me in the task of logging and transcribing field tapes. Margaret Binney, Rhea Gosset, Herbert Luthin, Margaret McPeake, and Rebecca Renfrew were among those wonderfully capable research assistants. I am likewise indebted to Anna Beck, a PhD candidate in the University of Wisconsin Department of Geography, for drafting the three maps included in this volume.

I have a particular debt to the University Research Expeditions Program (UREP) of the University of California for having sponsored four two-week group fieldwork expeditions in Scotland, two in the summer of 1986 and two in the summer of 1988, and to the volunteers who signed up for those projects. Those persons provided invaluable help by note-taking, taking still photographs, helping to catalog field tapes, running audio recorders or video cameras on occasion, and conducting certain interviews on their own. Just as importantly, those warmhearted individuals provided a receptive audience for the singers and storytellers whom we interviewed. Holly Tannen in particular, my field assistant in the summer of 1986, supervised a number of recording sessions while also enhancing the conviviality of our ceilidhs with her own music and singing. The names of all participants in these expeditions are provided at the head of the List of Transcriptions at the back of the book.

Two anonymous readers for the University Press of Mississippi offered a number of suggestions for the improvement of an earlier draft of the book. I am sincerely indebted to those persons for their astute and well-informed critiques and for helping me avoid errors and infelicities. For help with locating archival photographs and gaining permission for their use, I am grateful to Alison Diamond, the archivist at Argyll Estates, Inveraray, and, going back to the 1980s, to Hugh Gentleman and Mrs. L. Malcolm of the Secretary of State's Advisory Committee on Scotland's Travelling People, St Andrew's House, Edinburgh. Among others who offered encouragement, advice, or hospitality during my stays in Scotland were Sheila Douglas and her husband Andrew Douglas of Scone, Perthshire; Peter Hall of Aberdeen; Adam McNaughtan of Glasgow; Timothy Neat of Wormit, Fife; R. Ross Noble of the Highland Folk Museum, Kingussie; and Peter Shepheard of Kingskettle, Fife.

Other debts incurred in the course of this project are acknowledged toward the end of the following chapter. My greatest debt—one that I can never repay, though this book makes a gesture in that direction—is to Duncan Williamson himself, together with his wife Linda, for their unstinting generosity.

JOHN D. NILES
Boulder, Colorado, 2022

ABBREVIATIONS

♪♫	Flags a recording available at the Scottish Voices website: https://digital.library.wisc.edu/1711.dl/ScottishVoices
*	Flags an entry in the Commentary
§	Section
{ }	Marks words that are scarcely audible
ATU	Uther, Hans-Jörg. *The Types of International Folktales: A Classification and Bibliography, Based on the System of Antti Aarne and Stith Thompson*. 3 vols. Academia Scientiarum Fennica, 2004
BW	Betsy Whyte
Child	Child, Francis James, editor. *The English and Scottish Popular Ballads*. 5 vols. Boston: Houghton, Mifflin, 1882–1898
CN	Carole Newlands
DSL	*Dictionary of the Scots Language*, an online resource: https:/dsl.ac.uk
DW	Duncan Williamson
Greig-Duncan	Shuldham-Shaw, Patrick, and Emily B. Lyle, general editors. *The Greig-Duncan Folk Song Collection*. 8 vols. Aberdeen UP, 1981–2002.
HBN	Helen Beccard Niles

HT	Holly Tannen
Laws	Laws, G. Malcolm. *American Balladry from British Broadsides*. American Folklore Society, 1957.
LW	Linda Williamson
JN	John Niles
n., v., adj., pron., adv., interj., pl.	noun, verb, adjective, pronoun, adverb, interjection, plural (in lexical entries)
no.	number
OED	*The Oxford English Dictionary*, 2nd ed. Oxford University Press, 1989. Available online: https://www.oed.com/
Robinson	Robinson, Mairi, editor. *The Concise Scots Dictionary*. Aberdeen University Press, 1987 [first published 1985]
Roud	The Roud Folksong Index, maintained by the English Folk Dance and Song Society at the website of the Vaughan Williams Memorial Library, London: https://www.vwml.org/
SND	*Scottish National Dictionary*, an online resource: https://dsl.ac.uk
s.v.	sub verbo ("under the word")
TMSA	Traditional Music and Song Association of Scotland
Tobar an Dualchais	Tobar an Dualchais / Kist o Riches: a collaborative searchable online database that includes excerpts from audio recordings in the holdings of the School of Scottish Studies Archive, the University of Edinburgh: https://www.tobarandualchais.co.uk/
UREP	University of California Research Expeditions Program. Individual UREP participants are identified in the main text by their initials; their full names are provided in the List of Transcriptions.

LIST OF SONGS AND STORIES

1. SONGS

2. LEADING STORIES

WEBSPINNER

Chapter 1

WILLIAMSON AND THE TRAVELLERS

If friends of mine were to drop by and, to pass the time, we thought we would make up a list of geniuses that we had personally come to know, then my list would start with Duncan Williamson (1928–2007). Beyond any doubt, Williamson was the finest storyteller I have ever encountered. Other people who knew him and who heard him perform have had no hesitation in coming to a similar conclusion. By the time of his death in 2007, correspondingly, Williamson was widely regarded as the finest traditional storyteller in Scotland.

One of the great privileges of my life is that I was able to spend hundreds of hours with Williamson in a variety of settings during the mid-1980s, when he was in fine health and spirits and had only fairly recently come to be recognized by many as a stellar performer. During a series of visits to the United Kingdom from my home in Berkeley, California, I sought out a number of talented Scottish tradition bearers to record their songs, stories, and reflections on tape. This book is a selective record of the hours I spent with Williamson.

Almost the whole of the book—all of chapters 2 through 9—is Duncan's, not mine, for what it consists of is a set of faithful transcriptions of his spoken words, interspersed with songs and with occasional exchanges with other people who were present on these occasions. I have organized the transcriptions that make up the bulk of the book into a coherent thematic sequence, whether chapter by chapter or within each chapter. Only in chapters 1 and 10, as well as in the Commentary and other back matter, do I speak in my own voice at any length. What readers will therefore encounter here, as they survey the main part of the book, is a faithful record of the words of a single masterful storyteller as he reflects on his family background and upbringing, tells anecdotes based on his personal experiences while on the road and while making a living, and shares with his interlocutors an occasional song or story drawn from his deep well of memory.

My recordings were made not in the vacuum of a sound studio, nor in a concert venue (except on certain occasions), but rather in a series of relaxed, informal settings where Duncan was free to interact with his listeners from Scotland or abroad, some of whom were skilled singers, storytellers, or musicians in their own right. Most of the recordings were made in the comfort of one or another home, chiefly in Fife but also in the United States, in circumstances that ranged from the quiet and intimate to the boisterously convivial. As a result, there is no one monologic "Duncan's voice" on display here, but rather a variety of styles and linguistic registers, each one shaped to the contours of a fluid social setting. More information on this topic will be found in Appendix 1, "These Recordings and How They Were Made."

In Scotland, during informal sessions of this kind, periods of talk naturally alternate with the performance of songs and stories, often in an impromptu manner. I have made a point of imitating that flux of genres in my ordering of these transcriptions for publication. As much as is possible in the medium of print, with its constraints of word length and legibility, Williamson's performances are integrated into the social and intellectual matrix from which they arose, rather than being presented in isolation, while his comments or reflections are presented on an equal footing with his songs and stories. The book's design is thus unusual among publications of its kind, and it may possibly be unique.

Definitely unparalleled is almost all of the book's contents, for in choosing selections from my field collection that make for a coherent ensemble, I have tried to avoid duplicating material that is available elsewhere, whether in print or in audio publications. The result is a book that consists largely of reflections and anecdotes based on Williamson's personal experiences, told in a natural manner and transcribed faithfully. Correspondingly, the book reveals a great deal about Williamson's character and values as a man. The book not only shows how Williamson told stories, doing so often in an animated way in interactive social circumstances. It also reveals how he thought of his life in the world *through the medium of stories*, for they were his heart's blood, so to speak.

Just as importantly, for those readers whose interests extend to social history and ethnography, the book provides an insider's insights into what it was like for one person to grow up as a Traveller in the west of Scotland in the 1930s and 1940s, or to make one's living as the head of a Traveller family during the middle decades of the twentieth century. These aspects of Scottish social history may have vanished or may have been transformed practically beyond recognition, but they should not be forgotten.

My fieldwork was not initially undertaken as a study of one gifted individual, however, nor was it meant primarily as a contribution to Scottish social history. Rather, it was an attempt on my part to gain a more complete understanding of the art of oral, traditional storytelling itself: its social foundations, its cultural significance, its adaptability, its educational value in the home, the dynamics of

Figure 1.1 Duncan Williamson storytelling, Auchtermuchty, Fife, 1986. Photo by Leonard Yarensky.

its transmission from one generation to the next, and its interactive qualities in terms of performers and their audiences. I wanted to learn about this art not from books but from life. For me, that entailed going to a part of the world where this art was confidently practiced, in a language whose idioms I could readily understand. Scotland presented itself as an obvious choice for a North American of my background and education, especially given my special affection for Scottish balladry and my delight in the unvarnished, earthy language that is characteristic of much of the best Scots poetry and song.

One pragmatic aim of my research was to come to a better understanding of what changes are entailed when the words of an oral performer are transmuted into print, for I was not satisfied that this topic had been treated adequately in the prior scholarly literature. Too often, when I have come across studies based on a collector's interviews with a particular person, family, or group, the question has arisen in my mind: "But whose words *are* these, anyway: the performer's or the collector's? And why is this point not addressed more precisely? At what point, moreover, does editorial mediation merge into fraud?" Readers of the present book, by way of contrast, will be in no doubt whose words are whose.

Another of the aims that motivated my research, one that was more basic and more elusive, was to gain a clearer understanding of the role of oral art forms in shaping the mental world that human beings inhabit. I believed it was possible to see in some of the masterful traditional singers and storytellers of today a reflection of their counterparts in earlier eras, going back even to prehistoric times when all storytelling was oral storytelling. The potential significance of this topic is underscored by the observation that, as the prehistoric archaeologist Peter Boguki has observed, "Over 99 percent of the existence of the genus Homo to date occurred prior to the development of written records."[1] While the stories and storytellers of prehistoric times are obviously not available to us, something of their art can be recovered, I believe, through close attention to the literary records of ancient civilizations and of their medieval and early modern counterparts, as well as through close study of the living narrative traditions of various peoples inhabiting the world today.

Among the singers and storytellers whom I recorded in Scotland in the 1980s, Duncan Williamson stood out as someone in possession of a huge gift. He was also a person who never failed to gain the admiration of those who met him and who heard him spin out tale after tale relating to both the real world that we inhabit and imagined worlds of wonder and delight. It did not take me long to realize that I could not go wrong if I focused much of my attention on Duncan. At the same time, I continued to record many other talented singers and storytellers, including other Scottish Travellers, in part to provide points of comparison for my more sustained work with Williamson.

§1.1. INTRODUCING A REMARKABLE MAN

Duncan Williamson spent his childhood in poverty at the shore of Loch Fyne, Argyll, as a member of a denigrated social group, the Scottish Travellers, or tinkers.* He grew up in an environment where the shore was a constant presence, offering young people of his somewhat rebellious nature a refuge from the confining rigors of ordinary society. At the same time (as visitors to the western coastal regions of Scotland will be aware), the shore provides a luminous liminal zone poised between the land and the loch: the land, with the solidity of its hills, fields, woodlands, and settlements, and the loch, with the ephemera of its changing light effects, its abundant birdlife, and its "now you see them, now you don't" aquatic creatures, including both real seals and the seal folk of legends and the imagination. Williamson likewise grew up in an environment where the material poverty of the people of his parents' generation was offset by the richness of their oral culture, which was deeply inflected by Argyll's Gaelic heritage.* Since most of the Travellers of his parents' generation were unlettered (as was the norm for people of their social status going far back into

---

1. Boguki, *Origins of Human Society*, 1. Full publishing information about books and articles cited in the present study will be found in the Selected Bibliography at the end of the book.

the past), they relied on oral communication for almost all purposes, including entertainment and the informal education of their children.

Williamson absorbed additional elements of what eventually became his vast repertory of songs, stories, and other lore while in school in his native village of Furnace. He absorbed yet more of such lore throughout his life, after leaving home in his mid-teens to travel, work, or take up residence in various parts of Scotland, returning to Argyll periodically to visit his parents and other relatives while they were still alive. By the time that I first met him in 1979, shortly after he had turned fifty, he had become a standout performer at Scottish folk festivals and folk clubs thanks to his good voice, his deep well of knowledge about the Travellers and their way of life, and the ebullience that he brought with him almost everywhere he went. And by the time of his death in 2007, he had come to be recognized as one of the preeminent storytellers not just in Scotland but in the entire English-speaking world: some would ask, "Was he not the foremost of them all?"*

Like the gifted Scottish fiddler Aly Bain (b. 1946), from whose fingers music flowed as effortlessly as water from a Highland stream, Williamson became a master of his chosen medium chiefly by practicing it. In addition to being a person of strong individual character, he was also someone in whom the knowledge and capabilities of prior generations coalesced, doing so without fanfare or ostentation. This is what it means to be a tradition bearer, as distinct from those performers who project their own personality at the forefront of a stage. Of course, Williamson too was a consummate performer, but to my mind he was wholly unlike those well-educated storytellers who resemble stage actors in their style of delivery. Instead, he told stories because that was his calling—his inner, irresistible vocation—and because he wanted you as a listener to hear those stories, enjoy them, and learn from them. In this sense he was a natural-born teacher. Like other born teachers, he knew that there is no better means of education than stories that strike home and are heard with delight. So Williamson was *both* a tradition bearer and a consummate performer; and it is this conjunction of knowledge and talent that made him such a compelling verbal artist.

While functionally literate, having attended school as a child in the village of Furnace, Argyll, from age four to age fourteen for the legally required minimum of two hundred half days per annum, by the time that I first began recording him in 1984, Williamson had absorbed a huge repertory of songs and stories by ear, whether in his native Argyll or in other parts of Scotland. When one heard him tell a tale, one had the sense that what one was witnessing was far more than technical mastery of an oral art form. One was also aware of deep wells of knowledge that were fed, as manmade reservoirs of water are fed, by a fortunate conjunction of mountains, seas, winds, and human engineering.

To put this seemingly fanciful notion another way, Williamson was a *natural* performer in more than the ordinary sense, for ever since he was a boy growing up in a tent outside the village of Furnace, he had lived much of his life closer to nature than most of us will ever know.

Far from being a recluse who wished to escape into the quietude of nature, however, Williamson was an outgoing person who loved to join in a singsong, to open a tin of beer in the company of friends or acquaintances, and to "have a crack," as the Scots call it when they trade news, stories, and jokes with one another. More than that—turning into a virtue what in others might be a vice—he loved to be at the center of a group's attention, taking undisguised delight in the pleasure that he was able to bring to others through his seemingly limitless fund of songs and stories. Perhaps paradoxically, Williamson has also been called "something of a loner, a maverick," for he was a staunchly independent man who did not fit comfortably into the categories that other people might wish to impose on him.[2] If his personality had a dark side, as I believe it did, then in my own experience he never showed more than glimpses of it to others.

Williamson was not just a singer and storyteller. He was also a serious collector and critic of the songs and stories that he heard from others. At one stage of his life, influenced by the Folksong Revival, he had used a tape recorder himself to record the performances of other singers and musicians, though his tapes from the 1960s are now evidently lost.* More significantly in the long run, whatever he collected by word of mouth he stored in boxes in his head: "three thousand little boxes," as he liked to affirm when speaking of his mental thesaurus of stories alone. Correspondingly, when he heard a new version of a song or story, he had the ability to compare that version feature by feature with other versions that he had heard in the past. It is this ability that enabled him, at times, to gather scattered fragments from oral tradition and convert them into satisfying wholes.

I believe he was the best listener I have ever known. When another person was singing or telling a story in his presence, he gave that performer his unswerving attention. His encouragement of that man, woman, or child was invariably warm and enthusiastic, even if the person's performance had been less than brilliant. (Here I can speak from personal experience!) But if it was a good song or story, then no one enjoyed it more than he did, sometimes greeting it with whoops of delight. It was an easy step for him then to add that item to his personal repertory, as long as occasions arose when the person from whom he had heard it—"the owner," in his philosophy—was not around.

This matter of being a good listener is worth emphasis, for I believe it was the key element contributing to Williamson's brilliance as a storyteller. A good

2. Alan Bruford, "Duncan Williamson," *Tocher*, vol. 5, no. 33, 1979, p. 149.

voice helps a person have the confidence to stand out from the crowd; stamina can matter, and charisma never hurts; but a passion for songs and stories—a positive hunger to hear songs and stories, ones of the kind that one can live by—is the sine qua non for masters in an oral tradition.

§1.2. A TRAVELLER IN TWO WORLDS?

It is an understatement to say that Duncan Williamson became a celebrated storyteller during the last twenty years or so of his life. His reputation has not diminished in brightness since his death in the year 2007, and as far as I am aware, the Duncan Williamson chair—a real chair, not a metaphorical one—still holds a central place on the stage of the Scottish Storytelling Centre in Edinburgh.*

Correspondingly, at least three prior book-length studies have dealt substantially with Williamson's life and repertory. One of these is my own book *Homo Narrans: The Poetics and Anthropology of Oral Literature* (1999). This study draws selectively on my training as a medievalist and comparatist, as well as on the fieldwork that I undertook with Williamson and others in Scotland in the 1980s, to make a case for the foundational nature of oral narrative—and in particular, of the contrary to fact capabilities of storytelling—in shaping the human condition in a manner that is both pleasurable and saturated with meaning.

A book with related content is *Scottish Traveller Tales: Lives Shaped through Stories* (2002) by the American folklorist and storyteller Donald Braid. This account of the social conditions that make for a strong family tradition of storytelling is anchored in fieldwork that Braid undertook in Scotland chiefly during the late 1980s and early 1990s. The book draws on recordings the author made not just of Duncan Williamson but also of other members of Duncan's family or circle of friends, including Jimmy Williamson,* Duncan's oldest son from his first marriage, a fine singer and storyteller in his own right. Braid adopts the voice of an informed, sympathetic, academically well-trained outsider who probes how storytelling functions within Traveller communities, serving as a means of strengthening the bonds between individuals and their families and thus helping to maintain Traveller autonomy and identity in the face of pressures to assimilate into the settled society.

A study very different in style is David Campbell's pair of volumes *A Traveller in Two Worlds* (2011–2012). As someone who became a professional storyteller himself in the course of his life, Campbell writes of his complex and sometimes turbulent friendship with Williamson during the 1990s and later years. The collaborative relationship of these two men extended to Linda Williamson,* Duncan's American-born second wife, during a period when all three of them were active in the Scottish storytelling scene. The first of Campbell's volumes focuses on Duncan Williamson's experiences during his earlier life, while the second volume tells of Duncan's later life while also devoting close attention to Linda Williamson as a fascinating individual herself. David Campbell generously stepped in to help to promote Duncan's career as a storyteller in the schools after Linda's partnership with Duncan had broken off, for Linda and Duncan separated in the mid-1990s after a period of increasing strain in their marriage.

Campbell's and Braid's books make for instructive complements to the present one, as I hope is true in reverse, as well. I have taken care to see that there is very little overlap between our respective publications, though a limited amount of duplication of songs, stories, or personal reflections is inevitable and is indeed welcome. In those relatively few instances where overlap occurs, specialists may be interested in tracking down the parallels as evidence for the workings of variation: the soul of a vibrant oral tradition.[3] Moreover, Campbell's perspective as a native of Scotland and an active storyteller himself provides a welcome contrast to my own point of view as a North American university professor, now retired, whose visits to Scotland have necessarily been of finite duration. If Campbell and I could sit down together today, however—after complimenting him on his frank and openhearted tribute to Duncan—I would want to discuss his choice of a book title.

In my own view, to speak of Duncan Williamson as a "Traveller in two worlds" has only limited explanatory power when one considers the trajectory of his life as a whole. Perhaps a complementary criticism could be made of the tendency of certain writers to focus on Williamson and other Travellers as if they were inhabitants of a single closed world, that of their traditional cultural heritage; but it is the notion of some kind of existential binarism that I wish to address here. While Williamson himself may sometimes have thought in binary terms when contemplating the course of his life,[4] it was his habit in my interviews to make a distinction between the travelling people of Scotland as a collectivity and his own personal identity, customarily speaking of the culture of "the travelling folk" in terms of "they" and the past. This distinction can clearly be seen, for example, when he affirms that "they had their own tradition, and they lived in their little world, apart from the world outside" (see §7.1 below). By his birthright, he himself was one of that relatively isolated

---

3. In addition, variant recordings of a number of Williamson's songs are available in Scottish Voices, providing evidence for the dual factors of freedom and relative stability that are characteristic of living oral traditions.

4. See, for example, Williamson's comments to the effect "I've been to both sides of the street," as quoted by Braid, Scottish Traveller Tales, 44. Similarly, Campbell, Traveller in Two Worlds, 1.13 writes of Williamson giving his approval to the working title A Traveller in Two Worlds when it was first floated to him.

ethnic group, which he associated especially with his parents' and grandparents' generations; but he also looked upon that group with the eyes of an outsider who was a participant in a much larger and more cosmopolitan society. It is largely due to the conjunction of these two perspectives—that of the insider and that of the outsider—that he became such an outstanding communicator about Traveller lifeways during his later years.

To a person like me, having lived most of my life in the San Francisco Bay Area, Campbell's title phrase "two worlds" calls straight to mind the figure of Ishi (*ca.* 1861–1916), the Yahi Indian who grew into adulthood in a remote part of Northern California entirely on his own, in hiding, before he was "discovered" by chance in 1911 and was brought to San Francisco, where he lived out the relatively short remainder of his life. This story is told in Isidore Kroeber's haunting study *Ishi in Two Worlds*, a book whose title is suggestive of a drama in two acts separated by a rupture. That same language of two worlds, however, applies less forcefully to Williamson, a man who inhabited with remarkable fluency the multiple social worlds that he encountered, whether as a child in his homeland of Argyll or in those parts of Scotland where he travelled or resided as an adult. Williamson's emergence on the Scottish "folk" scene of the 1960s and 1970s could not by any means be mistaken for that of a Yahi emerging from the wilds.

Moreover, Williamson maintained close ties with some highly educated people during much of his adult life. These relationships began in 1958, when the poet and folk music enthusiast Helen Fullerton, later to be appointed lecturer at Glasgow University, called on Duncan's aged parents at the woodsman's hut where they were then living on the grounds of Inveraray Castle, Argyll.* Fullerton wished in particular to tape-record Duncan's mother Betsy, who was known for her fine diddling, or mouth music. Subsequently, in May 1967, Fullerton's friend, the Glasgow-based folksong collector George McIntyre, recorded certain of Duncan's songs, whether as wholes or fragments, both in Inveraray and, later that same year, in Fife. These archival tapes, as far as I know, are the earliest extant recordings of Duncan's voice.[5]

The fieldwork that Fullerton and MacIntyre undertook with members of the Williamson family during the period from 1958 to circa 1974 sparked Duncan's interest in the Scottish Folksong Revival,* which was then in its heyday. His encounters with well-educated non-Travellers sharpened his awareness that his own Traveller family, though subject to being stigmatized and ostracized by others, could lay claim to a special heritage. Through ensuing encounters with people active in either the Folksong Revival of the 1960s and 1970s or the

---

5. Fourteen tracks from McIntyre's 1967 recording sessions can be heard via Tobar an Dualchais by use of that website's online search engine. They provide valuable points of comparison with later recordings by other collectors.

Storytelling Revival of subsequent decades, Williamson gained esteem as an authoritative interpreter of Traveller traditions.

In this regard Williamson was not unlike the great Aberdeenshire ballad singer Jeannie Robertson.* After having spent much of her life in relative obscurity except among other Travellers, Robertson was "discovered" in 1953 by the poet and scholar Hamish Henderson.* Before long, thanks largely to Henderson's encouragement and sponsorship, she became the most prominent of the singers being introduced to the public at this time as custodians of a priceless Scottish oral heritage, one that was expressive of the genius of ordinary people rather than an educated elite.

In this way and in others, Henderson took to the next level a program of recovery that had been initiated by Alan Lomax,* the American folksong collector who did more than anyone else to promote appreciation of the richness of vernacular singing traditions not just in his native country but in other parts of the world as well. Those other lands included Scotland, where Lomax and Henderson collaborated in a program of fieldwork in 1951. In turn, Henderson became a leading light of the Scottish Folksong Revival, embarking on an ambitious program of fieldwork of his own and providing inspiration for the Edinburgh Peoples Festival (founded in 1951), the Blairgowrie Festival (founded by Peter Shepheard and other members of the TMSA in 1966), and other events where traditional singers of sundry backgrounds found an enthusiastic audience. Concurrently, Henderson spearheaded a successful effort to establish the School of Scottish Studies,* with its invaluable Archive, as an academic unit of the University of Edinburgh.

Thanks in part to Henderson's charismatic efforts to promote a wider appreciation of the role of nonelitist culture in Scotland's cultural identity, a number of singers of Scottish Traveller heritage or affiliation emerged from obscurity during the 1950s and 1960s to become known to the public through their appearances at festivals and folk clubs. One of these was the Aberdeenshire street singer and man of the roads Jimmy MacBeath.* Another was Davie Stewart,* a street singer and box player (or accordionist) who lived in and around Aberdeen, Dundee, and Glasgow. Two female singers of Traveller heritage who were "discovered" during this same period were Lucy Stewart* of Fetterangus, Aberdeen, and Jane Turriff* of Fetterangus and, later, Mintlaw, Aberdeen, two leading representatives of the domestic singing traditions of the northeast of Scotland.

The traditional singer whose role in the Folksong Revival was like that of no other save Jeannie Robertson alone, however, was Belle Stewart.* As longtime residents of the region of Blairgowrie, Perthshire, Belle and her family were active participants in the musical festivities associated with the annual season of berry picking in the fields round about Blair.[6] In 1955 her family came to the attention of the journalist Maurice Fleming, a pioneering folksong collector who introduced the Stewarts to Henderson.[7] Performing alongside her husband Alex Stewart, who was a fine piper and a dynamic showman, and their daughters, the singers Sheila Stewart and Cathie Higgins, Belle was the leading member of the group that became known to many as "The Stewarts of Blair." When Ewan MacColl and Peggy Seeger*—two singer-songwriters of commanding stature in the Folksong Revival—compiled their two major anthologies *Travellers' Songs from England and Scotland* (1977) and *Till Doomsday in the Afternoon* (1986), it was Belle's repertory of songs and other lore that they drew on more copiously than any other source.

My point in calling attention to these well-known developments is that they paved the way for Williamson's emergence on the Scottish "folk" scene in the 1960s, 1970s, and later years. As far as I am aware, this began with his participation, beginning in 1967, in the Kinross Festival and the Blairgowrie Festival, and it continued at such other venues as the Glasgow Folk and Ballad Club and the People's Festival in Edinburgh. While participating in such events as these, he would have heard or met firsthand many of the leading figures in the Folksong Revival, sharing the stage with some of them on occasion. These exchanges of creative energy had a substantial impact on his life and career. While Williamson never claimed to be a standout vocalist on the concert stage, he sang in a no-frills style that conveyed impressive authority, while his firsthand knowledge of the Scottish Travellers' traditional way of life was second to none on the Folk Revival scene.

In view of his lifetime of interactions among people of different classes and backgrounds, then, I am tempted to speak of Duncan Williamson as a sojourner not in two worlds, but simply in *the* world, the same large one that we all inhabit. This is not in the least to minimize the formative impact of Williamson's heritage as one of Scotland's travelling people. Far from it! For this element was crucial to his identity, as he and all who knew him were aware. His repertory of songs and stories remained grounded in the world of his Argyllshire childhood, whatever other influences he absorbed in later years. Much the same can be said of his confident, everyday Scots speech, whose grammar and idioms differ markedly from those of standard English.

Significantly, Williamson's worldview remained fundamentally that of a Traveller. What this meant in practice is that he made a habit of living from day to day, always poised to adapt to new circumstances while remaining attuned to

6. Henderson, "Folk-Song and Music," gives a lively account of the scene in and around Blairgowrie during these summer seasons.

7. See *Songs and Ballads from Perthshire*, a CD edited by Fleming in the Scottish Tradition series produced by the School of Scottish Studies. The album comprises music and songs that Fleming collected chiefly from Travellers, including Belle Stewart and her daughter Sheila.

the character and exigencies of his physical environment. What this also meant is that he valued companionship and conviviality above almost all else that life had to offer. While always attentive to economic necessities, he had scarcely a thought for the accumulation of material wealth. Other ingrained attitudes of his, as well, were consistent with what sociologists have found to be typical of the Scottish Travellers as a group. These attitudes included the high value he set on having and raising children; the low value he ascribed to their formal education apart from basic instruction in reading and writing; his resistance to institutionalizing or otherwise quarantining the elderly, the infirm, or the mentally impaired; and his core concept of marriage as an unconditional act of personal commitment rather than as a legal arrangement sanctioned by church and state.[8]

What I would still maintain is that Williamson was never *only* a Traveller. Even while a child, living in his family's winter tent in woods adjoining the village of Furnace, he rubbed shoulders with the children of settled families during much of the year, whether learning lessons beside them in the classroom or playing shinty or other games after school. From age fourteen onward, as he made his own way in the world by picking up work here and there, he rarely neglected opportunities to socialize with the next compatible person he met. These interactions with people from all walks of life, as well as from many different regions of Scotland, had an indelible influence on his repertory of stories and songs, for he was quick to absorb influences from all quarters. Moreover, as a person with basic formal education, he was perfectly capable of lifting what he wanted from books. Still, I believe he was speaking the truth when he once remarked to me that he had no use for books unless they were his own: that is, unless they were the ones that certain publishing houses brought out on the basis of Linda Williamson's recordings of his voice. The advances and royalties from those collaborative publications helped to float the family's finances, while Linda often made copies of the Williamsons' books, suitably inscribed in his somewhat wobbly hand,[9] available for purchase at events where Duncan was a featured performer.

---

8. On these aspects of Travellers' worldview, see Rehfisch and Rehfisch, "Scottish Travellers or Tinkers." The authors speak of this worldview as one that was confidently espoused, and they argue that it has been an essential element in the survival of the group over time.

9. The wobbly writing hand was not a sign of semiliteracy; it resulted from an injury that Duncan suffered while in his teens. See Figure 6.3 and the corresponding discussion at the end of §6.12.

§1.3. THE SCOTTISH TRAVELLERS AND THEIR
TRADITIONAL WAY OF LIFE

Williamson was a Traveller, then, although his identity was also shaped by his interactions with a wide range of settled people from his early years onward. Since most of his songs, stories, and reflections have to do with the traditional way of life of the Scottish travelling people as Williamson either experienced it firsthand or knew of it from the stories that he heard in his childhood, some preliminary words on that topic might be welcome here. In addition, readers may welcome some brief remarks on how this book relates to other books written by (or dictated by) Travellers themselves, especially since this book's Commentary draws on those sources to set Williamson's personal experiences and his repertory of songs and stories within a broader horizon.

Gypsies—also known as Romani or Roma—and Scottish Travellers* constitute two recognized ethnic minorities in Britain, while Ireland's Travellers* constitute a third minority of a comparable type. Each of these marginalized groups has its own traditions and culture going back at least several centuries. While the origins of the Scottish Travellers are lost in the past and conceivably extend back into prehistory, the arrival of Romani as migrants to Britain can be dated to the late fifteenth century. Since that time there has been some intermarriage between these two groups, while other sorts of interchange can be identified as well. Certain words or phrases in Travellers' cant, for example, such as the word *gadgie* meaning "man" or originally "horseman," are of Romani origin. But there are significant differences between the two groups other than ethnic ones. In prior centuries, Scottish Travellers tended to move from place to place on foot, often using a pushcart, pram, or donkey-drawn barrow to transport a few lightweight possessions rather than relying on heavy horse-drawn wagons that were literally houses on wheels, as the Romani did. Vehicles of that last type, often stylishly painted, may have been well suited to the highways and byways of southern England and the Continent but were scarcely practical conveyances in those parts of Scotland where passage overland from point to point was almost impossible except by footpaths or by the old drove roads by which cattle were formerly driven to market.

While, traditionally, the rhythms of the calendar year have shaped human activities in all times and places, they had a particular impact on those Scottish men and women who lived on the land in former days, travelling light during the summer while constructing a more capacious shelter, or living in rented houses, during the long, dark winter months. This was a practical way of life in the more northerly parts of Britain before the advent of steam power, petrol, conurbations, high-rises, and motorways. At least until the early 1940s, when open-air fires were banned at night in keeping with wartime blackout regulations, Scottish Travellers were able to live seminomadic lives in this manner, hawking handcrafted items from door to door; mending tinware, wicker ware, and ceramics; sharpening knives; cutting hay; engaging in other seasonal labor such as thinning turnips, lifting potatoes, and picking berries; and otherwise making valued contributions to the economy of rural areas. As itinerant craftsmen, peddlers, and seasonal farmworkers, Travellers often met with a cordial welcome, especially among rural householders who had met them before and knew them by name. At the same time, as internal strangers* in their own society, Travellers were also deeply mistrusted by many, even to the point of being despised by some with a vehemence that is hard for outsiders to comprehend.

These seasonal rhythms provide the framework for the justly celebrated book *The Yellow on the Broom* (1979) by Betsy Whyte,* an autobiographical account of the author's early years. Betsy Whyte (also known as Bessie) was born in Perthshire in 1919, nine years before Duncan Williamson was born in Argyll. Her way of life during her childhood years was much like his, with the difference that her family lived for most of the year in rented lodgings in one or another town in east central Scotland, while Duncan's family lived in tents on the west coast of Scotland, a region with a more distinct Gaelic-speaking heritage. Betsy and her husband Bryce became fast friends of Duncan and Linda Williamson after the four of them met in the 1970s in the course of Linda's musicological fieldwork. Betsy was a woman blessed with razor-sharp intelligence as well as a keen memory, and she writes about her experiences during childhood with both psychological insight and an ethnologist's precision. Her memoir became an icon of the Storytelling Revival, many of whose participants had a deep appreciation for the contributions of Travellers and Romani to the oral cultures of Britain and other parts of the world. A sequel to this publication was Whyte's 1990 book *Red Rowans and Wild Honey*, which carries the story of her childhood forward into her adolescence and the early years of her marriage.

In *The Yellow on the Broom*, Betsy Whyte recalls the restless anticipation with which, when a child, she looked forward to the time each spring when the bushes of yellow broom that flourish on Scottish hillsides would burst forth in a profusion of blossoms. This was a sign that Traveller families too, including her own, would soon be breaking out of the confines of their winter quarters to take to the road for the summer months. Long summer days afforded enough hours not just for seasonal labors, an essential source of income, but also for long periods of leisure, with their opportunities to meet with friends or relatives whom they might not have seen since the year before. There would be time to exchange news, to play and flirt and court, to make a bit of mischief perhaps, to obtain fresh berries or other seasonal produce, and to get fresh milk from a farm or draw drinking water from a well. There was time too for an occasional ceilidh,* where instrumental music, song, and stories might continue long into the night to the accompaniment of cups of tea and often, for the adults, stronger refreshments.

Whyte's memoir gives its readers a vicarious sense of what it meant to be a girl growing up as a Traveller in the early decades of the twentieth century. Since it is just one person's story, it is best read in conjunction with books providing other perspectives on the Travellers' way of life. Fortunately, other writers of Traveller heritage have told their life stories in recent years, whether writing them themselves or completing them in collaboration with others; and as a sage observer has remarked, "The best resources available for studying Traveller tradition are the Travellers themselves."[10]

A noteworthy achievement along such lines is Roger Leitch's *The Book of Sandy Stewart* (1988), a self-portrait of a Scottish Traveller who was born in 1920 in the town of Kircaldy, Fife. Based on tape recordings made between 1981 and 1983 by Leitch, a scholar affiliated with the School of Scottish Studies, Edinburgh, the book is expertly annotated and is a linguistically precise record of Stewart's idiolect. In the introduction to his book, Leitch provides an informed overview of the Travellers' traditional way of life while also discussing the human dynamics by which a collaborative work of oral autobiography is made.

A more narrowly focused publication is *The Horsieman: Memories of a Traveller 1928–1958*. This is Duncan Williamson's oral memoir, as told to Linda Williamson, of his years on the road from the time of his marriage at the age of nineteen to his first wife, Jeannie Townsley, who died of a weak heart in 1958, to the time when, after her death, he sold his horse and cart and bought his first motor vehicle. This is just one of a number of books that Duncan and Linda Williamson produced on the basis of her recordings of his stories and reminiscences. While those other books are collections of folktales, some of which are set in a wonderland of the imagination, this one is based in the real landscape of Scotland and on Duncan's personal experiences at a time before the motorcar replaced the horse cart, donkey cart, or handbarrow as the Scottish Travellers' chief conveyance while on the road.

More flamboyant in its literary ambitions is the 1988 book *Exodus to Alford*, by the Aberdeenshire Traveller Stanley Robertson.* This experimental synthesis of autobiography and storytelling is accompanied by visionary illustrations by the artist Simon Fraser. While the inset stories that comprise the main part of Robertson's book are composed in Scots dialect to provide a semblance of actual speech, the "framing" parts of the book are written in standard English. In his choice of the title *Exodus to Alford*, Robertson plays off the notion that the journey (the "pilgrimage") that his own Traveller family made in the

10. Douglas, "Narrative in Traveller Scotland," 55.

summer of 1946 from the city of Aberdeen to the village of Alford, located between the rivers Don and Dee in the fertile northeast region that Robertson liked to call "little Mesopotamia," offered a modern parallel to the biblical story of the exodus of Moses and the Jews from bondage in Egypt to a promised land of milk and honey. Robertson was a self-taught scholar. For three years, toward the end of his life, he was employed as a key worker on a project having to do with Scottish Traveller traditions sponsored by the Elphinstone Institute, a leading center for the study of ethnology, folklore, and ethnomusicology at the University of Aberdeen. Correspondingly, in 2008, the University of Aberdeen awarded him an honorary degree.

Complementing the books just mentioned is a cluster of publications dating from the period 2002–2011. Noteworthy among these is *Last of the Tinsmiths: The Life of Willie MacPhee* (2006), by the Perthshire singer and collector Sheila Douglas.* Douglas was a noted singer herself, as well as being a staunch promoter of the Folksong Revival and the Storytelling Revival, while Willie MacPhee* was well known among the Scottish Travellers as an outstanding piper and storyteller. Since MacPhee and Williamson were close friends, one is not surprised to find some overlap in the repertories of these two men. Another valuable witness to Traveller lifeways is the 2006 book *Queen amang the Heather: The Life of Belle Stewart.* This biographical tribute was written by Belle's daughter Sheila Stewart,* whose own autobiography, *A Traveller's Life* (2011), is a forthright and gritty account of her childhood and her experiences on the "folk" scene. Somewhat more novelistic in style are three autobiographical books by Jess Smith,* a popular author of Traveller background: *Jessie's Journey* (2002), *Tales from the Tent* (2008), and *Tears for a Tinker* (2009). This trilogy bears comparison with Betsy Whyte's pair of memoirs for its sympathetic account of the older way of life of travelling people of Scotland as seen from a female perspective.

Taken together, the publications just cited are important complements to the present one, for they provide insights into the travelling way of life as seen from several different perspectives: male and female, younger and older, east coast and west coast. They confirm that when Duncan Williamson speaks of his personal life, he is giving voice to experiences and attitudes that are deeply entrenched in Traveller culture as a whole.

None of these books came out of a vacuum. Looking back seventy-five years or so, and leaving aside the work of nineteenth- and early twentieth-century folksong collectors,[11] the single most important impetus for most of them was the invention of the portable reel-to-reel tape recorder.* This development can be traced to the era of World War II and the desire on the part of both Axis and Allied forces to exploit the potential of audio technology for radio

---

11. The most comprehensive of these earlier collections is Shuldham-Shaw and Lyle, *Greig-Duncan Folksong Collection,* edited in eight volumes (1981–2002).

broadcasts serving propagandistic purposes. When the same technology was later converted to commercial and academic use, linguists, musicologists, and folklorists (including Alan Lomax) pioneered the use of portable reel-to-reel tape machines to make high-quality recordings of the oral art forms of people whose talents might otherwise have gone unnoticed. This goal fit in well with the celebration of the common man and woman that, on both sides of the Atlantic, was a core value for Lomax, Henderson, and other intellectuals of the time, many of whom made no secret of their left-wing political sympathies.

One danger attendant upon books that celebrate the vanished way of life of the itinerant ethnic minorities of Britain or Ireland, however, is that either the authors or the readers of such books may be tempted to romanticize the past. One should therefore keep in mind that hunger, need, hardship, disease, bereavement, domestic violence, assaults, alcoholism, insanity, industrial or agricultural accidents, pedestrian deaths, and other forms of suffering or trauma have been inseparable from the Travellers' experience of life over the years. Moreover, the hardships that go along with life on the road or in ghettoized housing have often been intensified by social stigmatization, by the cruelty or indifference of members of the settled society, and by the draconian measures by which governmental authorities have sometimes attempted to regulate Travellers' lifeways, as readers of the following chapters will be well aware. To note just a few examples illustrating this point,[12] two of Duncan Williamson's siblings died in infancy. His oldest brother Sandy, when still a vigorous adult, committed suicide by drowning himself in the River Tay after learning that he had contracted cancer. Williamson's Aunt Rachel likewise drowned herself in Loch Fyne at age forty-seven, possibly while suffering from delusions regarding her affinity with the seal folk. Duncan's maternal grandfather Big John Townsley ended his days confined to a mental hospital as a victim of alcoholism or alcohol poisoning. Duncan himself, when in his teens, was seriously injured in one hand when a hook from a heavy fishing line tore out both flesh and bone, while he too suffered from alcoholism in later life. A remote Williamson ancestor—though there is no way to verify this legendary account—is said to have fled from the Orkneys to the Inner Hebrides after his involvement in a fratricidal murder. This list of traumas, which could easily be extended, serves as a reminder that the life of impoverished itinerants, like life in general but more intensely so, involves real suffering, hazards, and tragedies.

A related point is that the publications to which I have called attention provide only glimpses of a larger picture involving sociological perspectives on the Gypsies and Travellers of Britain.* That picture has much to do with demographics, economic stimuli, social work, land use, public housing,

---

12. Certain of the following details are drawn from vol. 1 of Campbell's *Traveller in Two Worlds*, as well as from my own conversations with Williamson.

sanitation, medical facilities and treatment programs, and legal protections for the homeless, among other factors. Moreover, a number of official Scottish governmental reports have been issued over the years documenting the living conditions of Scotland's Travellers with an eye toward maximizing their welfare while minimizing the frictions that arise when the interests of the dominant society conflict with those of itinerants. A passage from one of those reports (Gentleman and Swift, *Scotland's Travelling People: Problems and Solutions,* 1971) is the subject of remarks by Duncan Williamson that conclude chapter 9 of the present book.

Official reports documenting the conditions under which Scottish Travellers have lived in recent decades underscore the point that the traditional way of life of the travelling people of Britain and Ireland has not altogether come to an end. Rather, it has undergone a metamorphosis. The Scottish Travellers have not died out. The older generations to which Duncan Williamson, Betsy Whyte, Belle Stewart, Willie MacPhee, Stanley Robertson, and other outstanding tradition bearers belonged may no longer be among the living, but their descendants are. Social conditions have changed, however, so that Travellers are now more likely to be found living year-round "hoosed up" in towns and cities, where influences encouraging their assimilation with the rest of society are often intense but are also often resisted. Some Travellers live in motor homes in caravan sites or makeshift areas where their presence is legally permitted, even if in the teeth of local opposition. Depending on the time of year, as well, Travellers who are mobile may be heading for parts of Scotland, England, Wales, or elsewhere to pick up seasonal farmwork while meeting with friends or relations. Patterns of seminomadism whose origins may extend far back into prehistory are thus echoed in the present day.

§1.4. FROM THE FIELD TO THE PRESENT BOOK

As I have stressed, Williamson was a consummate performer. As such, he tailored each of his songs or stories to his audience of the moment, taking note of listeners' ages and backgrounds and anticipating their expectations, tastes, and degree of familiarity with the Scots language. Moreover, "the performance of everyday life" has become a commonplace theme of academic writings, heightening awareness that when we live and act in the world, we are performing roles that are expected of us by others.[13] For the most part, though some-

---

13. Erving Goffman's seminal 1956 book *The Presentation of Self in Everyday Life* mounts a strong argument in this regard. Elements of this line of thought have been nuanced and amplified in a large body of more recent work in performance studies, for example, Abrahams, *Everyday Life.*

times with flashes of rebellion, people aim to perform those roles reliably and well because they know that success in doing so confirms one's social identity while at the same time manifesting respect for others. Williamson was like many other skilled performers in these regards, deeply attuned to the nature of his audience and always, as far as I can judge, aiming to speak truth to his interlocutors in a manner to which they could relate.

What this means in practical terms is that I made an effort to tape-record Williamson's words in a number of different social contexts, being well aware that he would adjust his performances accordingly. Moreover, while a professional stage actor may repeat the same script thousands of times with only slight variations, each recording session with Williamson was unique, for it evolved on the spot in unanticipated ways in response to the reactions he received from members of his audience. I was happy to encourage such feedback, knowing that his relationships with others were the mainspring of his creative energy.

Since, by definition, a tape-recorded interview is a staged event subject to self-censorship and other forms of regulation or control on the part of those who take part in it, and since one sometimes hears remarks to the effect that all ethnographic fieldwork is a tainted intervention by clinically minded academics into the lives of unwilling subjects, I wish to emphasize that Williamson was at all times an active and willing participant in the sessions that I organized. He was no stranger to microphones, and it was he who several times remarked to me words to the effect, "Is it on? Is the tape recorder on? This is something you must have for your collection!" It was likewise he who volunteered the remark, "You know, Jack, you get the best stuff when you just keep the tape recorder running." Williamson was a natural performer and, indeed, a kind of untutored folklorist himself, as is not unusual among masters of traditional art forms. Despite his disdain for certain aspects of academia, he was a scholar of his art. Even if seemingly oblivious to the fact that he was being recorded, he wanted his words for me—and thus, potentially, for posterity—to be accurate and, when it came to songs and stories, to be the best versions that he could provide, on the spur of that particular moment at least. His passion for truth and accuracy in these recordings was manifest regardless of whether he was recounting a memorate (an anecdote based on his personal experience), providing an account of some incidental feature of Traveller life (such as how to make a makeshift potato lamp), or singing one of his big ballads. Moreover, reviewing my corpus of field recordings now after the passage of some years, I can perceive more clearly than ever how much delight Williamson took in entertaining his audiences, doing so with acute alertness while urging our sessions on. As for myself (for what this observation is worth), the hours that I spent with Williamson were among the happiest and most rewarding of my life.

Figure 1.2 John Niles, Auchtermuchty, 1986. Photo by Leonard Yarensky.

As for the settings in which these recordings were made, most sessions were recorded either in the sitting room of the home where the Williamsons were then living or at a house that I was renting at the time. The circumstances of recording were usually informal, with tea or beer being served from time to time and with occasional breaks in the recording that resulted from interruptions of one kind or another: peoples' comings and goings, children's needs, a farmer's knock on the door when a cow or its calf needed immediate attention, and other unanticipated events of that sort. Certain evening sessions consisted of ceilidhs involving other singers, storytellers, or musicians who were able to join us for the occasion. Several times, thanks to the portability of my recording equipment, I recorded Williamson literally on the road, whether in the interior of a car or at one or another site that we accessed on foot. At other times I recorded him in a folk club, a concert hall, a classroom, or a pub that served as an ad hoc concert venue. The technical quality of the recordings therefore varies a great deal. All of these contexts were what folklorists call "induced," in that my presence (and that of my tape recorder, or of other persons) encouraged Williamson to enter into a performance mode that surely differed from what his behavior might have been when no collector was present; but unwitnessed natural contexts remain undocumented, of course, by their very nature.

When directly quoting Williamson's words, I cite the tape number from which the passage in question is transcribed so that anyone with access to that recording can gain a sense of the context in which he is speaking. At the

Figure 1.3 Linda Williamson, Auchtermuchty, 1986. Photo by Leonard Yarensky.

back of this book will be found a list of the tape-recorded interviews from which these transcriptions are drawn, with information on when and where a recording was made and who was present on that occasion.

Many people helped to advance the fieldwork that resulted in the present book, converting this into a team project rather than an individual one. As such, the book provides a model of a new kind of ethnography, one that is based on the collective efforts of many people wanting to advance certain aims in consort with one another rather than on the experience of a "lone wolf" ethnographer working more or less on his own. Certain of the people who contributed to this collective effort did so in exceptionally selfless ways, and I want them to know of my gratitude for their acts of generosity. One of those individuals is Linda Williamson, a woman of extraordinary magnanimity and courage. Put simply, without Linda's active and generous support, and without the warm personal hospitality that she offered to members of my UREP teams as well, there would have been no successful project and no book. Her exceptional knowledge of the traditional way of life of the Scottish travelling people, together with her professional expertise in Scottish folksong and storytelling traditions, is something that I am thankful to have been able to draw on again and again.

Another person who made exceptional contributions to my research was Leonard Yarensky (*ca.* 1925–2012), who, with his wife Jeppy, can stand in for the whole set of UREP volunteers who assisted me in 1986 and 1988. Len and Duncan hit it off at once as if they were long-lost friends, enlivening many

Figure 1.4 Leonard Yarensky, an active participant in the 1986 UREP field project and a skilled amateur photographer, Auchtermuchty, 1986. Photo by Jeppy Yarensky.

Figure 1.5 Carole Newlands at the Auchtermuchty Festival, Fife, 1986, with our son Alan, the youngest member of the team. Photo by the author.

sessions with their infectious laughter. Len was a skilled amateur photographer with a gift for capturing his subject's moods and facial expressions, and many of the photos included in this book are his.

A third person who played a key role in this collective enterprise is my wife Carole Newlands. A native of Glasgow, she was my partner in the field from start to finish, invariably offering me the soundest of advice while also ensuring that the needs of our guests from either side of the Atlantic were met. Also, and importantly, she often helped to provide a receptive family-style audience for Duncan's songs and stories, abetted from time to time in an unselfconscious manner by our young son Alan and by the Williamsons' two children Betsy and Thomas.

Given Duncan Williamson's extraordinary talents as a storyteller as well as his highly unusual upbringing, the present book, called *Webspinner* for reasons that will be made clear in the concluding chapter, ought to be of interest to a wide range of readers. Those who come to the book wanting to learn more about the Scottish Travellers will find a treasure trove of information here. Indeed, this is one of the main reasons I undertook this project in the first place. At the same time, Williamson's vast web of narratives was spun out of an exceptionally wide range of personal experiences, while countless other voices coalesced in his. Anyone who has an interest not just in the Scottish Travellers, but also in Scottish folklore, social history, and oral traditions, or in the foundational role of oral narrative in shaping the human condition, ought to find much here to savor and enjoy.

Map 1 Scotland (less the Orkneys and the Shetlands), showing place names mentioned in the text

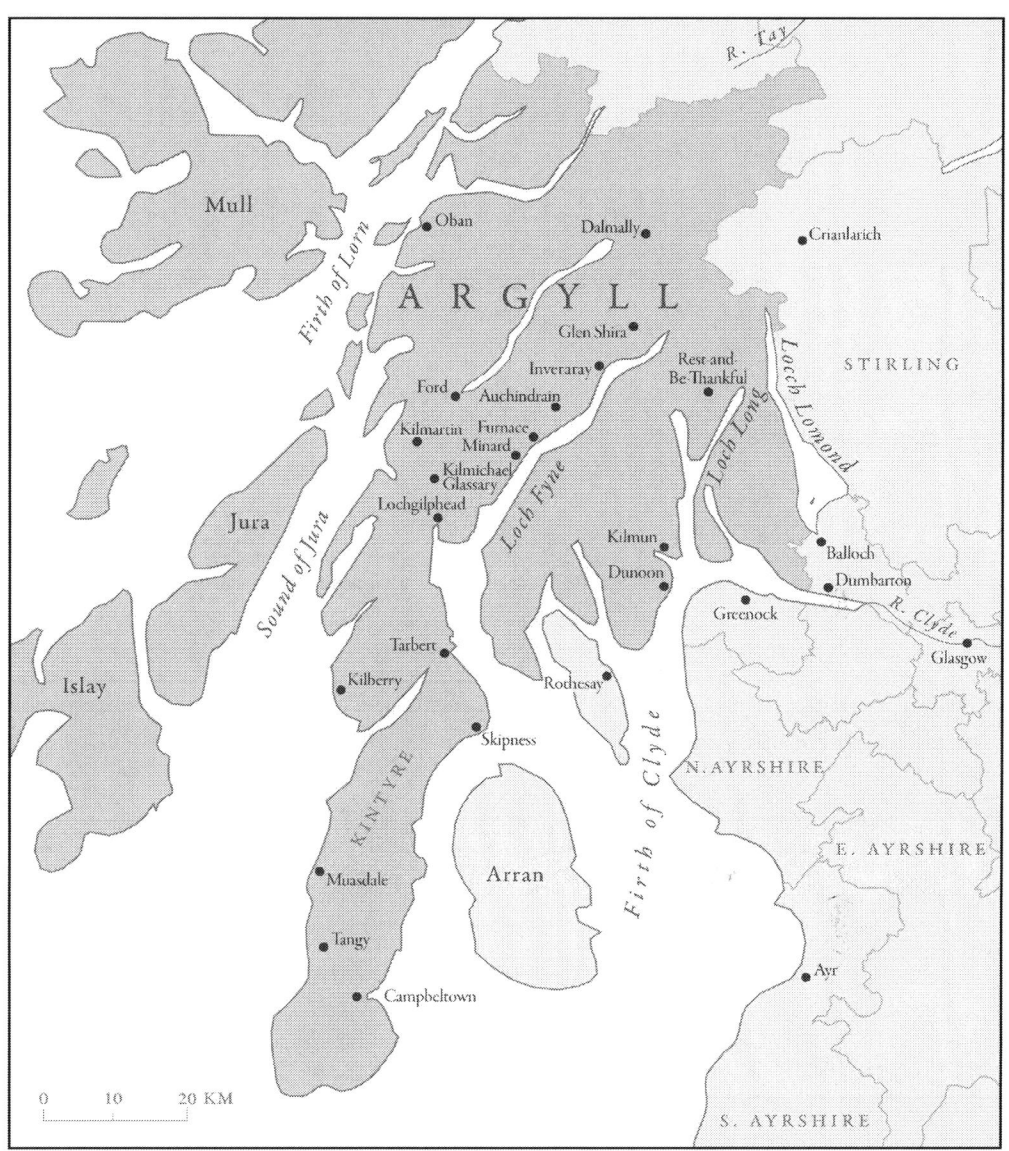

Map 2 Most of Argyll, showing place names mentioned in the text

Map 3 Fife and its environs, showing place names mentioned in the text

Chapter 2

THOSE WHO WENT BEFORE

§2.1. BETSY TOWNSLEY AND JOCK WILLIAMSON
ARE MARRIED AND SETTLE DOWN

Well, to tell you first, to tell you to start with, it goes back a long way till 1896. My mother was born in a cave in 1896.[1] They didnae e'en have a tent. She was born in a cave in 1896. And at the age of fourteen she married my father.* She was fourteen years old. And that was aboot the beginnin of the war, and he was three years older, and he was called off to the 1914 War.

They got married in 1914, and then he served his time in the war. He was a cook in the Black Watch and a piper forbyes in his spare time.[2] An he was a great piper, an a cook, and he was three years older than my mother.

And after he came home from the war, things was very hard on the west coast of Argyll. They were really tough. And he settled there in the west coast of Argyll in a place called Furnace, on the shores of Loch Fyne. An he made up his mind [to settle down there] because he could neither read nor write, and neither could my mother.

My father used to get soldiers to write letters for him because he could not read nor write, an he said, "When I go home," he told me this often, he said, "if I have any family, I'm gonnae make sure that they're gonnae no need no one to write them a letter." So he stayed in one place when he came back from the war in 1918. He settled in a little place in the Duke of Argyll's estate, in a little place called Furnace in Argyll in 1918. And then he reared up his family there.

And the old Duke was the eighth [rightly tenth] Duke of Argyll,* who owned all Argyllshire. I mean, not an estate, but a whole county, rangin for over about 150 square miles of land. The Campbells of Argyll owned the whole lot.

---

1. Duncan later identifies the date of his mother's birth as 1889 rather than 1896; see §2.2.
2. "A cook in the Black Watch": that is, in an infantry battalion of the Royal Regiment of Scotland that has commonly been known as the Black Watch (the Royal Highlanders). "A piper forbyes": that is, a piper too.

Figure 2.1 Niall Diarmid Campbell, the tenth Duke of Argyll (1872–1949), in a photograph dating from 1921. The Duke occasionally called on the Williamson family at their winter barrakit. From the Argyll Papers, Inveraray Castle, reproduced by kind permission of the Duke of Argyll.

An my father was a great friend after comin back from the war because he was in the Black Watch, which is a Campbell clan. And then he went to the Duke of Argyll, and he said, "Luik, Mr. Campbell"—Duncan was his name, the same name as myself—he said, "I want to stay in one place an school my children."

"Well," he said, "Mr. Williamson," he said, "you stay there as long as you like and school your children, and I'll pay you a visit from time to time."

(86DW03 @ 14:40.)

§2.2. BETSY TOWNSLEY IS BORN IN A CAVE IN MUASDALE

Ma father was born in Tangy,[3] and when he was seventeen he ran away wi my mother. She was thirteen. She had her first baby when she was fourteen, an it died. And she was born in a cave, in a rock face. You know, a cave, a rock cave.

They were travelling along the roadway, the old man.[4] They were very puir, these folk, the auld travelling folk, very puir, an all their possessions was on their back. It was a lot tae carry. You had an anvil for makin tin,* and ye had a set of tools for makin the tin. And ye had a roll of canvas, some sticks,[5] some blankets, some bedclothes, some spare clothes for any children you had. It was a good big heavy bundle. And these old men used tae carry it, an the women always carried a big square basket. She carried all the cookin utensils and the food in the basket, knives and spoons an tin cups. I mean, they needed very little.

But it was a late rainy night they came to Muasdale. Muasdale rock cave* is still there where Mother was born.

I think she was born, she was born in 18 . . . let's see, what age would she be now? She was born in 1889, on the fourth o May in 1889. Yeah. And as I was tellin you, they came late that night to the cave, and it was dark by the time they got there. And the old beggar men used tae stay in the cave,[6] ye know, and they pulled brackens and put dry grass in it, ye know. What the Travellers used tae do is—all the dry bracken and bits o withered grass, they set fire to it first before they slept in there, you see. No one would walk intae a cave that's full o dried grass an brackens and think to bed down in it, cause there could be an adder or a snake crawled in. What the Travellers used tae do is put a match to it an stand back and let it burn itself out, and then sweep out the burned pieces, and then the cave was clean.

Well, as I say, they cuidnae put the tent up that night because it was wet and rainin, so Grandfather just put the match to it and waited til it was cleaned, and then they bedded inside the cave, which was a big place made in the solid rock. And during the night my granny had my mother in the cave, ye know?

And my grandmother was at *my* birth; she was *my* midwife. She just done her own thing, ye know? Tuik the baby and done everything to it, tied its navel

---

3. Tangy Glen, near Campbeltown in Kintyre. Tangy Mill is the setting of Duncan's song "My Wee Maggie," for which see §5.3 and §5.4.

4. "The old man": this would have been Duncan's maternal grandfather, "Big John" Townsley, also known as "Johnnie." His wife, Duncan's maternal grandmother, was Bella MacDonald, also known as Belle.

5. "Some sticks": that is, some poles, usually made of alder, that could be bent and fixed in the ground to form the framework of the bow tent, which was then covered with canvas.

6. "Old beggar men": Duncan distinguishes between solitary beggars, or tramps, and Scottish Travellers, who typically moved from place to place in family units that often comprised multiple generations.

Figure 2.2 "Tinker's Cave," Wick, Caithness. Williamson's mother Betsy was born in a cave at Muasdale, Kintyre. Plate I of the "Report of the Departmental Committee on Habitual Offenders, Vagrants, Beggars, Inebriates and Juvenile Delinquents 1895," courtesy of the Secretary of State's Advisory Committee on Scotland's Travelling People.

and everything herself.* Next day they just packed up the babe in her shawl and walked down the road with it, ye know. No problem at all.

But the wonderful big sons she [my grandmother] had! My grandmother had seven sons, and not one was under six foot. I lost two uncles in the war, in the 1914 War. And their names is up on the stone in Argyll,* lost in the '14 War. And Father lost two brothers in the War.

(86DW19 @15:10)

§2.3. BETSY TOWNSLEY GETS TATTIES TO GO
WITH HER HERRING

But they [my parents] were well known in Argyll. Everybody knew them. Everybody knew them from Furnace to Inveraray to Lochgilphead right to Campbeltown. All the local people, fishermen an crofters an small farmers, they knew my father and mother well.

❧

You know, my mother lived till she was eighty-seven, and she cuid not tell the time?* There was only one time that my mother could tell the time, was when the two hands [of the clock] were on twelve. She knew it was twelve o'clock, ye know? But she was a wonderful woman. She was a great seer, and she could tell wonderful things, ye know. She was classed as a witch: a white witch, yes, a white witch.

❧

♫

She made her own cures, and she taught them [the villagers] all these things. I mean, she teached the people everything, ye know.

She used tae spit on my hook when I went to fish. I wouldnae go tae fish without ma mother spittin on my huik. I would not go tae fish. Fishin for sea trout an salmon an—on the sea. I says, "Mother, spit on that." [*Makes spitting sound.*] She spit on ma huik. That was me for a day. I was sittin out, an nothing in the world Ah cuidnae—I got loads of fish.

So. From our village was eight miles to the large town Inveraray. So, her an I was up—we're doin a job, you know, shinglin turnips for the farmer,* and we'd to walk the whole eight miles home. So in these bygone times, they used tae bring a lot of fish by road; herrin on lorries, an this lorry had went off the road, an all these boxes of fish were couped on the road,[7] ye see? And ma mother went up tae the driver, and she said tae the driver, she says, "Can we have some fish?"

"Oh," he says, "help yourself. Take as many—they're going to be destroyed. Ah cannae get my lorry back on the road, help yourself." They were spewed across the road.

So my mother and I fulled a basket of herring, you see? And we had eight miles to walk home from Inveraray to Furnace. [*Speaking in an aside:*] I hope

---

7. "Couped on the road": overturned on the road. See Robinson, *Concise Scots Dictionary*, s.v. "coup, cowp, coop," v., sense 1: upset, overturn.

you all get to Argyll sometime; it's the most beautiful country in the world. It's the land o the Campbells, an it's the greatest country in the world.—And then we walked on, and Ah'm carryin this bag o fish, and lo and behold, past us comin was a lorry, an old Bedford lorry, and it was loaded with bags o potatoes, see? An it passed us by. Noo this is square on my mother's grave, I mean, I'll be dead tomorrow if I'm tellin you a lie. My mother said, "We've fish," she said, "and there's a load of potatoes. Wouldn't it be happy," she said, "if we could get some potatoes to go along with the fish."

And I swear on my dear mother's grave, we come round the next bend, and here he was, right intae the ditch, upside down, and all the bags o potatoes on the road! There was the lorry. The driver wasnae hurt, and he's standing there, and he's looking—his lorry is in the ditch.

"I don't know what happened," he says. "I just—off the road," he said.

There was the bags o potatoes scattered across the road. Mother said, "Can I have some of these?" He says, "Help yourself," he says, "they're goin to lie there."

We picked up about half a bag o potatoes. Ah carried potatoes, she carried the herrin, and we got a wonderful supper that night, but the man was standing there beside the lorry.

"Mother," I said, "luik," I said. "You put a spell on that man when he passed us back near the road a bit."

"Well," she says, "he wasnae hurt," she says, "was he?"*

That's all the words she said. I'll swear on my mother's grave.

(86DW04 @ 19:21; the first paragraph is from 86DW28 @ 23:24 and the second one from 86DW03 @ 15:53.)

§2.4. BETSY TOWNSLEY SEES A FRECHT

♪♫

I remember my mother tellin me one time: we were sittin all over the tent wi a big fire in the floor, ye know, and the sticks was sparkin. We always used sticks that never sparked, an the smoke was goin straight up through the chimney. Father was sittin and he was sharpenin his razor,* and Mother was sittin over tae the side, and the kids were all doin other things, you know. They're arguin and fightin and carryin on. And she said, "Children, quiet!" she says. "Something terrible has happened."

When Mother spoke, we always listened. She said, "Something terrible has happened." She says, "I saw your uncle has gone for a pail o water."

"Mother!" we said. We'd never saw our Uncle Johnny for years.

She said, "Your uncle is away for water." She said, "I saw him walkin across there." She said, "He's away with a pail for water. Go and tell him—maybe he thinks we need some water."

We'd never seen him for years. And we said, "Mother, we never saw wir Uncle Johnny for years." He was my mother's brother, you know, an auld man. He used tae come with a horse and cart travellin the country, and he came every summer.

"Well," she said, "he hasnae got his cart with him this time." And we didnae even believe it, you know. She said, "He's goin for the water."

So aboot two days later ma mother got a telegram sayin that Uncle Johnny had walked for a pail o water to feed his horse, and [*claps his hands*] he went down like a shot. Died wi a heart attack, you know. He had aa kept ponies,[8] you know, and he carried the water to give the pony a drink, and he walked wi the pail in Glasgow, which is aboot ninety miles away from that place, and she had a vision. She saw her brother go with the pail tae the well for tae bring back water. But she never saw him die. And she said, "Ah saw my brother goin to the pail," she said. "He's away for a pail o water." Cause where we stayed there was a river, and opposite the river there was a campin place where all the travellin people used to stay, and they could walk across the river when the river was dry and came up to our place wi a shortcut, and she thought her brother had jist come up and said, "I'll go for a pail of water," an she had saw this. But he had died ninety mile away with a heart attack. At the present moment that she had saw him goin for the water, he carried the pail tae feed his horse, and he never got the water. He died before he picked the water up tae feed his pony, and she had saw this and told us that he was there. But he had died.

At was what we call a frecht.* He was there before; she had seen this happenin.

(86DW04 @ 16.28.)

§2.5. A DANDLING SONG ("BONNIE ONE")

♪♫

JN: *Well, how about now, "Bonnie Wee Thing?" You know, we haven't heard that yet. That was one of your mother's, wasn't it?*

Oh, wait a minute and let me get that tune again. It was on my head this morning. [*Pauses, whistles tune softly.*] How does it go again? [*Sings under his breath:*] "Puir, puir wee bonnie one—" Whether my mother had known this as—haird it as a tune, and uh—was it a Gaelic song, or a Gaelic air? But she used tae set wi the babies in her lap, an she used tae sing. [*Sings:*]

1   Wull you come—

---

8. "He had aa kept ponies": he had always kept ponies.

[*Starts over:*]

Where're ye gaain, my bonnie one, bonnie one?
Where're ye gaain, my bonnie one, oh?
Oh can Ah come with you, bonnie one, bonnie one,
can Ah come with you, bonnie one, oh?

2   You can if you want to, bonnie one, bonnie one,
can if you want to, bonnie one, oh.
You can if you want to, bonnie one, bonnie one,
can if you want to, bonnie one, oh.

3   Oh what is your fortune, bonnie one, bonnie one?
What is your fortune, bonnie one, oh?
My face is my fortune, bonnie one, bonnie one,
face is my fortune, bonnie one, oh.

4   Then I winnae come with ye, bonnie one, bonnie one,
winnae come with you, bonnie one, oh.
Then I winnae come with you, bonnie one, bonnie one,
winnae come with you, bonnie one, oh.

Bonnie One

verse 1

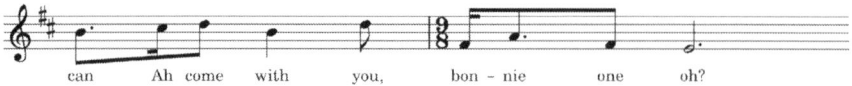

Granny used tae sit with the babies in her lap wi that all the time.[9] But I never haird no more of that. And the tune. . . . I was just settin here and sometimes the tune comes intae my head and sometimes it's gone. Ah mean, Ah've never diddled that for years.[10] [*Begins diddling, to the same tune as before:*]

   1   Dúm-da-dum dáy, dum dúh-da-dum dúh-da-dum,
         dúm-da-dum dóo, dum dóo-diddum dáy—
         ti-díddie-ti dée, dee dái-diddum dów-diddum,
         díddie-ti dáy, ti díddie-dum dáh.

Then she would go on:

   2   Ay-dáy-diddum dó, dáy-diddum dá-diddum
         dúm-diddum dóo, dum dóo-diddum dái—
         ah-dídda-ti dí diddie dów-diddum dái-diddum,
         dídda-di dúddíe-di, díddie-dum dáh.

That was all she ever done wi it. I don't know where it come from. That's a way back, back in the thirties, when Granny—my mother—used tae take the babies in her lap, ye know? And then when the babies got a wee bit older, when they'd come to about a year and they were sittin up, she'd take one of the baby's foot in each leg, an she sat crossin her legs. And she would diddle all the tunes to the baby wi the baby's feet. All Traveller women have a great habit of that.

And, eh, Ah was in Perth, and Ah was doin a storytellin for the Scottish Language Society in Perth. There was a good crowd there. Sheila and Andrew was there; it was they were runnin it, of course.[11] And they asked me to do some storytellin, and talk aboot my travels and languages in Aberdeenshire, and Argyllshire, and the Highland tongue an the Highland accent, and a few Gaelic words an talk, but Ah did some storytellin in between.

And this woman had a wee baby aboot—oh, a wee bit older than your Emily.[12] And it was cryin to break its heart, you see? And Ah knew she [the mother] was interested; she'd come from Glasgow, and her husband was there. And Ah walked over, and Ah picked the baby up and Ah tuik it in my lap. And

---

9. "Granny used to sit": Duncan often referred to his mother as "Granny," thinking back very likely not just to his own childhood but also to the times, during his first marriage, when he and his wife Jeannie and their children used to visit his mother in Argyll.

10. "Diddling": a term for singing a tune using only vocables (meaningless syllables). See also Duncan's story "The Silence Wager" (§8.9).

11. "Sheila and Andrew": the reference is to Sheila Douglas, the Perthshire singer, collector, and educator, and her husband Andrew Douglas, an educator and poet.

12. "A wee bit older than your Emily": this recording session took place in October 1987, when our daughter Emily (or Skye) was just four months old.

Ah started—one foot in each hand—an I started diddlin to it. [*Diddles, to a new tune, in march time:*]

> Doodle dúddie, dum-da-dúm, da-doodle-dów da-diddle dóo
> diddera-dóo, dowdle-dów-dum, tóodle-doodle-dúm
> toodle díddie dum-da-dúm, da-doodle dówdle-didden dów
> diddera-dáh, diddie-dó diddum dóo-rá—
> tidderie dóodle-dóo, da-dóodle dum-da-dóo
> diddie-dáy daydle dóo-diddum, tóodle-toodle dúm
> toodle-díddie dum-da-dúm dah-doodle dóodle-didden dóo,
> diddera-dá diddle, dów-diddle dóo-rá.

And that wee baby started tae giggle an laugh, and I passed it back to its mother, and she was over the moon! Because she thought she'd have tae take it outside. And it never said another word more the night.

(87DW12 @ 26:36.)

§2.6. THE DUKE OF ARGYLL USED TO CALL ON JOCK WILLIAMSON*

JN: What about your own family connection with the laird? You had a connection with the laird—was it the Duke of Argyll?

The Duke of Argyll, yes. My father was wi the Duke of Argyll for thirty-seven years. We were stayin in the Duke of Argyll's estate, and we had great connection with the Duke of Argyll, ye know? An we stayed in his wood, an we had this large tent built in the wood. And the people in the village, a wee small village, always complained. They came up at night an they cut trees, you know? And when the forester came round, he said, "Oh," he said, "it's the tinkers cuttin the trees."* You know? So they sent word up to the estate, the forester o the estate, that the tinkers is cuttin trees.

And they sent word to the old Duke, and the Duke came himself to see ma father. He came down with his old-fashioned car, he drove up right through his estate, right in the wood, in the forest, and he driv up. He said, "Mr. Williamson, we've had complaints in the office that you were cuttin some trees."

My father said, "Look, Duncan." He called him by his first name, Duncan. He said, "We didnae cut any trees," he says. "We burn the *branches*. Your people in the village, the ratepayers, cuts the trees, and we get the branches. We dinnae need trees to build fires, cause we cuidnae burn trees."[13]

---

13. "We couldnae burn trees": that is, the family could only burn relatively small sticks inside their barrakit.

"Oh, Mr. Williamson, I'm thankful you told me that." But he says, "I brought some lollipops for the children." And he had a big tin, an old tin, a monster tin that was full o lollipops, and he says, "I'll pay the doctor's bill the next time I'm back. Mr. Williamson, if you feel like a fire, you cut the tree. And if anybody stops you, you tell em I give you permission."

My father was there for thirty-seven years in his estate, thirty-seven years.

∾

I loved the Duke of Argyll.* The Duke of Argyll was my pal, eh. He was my old pal. Brung me lollypops when I was a wee boy. Let me take salmons fae his river. He was an old angel, old Duncan. And my father stayed in his ground all his life. I loved old Duncan Campbell, he was a great one. "Ah'll pay your doctor's bill next time, Mr. Willy," he said, "Mr. Williamson."

Great old man. And his kilt was full o moth holes! An his sporran was full o verdigris.* I mean, he went like a tramp! And his Balmoral bonnet was full of moth holes, you know. One of these Balmorals with a red tassel on top, and full o moth holes! A gray bonnet, ye know? Great old man. And these big buckled shoes, you know, he wore, and long stockins up his legs, with a kilt. And I guarantee that the eyeholes in his [shoes]—the laces—had never been moved for twenty years. You know? Big heavy brogues. A great old man.

∾

JN: Your father must have been very attached to him.

He was. He loved to cut his corns wi a razor. Pared his feet.

JN: How's that, Duncan?

Pared his corns wi his razor. My father, wi his razor, was shavin his face. An auld open razor. Well, ye ken when old people gets corns on their feet? They get hard corns, hard skin. He [the Duke] cuidnae walk wi the corns on his feet. And he used tae take off his shoes, and my father used to set there with old Duncan's—the Duke of Argyll's—foot on his lap, and pare the corns with his razor and gie him relief. He would pare them right down. Corns are a sore thing, you know? He'd a corn—maybe he had one on the side o his big toe, here, or there, and he had another one on the side o his heel. And he'd take off his old sock and he set there, his foot in my father's lap. My father was sittin, cuttin away, parin his corns wi his open razor.

JN: Would he come and call on your father, that way?

Aye, he came, aye! In an old Bentley car he had wi a quilted top, you know, a cloth top. These old cars, the bonnet could go back like a pram. Yeah, that's the kind o car he had. Great old man. A real gentleman, you know. He was just—

JN: You don't see them like that anymore.

You disnae get them like that anymore, never in a million years.

(Tape 84DW04 @ 1:21:48 for the first 6 paragraphs; then from 87DW14 @ 1:20:56 and @ 1:24:44.)

§2.7. THE OLD DUKE IS TAKEN AWAY BY THE FAIRIES

♪♫

Across from Inveraray there's a wee hill. We call it "Fairy Knowe." It's a high peak.

JN: Across the water?

Across from Inveraray, just above Strachur. It's called "Fairy Knowe." Noo, auld Campbell was a great believer in fairies. He believed in fairies all the days of his life. And he would cross that—get Douglas, in his motorboat, to take him across wi a basket, wi tobacca, whiskey and things, to put them on the top o the knowe for the fairies. He done this, oh, in Strachur Bay, until he got too old, he cuidnae dae it. And people laughed at him. And some say the shepherds took his stuff away; you know, the shepherds on the hill took his stuff away. But anyhow, this is a true story, Jack.

Now, old Duncan Campbell died on the third of June, about 1952; '52 or '53.[14] It was a beautiful summer's day, and Loch Fyne was just like a band of silver between the hills at Inveraray. Now the boat has got tae sail down Loch Fyne, go right round, and come into the Holy Loch where all the Campbells are buried, right?[15] Ah'll tell you where the Campbells are buried now: at Kilmun, the other side of Dunoon.[16] It's got to sail down Loch Fyne, then right roon.

They took his corpse away from Inveraray in a boat—motorboat. There were a lot of people, down Loch Fyne, and then the mist came down. The mist

---

14. "About 1952": the actual year of death of the tenth Duke of Argyll, whose proper name was Niall Diarmid Campbell, was 1949.

15. Holy Loch: a small loch in the great outlet of the River Clyde, near Dunoon. It is accessible from Inveraray by boat by sailing south down Loch Fyne, then eastward around the Isle of Bute, then north as far as the mouth of Loch Long.

16. "At Kilmun": the private mausoleum of the Dukes of Argyll is located close by the ruin of a twelfth-century church at Kilmun, on the north shore of the Holy Loch, on the Cowal peninsula.

came down, right? In the middle of June! And that loch was black and that boat was lost for three hours! They had tae send another boat tae look for it. The fairies come for him and tuik him away! There was nothing in the coffin, nothing never buried—old Duncan never was buried. No, no, no. He was like Thomas, like Thomas the Rhymer*; he was away.

Yeah, nobody was convinced but Father, God rest him. He said, "Duncan Campbell—there were nothing in the coffin when they buried it in Kilmun." They took him around to Kilmun, to bury—all the Campbells are buried in Kilmun, you see, the private tomb in Kilmun. And Father says, "Ah bet ye a pound there were nothing in that coffin when they tuik it away."

JN: [Laughs, then realizes that Duncan is serious.]

Old Campbell was gone wi the wee fellas, yeah. He was guid tae them, he took tobacco an stuff up the Fairy Knowe tae them.

That's a true story. And there never was known, though, for mist to be in Loch Fyne in the month of June. And the loch was black wi mist, completely, and the boat was lost in the mist. Cuidnae see where they were going. In the month of June! See, it was the fairies.

(87DW14 @ 1:22:10.)

§2.8. HOW JOCK WILLIAMSON MADE ENDS MEET

JN: Do you take after your father?

Ah, well, maybe a little. A little, I would say. He was very fond o stories like mysel, ye know. Yeah, he tellt a lot of stories. Aye. He told stories tae his children, and other people forbyes, ye know, when he was in company, like. But I could never play the bagpipes with him.[17] He was a good piper.

∾

JN: The quarry where your father worked[18]: was it owned by the Duke of Argyll?

Well, *all* Argyll was owned by the Duke of Argyll at one time. But it was a company had the quarry, a company the name of Simm. They had it back in

---

17. "I could never play the bagpipes with him": that is, "I could never play the pipes as well as he could."

18. "The quarry where your father worked": the reference is to the stone quarry just outside Furnace, where, for a number of years, Duncan's father worked during the day while Duncan's mother hawked the houses up and down Loch Fyne.

the thirties, ye know. When my father worked in the quarry, it was back in the thirties, ye know? 1935, '36, '37, '38, up tae the war. But then, in 1940, when the war was goin, they started buildin the naval bases. And wages were beginnin tae get a little better, so my father finally left the quarry and went to work with buildin the naval bases for the ships—tank landing craft—along the Loch Fyne side. So he never went back to the quarries there anymore. It was too hard work in the quarries, breakin stones.

Figure 2.3 Williamson at the quarry on the outskirts of Furnace, Argyll, where his father worked during the 1920s and 1930s. Photo by Dorothy Leese, 1988.

We always got as much as kept us alive, ye know. Father an mother tried their best. It [poverty] was no disgrace tae them. They tried their best to bring us up the best that could be. At least we could look forward to food sometimes because of my father's work, and they always got a few shillins. But some people travelling in Perthshire and Aberdeenshire and all over, sometimes they went without food for days, ye know? So in a way we were better off because we had the seashore. We had plenty o fish in the burn. We had fish, we had plenty o shellfish, and we never really got terrible hungry. [We could] always get somethin tae eat, you know? The people who were travellin in the mainland cuidnae do these things, ye know?

JN: Right.

And we never travelled in the winter. They travelled in the winter. So we were never really as cold as they were, because we always got a tent and a good fire, ye know, in the wintertime. Father would see to it that we had a good fire and a warm place to sleep.

JN: What did your mother do for the most part, Duncan? Did she raise the children?

Yeah, and she hawked some of my father's [wares]. But after the children left school she went to work in Inveraray, to the Duke's castle in Argyll, in the kitchens. After the children left school, when the youngest girl left school. They moved up to Inveraray.

JN: Your father and mother both?

Father and mother both. An the Duke of Argyll gave them this great big wooden cabin to stay in. You know, a wooden cabin with a fire. They gave it to them free for to stay for the rest of their life. And my father worked on the estate among the timber and, ye know, cleanin the young trees.

JN: So he gave up the work in the quarry?

Yeah, to work on the Duke's estate. I was gone by that time, but I used tae always go back to visit them in Inveraray. They moved from Furnace, eight miles up the road. But we all went to school in Furnace. It was only when his children left school that he moved away from Furnace. But as long as we were small, he stayed in Furnace in the one place all the time. He gave us a little schoolin and as much as he could afford to do.

Figure 2.4 Inveraray Castle from the air, as it was in 1933 or 1934, amid some of the estate's woodlands. The shore of Loch Fyne is to the left. Williamson's mother and father lived in a woodsman's hut on the Castle grounds in their old age. From the Argyll Papers, Inveraray Castle, reproduced by kind permission of the Duke of Argyll.

JN: So they got along all right with the Duke of Argyll?

Yeah. The factor of Argyll, the Duke's underfactor, was at my father's funeral. The factor of the estate was at my father's funeral. Ah remember the old Duke of Argyll, old Duncan himsel, who had never married, comin down to visit my father. He was a great old man. He had never married. He was a bachelor all his life. And we stayed in the forest with the permission of the factor. Nobody could move us on because we had a rental certificate from the factor allowin us to stay there as long as my father lived, until he schooled the children and he wanted to move closer up to Inveraray.

My mother went to work in the kitchens in the castle, and my father worked on the estate. When they cut trees, he cleaned up, burned up all the branches, and sorted the drains[19] and sorted the fences, you know, where the people were cuttin timber on the estate. He did a lot of work there.

(86DW28 @ 23:40, @ 22:17, and @18:18.)

---

19. "He sorted the drains": that is, he cleared out the ditches that carried runoff groundwater through the Inveraray estate down to Loch Fyne.

§2.9. DUNCAN'S SISTERS AND HOW THEY WERE NAMED

All my sisters is called after the local people in the village, ye know. My mother never called any o my sisters after any of our own family, because she hawked aroond the little village where we lived, ye know, and she had good friends, people who were good to my mother. She was a friend, she tuik their hand and set for a cup of tea wi em, an would mend their baskets and give them clothes-pegs and have a crack wi them.[20] She was jist one o them, you know? John an Betsy'd come in for a crack, ye know, an have a cup o tea wi them. She brought them baskets and mendit their baskets, and she told their fortunes. She had a wonderful time. She gave them help wi cures, and everybody loved old Betsy.

And, eh—"You're having another baby, Betsy?"

"Yeah."

"You're going to call this one after me?"

So she naturally did, ye know? And Ah've a young sister who's got five Christian names. Her name is Mary MacNichol McClure MacLain MacDonald Williamson. [*General laughter.*] No, sorry! Mary *Joe-Maima.* She [the villager] was Maima, her man was Joe, and she [Duncan's mother] called her [her daughter] "Mary Joe-Maima MacNichol" (was her mother), "McClure" (was her father-in-law), "Williamson." All in the one name, ye know? It's amazing, but it's true. It's amazing, but it's true.

(86DW41 @ 1:08:40.)

§2.10. ON DUNCAN'S UNCLE DUNCAN AND HIS GRANDMOTHER BELLE MACDONALD

JN: You say your Uncle Duncan—

He was a wanderin piper. He played. That's how he kept him and Granny alive in the summertime. He played round tae the big houses and hotels and shootin lodges for pennies tae keep enough food for him and Granny tae keep them alive. In the winter months he would always come back to Argyll an spend the winter wi us. Ma father would just fix another tent in beside ours for him, ye know? And then they would stay wi us for the winter.

Now when the cold winter was over, he would take off again with his mother. They would travel. Sometimes they would go down tae Campbeltown for the summer and then come back up. Sometimes they would go away back up to Perthshire. Sometimes they would go away to Dumbarton, you know? But they would always come back in the wintertime.

---

20. "Have a crack wi them": that is, have a chat with them, exchange news or stories.

He was a good piper, Duncan, a good storyteller, a great storyteller, fantastic storyteller. He collected stories galore. You have no idea. Yeah, because he was around many campfires as a young man. Him and Granny used to go out. But Granny taught him a lot o stories too. His mother taught him a lot of stories. She was a good storyteller. Aye, she was a great storyteller.

(86DW28 @ 24:20.)

§2.11. WILLIE WILLIAMSON MAKES A BIG MISTAKE

I don't remember my mother's father.[21] He died the day I was born. But I remember my father's father, my other grandfather.[22] He stayed at Tarbert, Loch Fyne, all his life, since he married my grandmother.[23] An he brought up his family there, an he died about 1945. An my grandmother died about 1946, I think. He was an old tinsmith. And he workit there, and he made—eh, he mendit umbrellas. He was an umbrella mender,* an he was just a little man.

But my granny was a big woman. She was well over six-foot tall. An he was jist a little man. And one day, many years ago, Grandfather had went and made the biggest mistake of his life.* He went to mend one woman's umbrella, and he mendit it for her. And she knew him well, and she asked him in for a cup o tea. And he made a simple mistake of walkin in for a cup of tea, and he left his wife, ma granny, standing on the roadside, waitin on him comin back. And from that day on, they never stayed together from another night onwards for the next thirty years. They built their separate tents. They made their own food. They stayed close tae each other, but they never slept another night together in their lifetime, because he walked into that woman's house and had a cup o tea with that aul woman in the house. Granny an grandfather were parted for life. Not actually parted, but just talkin friends, but that was all. And they were only young people at that time. Their family was there. They had sons an daughters. But father an mother never speaked, never talked, and never was—never was friends again. My father told me that as a true story.

JN: And your grandmother was so upset—

So upset by my grandfather goin into this lady's house and acceptin that. He'd broken the code, you see?

JN: Just to go in for a cup of tea?

---

21. "My mother's father": this was "Big John" Townsley.
22. "My other grandfather": this was Willie Williamson.
23. "My grandmother": this was Duncan's paternal grandmother, Bett (or Betsy) MacColl.

Yeah. She asked him in and it was a cold day. He'd mended her umbrella, and she'd asked him in. He broken her—he'd broken the code. She was a MacColl herself. She was a Betsy MacColl, a big woman. And her father was from Irish descent, and they had a strict code, ye know? If he'd have said tae the woman, "Well, that's nice, but can my wife come in with me for a cup o tea?" But he left his wife standing in the road and he walked in. And from that day on, for thirty years, they never slept another night together. Never forgave him till she died. He died a couple o years before her. That's true.

So that tells you how strict a code these old [people had]. And my father, when he was young, he had a younger sister, and she ran off with a man, a runaway marriage. And the man left her the next morning. My father was married with two children. And my father trailed him for over fifty miles and near killed him.

They had a strict code among themselves, these people in olden times, in bygone times, ye know? Not like the Travellers that's in the country nowadays. They dinnae seem tae mind much. They've changed wi the times, ye know? But the old Travellers are very strict. They had strict standards and strict codes that they stood by, especially in my grandfather's time and my granny's time.

(86DW28 @ 1:00.)

§2.12. WILLIE WILLIAMSON MINDED THE DUMP AT TARBERT, LOCH FYNE

When we used to leave Furnace in the spring, my father's first stop was down tae Tarbert, where his father stayed. And we'd camp beside the fire for about a week, you see, because he always liked to go tae Tarbert tae spend a while with his old man and his mother. And he put his tent up in the old village dump, beside my grandfather. See, my grandfather took care o the dump, the village dump. And he was allowed on that dump, only himsel. But that dump was [in] a big forest, you see, and one part of it was a big wet hole, and all the village rubbish went intae the dump.

My grandfather had his tent apart away, and his gelly.* And my granny's tent—she lived by hersel, after all those years I was tellin you aboot, up on a nice drive up away from the dump. But he took care of the dump, kept people off it, and he poisoned rats, and he set traps for rats, and he taken up the blowin papers. And he never got any wage for it. He got permission to stay there as long as he liked, see what I mean? And he got many good little things at the dump. He got all this stuff. He saved up all these bits of brass, and he saved up bits o copper. He collectit all the bits o stuff, things that he needed, that came oot in the dump that people didnae need. Round his camp was like Aladdin's Cave with stuff he'd gaithered off the dump.

JN: [Laughs.]

And he'd collect all the good boots, good boots he'd got in the dump. "I'll save this for the wee grandchildren." We'd come down there—any good clothes that'd come oot, bags of clothes, he'd pack up the clothes and he'd keep them. An he had two or three tents, you see, and he'd pack all that stuff. And we'd come doon there, Grandfather would say, "Ah've saved up some clothes for the kids," and Mother would get all these clothes for us to wear to school in the wintertime. People were throwin away good stuff! And boots, ye know. Plenty of boots and shoes, back in the thirties, when things was really hard. And he saved up all these boots and shoes for the kids.

I mind one time we went doon an he had two big jars of suckers. Now these were clean jars, and it was these struppit balls, ye know?

JN: It was what—?

You know those struppit sweeties you get, struppit balls? Strupped balls. It was like a big marble, but full of stripes. And the more you sook it, it went into different colors. And because it got soft and sticky in the shop, they were throwin it oot. And these struppit balls, they went in your jaw and they'd sit there all day, ye know.

JN: [Laughing.] We called them jawbreakers, and they'd last all day.

That's grandfather, you know. Grandfather got us two jars, as big as that log [*pointing to a log destined for the fire*].

(87DW12 @ 23:08.)

§2.13. HOW WILLIE WILLIAMSON RECOVERED A LOST RIVETING TOOL

♪♫

Old Wully, he was a clever old man.[24] They called him a doll, when he was young. That's why old Bett McColl was so jealous, they called him a doll. He

---

24. "Old Wully": this spelling of the name gives an approximation of Duncan's pronunciation of "Willie," with a lax initial vowel, much as Duncan often pronounces "little" in a manner that sounds more like "luttle."

was so beaut—"The Doll," when he was a boy. He was small, fair hair—fair, fair, fair—and eh, he was a nice luttle man. He was only about five foot tall, and he used tae go out wi the fishermen.

He told me a story oncet, a long time ago, when I was a wee boy. An he was settin makin tin. Now he used tae make these floats for the nets. Ken, there were nae plastic floats in they days, you know, the floats for the nets. He made them of tin; sold them and made floats to keep the nets afloat for the fishermen in Tarbert. Because fishermen in these days in Tarbert, back in the thirties—it was all fishin skiffs. That's what they lived off, fishin boats. Boats lay in there, dozens of them, the whole pier. And old grandfather Wully used to make the floats.

Now, he told me, he had a luttle drill, a little thing like what they called a nail tool, for makin his own rivets. It was a little bar o iron that he made himself, with holes in it, different types of holes for different sizes o rivets. Noo, he made his own little rivets for puttin on handles an things like that, and he'd made one o the floats, and he said—Noo, this was in Tarbert, and eh, after he made the float, with another two or three for someone, he went and tuik them back to the fishermen who wanted them. An he gave them away to the fishermen. But when he come back, he searched for his nail tool high and low, but he cuid not find it; he cuid not find it. Now that was in Tarbert. Now jist listen tae this story.

If you stay in Tarbert, there is Loch Fyne, right? Where the fishermen fish. Now if you go on round the Mull of Kintyre, right round the Mull of Kintyre, you've got to go tae Campbeltown and come back up the other side, up the Kilberry side, which they travelled in the summertime when they left town.

Now, [see] this cigarette here. [*DW maps out the geography on the floor, using a cigarette as a pointer.*] That's down from Tarbert, down, right round to Skipness, right round to Campbeltown, round the Mull o Kintyre, and back up here to Kilberryside—that's Kilberry. Right round the point, round the peninsula, right round the point. So he searched, but he cuidnae get it. And, eh, he was searchin high and low, cause it was a favorite o his, you see?

Anyway, he said, "Well, your Granny," he said tae me, "an the bairns, we used tae go away for a wee holiday in the summertime. So," he said, "we went away to Kilberry, an we put up a tent in Kilberry. And I said, 'Come on, weans, away and get us some sticks for the fire, driftwood for the fire.'"

Noo, frae Kilberry to Tarbert is about fifteen miles, down the Kilberry road, and they camped their tents beside the shore there. And I think it was Aunt Rachel (who drowned herself),[25] a lovely lassie aboot, maybe ten or twelve? And they were gatherin sticks. And one o them picked up a float, an they brung it back, an they shaked it, an they brought it back to their faither. Said, "Father, we found this float." An it was rusty by that time, you know? Tin rusts very easy.

----

25. "Aunt Rachel who drowned herself": this tragic event occurred some thirty-five years later.

He shaked it, an he sat down an he took his clippers, his tin clippers, an he opened the float up, and there was his nail tool, inside the float! He had soldered it inside the float, and that float had broke away from that net, travelled round the whole coast, floated round Kintyre—round through Skipness, on through Campbeltown, right up an back into Kilberry—and was washed in the Kilberry tide. Come in wi the tide. About six month later, an he got it back. After six month in the sea! Now, that wee float must have travelled all around Kintyre: the wee buoy, the wee float, like a plastic ball made o tin. And that's a true story he told me.

"Now," he says, "you'll no believe that." And he took out of his luttle bag. He had a little, long mason's kind o bag made of sheet for holdin his tools in. He said, "There, it's in there, that's it." As if somebody had driv it, somebody had steered it, right round the Mull o Kintyre. And he got it back after six, maybe eight months or something.

JN: That's amazing.

That is the God's truth, now. The old man told me that for the God's truth.

(87DW04 @ 25:40.)

§2.14. A FAMOUS FIGHT ON THE GREEN AT ABERFELDY

♪♫

The worst fight I never saw—the worst fight I ever *haird* of among the Travellers—It's a true story. My grandfather was known as "Snorin John" MacColl.[26] He was a MacColl from Ireland, ye know? And when he went to fight, he— [*makes snorting sound*]—snored like a bull, you know?[27]

So, he was only a young man when he met my mother's father, Big John Townsley, Piper John Townsley. They met in Aberfeldy, in the green at Aberfeldy. An all the Travellers used tae gather together there, and they sat on the green havin a drink, and the local community never paid much attention to them. So along comes Snorin John MacColl, ye know. He would be in his twenties, maybe twenty-five, maybe thirty. Noo my grandfather, Big John, was about six-foot six. He was a piper. So, they got in an argument between them, you know. Now, John MacColl could not play the pipes, though he came off pipin

---

26. "My grandfather": Duncan is actually referring to his great-grandfather, Bett MacColl's father.
27. "He snored like a bull": that is, he snorted like a bull. "Snorin John" means "Snorting John." See the *OED*, s.v. the noun *snore*, sense 1: "a snort; snorting" and s.v. the verb *snore*, sense 1: "of animals, esp. horses: to snort."

stock, but my grandfather was a good piper, so an argument set up. A fight, came tae be a fight.

"Well," he said, "MacColl," he said, "I haird you can fight."

And he [MacColl] said, "I haird that ye can tae, *Red-Nosed* Jeck," he said. (He had a red nose, ye know? It was always red from drink.)

So, "I haird you can fight, but," he said, "there's nae sense in us wastin wir dukes." (Their dukes are called their fists, ye know?) He said, "The best thing we'll dae," he said, "let us have a *real* fight."

So each man had a luttle handcart, and they had this luttle thing we use for boilin the pot, you know, the snottum.* And Jeck—my grandfather always carried his stowed in the cart.

So they tossed a coin, a penny, for the first "wholp," they called it. And Big Jeck won the toss. An he says, "Where dae ye want it, MacColl?"

"Well," he says, "put it across my shoulders," he said.

And he took this piece o iron, and he het him across the shoulders. He het him across the shoulders, and he was six-foot six, my grandfather! An MacColl just gruntet like a pig.

"Well," he said, "Big Jeck," he said, "You hut me there, but," he said, "you never touched a muscle." Now, it was *his* turn. MacColl said, "Now, Red-Nosed Jeck, it's your turn," he said. "You het me across the shoulders," he said, "but you never hurt a muscle."

An my grandfather turned roond, and he said, "Look," he said, "MacColl," he said, "I'll tell you something. Het me where you like, but dinnae hit me in the airrums," he said, "because I'll no be able tae play my pipes."

"No, but," he said, "I'm gonnae het you somewhere else." An he het him across the legs, and they broke—the two of them, across there! [*Gestures toward the shins.*] Two! And Granny had to hurl him in a wheelchair for six month. An that was the end o the fight. And that was the fiercest fight, an no one was involved except the two o them. An that fight was talked aboot for many, many years to come. Imagine standing, with someone hittin a piece o iron across your legs, and you cuidnae do nothing! That was like, "Turn an fire," you know? "One, two, three"—ye know, when they challenged each other in olden days.

LW: A duel.

That was a duel, yeah. My mother's father an my father's father. [*Corrects himself.*] My mother's father an my father's *grand*father. And that was in the green in Aberfeldy. That was in about—oh, about 1912, just afore the First World War.

HT: Duncan, why couldn't they just fight with their hands?

Because they were too guid for each other! They didnae want—they was too guid. They was too guid for each other. Because Snorin John MacColl could fight anything, ye know?

(86DW41 @ 58:21.)

§2.15. JOHN MACCOLL BREAKS THE WATER PUMP

♪♫

Ye know, we used tae have all these—Scotland had these outside pumps, ye know, for pumpin water. There was a lion's face,[28] made o steel, an a handle where you pump, behind his face there.

So there was a man known as John Reid. And, eh, he fell in an argument wi John MacColl: Snorin John MacColl, my father's grandfather.

And they started in arguin, ye know? And MacColl said, "Look, man," he said. "Step back," he said, "I dinnae want tae hurt the pump." And Donald, Curly Donald, put his arms roond the pump.[29] And Snorin John made a kick at him wi his tackety boot, an he hit the pump an he knocked the faucet pump right off! He het the pump under the lion's chin! He missed Donald Reid an he het the pump.

These people could kick, you know. He het the pump! Size ten, a tackety boot, a shepherd's boot. Steel toe-cups. He het the pump, an the pump went *PFISSHT!* [*Mimics the sound of spurting water.*]

Donal, big Curly Donal, turned around and he says tae him, "That's a good job, MacColl," he said. "You'd a hurt me." [*Laughter.*]

And that's all! They shook hands, an that was the end.

(86DW41 @ 1:02:17.)

§2.16. BETT MACCOLL RINGS THE BELL AT TARBERT

♪♫

Bett MacColl was his daughter [John MacColl's daughter]. Six-foot two. My granny, my grandmother. She wore a man's size ten boot. I'll tell you what she done. At the fair, in the market, where you walked along tae the Tarbert fair, ye know? You took a hammer, and ye het the—and the bell rung—do you know these things?

---

28. "A lion's face": this decorative feature evidently served as the base of the spout.

29. "Curly Donald" Reid: this is apparently the same man whom Duncan previously refers to as John Reid. It is not clear where Duncan thought this incident took place; perhaps at Aberfeldy, as with the preceding anecdote.

HT: Yeah.

Big Bett MacColl comes along, twenty-one years of age, a baby on her back, ye know? Her husband, my grandfather, was just a wee man, you know. And he was a fisherman, sailed on a boat for the fishin. And all the fishermen knew them, you know. They were there all their lifetime, they never travelled. And they had stayed in this village [Tarbert], and it was market day, and Big Bett came along. Beautiful big woman, blond hair down her back, two big plaits, you know. She was a beautiful woman. But she was tough.

They said, "Come on, Bett!" All the fishermen, you know, half-drunk fishermen. "Gie us a wee bit for the hammer," you know.

She had a baby on her back with a shawl, and these little things she'd sewn, and the skiffers across it holdin the shawl together, you know?[30] She come along. She spit in her hand, you know. [*DW simulates her spitting on her hands and rubbing them together.*] She took the hammer, and *bopp!* Clean off the top! [*Laughter from all.*] The bell went right off! "*Cling!*" the bell went, and it disappeared.

They're still talkin about that, too. Six-foot two, an built like a tank. Big handsome woman. And that's because she came off Scandinavian stock, ye know, the big blond women.

(86DW41 @ 1:03:34.)

§2.17. ON TRAVELLERS' SURNAMES AND THE ORIGINS OF SOME TRAVELLER FAMILIES

JN: Do you ever meet any Travellers who are still keen on the Jacobite cause? Who like the songs of the Jacobites, you know?

No, not really. Didnae have much meaning to them, didnae have much meaning to them at all. No, it's a thing they never talk about.

JN: Because they say that some of the Travellers may have come from the Jacobite times.

Some of the Travellers did come from the Rebellion. Especially the young ones, who absconded and deserted from the army. Ones that was wounded, and were took—they sought help in the bands o travelling people. Food and help, and cloth to tie up their wounds.

---

30. Skiffers: see the Commentary on §9.8, "These silver skiffers."

JN: That was a long time ago.

That was a long time ago, yeah. So they joined up. I think that's where you got all these good names in among the travelling folk, like MacDougalls, MacMillans, MacLeans, Stewarts, MacPhersons, McFaddyens, Whytes, Robertsons, Campbells, MacDonalds, in among the travelling bands. I think that's from the Rebellion times, the Jacobite Rebellion, these names went in among the travelling folk. See what I mean? I think that's where they come frae. And the Clearances,* ye know?

JN: Do you think there are any names that go back before that? Any clans, any families?

I think back before that was MacPhees.[31] MacPhees and Burkes. And Williamsons. Yeah, they're very old names. The MacPhees and the Burkes and the Williamsons is very old names. And the Johnstones; they were very old. Johnstones goes back a long, long time. But I think some o these other names, like MacMillan, MacGregor, and Cameron, Stewart, I think they come in after the Clearances. They joined the travelling people after the Clearances. Some o the young soldiers married in among the Traveller lassies.

(87DW14 @ 44:45.)

§2.18. GREAT-GRANDFATHER MACDONALD RUNS OFF WITH THE TRAVELLING PEOPLE

♪♫

You see, my granny's father, he was a MacDonald from Appin. He was crofting folk. My granny was a Traveller, see? My granny's mother was a Traveller, I should say; my great-granny was a Traveller.[32] But he came up—he was a piper in the Perthshire militia—and he came intae a travelling band somewhere about Crieff, wi his pipes under his arm. An they give him shelter, and they give him something tae eat. An he played his pipes tae them, an they sat round the fire—I made my granny tell me—an he played all night tae them, because he was a guid piper, and that was very interestin tae the travellin people, tae hear a good piper. And my great-granny was a young lassie, about sixteen. Bonnie

---

31. MacPhees: also known as the McPhees or Macfies, from the Gaelic name *Mac a'Phi*.
32. "My great-granny was a Traveller": this is Duncan's great-grandmother on his maternal side, the mother of Bella MacDonald, Duncan's favorite grannie, who lived with the family and was a captivating storyteller.

young woman. An she'd two sisters who were deaf an dumb. And then the next mornin he was gone, and so was my great-granny!

JN: [Laughs.]

And he never went back tae his brithers. He tuik tae the road and became a piper for his livin. He liked the travellin life, so he took it. Roderick MacDonald was his name, Roderick.

(87DW14 @ 46:51.)

§2.19. ON TRAVELLERS' FUNERALS AND FUNERARY CUSTOMS

You see, Jack, even the old travelling people, back in my father's day, they never even registered their child when it was born. An, if a child died, they jist buried it in the moors, in the open.

JN: Would they keep to any special burial ground or area?

No, there's nae special burial ground, not in my father's day as much. They do now. Since the thirties they've kept to the burial ground. But I'm talkin away back when ma father was jist a—I mean, if my father was livin today he'd be well over a hundert, and he was a child.

Ah remember my father telling me that there were Travellers—a wee boy could barely remember it—an they were goin up to a place, some place in Kintyre, and one o the wee babies died. And they tuik it out tae the forest an they buried it in a nice wee place. An they stuid all around and some old man muttered a few words or something; I don't know. But then they kindled a fire on top o the burial site, and they said if anybody passes by they'll just think it was somebody kindled a fire. The wee baby was buried. It died when it was young, only maybe a couple weeks old. They buried it in a nice wee place there, and they kindled a fire on the top.

The Indians, the American Indians, have the same habit of daein that. That's funny, isn't it? They first buried the baby and then they covered the wee grave up with nice clods, maybe put some stones in, and then covered it up. An then they kindled a fire, a great fire on the top o the grass where the baby was, so that that fire would destroy every marks o where it's been dug. Noo, I read that in a book years and years and years ago that some o the American Indians used tae do the same thing. They buried their people in the ground, and then they kindled a fire so people would jist think it was a fire. See, there could be another cause for that, Jack. That's stray animals, ye know, diggin up things in the ground. Well, the smell of burnt fire would keep em away from it. That could be another idea. Well, that was the Americans' idea, the Indians' idea, but—

JN: Would they do that with older people too?

No, no older people, no. Jist babies. I remember, my mother—when old people died they took them to the graveyard and they buried them, but they threw in a cup—a tin cup—and a piece of bread and a coin.*

JN: Always these three things?

Always these three things.

JN: Why, do you think?

Well, my mother tried tae tell me. The coin was supposed tae pay the way wherever they went; the piece of bread was tae keep their soul alive till they got there; an the cup was for his drinkin while on his journey, wherever, tae some other land he was goin to. An then there was a great thing aboot travellin people: old pipers got buried with their pipes on their coffins. Their bagpipes was buried with them.

JN: Now the pipes could be valuable, right?

Yeah, pipes were valuable.* And the old woman's jewelry was put on her.* All her beads, all her jewelry, all her brooches, all her possessions was put on her, an she was buried with em. They never kept—maybe the daughter would keep one wee thing.

JN: Would they do that in the church graveyard?

In the church graveyard, yeah.

JN: I see. Was there a minister, you think, they had with them, or—?

Oh, a minister, yeah; they all got ministers. They all got a minister to give a wee sermon for them, yeah.

JN: Because I don't know what the minister would think about this.

I don't know, but, you see, they made sure that they buried everything with them—with the cup, an the things within the coffin with them when they were buried, you see. And so wi the jewelry. All the minister knew was that they were jist buryin a coffin, he didnae know what was in it, ye see.[33]

JN: Do you remember any funerals that stand out in your mind? Like big Traveller funerals, with somebody important?

Yeah. A big Traveller funeral was all-important for an old person who was well known. An old person 'at was well known was—they gathered—Travellers come from all over. The most important thing aboot Travellers' funerals is a child, a wee child, belongin tae some of the travelling people, or an elderly person: that gathers the most people.

JN: The wee child as well?

The wee child. Afore it's only weeks old, that wee baby child can have as big a funeral as what the old person would hae, you know? Especially if the old people was well known. . . .[34] [There's hardly a Traveller] that's not related to MacPhees in some way or other. Now Ah've got MacPhee blood in me. So does all the Travellers, in some way connected, if ye go back far enough, by marriage or through generationship, ye know? Now say that an old man MacPhee was to die. There's one o them now, he's related tae the MacPhees, he's in his eighties, about eighty-six. And he was a piper.[35] When he dies, I guarantee ye, half the Travellers of Scotland will be there.

JN: What's the biggest funeral you've been to, would you say?

The biggest funeral I've ever been to in my life was an old man called Johnny Whyte, from Aberdeenshire. He was a cousin of Bryce's.[36] There were three pipers there. He was buried in Banchory, in Aberdeenshire. And every Traveller in Aberdeenshire come down. Of course Ah was there too, wi many o my relations from Banff. There were so many Travellers there that some of them cuidnae even get tae the graveyard. They cuidnae get room to stand aroond in the graveyard. Some of them had tae just stay out on the roadside with their cars; they cuidnae get in. But they put in an appearance at the funeral. Even though you never was actually at the site, as long as you were there.

---

33. Some talk about Viking Age ship burials is left untranscribed here.
34. There is a short break in the recording here as the tape reverses direction.
35. Duncan is probably referring to his friend Willie MacPhee, who is discussed in chapter 1.
36. "A cousin of Bryce's": the reference is to Bryce Whyte, Betsy Whyte's husband.

Well, you see, the most terrible—it's like, if you don't go tae my relation's funeral, I don't go tae yours. You see, that's a great stigma on the travelling people. Unless you've some reason that keeps you back from being there; that's accepted. Say your wife's ill, or some of your children's ill, and ye cannae get [there], or your car broke down, or you've something else, you're forgiven. But not tae turn up, and say "Och, to hell, I'm nae goin there"—that is a terrible insult, ye know what I mean? Because ye don't know among your own family when some of you are going to loss some o your own people. An it's a very puir thing when a Traveller gets buried and not many people are there. It's a kind of an insult, see what I mean? Specially when people you've known all your life, when you're alive, disn't turn up tae your funeral.

JN: After the funeral, would there be family get-togethers?

Family get-togethers—they'll split up an maybe they'll go inte the pubs and they'll have drinks together.* Some will drive home in their own caravan and they'll have a drinkin session. But I've been tae a lot o funerals among Travellers and very rarely have I seen anybody drunk at funerals. But afterwards, yeah. It's a kind o insult forbyes to come tae somebody's funeral when you're drunk; you're no showin them very good respect.

JN: What about beforehand? Do you have a wake for the body?

No, no. No. We never sit up wi the bodies, we don't have no wakes. Travellers didnae have any wakes. The Irish Travellers do.

JN: Would you hire someone to keep the body?

No, the body is off, the body is off tae the church; the undertaker takes it off tae the church. Some o them now have a ceremony in the church, before they take it off. Now if you go to the church ceremony, you don't need tae go to the graveyard. See what I mean? Say an old Traveller was died in Perth, and his home ground was in Argyllshire or Dumbartonshire. They'll have a ceremony in a church for the people who cannae go there, and then the hearse'll take him off, but wi people waitin at the graveyard who've never come to the ceremony.

JN: You mean they might have a church service where he died, but they'd want to be buried back where they were from?

In their old home ground. If somebody's buried there, if their family members is buried there, they all go back tae where their family is.

(87DW04 @ 40:05.)

§2.20. HOW MUCH LAND DOES A MAN NEED?*

🎵

JN: Do you have a family graveyard?

My father—I'll tell you a wee story. When my wee sister Cathie died, we were very puir, back in the thirties. Everyone was; it was no shame tae be poor, it was everyone was the same. My mother was down to Captain Campbell, who owned the churchyard, the graveyard. He owned Crarae Estate,* he owned Minard, he owned [this] whole district of Argyll, Captain Campbell. And she

Figure 2.5 Williamson at his mother's unmarked grave, Minard churchyard, Argyll, 1988. Photo by Dorothy Leese.

goes up for Captain Campbell and she asked for the Captain, and he came out himsel. He was a big tall man, army man, with a great mustache. I remember him fairly well.

"What's the trouble, Betsy?" he said. He knew my mother well.

"Well," she said, "look, Captain," she said. "I cannae afford tae get my baby buried and it died, wee Cathie died." (That was one of the ones what was born in hospital.)

"Well," he said, "what dae you want me to dae for you?"

She said, "I want you to get me a wee bit of ground in the cemetery for my baby."*

"Well," he says, "Luik. I'll get a piece of ground in the cemetery that will do for yese all, an it will be your own. Don't worry about it. I'll get in touch with the gravedigger," he says, "and I'll dae everything for you."

And my father carried that wee baby on his back, five miles, on his shoulder, in a little white coffin. We all walked behind him to Minart, fae Furnace to Minart, which is five miles. And she was buried in there. My brother Charlie's buried in there, my mother's buried in there, and my father's buried in the same churchyard. And I suppose any other member of the family who at that time stays in Argyll, like my old brother Jock and some o his friends, they'll all probably end up in the same graveyard, because it's their own.

Now, Ah was stayin with Linda's grandfather, old Don Cass,[37] and I says, "Don, how far does your land go?"

He said, "As far as you can see with your eyes, that's my land." He says tae me, "You need land, you know." He said to me, "Do you have any land in Scotland?"

Ah said, "Yes, Don, I've got land in Scotland. My own land in Scotland."

He said, "Is it big?"

Ah said, "No, it's no very big. It's aboot six feet long, four feet broad." An Ah said, "It was bought for my mother because she was so puir she cuidnae afford to bury my wee sister." I said, "She got it free from the laird. And," I said, "my mother's in it, my father's in it, my sister and brother's in it, and," I said, "I hope someday I'll get it. 'At's all the land I need."

(87DW04 @ 50:08.)

---

37. "Linda's grandfather, Old Don Cass": Linda Williamson's maternal grandfather, Don Lynn Cass, was a great landowner in southeastern Wisconsin; see Campbell, *Traveller in Two Worlds*, 2.35.

Chapter 3

A CHILDHOOD IN ARGYLL

§3.1. GROWING UP IN THE WOODS OUTSIDE THE
VILLAGE OF FURNACE

Now we lived in a forest, right in the center of a oak forest. It was a oak wood forest. And beside us was a little village wi about five hundred people, one post office, two shops, one butcher shop, nothing else. The nearest place was maybe eight miles away, the large village called Inveraray in Argyll, where it was the home of the Campbells.

So ma father there built this large home-constructed tent. Nowadays no one would ever believe that anyone could live in such a place. And in this forest it was *dark*, really dark. It was dark when the leaves were on, [though] the trees in the summertime was really nice. By wir place ran a river, and this river was always full of plenty salmon and fish. We had the river and we had the sea beside us, which was about a quarter of a mile from where we stayed. And then there was a stone quarry not far away from that place.

So ma father tuik up employment in the quarry, in the stone quarry. Forty pence a day; that's two pound a week. And then he started to havin a family. Now he brought up sixteen children.* Well, not sixteen, I'm sorry, thirteen children. Three died as infants. And every one of those children were born in the tent. The children who were not born in the tent had died. They were born in hospital because my mother was sae serious ill. She had a child every year. They sent her to Oban hospital, which was just a common hospital, ye know. And the children that she had in the hospital died, which left thirteen.

Now, all these thirteen children are all alive today, except one. The oldest brother had joined the navy and came home from the war after five years in the navy; [he] tuik up employment in a place called Stanley in Perthshire. He never smoked. He never drank. He reared up his family. And then, at the age of forty-seven, he tuik ill, an he went tae the hospital, and they found that he had cancer in his lung. An it was a type of cancer he could've lived all his life

61

for.[1] It was not a serious type o cancer, the doctor told him. But he jist walked down tae the river an committed suicide, drowned himself.

Now, life in this great tent my father had built many, many years ago was wonderful. It was really good for us because we had wir old grandmother there, and we had some of the old uncles would come for a visit, and they would stay, and my father would put another extension intae this great big place, and they would have their own privacy and their own place to stay.

And the only problem was, there was not another Traveller in the district in the winter months. And us children had no one to play with except the village children. And if something happened—now my mother used tae walk around the village, and she had many good friends in the village. And she got to know these people, an she knew them well. But if anything happened in the village, we got the blame, cause we were livin in a tent in the forest. I cuidnae fight in school. I cuidnae hurt anyone. I cuidnae touch nothing. I cuidnae dae nothing wrong in school, because if I did, when my mother hawked the doors round, seein her friends, and she [the friend] said, "Your son done this," then my father come an he beat me.* Even suppose it was not my fault, if something went missin in the school, oh, we naturally got the blame, even supposin we're innocent.

We were persecuted at every turn.* Every turn, we could not do nothing right, because we were travelling folk, and we were the only travelling people in the district. Even though ma father had permission to be there, many people tried tae get us moved, but the Duke wouldnae have it. The Duke of Argyll wouldnae have it.

(86DW03 @ 18:01.)

§3.2. LIFE IN THE WILLIAMSONS'S TENT

CE: When you went to school, did the other children ever come into your tent?

Yes, we used to bring children up to the tent, and the children loved it. But their mother and father was against it, you see. They didnae like bringin the children up to the tent. But the tent was lovely.

❧

---

1. "He could've lived all his life for": that is, he could have lived for the rest of his life with this type of cancer.

Figure 3.1 Williamson at Loch Fyne, 1988, standing near his birthplace at the shore, with the village of Furnace in the background. Photo by Dorothy Leese.

My father would not allow to have a fire inside the tent except it was on the floor, and a hole in the roof just to let the smoke go up, ye know.[2] And we had what ye call cruisies, an these lamps hung from the ceilin on pieces o wire.* And when the girls came to change theirself or do things, they had their own privacy. There was a curtain hung down, and this was a big place. You know, they could do anything and have their privacy there. But it was all outside toilets.

And a river used tae run by the campsite, so we collected all the water from the stream in pails, in a homemade pail my father had made. You made these pails of tin; he made them from tin hisself. He was a tinsmith forbyes, and he made these pails. And he made clothes-pegs for my mother and all these things.

Now the local villagers were upset because we were always healthy and strong. The main reason that we were healthy an strong was because wir life relied on shellfish. We ate whelks, we ate mussels, we ate cockles, we ate everything that crept, hopped, and jumped! When we would come intae school every morning, sometimes holes in wir knees, no backside in wir pants, you know, just castaway clothes that my mother would collect from around the village, from other women that she knew, friends of hers.

Now you can imagine, there were no school dinners. There were no free meals. There were nothing. No social security, no nothing at all in these days.

---

2. Here, during about four minutes of talk, Duncan draws a diagram of the type of tent that his father built for the winter months and comments on its structural features, including its earthen floor and its central hearth (see §3.3).

And we were so hungry at school! I mean, there were nine of us goin to school all at the same time, nine. We came home sometimes. This place was empty at dinner hour. The children went home to have their lunch with their mommy because it was only about a stone throw from the school to where we stayed. We come home—this [tent] was empty. Father was workin, mother was goin visitin her friends tae see if she could find something from them, ye know, around the doors? She wasnae beggin, but she was just visitin her friends, and if they had anything to spare that they didnae need, they would give it to her, ye know?

So this is how I spent my childhood. My father was a tinsmith an a basket-maker,* and during the weekends he would make baskets. And in these days he would make utensils. He would make toasters for the fire. He would make ladles. He would make graters for gratin the vegetables. And Mother would trade them around the doors for secondhand clothes and for food and things. She wouldnae sell em. Well, if she didnae trade them, if somebody had nothing to give her, they would pay her, maybe a sixpence, maybe threepence, for some of these things. And he [Father] made them on the weekends to keep us alive.

So we grew up like that. You left school at the age of fourteen in these days,* fourteen. Hunger was the only thing was wrong with us. We were healthy enough, but we were so hungry! Because if our mother had any food, she gave it tae the younger children. I mean, you cuidnae feed everyone. When you came seven, you were supposed to feed yourself. Ye had to take care o yourself.

(86DW03 @ 27:23 and @ 29:33.)

§3.3. DUNCAN IS BORN BY THE SHORE OF LOCH FYNE[3]

So when it came the month of March, Father burned the tent, the big barrakit.* Tuik a piece o canvas an said, "OK," he said tae my mother, "take the children fae school," the first of March, that was near finishin school in March. We'd been tae school all winter long—Geordie, Jimmy, Susan, Ellen, Mary—we'd all been tae school. We were dyin to get on wir way, right? "We're off."

We didnae have a horse, we just had a couple prams, ye know, packin all our stuff on. Daddy would pick the best sticks, the best piece o canvas, the cookin utensils, and the blankets and clothes that we needed tae go off for the summer. So we left Furnace. My mother was expecting—with me!

She didnae have many children [at] that time; maybe seven. See? I was the seventh, right? So she came down here [to a place by the shore of Loch Fyne], and by the time she reached here she said to my daddy, "I cannae go any further.

---

3. This recording was made in the open air, at first in the woods to the north side of Furnace, where Duncan's father built his winter tent, then at the place where Duncan was born, a short walk south of the village.

Ah'm in labor." It was only a short walk from Furnace to here, but by the time she got here, she was in labor. So he pulled his luttle pram in here [*points to an area by a scrub tree at the shore*] an he put up his tent. Ma granny was with us. Her husband had died and she stayed wi us all the time, the old storyteller, old Belle MacDonald. She was with us, so she said, "Johnny, put up your tent. Your wife's goin tae have a baby."

So they put up their luttle tent, an mother went in an she made the bed, an I was born there. And Granny was my midwife. There was no doctors, no nurses, no midwife. Granny cut my cord, takin up everything, and put me to sleep in my mother's arms and put me at my mother's breast, in that luttle tent under that tree. And my mother stayed in there for two days. The next day she tuik me in her airms; two days later she walked down tae the village, showed all her friends her new baby. A sixpence here and a thrupenny piece there. By the time she got to Lochgilphead, she'd collected about a pound of money. You hansel a new baby, you hansel a new baby with silver.*

Two days old; that was me! An she had me in a shawl, the way the Travellers' carried them in a shawl, ye know?

Daddy packed up his tent—two days! She lay in there for two days, and she had tae drink her milk or her gruel or porridge, whatever Granny made for her. Two days, and this fit young woman had the baby, wrapped the baby up in a wee shawl, and tuik her shawl on her shoulder an a big silver pin in it, and—"Right, let's go!" Walked to Lochgilphead—sixteen miles. But they stopped at Minard; they would stop at Minard. She would go and show all her old cronies—her friends, you know?

She was well respected here, Jack. She was known. She was born here, ye see. Well, she wasn't actually born here [at Furnace], but she spent all her life here. And Grandfather, her father, was born at the bridge there.[4] Grandfather spent all his life here.

(88DW09 @ 1:08:04.)

§3.4. A WALK THROUGH THE WOODS WHERE THE WILLIAMSONS HAD THEIR BARRAKIT

JN: What's the name of the burn coming down here, Duncan?[5]

---

4. "Born at the bridge there": this is a bridge in the village of Furnace that spans the River Lechen. Travellers visiting the area used to put up their tents nearby. Duncan's mother's father was "Big John" Townsley.
5. This tape was recorded in the open air, on a walk through the woods outside Furnace, where Duncan spent much of his childhood.

Eh, the Lechen. The River Lechen. This was all oak here at one time. This was all oak. We can see where I spent my childhood. This is the bridge terrace here, dae ye see?[6] That's known as the bridge terrace. It's houses, separate houses. There was no electric pole here when we were there. That was all oak; there were no conifers there.* Big spreading oaks, you know, like a estate.[7] And we had wir tent right in the middle, and, eh, we had paths leadin all the way through the forest, and a luttle river coming down here.

We got wir fresh water from the river. Mother used to wash her clothes in the river every Saturday afternoon. And, eh, we had no conifers here—spruces, they call it now. It was all these great big oak trees, ye know, and the branches touched down to the ground, and the rabbits had eaten the grass short, and there were no weeds, none o that young stuff there. It was like livin in a estate. It belonged to the Duke of Argyll, and he had a forester taking care o this, and dare you ever even write your name on a tree and you were in trouble!

So that's where we were reared up, here. We'd walk from here tae school. It was a short walk tae school, just about a quarter of a mile. A lot o my brothers and sisters was born in here.

JN: Here in the woods?

They were born in the woods. Jimmy was born in here, Susan, Mary, Rachel, Nellie, Jeannie, they were all born in here. Willy was born in here. Ah was the only one that was born [elsewhere] in the spring, because we took off. Father had said, "We'll go off for the summer, to Lochgilphead for a while." And, eh, my mother was pregnant. We only got the length o the shore when they had tae stop an put their tent up. She didnae know her time; she thought she was goin tae have a baby in May, but it was comin in April, you see?

April was a lovely early spring that year, 1928. When it was lovely in the spring my father said, "We'll go off an we'll get an early spring down in Lochgilphead," ye know. He would probably be cuttin hay round some of the crofts with his scythe, you know.

He was a good scythesman. He contracted cuttin hay with his scythe, so much per acre. He carried his own scythe an his scythe stone. Could cut anything. He tuik that with him. And even the minister who buried him—Duncan MacKenzie buried him—when he gave a sermon at the graveside, he says, "We're buryin one of the greatest scythesmen ever lived."

But that old tree's still there; that was one of them [*pointing*]. They were all like that.

---

6. "The bridge terrace": the reference is to a row of houses where the parents of some of Duncan's schoolmates lived and where the village children used to play.
7. "Estate": pronounced with extended vowel length (stress) at the first syllable.

JN: They were all like this big oak tree here?

They were all like that big one there. That one was never touched.[8]

∾

JN: Would you have any reason to go off far in the other direction, away from the village?

No, unless you went for firewood. And huntin for the hares—rabbits.* Up the hill behind you, there, Collechan. Collechan is a hill wi heather. Heather for scrubbers, and heather for makin heather besoms. We collectit all the heather up there, and Father would make heather besoms and heather scrubbers from the hill. And collectin firewood. That's the only reason—and hunting rabbits, in the cliffs an the rocks up there. Oh, that hill goes back all the way tae Inveraray.

This old road [*pointing to a dirt track*] only goes to an old Gaelic farm. There's an old Gaelic farm up there. The Forestry bought the farm and plantit the whole farm, the estate. And the house is all in ruins, ye know. It was a beautiful farm at one time. There's nobody livin on it anymore. It's called Collechan.

JN: Was the road here when you were a boy?

Yeah. It went right tae the farm. Old Donald Monroe used tae come down there with his two cans of milk. He used tae carry the milk by hand. And he used tae hum away "The Swanee River,"[9] and he come to the river and he would take his luttle juig, and he put a couple of juigs o water in his milk, ye know, tae make it go further. [*Laughs.*] He'd sell it at the village to the people. [*Duncan hums the opening bars of "Swanee River."*] I watched him many times. He just had cans, you know? These big cans, with the milk.

He had two cows and he milked them, him and his old sister Betsy. And she had a string of chestnuts, ye know? Conkers, we called them. Boys played with them. She had a string of chestnuts round her neck when she was three year old till she was eighty-five. She wore them all her life. She slept wi them on, she never tuik them off all her life.

She never married, none of the two. Old brother and sister, they stayed in a small farm up here, and they kept some sheep and a couple o cows. And

---

8. Omitted here are some remarks relating to Ian Campbell, the eleventh Duke of Argyll, and his fruitless attempt to recover treasure from a ship of the Spanish Armada that was sunk in Tobermory Bay.

9. "The Swanee River": this is the name by which the song "Old Folks at Home," composed by Stephen Foster in 1851, is commonly known after its first line, "Way down upon the Swanee River." The river is known today as the Suwannee River.

he sold his milk in the village from a couple o cans, and he walked wi them. And there's a wee river that crosses up there, and there's a wee pool, and he used to go—[*hums bars from "Swanee River"*]—all the time and put a couple of dabs of water intae the can tae make the milk go farther. Penny a pint, ye know? [*Laughs.*] The people jist bought it for their cats, I think. They weren't even that interested in it. He would sell his two cans of milk an go home with about fifty or sixty pence, ye know; he was quite happy wi it. And his sheep all ran through here, ye know? The sheep wanderit all over. Old Donald Monroe, yeah. Funny old fellow.

JN: How would you catch the hares?

With snares; we set snares. See, the hares in the heather—*white* hares. The white ones. They have tunnels under the heather, ye know, and they cannae run fast in these tunnels. We could outrun them. You saw them under the tunnels and just—[*gestures*]—dive on top o them, ye know?

JN: Oh, you could just go after them?

Yeah, go after them in those tunnels, with our hands. But the rabbits—we used tae dig for the rabbits up in the cliff. Rabbits had their nests in the cliff face, in the rocks. And you'd pull out the stones so they cuidnae go in any further. And then you've got em. "Wee, wee, wee!" [*Mimics their cries.*] We sold two in the village, one an six a pair.[10] And, eh, we'd keep another two for the pot. And then, for the one an six, we could buy a little bread an butter an tea an sugar an cigarettes. And that was good for the night, with another couple in the pot, and then the next morning—up the river and get a couple o salmon. Sell one, and put one in the pot, ye know?

JN: The salmon you had to just nab, right?

You had to nab them, oh yeah. It was illegal but we had a way o getting them, you know. A way o gettin them. Millions of salmon were killed up that river.

JN: So is this something all the children would do? Getting the hares—?

Yeah, the kids. My sisters were good at rabbits, with the hares and rabbits, yeah.

JN: Getting the salmon—?

----

10. "One an six a pair": one shilling and sixpence a pair.

Yeah. We had learned to do that from an early age, ye know? You got good at it through time. If you do anything often enough, you really get good at it.

JN: You wouldn't ever get deer, would you?

Never had a deer, no, unless the farmer shot one and gave my mother a piece. That was the only time we got one. Farmer would shoot them coming in these little puckle patches o corn. They would come and eat this wee puckle of corn, and—[*Duncan makes a noise like a gun going off*]. And it was too much for the whole o them to eat, so he would say, "Betsy, would you like a piece?"

JN: He couldn't keep the meat, right?

Cuidnae keep the meat, there were no fridges or nothin. He just shared it with anybody who needed it, ye know? Maybe tuik a haunch for himself an his wife an family an shared the rest of it wi anybody that wanted it. To keep them off his wee puckle corn, ye know?

JN: Right.

So that was the whole story. He was happy tae get the meat for a bite, for himself. And they killed a sheep. And then they always killed a pig in Auchindrain, and every year my mother got the pig's head. That was all she got, the head every year, from Eddie McCallum, who owned the Auchindrain Museum* there. Because she worked [there], we got the pig's head every Christmas. Killed the pig every Christmas, and we got the head o the pig. The pig's head. It was really good.

(88DW10 @ 55:01 and @ 1:00:15.)

§3.5. OWN SONG, "COLLECHAN"*

🎵

But you see, where we stayed [near Furnace] was a place called Collechan. Collechan was under a mountain. My father an mother used tae wander there in the evenings. They would go by theirsels, collectin sticks for the fire. And when Ah went back there an the woods were all plantit and the forest was gone, Ah made—Ah put a few words tae the tune of "Mother."[11] And, eh—[*Sings:*]

---

11. "Mother": a well-known Gaelic air, *Mo mhàthair*, composed by Neil MacLean of the Isle of Mull and available in Gillies, *Songs of Gaelic Scotland*, 297–99.

1   Oh my Johnny, oh my Johnny
     I was young and I was bonnie
     when we wandered round Collechan long ago.

Collechan was a hill where they used tae collect the heather for the scrubbers, and him and her would go for a walk through the hills and bring back sticks, and bring back some heather for scrubbers. [*Sings:*]

2   And the purple, the bracken—
     but it's now my hairt is breakin—
     when we wandered round Collechan long ago.

Collechan

That was just words I added to that tune. My mother and father used tae like that tune called "Mother." He used tae play it on the pipes, ye see? An I just put a few words to it. It's a nice tune.

JN: Is there more to it, Duncan?

No, there's no words more to it. No, just that, just that wee bit. I don't sing it very much.

(87DW12 @ 58:40.)

§3.6. DUNCAN WAS CHRISTENED MANY TIMES

DY: How old were you when you got christened?

Wait till you hear this! This is something you must understand. When you went to get christened, the minister then paid the mother half a crown. Two and sixpence. So Ah was christened three times! Ah was christened at the age of one. Ah was christened at the age of two. Ah was christened at five year old. It wasnae for the christenin, it was for the money. Because we was so poor, you see, mother said, "Come on, I'll get you christened," because she was broke. She had no money and maybe needed a loaf of bread or something. And there was the minister's house, an open invitation, you see! She said, "Come on, I'll get you christened." I was five year old when Ah had my fourth christening. And he put the holy water on my head, and he said a few words, and he gave my mother half a crown, two and six, about thirty pence, ye see?

I'll tell you something. We must have had about thirty christenins in wir family. [*General laughter.*] The minister didnae know one girl from the other or one son from the other. You see, the minister never knew who was Duncan, and who was George, who was Jimmy, who was Willie, or Rachel, or Susan, or Ellen.

She [my mother] said, "Come on, laddie."

I says, "Mommy," I said, "I was there last week!"

"Come on, he'll no ken the difference." And he tuik me in, an he got his wee wooden bowl, and, ye know, he dupped his fingers in, an he put it on the head, and he said a few magic words, and—"Your name?"

"It's Duncan."

"Oh, yes, Duncan. Yes."

Old MacKinnon, old Master MacKinnon. He was a great old minister, ye know, and he would go tae his wee box, and he would take a sixpence and two shillins, you know, give it to my mother. She would go and buy—that would get us messages for one day.[12] I mean, a half a loaf of bread was only two and a halfpence, and a dozen eggs was only about two and a halfpence, ye know. And that was food for us for a full day.

So then they used to go tae the priest. There were a priest there. And I've been before both, ye see what I mean? She'd take me to the priest and all, you see. Just for the money. We're not Catholics at heart. I'm not against Catholics, now, don't think I am! I'm not against Catholics. I think they're the wonderest people in the world. And, eh, they've their own religion. I've nothin against their religion. It was jist a way o gettin some money for tae buy some food. So Ah been christened, Holly, at least five times.

(86DW03 @ 52:58.)

---

12. "Messages for one day": that is, groceries for a day.

§3.7. STRUCK DUMB ON A PICTISH STONE

♪♫

When we used tae travel down through Lochgilphead in the summertime, we took off in the springtime. My father was back tae the same farms every year tae thin turnips on your knees, ye know, big fields o turnips. They grew them thick in bunches, but ye had tae crawl on your knees an separate them so they would chance tae grow. Probly single them out aboot four to five inches from each turnip, and pull away all the weeds, and pull away all the other turnips that grew around them, because they sowed them very thick. Nowadays they have a certain seed that doesnae need that.

So father was standin in the field an we started thinnin turnips. The farm would have maybe six or seven acres. When that was finished, we'd move on tae the next farm. Now we were very small, and the corn was just starting tae grow,[13] the green corn just startin tae come up. And there was a great big Pictish stone* in the middle o the field where we were camping.

Noo, father warned us. He says, "Look, don't interfere with the stone, boys, in any way. You can luik at it an admire it, but," he says, "don't touch it, an don't do anything to it. Don't climb on it."

So Ah never listened to my father's word, and I was a bit, a wee bit bigger than your Alan.[14] Maybe five or six—well, it wouldn't be six; it'd be five. Ah climbed up the stone. And I sat at the top an I went, "Coo hoo, look at me!"

Father says, "Come down there, boy!" He says, "Ye know what'll happen to ye. Something bad'll happen to ye," he says, "if you dinnae come doon from that stone."

So he couldnae come up; Ah didnae come doon. But I got fed up climbin up the stone, and then—and then Ah came down. It was a very sunny hot sunny day. And I said to Mommy, "I want a penny." And Mommy said, "I dinnae have a penny." There's a wee shop [where I] used to get the McCallard's toffee. Big bite of toffee for a penny. So she hadnae got a penny to gie me. "Well," I said, "I'm going away. I'm no comin back." And I took [to] the middle o the field.

The corn was only jist aboot six inches high. They were busy thinnin the turnips. What we used tae do is go in front o my mother's dreel and scrape a wee bit around it and try tae help her on, you know?[15] Well, I went out an I lay down in the sun. And the sun came up full strong. They searched for me all day and never found me; Ah lay there all day. They thought I fell in the burn,

---

13. "The corn was just starting to grow": that is, the shoots of hay, oats, or other crops were just starting up.

14. "Your Alan": the author's son Alan was four years old in October 1987, when this recording was made.

15. "My mother's dreel": that is, "My mother's drill," or row of turnips.

because a great big river runs past the field where we stayed, the River Add, which is famous for salmon.

But they found me at midnight. And that was—I would say it would be the first week in June. They got me there in the middle o summer. I was very sick, ill. I remember nothing else; I was sunstroke.

And the next thing I remembered—Jack, this is the God's honest truth, I swear on my mother's grave—my brothers was catchin seagulls. And—to catch a seagull, you have a little can with a lid, you see, full o water. And a bit o string and a bit o bread, and the seagull swallowed the bread, and he cuidnae take away this string. We caught the seagulls and then we let them go again. Willie and George. They were older than me, maybe a couple of years older than me each. And I was lyin in the tent, completely sick. I was lost! I had no memory, no brain, no nothing! Oh, my mother took me tae the doctor's, and he give me some kind o tablets or something, but as far as I was concerned I was completely finished. The doctor said I was completely sunstroke. He said it was lucky I had lain on my back and it struck me in the forehead. He said if it'd hit me here in the back of the head, it wouldae killed me. That's what I learned later.

And Ah wakened up, and they had me in a wee bit blanket in front o the tent, an the first thing I remember was watchin the gulls. Frae the day I come down off that stone tae the day I wakened up watchin the boys catchin gulls, that was exactly two month or more. The corn was full grown and ready tae be cut, an the only thing I can remember was going there and lyin down in the corn six inches green, just comin through the earth, six inches green. And the next thing I remembered—[pauses]—was the corn gettin cut, and my father takin the horses around the field, and my mother stookin.[16] An that was the month of August.

I was back to where I started, but I cuidnae remember anything. I remember climbin the stone; I remember comin doon off the stone; I remember lying down in the field; but for two month of my life, for two and a half month, I know nothing. They had thinned the turnips, they had wandered all through the country and hurled me in a pram and took me tae doctors, took me to places, but I knew nothing.

(87DW04 @ 1:11:33.)

---

16. "My mother stookin": that is, my mother piling the hay into stooks, or stacks.

§3.8. DUNCAN'S TEACHERS WERE WONDERFUL;
SOME OF THE VILLAGERS WERE NOT

SL: Did you get along well with the teachers at school?

Oh, the teachers was wonderful. The teachers was wonderful teachers.

CE: So there was no prejudice against Travellers?

The teachers were never prejudiced. The teachers regarded us as jist natural children. We had a Miss Crawford, an a Miss Smith from Tarbert, an she knew my grandmother and my grandfather well because they were residents of the place for many, many years. And Miss Smith was a wonderful teacher; she just treated us like the rest of the children. You know, we were jist accepted. An the children treated us just like children.

The only problem we had was the *parents* of the children. The parents of the children was thinkin that we were goin tae teach them [the settled children] bad things. But we were teachin them about flowers, and we were teachin them about nature. We were teachin them about fish, and we were teachin them how to guddle trout,[17] and hunt rabbits, and cuik shellfish. We were teachin the children how to stay alive!

SL: So how did you feel about the parents of the kids you were playing with?

I hated the people in the village. Well, some of them were very reasonable. But some of them were very—some of them were a bit—Especially the older ones were really good; say, the old pensioners. They were really good. They understood. And they used tae come up to us on a Sunday and get their corns pared by my father. My father used tae pare their corns with an open razor, pare their corns on their feet, ye know?

(86DW03 @ 50:52.)

---

17. "How to guddle trout": that is, how to catch trout with one's bare hands while wading in a stream.

§3.9. "I COULD LEARN NOTHING AT SCHOOL"

JS: You went to school when you were real young?

Four till I was thirteen past. But I never got very—I only wantit tae learn tae read an write. That was all. That's all the Travellers wanted, jist tae learn to read an write. Still the same thing yet. I mean, they don't want anyone teachin their children. I mean, the great man, the great scholar who was a great scholar himself, once wrote, "Don't let readin or writin interfere wi your education!"[18]

I mean, Ah cuidnae learn to cook shellfish. I cuidnae learn to survive in school. I cuidnae learn tae make flowers.[19] I cuid not learn tae make baskets. I could learn nothing at school.* These were the most important things for the travelling folk. The art of survival was learned at home, not in school. And readin an writin was not the most important thing. It didnae mean nothin because they werenae gonnae be taught to be teachers, or ministers, or doctors, or nothing. They werenae goin tae go to college. Why did they bother about education for? I mean, ten percent of the travelling folk can neither read nor write till this present day. They're still well off. They're rich enough, an they've got new cars and new lorries an new caravans, an they've got plenty o money. But they still cannae read nor write. So it's never been a drawback to them in any way.

HH: Did anyone in school show any interest in learning anything you could do, like making flowers or baskets?

No, not in school, no, no, no. See, Father wouldnae allow us to do anything. When we went to school, we had to do what was done in school. We weren't allowed to bring wir own crafts intae school or anything like that. We were supposed to do all that at home. I watched my father sittin makin tin, making baskets, makin toasters for the fire, makin ladles, graters for the vegetables, makin flowers, makin leather laces from old boots. These were the things that was most important to us. Makin clothes-pegs, which we never learnt in school.

You see, if I was on my own, travelling on my own, and I was down and broke, I could sit down beside an elderberry bush and make mysel a half a dozen flowers, go intil a house, give them tae the lady, trade them for something to eat or get a couple o pennies for them. I cuidnae do that with anything a

---

18. "Don't let readin or writin interfere with your education": a saying that is often attributed to Mark Twain, who was fond of it even though he may not have coined it.

19. "Learn to make flowers": that is, learn how to whittle artificial flowers out of a piece of wood, or how to fashion them from tissue paper, so that they could be hawked around the houses or given as gifts.

teacher taught me in school. I cuidnae go up to the house and say tae the lady, "Look, Ah can read and write, is it any help to ye?"

So the best thing was for me tae learn something that would stand me in good stead through my intire life. Now Ah learned this from my father, back fifty years ago. I'm still doing it now up there at the Traquair Fair, and I make my living off it, still at this present moment.[20] But the schoolin I've gotten at school, what has it done for me? Nothing. Ah could read a book or read a paper, which I never do very often. So schooling doesnae mean nothing to travelling people, nothing at all.

(86DW12 @ 30:53.)

§3.10. FINDING TWO DUCKS THAT WENT MISSING

♪♫

*JN: Were you treated that badly other times when you were a boy?**

Oh, Jack, you've no idea! You've no idea. You can imagine. There was seven sons and nine daughters of us, sixteen children, ye know. The two older brothers were gone, but there'd always be twelve at home. Twelve children in this little camp in the forest, ye know? And anything that happened in this village—the village wasn't very large, maybe about half the size of Strathmiglo[21]; couple o shops, butcher's an the baker's an that, ye know—if anything had happened, if anything went missing, we'd get the blame of it.

And this woman who owned the grocer's shop, she kept ducks, ye know, an lo and behold, two of her ducks went a-missin. Right? We got the blame of her ducks. Now you know what ducks are. Ducks will travel far and wide an get in the river. They'll fall in the river, you know. And they'd go out to the sea, because the river ran intae the sea.

She sent for the police. The police come lookin for feathers around wir fireside. Two ducks had went missin; lookin for feathers. But if we'd have took a duck, she'd have never saw a feather, anyway! [*Laughter.*] We'd have burned all the feathers before we'd have done it, you know. We'd have cooked it with the feathers on so there wouldn't be one feather. But we never touched the ducks, I swear.

But one day, as I was telling ye, I used to gather the driftwood comin in with the tide. And there was lots of ducks on the shore. But I saw these two

---

20. "Up there at the Traquair Fair": During the mid-1980s, Williamson set up a bow tent and made wooden flowers at summer fairs held at Traquair House, in the Borders, to demonstrate the traditional lifeways of travelling people.

21. Strathmiglo: the village in Fife closest to where this recording is being made.

particular ducks by themselves, a duck an a drake. And they were out in the sea, swimmin in the sea, about half a mile from where the lady lived. Ah said to myself, "If I'm not mistaken, they were Carky Campbells." You know, the Carky Campbells?[22] Ah said, "That's Mrs. Monroe's ducks. They must have come down the river and they got intae the sea and they didnae know their way back." So I went [up] tae the waist, there, after the ducks, and I got them on dry land and I chased them and I caught them. Caught them both, and I took them back. That was about a week later.

And I walked up tae the shop, an I said, "Mrs. Campbell,[23] I've got a present for ye." And she was very thin, you know, and she says, "Well, what have you got, what have you got?"

I said, "Your ducks."

"Oh, do you know where my ducks went?"

I said, "Aye, I know where they went." One under each arm! I said, "Now, there are your ducks." I said, "You accused me of eatin your ducks."

"Oh, you found my babies."

I said, "Yes, I found your ducks. There they are. Take them round the back. Put them in their pen."

She walked to the shelf and she picked up a scone; a single scone! That size [*gestures*], what you call a cookie. She said, "There you are, and thank you very much."

That was all I got. A scone about that thickness, about three or four days old. "Thank you very much," she said, "for that." A wee little scone with a few raisins in it! "Thank you very much."

I said, "You accused us of stealin them."

I wish to God I *had* ate them! I should have taken them home and put them in the pot! [*Laughter.*] If I had been sensible enough, I should have taken them home and put them in the pot and I would have got as much thanks for that, because she would have forgot about em by that time anyhow. I should have taken them home and put them in the pot!

And these big fat lambs, you know, used to walk around our campin place, big fat lambs, and they would come and eat the grass around the tent. And Father wouldnae let you touch one. We should have killed them and put them in the pot! He would let you kill a rabbit or a pheasant, ye know, but he wouldnae let you touch any o the landowner's lambs, cause he worked for the Duke of Argyll, ye see. And, eh, we used tae feel like puttin the lamb in the pot many times. We were hungry, you know.

(86DW29 @ 1:14:36.)

---

22. "Carky Campbells": Duncan's reference is to the Khaki Campbell, a breed of domesticated duck that was first developed in England.
23. "Mrs. Campbell": evidently a slip for "Mrs. Monroe."

§3.11. ABSCONDING FROM SCHOOL

The only consolation we had was the seashore, because we could get to the sea. And I used tae—sittin there in the schoolroom, the teacher is talkin about Gaelic, an talkin about poems and all and history and Bible, ye know, and I paid no attention. I was too hungry: stomach rumblin wi hunger. Bare feet, nae backside in my troosers, just a jersey on, ye know, and nothing under it. Short pants, knees full of warts and scabs from playing football and shinty. Bare feet, maybe the toes full of muck in between, you know, sittin in class. A real urchin.

"Please, Miss."

"Yes, what is it?"

"I want to leave the room, Miss."

"Right, don't be long."

I was off! Climbed the dike, an—off! Down tae the beach.

There's an old fisherman, sittin, sewin the nets, ye know? An old fisherman walkin along. I was at home with the little old fisherman smokin the clay pipes.

"Could you spare me a match?"

The man gie me a match, ye know. Ah'd go along the shore an gather sea-weed, driftwood, kindle a wee fire. And then Ah'd pick up an old tin, maybe a soup can or a jelly tin, ye know? An Ah'd go and get cockles an mussels an whelks an all the kind o wee shellfish, and I put them in the fire. And Ah was at home, sittin back there in ma bare feet beside the fire. Bringin them a-boil, ye know. Sittin there, and children still gettin their end of school.

I never came back! No way was I goin back tae school! [*Laughs.*] How could you sit in school class when you're hungry, dyin with starvation, sittin in a class where the teacher would go home to her tea and have all these nice wonderful things?

And my sisters would say, when I went home, "Daddy, Duncan absconded frae school and never come back." I cuidnae go home. My father beat me. So the old fishermen used tae take their boats, you know, and they turned them upside down an put them on the seashore. And that was ma favorite bed at night, under the boat. So I would cuik shellfish all day. At nighttime I got under the boat. The boat was turned upside down, ye know what I mean? The rowin boat.

(86DW29 @ 1:18:21.)

§3.12. THE LONG LONG COURTSHIP

♪♫

And I remember one night, a long time ago, I must have been about nine. I had been away from school for three days on my own, just like a wild cat or a wild dog runnin around the village, ye know? Gatherin driftwood; sellin it tae the ladies for a penny; buy a cookie or a biscuit, and kindle the fire, cookin shellfish, ye know? An back to my bed under the boat at nighttime.

I popped under the boat, up under the seats and down to sleep. No blankets, no nothing, just the clothes you wore on. You washed your face in the river and you washed your feet. That was all you done. No soap, no nothing.

An one night, about twelve o'clock, a man came and he sat in the boat and he smoked cigarettes, ye know. Sat in the boat and he's talkin tae himself, mutterin to himself. You know, he's lookin up intae Loch Fyne side, like a long valley, Loch Fyne side. And he's talkin to himself. Ah knew the chap well, later on. An he's all on his own; he's discussin a love affair to his girlfriend, ye know. "Why would she do this to me? Why?"

And I'm lyin under the boat, ye know! About two inches of black between him and me. So this woman who he's discussin, her name was Mary Black, and she worked in the village store. And, eh, Mary was a big stout woman. His name was Willie Ling. And he sat in the boat, and he smoked cigarettes. Ah didnae smoke in these times, thank God. An he said, "Why? Am I not good enough? Where have I went wrong? Where have I—maybe I'm doin the wrong things."

So Mary—when Ah had a penny, Mary Black was good to me. You know, she was good in the shop. You had a penny, you got a penny's worth of broken toffee or broken biscuits, ye know. So, eh, Ah told her the story. But Ah didnae tell her Ah slept in the boat, cause if Ah had, I'd have given the show away, you see? I said, "I haird Willie discussin his love affairs with you, Mary."

"What was he sayin aboot me?"

I said, "He was sayin a lot of good things about you," I said. "A lot of bad things too."

"Well," she says, "I'll see him today when I meet him."

They courted for thirty-five years and they never married. That's true! An I remember one time they were sittin at—we'd call it a "cuddie," for cutting sticks on.[24] And Willie was a great man to cut logs for his fire, ye know. And Mary come up. She says to him—she was definitely wantin tae marry Willie. Willie had a good cottage. He worked in the quarry, ye know. Cuttin sticks; I used tae help him cut sticks. He was good at givin me a couple of pennies. But he didnae know I was under the boat. And he says to her—she said, "Willie, why don't we get married?"

"Och," he said, "it's all right gettin married. But who would have us?"

_____
24. "We'd call it a 'cuddie'": that is, a carpenter's bench or trestle, named after a donkey.

All: [Laughter all around.]

After thirty-five years of courtin! Now, that's true. "Och," he said, "it's all right gettin married. . . ." And I swear, Jack, on ma mother's grave, I was helpin Willie. Because we pulled the crosscut saw, ye know, and I was at one end and he was at another, sawin logs. And Mary come up. She was stout and wore glasses. She would be in her late forties, you know. He would be about maybe thirty-five.[25] He was a bit younger than her. She says, "Willie, I think it's about time that we get married."

"Och," he said, "we cuid get married, Mary. But who would have us?" [*Laughs again.*] I swear on my mother's grave, that's true! After thirty-five years. And I'm not lyin tae you about it, Jack, I'm tellin you God's honest truth.

(86DW29 @ 1:20:30.)

§3.13. THE DUKE RESOLVES A POACHING INCIDENT

♪♫

So there's a river, John, passin doon through by wir tent where we stayed, and the salmon used tae come up there, up this wee river. And when the burn went dry, the salmon was left in wee pools. So me and my brother George, we went up. We took two big salmon from the burn; we took a salmon from the burn, each. But the gamekeeper saw us, and we hid it in a bush, and we were on our way up the road. But he tuik it, and he tuik it up tae the chamberlain's office in Inveraray an put it in the chamberlain's office, the salmon we took oot the river.[26]

So it was the summer time, and ma mother and I walked in tae Inveraray, eight miles, to thin some turnips on the laird's farm. An we thinned the turnips on the laird's farm, an when we come out o the farm—we've finished, worked all day, thinnin the turnips with wir hands—we come out, and who's come walkin down the street but old Duncan Campbell.

Ma mother says, "Here's old Duncan comin," she said. "I'm gonnae talk to him and see if he gies me a couple shillins," ye know? And he had this sporran roond his waist, and his kilt was full of moth holes, ye know? And he had a dog wi him; he had never married a wife. Ah was aboot fifteen and George was aboot seventeen. Two young boys helpin with thinnin the turnips. So she says, "We'll get a couple o shillings fae old Duncan."

---

25. "About maybe thirty-five": perhaps a slip for "about maybe forty-five," a figure that squares better with the notion of a thirty-five-year courtship. But the numbers are approximate.

26. The number of salmon is a bit confusing here: is there one or are there two? What Duncan may mean is that the boys took two salmon and then stashed them in a bush, bundled together, and the gamekeeper then took the stash up to Inveraray.

Old Duncan come oot frae the castle. Stopped us. "Hello, Mr. Campbell," she said.

"Hallo, Mrs. Williamson." He was good English folk, ye know; he was related to the Queen. The Queen's father, anyway. "Hello, Mrs. Williamson, were you thinning your turnips?"

"Yes," she said. "Mr. Campbell, we thinned the turnips in the fields," she said.

"Terrible dirty job, they're very dirty. You'll not be gettin much at them."

"No," she says.

"Well, I'll see if I can help you."

So he opened the sporran, an his sporran buckle was full o verdigris, an he took oot two shill—two *florins*, and he gave them tae my mother.[27] Four shillins.

He said, "Is this your boys? Nice young boys, yes. Eh, is this the boys that was taking the fish out my river?"

All: [Laughter.]

Truth, Brycie,[28] I swear on your dear brother Johnnie's grave, I'm no telling you a lie. "Is this the two boys that were takin the fish out my river?"

Noo, I thought that Georgie an me was goin to *jail* for this. He said, "He's caught a nice salmon in my river, didn't he?" It was his river, you see, his estate. All Argyll belonged tae him.

She said, "Mr. Campbell, they caught a fish, but they never enjoyed it," she says. "I was *needin* a bit fish."

"See, they took it up to my office," he said. "They took it up. I thought the boys were very clever! Catching a salmon."

After that, Georgie an me, we cleaned the burn every night! Cleaned the burn snaring em, cleaned the burn every night, two or three every night. And nobody ever stopped us.

All: [More laughter.]
LW: Is that with snares you got them?

Snares, ken. A kind o rabbit snare. You got a rabbit snare, a wire snare, and the salmon is lying baskin under the bank, ye know, in the river. An you put a rabbit snare over his head and you pulled it tight and tighten it around his tail, you know? We killed hundreds of salmon when the water was low, you see? Cause they had no place to hide.

(84DW04 @ 1:23:40.)

---

27. "Two florins": the florin was a British coin worth two shillings, issued from 1849 until 1967.
28. "Truth, Brycie": Duncan is addressing his friend Bryce Whyte, Betsy Whyte's husband.

§3.14. CUMULATIVE RHYME, "THE HOUSE THAT JACK BUILT"*

♪♫

But then we had, Jack, an even more interesting one which I'd love to do for you.[29] You've probably never heard it sung before. And this is a song called "The House That Jack Built." This was sung among children in my time. And we used tae gather hands in the schoolroom and make a ring, you know, in the school playground. And we'd put one [child] in the center, and everyone would run round in the ring, and we would sing the song, as children, ye know, a long time ago, long before your day. [*Sings:*]

1   Oh this is the house
     oh this is the house
     oh this is the house that Jack built.

2   And this is the rat that ate the malt
     that lay in the house that Jack built.

3   And this is the dog
     that worried the cat
     [that killed the rat][30]
     that ate the malt
     that lay in the house that Jack built.

4   And this is the cow with the cruiket horn
     that chased the dog over the burn
     that worried the cat that killed the rat that ate the malt
     that lay in the house that Jack built.

5   Oh and this is the maiden all forlorn
     that milked the coo with the cruiket horn
     that chased the dog over the burn
     that worried the cat that killed the rat that et the malt
     that lay in the house that Jack built.

6   Oh this is the man all tattered an torn
     that kissed the maiden all forlorn

---

29. Duncan has just been talking about children's rhymes.

30. While never missing a beat, Duncan stumbles a bit at this moment in the song, at first leaving out the phrase "that killed the rat" and then backtracking quickly in an attempt to make up for the omission.

The House that Jack Built

verse 6

♩. = 132

Oh   this is the man all   tat-tered an torn that   kissed the mai-den   all for-lorn that

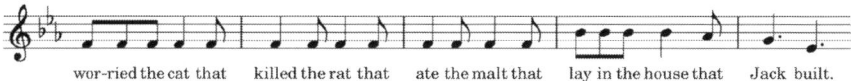

milked the coo with the   crui – ket horn that   chased the dog   o – ver the burn   that

wor-ried the cat that   killed the rat that   ate the malt that   lay in the house that   Jack built.

> that milked the coo with the cruiket horn
> that chased the dog over the burn
> that worried the cat that killed the rat that ate the malt
> that lay in the house that Jack built.[31]

7   Oh this is the minister shaved and shorn
    that married the man all tattered and torn
    to the maiden all forlorn
    that milked the coo with the cruiket horn
    that chased the dog over the burn
    that worried the cat that killed the rat that ate the malt
    that lay in the house that Jack built.

8   Oh this is the cock that crowed in the morn
    that wakened the minister shaved and shorn
    that married the man all tattered and torn
    to the maiden all forlorn
    that milked the coo with the cruiket horn
    that chased the dog over the burn
    that worried the cat that killed the rat that ate the malt
    that lay in the house that Jack built.

9   Oh this is the farmer sowin the corn
    that fed the cock that crew in the morn

---

31. Duncan sings stanza six twice; it is transcribed here only once.

that wakened the minister shaved and shorn
that married the man all tattered and torn
to the maiden all forlorn
that milked the coo with the cruiket horn
that chased the dog over the burn
that worried the cat that killed the rat that et the malt
that lay in the house that Jack built!

[General laughter.]

We all catched hands in a ring, first, and we put one in the middle. He was Jack, and Jack stood in the center. Everyone sang, and the ring ran around Jack. And then, when Jack said, [*sings:*] "Oh, this is the man all tattered an torn," he had to leave the ring and come intae the center of the ring, ye know? And no one wanted to be the man tattered and torn. And we all stepped out in the ring, till at last there was hardly anyone left. They were all in the center of the ring. You understand?[32]

Everyone took a part and sang it. You done one part, we done this part, you done another part, some was this—this, eh, the tattered man, the maiden all forlorn, the cow with the crooked horn, the dog and the cat, you know? Everyone took a part. It was played as a party game, ye know? But it was sung forbyes.[33]

(86DW29 @ 05:24, with video 86V01; last paragraph from 86DW38 @ 30:52.)

§3.15. CHILDREN'S SONG, "THE MOUSIE'S WEDDING TO THE FROG"*

♪♫

This song was sung back fifty years ago when I was a child, ye know? I learned it way back fifty years ago in my primary school. And the story is about a frog who went a-courting. Would you like to hear it?

JN: I'd love to hear it.

Now, I'm not a singer in any way. [*Sings:*]

1   A froggie would a-wooin ride
        oh-ho, ho.
     A froggie would a-wooin ride

---

32. Some of the words of this paragraph have been editorially rearranged for the sake of greater clarity.

33. "It was sung forbyes": that is, it was also sung on its own.

wi sword and buckle by his side,
>   oh ho.

2   Oh first he came to a mouse's den
>   oh-ho, ho.
>   First he came to a mouse's den,
>   he said, "Miss Mouse, would you let me in?"
>   oh ho.

3   So he took Miss Mousie on his knee,
>   oh-ho, ho.
>   He took Miss Mousie on his knee,
>   he said, "Miss Mouse, will you marry me?"
>   oh ho.

4   She said, "Where will the marriage service be?"
>   oh-ho, ho.
>   "Where will the marriage service be?"
>   "Down at the hollow by the old oak tree,"
>   oh ho.

5   She said, "What will the marriage supper be?"
>   oh-ho, ho.
>   "What will the marriage supper be?"
>   "A slice of cake and a cup o tea,"
>   oh ho.

6   Then the first came in was Mrs Moth,
>   oh-ho, ho.
>   The first came in was Mrs Moth,
>   she come to lay the table cloth,
>   oh-ho, ho.

7   Then the next came in was Major Dick,
>   oh-ho.
>   [*Spoken aside:*] Major Dick was a grasshopper.[34]
>   The next came in was Major Dick,
>   he et so much that he fell sick,
>   oh-ho, ho.

---

34. Duncan includes this spoken aside in each of my recordings of this song. Though extraneous to the meter, it is integral to the song as he sang it.

8   So they had to send fir Doctor Fly,
        oh ho.
    They had to send for Doctor Fly
    for fear that Major Dick would die,
        oh ho.

9   The next came in was a squirrel with a curly tail,
        tail.
    The next came in was a squirrel with a curly tail,
    He tore his head on a rusty nail,
        oh-ho, ho.

10 Next came in was a big brown snake,
    oh, next came in was a big brown snake.
    He coiled himself round the weddin cake,
        oh-ho, ho.

11 So they all went sailin down tae the lake,
        oh-ho, ho.
    They all went sailin down tae the lake,
    they were gobbled up by a big fat drake,
        oh-ho, ho.

The Mousie's Wedding to the Frog

verse 2

Oh   first he came to a   mou - se's den, oh   ho   ho - o,

First he came to a   mou-se's den, he   said, "Miss Mouse, would you   let me in," oh   ho.

That was "The Mousie's Weddin to the Frog." [*General laughter.*] The Travellers used to sing that round the campfire all the time, you know.

JN: That's the best "Froggie" song I've ever heard.

(86DW38 @ 25:53, with spoken comments from 86DW29 and 87DW13.)

Chapter 4

MAKING A LIVING

§4.1. A TRAVELLER HAS MANY TRADES

Ah can make baskets, Ah can make tin, Ah can make laces, Ah can make anything in the tradition. But someday you might no have the time for that, and you might have no willows for baskets, you might have no tin for tae make tin, then you're left all alone an you've got nothing else in the world. Father said, "Look, well, you can go sing for your living." You see what I mean?

Everything in the world, you must learn everything to be a travellin people! You must have every trade in the world. Even though you're no guid at it, ye can try your best.

(84DW01 @ 1:32:54.)

§4.2. ON CUTTING BACK WILLOWS FOR MAKING OR MENDING BASKETS

I know where tae get some good willows along the other side o Dalmally.* They should be growin along the roadside at Dalmally, some nice willows. We never actually picked willows off trees; we liked to get wir willows growin from the ground, like grass. They came up long and straight: year olds, the first growth. See, someone cut a bush, and then the young growth's comin up from the bush. These are the ones that are more supple. But if you take them off a tree, they tend to be brittle because they're old.

JN: So would you cut a bush back down to the ground?

Sometimes we'd cut a bush back to the ground there, and next year come around, it'd have willows, ye see? We'd cut it right tae the ground. If we stayed there all night, we'd hack down a bit, right tae the root. We'd come back next spring, an all these young ones were growin up from the root, ye know? Any-body else would do the same thing. You would come and get willows from a bush someone else had cut. Everybody, even though they never made a basket, would cut the tree down so some chap could get some good willows there next year. You know what I mean? Cuttin it from the root. Yeah.

There's a nice place for willows along the side of Dalmally. I think they grow along the roadside. We could get—we'll pick a small bunch of them. We'll get a quiet place, and then we'll do it all over again. The next fine place over here on the road, we'll get a stop.*

JN: So what would you need for making baskets? Just a jackknife?

Just a pocketknife. That was all you needed. Nothing else; nothing at all.

JN: Could you make them one day and sell them the next?

You could make em in the morning and sell em in the afternoon! The most important thing was that women went round the doors and asked the women if any basket was needin mended. They did a lot of basket mendin. Say you had a nice basket that belonged to your mother or your granny, and the handle fell off. Oh yes, she would sit in the house and she would say, "I have a basket here that needs to be mended; the handle's come a-loose. Would you put a new handle on for me?"

Well, a new handle was two and six—two shillins if you were pushed, you know?—for puttin a new handle on someone else's basket. So they did a lot of mending baskets. Dog baskets, washin baskets—the handles came loose an you put new handles on them, ye know? So you went from door tae door with a bundle o willows under your arm, asking the ladies were they needin any baskets mended. Basket mendin was a great job.

JN: Would you take them back overnight and bring them back the next day?

No, you could sit down at the door and mend it at the house, mend it right at the door. You had a bundle of willows under your arm, an your pocketknife, an you just went from door to door, askin them were they needin any baskets mended. Dog baskets, fish baskets, clothes baskets, message baskets[1]—you mended them at the doorstep. We used to have a luttle shout, a luttle thing that you shout in the street. We used to—[*calls out:*] "Baskets to mend; all kinds o baskets to mend! Clothes baskets, chairs, mendit at your door!" You know? We sat and mended them at the doorstep. Eh, what was the thing we used to—"Cheaply,

---

1. "Message baskets": grocery baskets.

neatly, repaired at your door!" That was it. We'd sing it out in the street, in the back streets. "Neatly, cheaply, repaired at your door!" That's what we used tae shout in the streets. You and maybe two pals, three boys would meet up with a bundle o willows each, and you would go up *that* street and I would go up *that* street. You could hear the voices in the distance, you know, and when you heard the voice, you'd say, "There's somebody up there already; I'll no tak that street, I'll take the next street." Ah sometimes made two pounds, that's before noon. Mendin baskets in the street, you know.

It was a good job, yeah. An that was the kind o job you could do all year round. You could do that in the middle o winter, providin you had the willows. Maybe you got a leg of a chair—ye know, a cane chair, if the weavin come apart in the leg, ye know? You'd cut out a piece o wood and put another leg in and weave it in. We would do up a chair for maybe two an six, half a crown. Two shillings, yeah.

JN: Did you have to know how each type of basket or creel was designed, was put together?

Oh, you learned all the baskets. You made creels and baskets and all kinds of stuff, ye know? The black willow was the best willow for makin baskets. It was more pliable, more supple. Better for weavin.

JN: What's the last time you made baskets to sell, would you say?

The last basket I made to sell—the last baskets I made was two luttle baskets for holdin rolls in the breakfast table for Sandy and Linda's father for the States.[2] Just small ones, ye know? That was the last baskets I made. That was just for a gift. I've never made any to sell since I married Linda. I made plenty—there were plenty o willows, we never longed for willows. Other side of Dalmally is a great place for willows. They grow along the roadside there.

JN: Is that something that the children would do, help with the willows?

The children would help peel the willows with a slipe.* And maybe the boys would be peelin them and the girls would be gradin them, separatin the big ones from the small ones, and puttin all the weavin ones to one side and the thick ones to a side, you know, and Daddy would just reach over and pick one from the pile he needed, from the bundles. It was a good help tae the father, ye know?

---

2. "Sandy and Linda's father for the States": Duncan is referring to members of Linda Williamson's family whom he met when visiting the United States for the first time, as is discussed in Campbell, *Traveller in Two Worlds*, 2.76–86.

Figure 4.1 Williamson making a slipe at the shore of Loch Fyne, close by the village of Furnace, 1988. Photo by the author.

JN: I see. So was your father the basketmaker?

He was a great basketmaker. He was one of the best in Scotland. Anyone will tell you, he was one of the best basketmakers. Now Grandfather—my father's father, old Wully Williamson—he made a crill. A creel. You know what I mean? Those handcreels? To hang from a man's watch, a fisherman's watch. That's how clever he was; that's true. Tae hang from his watch chain. A crill, a wee crill. And he made a toaster, a slidin toaster, ye know? Your old toaster's made of tin, and you cooked them on the grate; that's how you put a piece of toast on. And he took two hairpins—you know, ladies' hairpins, for their hair?

JN: Right, right.

And he made a slidin toaster from two hairpins—

JN: [Laughs.]

—for an old woman, un-huh! He was a very clever old man, old Wully Williamson. He was a—he was gifted, of course.

(88DW07 @ 54:15.)

§4.3. STORY, "THE ELF AND THE BASKETMAKER"

♪♫

HT: Another thing that I've been wanting to ask you about was something about—eh—the Williamsons getting their gift of basketmaking?

Well, ye'll get the whole complete story in Ailie Munro's book.* It tells you how the old Traveller Williamson man came to this little place every particular year tae cut willows for his baskets. Him an his aul wife. They didnae have any children. An when they came tae this particular place of Scotland—an it might be the west coast, it might be in Aberdeenshire or Morayshire or anywhere—he always came back in the summertime to the one particular place tae cut the willows every year. An he knew that within nine month they would be ready for cuttin again.

An one particular day he comes up, and there, lo and behold, is a little man, a little elf, sittin on the root of a tree. An he convinces the aul Traveller man that he must make a cradle for a elfin child. Ye know? And the aul man said, "There's no way in the world I'm gonnae make a cradle for an elfin child!"

He says, "John, you're a basketmaker, a great basketmaker." Now in these bygone times among the travellin people, knives were very hard to get. They used any kind of cookin knife—table knife, ye know?—they made themsel. And to have a wonderful knife was a gift, ye know? So the little man said:

"Ah know about you, John. Ah know how you come over here. Ah know your aul wife is away hawkin her baskets. Ah'm goin back home wi ye tae your tent."

An auld John says, "You can't come back with me." He said, "It's impossible. I've haird of youse little people, but," he says, "I've never saw you."

But John got up his bundle of willows, and the little man jumped in the bundle, and he walked back with him to his tent.

So when he come back, he spoke in cant tae his aul wife, who was home from her hawkin door to doors. He said to his aul woman, he says: "Mary, can ye deek the wee gadgie?"[3] Meanin the little man.

She says, "Ah dinnae see nothin." Ye know? "I dinnae deek nothin," she said.

He says, "Deek under ma airum." He says, "Deek the wee gadgie."

An the aul woman luiked, an she saw the luttle elf sittin on the bundle o willows.

He said, "Allo, Mary!" He said. "Ye don't know bout me."

She says, "Look, Ah've haird ma granny an ma grandfather talkin about ya, but Ah've never actually seen one before."

"Well," he says, "Ah've come for help."

---

3. "Can ye deek the wee gadgie": that is, "Can you see the little man?" The old man speaks to his wife in cant while in the presence of the elf, a potentially dangerous stranger.

An the two old people said, "Whit help can I give you?"

He says, "I want you to make a cradle for the Elfin King's child."

But he said, "How small would it have to be?"

"Oh," the elf said, "About that size." [*DW gestures.*] "Three or four inches."

Now John said, "There's no way in the world can Ah get willows tae make a cradle as small as that."

So the luttle man—they were makin some tea in the old can, "tea can" as they call it. The luttle man said, "How bout some tea?"

So, he was so small the aul woman didn't have a cup small enough, so she tuik the little lid of the can, she filled it, an the little man drunk it up. An he says, "That was good!" He said tae Mary, "Would you like tae help your husband make this basket, this cradle for the Elfin King? Because the Elfin King has just brought himself a new queen, and she's goan tae have a baby. An because he never invitit—he invitit everyone in Elfland except one aul particular woman who never got an invitation.[4] An she put a curse on the newborn baby that it will never be right until it's rocked in a human cradle, made by human hond. A mortal. And we find that there's no one better than you."

But old John said: "Ah can't make one the size that *you* are! You're only about six inches high. How small is a baby gonnae be? And where in the world would Ah find willows fine enough to make this cradle?"

An the little man comes up an he climbs on old Mary's knee, an he takes a look at her, an she has long lovely dark hair. He said, "John, Ah'll help you best way Ah can." So he went up to the old woman's hair, an he puu'd out a hair from her head, one long strand of hair. An he said, "John, how would that weave a cradle?"

But John said, "That's a hair. That's not willow or cane for anything."

"But," he said, "watch." An the luttle man pointed his finger, an lo an behold, there became the [most] beautiful long fine strip o cane you ever saw. An old John took it in his fingers, turned it round in his fingers like a piece of thread. He had never in all his life saw anything so beautiful. He said, "Ah could make anything with that!"

So the luttle man said to aul Mary, "If you wanted for to help—would you love to help?"

The aul woman said, "Take as much of my hair as you want."

An the luttle elf sat there, an he puu'd an he puu'd till he thought he had enough. An he left em down there.

"Now," he said, "Ah'm goin off. But tomorrow you shall bring this cradle to the place where ye cut the willows, and you shall be rewarded." An at that, the little man was gone.

---

4. The motif of the curse spoken by a woman who fails to receive an invitation to a royal feast is a familiar topos in fairy tales, for example at the start of classic versions of "Sleeping Beauty."

The old man and woman sat there and they were amazed. But they had this beautiful stuff made from Mary's hair. She says, "John, d'you think you could do it?"

He said, "Of course Ah could do it." He said. "With *that* Ah could make anything." He said, "You go off tae your hawkin, take your baskets off, an Ah'll sit home an make the cradle."

So the old man sat an he made the cradle. Small little cradle. An 'e cut little pegs for it, little rockers, an he made a cradle about four inches long. Beautiful hood on it, made from this stuff. An he tied it with his finger on a little piece of board, an it rocked back an forward. An a little hood on it, you know? Old-fashioned cradle. Beautiful.

He sat till his old woman come back. She came back; she had sold her baskets within an hour! She came home, they had some tea. He said to her, "What do you think o that?"

She said, "John, it's beautiful! It's the smallest I've ever seen you makin."

"But," he said, "Mary, we cannae put a wee baby in it on willow." He said, "Luik in your basket an see if you've onything I could line it with." See?

So the old woman used to sell ribbon—long strips o ribbon—around the doors, ye know, for women who want tae buy ribbon. An she took oot a purple piece of ribbon, an she gave it tae the aul man, and he lined the cradle beautiful. An he tuik it in his finger, and he walked away back—no, sorry. The old woman said, "Jist let me see it a minute, John," she said, "before you go away." An she luiked at it. But unknown to her aul man—these old women used to carry what you call a "pocket" round their waist. It had a large belt, an a thing like a holster was a pocket. An they kep their loose change, an their pipe, an their knife, an their cut o tobacca. And she took her hand in her pocket, and she slipped a silver thrupenny piece—you know, the little silver thrupenny pieces; Ah think we have some lyin around here somewhere—an she put it in the cradle. This is what you call hanselin the new baby: bringin the new baby luck. Ye always give a newborn baby something silver.

Aul John never noticed this. So he tuik the cradle an he walked back an he put it on the same stump o the tree where he had met the little elf. An he walked home.

So he said, "Ah hope," he says to his old wife, "they're pleased with us."

"Well," she says, "they're bound to be. You know," she said, "it's not often we come in contact with little elfs," she said. "Ah haird ma granny an ma mother talkin about them, but Ah've never met one before."

"Well," he said, "tomorra I'll go back an see."

The next mornin John walks back, an lo an behold, there settin on the little block of a tree was his cradle. And the old man was upset. He said, "Why didn't they take ma cradle?" He said, "It's not good enough, Ah know it's no good

Figure 4.2 Williamson holding willows that he has just gathered and peeled, Loch Fyne, 1988. Photo by Dorothy Leese.

enough." An he picked it up, an he luiked in it, an there was a thrupenny piece. An the aul man knew the old woman had made a mistake. You must never give a fairy money; you must never give a goblin silver in any way.

He was rantin, rantin an ragin, when he come back. He said, "Woman, you've destroyed it! You finished everything. They wouldnae take it."

She said, "John, I didn't mean any harm." She said, "Ah was only hanselin baby with a piece o silver."

He said, "That's all right for humans, but not for fairies an goblins. Now," he said, "we're cursed!" An he said, "Ah'll have tae break the curse." He said, "Get ye to yer callin, aul woman, an don't come back an bother me anymore."

So the old man, forbyes a basketmaker, was a tinsmith.[5] He tuik the thrupenny piece an he kindled up the fire, an he put it on his nippers, an he burned it till it was red hot. An he put his little anvil between his legs, an he sat down, an he filed an he cut, an he clupped an he filed, an he clupped an he clipped an he polished, till lo and behold, he had the most beautiful selver butterfly you ever saw, that size [*gestures*], made from a thrupenny piece. An original silver butterfly, made from a thrupenny piece.

He polished it. When the aul woman come back, he was kin' of—more pleased, ye know? An he said, "Woman, dae ye have any pins?"

---

5. "The old man, forbyes a basketmaker, was a tinsmith": that is, "Besides being a basketmaker, the old man was a tinsmith."

Now the auld travelin women used tae sell little brass pins of all descriptions. An he tuik a little pin, an he soldered it onto the silver butterfly. He tuik it, an he pinned it inside the little basket for the baby. Ye know?

"Now," he said tae the aul woman, "don't again ever bring me bad luck."

She says, "Ah didn't mean any haarum."

So he took the little cradle once more on his finger, an he walked back to the same place, an he put it on the root of the tree, an he walked away. He come home. He'd a worried night. He said, "Woman, you've brought me bad luck, but thank God Ah knew what tae do."

So the next mornin, after he got up, had a cup o tea, he walked back to the little tree stump. The little cradle was gone.

Then while he was cuttin the willows, he turned away an he saw something shining, stuck to one of the bushes where he cut the willows. An he walked up, an there an behold was the most beautiful pocketknife he had ever saw. It was made of silver, it was inlaid with mother-o-pairl, an it had a five-inch steel blade on it. An John looked at it, an he opened it up, an he said, "This must be for me." He says, "This must be the gift from the little people." An he walkit back with it.

Now, tae have one o these kind o knifes was like havin a Rolls Royce among the travelling people! Ye know?

All: [Laughter.]

Everyone comin would luik at it an were amazed where it ever come from, because nobody had its equal all over the country. And also, it was gifted. Whenever John cut willows, he made his baskets, aul Mary sellt them. Everyone wantit a basket. An John kept that knife, and all the travellin people came to see it. An when old John died, it passed down to his son. An it passed to the grandson an the grandson. And also passed the gift. And even *my* son today has baskets as off tae America, an he only taught himself—I never taught him—to make baskets.

An that's how the gift passed among the travelling people, especially the Williamsons, to make baskets. It was a gift from the little fella. An that knife is still in circulation yet. It might be somewhere, but who knows where it is? But Ah'm sure it will turn up some place, somewhere.

An that is the story of the elf an the basketmaker.

(86DW41 @ 05:55.)

§4.4. WORKING FOR THE STONEMASON NEIL McCALLUM

JN: So how did you take shelter here on the hill in bad weather?[6]

We had a luttle hut made o canvas, and we carried it like a stretcher. It had handles on each side, and you carried it with you when you were working. When the night moved on, you went back and carried your little hut with you, and if it come to rain, you sat inside it. And while we was waiting for the rain to go off, we told stories tae each other. It took me a long time to get him to tell a story to me. But once I knew he had a world of knowledge within his head, I tried to get all his tales.* I'm pleased today that I did; otherwise he would have died and the stories would be gone forever. Thanks to me, they are still alive. I mean, I was only fifteen, and he was in his fifties!

JN: I see. Had he been a drystone dike builder all his life?*

A mason, a stonemason. His two brothers run the farm, but when they were not workin the croft there were three of them. So he became a mason. I was an apprentice tae him. I'll tell you the story about how I met up with him.

Mother and I were walkin down to Achnagoul one day.* My mother smoked a pipe at this time; she was young, and she smoked a pipe, and Neil smoked a pipe also. And she asked Neil for a bit o tobacca. And "Neil," she says to him, "that's a lot of work for yoursel," she says. "You never get anybody to help you."

He says, "Betsy, where am I goin to get anybody to help me? Nobody wants to help me," he says, "for all the money Ah could pay them."

She says, "Duncan here, my son, would like tae help ye, if you could give him something."

"Well, I cuidnae pay him much," he says. "If he wants tae help me and learn a trade, I'll pay him two and six a day."[7]

Well, two and six a day was a lot o money then! I mean, my father was earnin forty pence a day, and I was gettin two and six, and I was only fifteen years old, ye know what I mean? So I stayed with him for eighteen months.

(88DW09 @ 40:17.)

---

6. Duncan and I are looking toward a hill, overlooking Loch Fyne, where, as a teenager, he worked for some months as assistant to a local mason, Neil McCallum, a Gaelic speaker. The dike they built still stands, though in a somewhat tumbledown state.
7. "Two and six": two shillings and sixpence. One shilling was divided into twelve pennies. Duncan's wages as an apprentice therefore came to thirty pence a day.

§4.5. AN UNCANNY SIGHT NEAR ACHNAGOUL

I was workin for a farmer in Achnagoul.[8] There's a shortcut when you left the farm; I'll show you a wee place you could cut across the hill. It would save you a couple o miles and cut out the road in front o you, because the road took a big turn. And old Duncan MacVicar was an old bachelor, and he used tae pay me five shilling a day for workin, and he paid me every night, five shillins for workin all day along with him. Cuttin the hay, and milkin the cows, and helpin around. Makin his tea sometimes and boilin potatoes for him, sweepin the byre, keepin the house clean, washin the dishes at night, ye know? He was an old bachelor, he was in his sixties; I would be fourteen. Just got oot o school.

So he said to me one night, [looking at] his old pocket watch there: "Duncan, it's gettin kind o late. I think you should go away home." He said, "Have a wee cup o tea before you go." He had a big metal kettle we used to swing on a swey at the fire, ye know?[9]

We had a cup o tea, and I says, "Ah think Ah'll take the shortcut."

He says, "Well, it's gettin kind o late. I don't think you should." Old Duncan looked at me: "I don't think you should." He says, "Take the road home. There won't be many cars on the road."

So I cut across,[10] an jist when it was gettin a-gloamin—we call it gloamin, just dusk, as you would say. And where you pass through, there's heaps of brackens. But this was the October month, Jack, and the brackens were all withered an brown. And I had tae walk through this heap of brackens tae get through to where I was goin, through the path to take me out tae the road with the shortcut. Saved me a couple of hours' walk, because it's five miles from his place to Furnace.

JN· Yes, yes.

An then I haird whustlin in the brackens.[11] And then a deer got up. And it stopped about—from here to that steel post here it stopped.[12] I looked, and, Jack, it had a deer's body, I swear on my mother's grave, but it had beautiful long hair an the face of a beautiful young lassie, an her hair—pieces of bracken stuck in her hair, never been combed for months or years. Pieces of bracken.

---

8. According to Linda Williamson ("Narrative Singing," 306), Duncan worked at Achnagoul occasionally from 1935 to 1955. The farmer there "treated him like a son," Duncan told her.

9. Swey: a chimney crane (also called a *swee*): a horizontal bar, from which chains or cooking vessels could be hung, working on a pivot fixed at the side of a fire.

10. "So I cut across": that is, "I took the shortcut."

11. "Whustlin in the brackens": the Scots word *whustling* can refer to any low sound without melody, as with wind rustling through dry leaves or grasses. See the *DSL*, s.v. "whistle."

12. "From here to that steel post": Duncan is looking out the window of our car to a steel post about fifteen yards away.

And it shook its head back an front, an it looked at me straight, an then it was gone. And I went over and I—[*gestures as if patting the ground*]—where it was lying and I felt the bed, and it was warm, where it was lyin. And I said to mysel, "That's not—that's a warnin for me. I'm not going home on that road tonight." I goes back to old Duncan, I tells him the story.

"Och," he says, "you were seein things."

Well, ma sister stayed near Inveraray, in a caravan, and her husbant was workin in the Forestry, a sawmill. Ah said, "I'm not going home tonight." I walked back and I stayed that night with my sister. And I told her.

JN: Uh-huh.

And you're the second person I've ever told it to. Beautiful face, and it shook her little head like that. A little head, a wee fourteen-year-old girl on a deer's body, and brackens stickin to her hair. And then it was gone. I felt the wee bed where she was lyin; it was warm where she was lyin among the brackens. That's something I saw. Ah cannae explain it to ye, I don't know—I'm not lying to ye, I cannae explain it. And that's the God's honest truth.

JN: Well, there's plenty in this world that no one is going to explain.

Yeah.

JN: And it doesn't do any good to say that it doesn't happen, it didn't—

Exist. Yeah.

JN: Because sometimes it's more real than real, and you don't know what it is, and no one else knows what it is.

Yeah. I cuidnae explain it, Jack. Tae tell you the God's truth, I could not. Well, it actually happened.

(88DW09 @ 09:02.)

§4.6. SETTING OUT FOR BLAIRGOWRIE AS A YOUNG MAN

This Betsy [Betsy Townsley] stayed with Granny and Grandfather in Tarbert until she became a young woman, an then she ran away wi my brother.* Now, brother and her went away to Perthshire, and they were away for many years. They didnae come back till I was about fifteen. And he come back one night, and he camped beside my father, and he sat and tellt me all the wonderful stories about Perthshire and about Blairgowrie and the berry fields of Blair and all these places. Ah had never been there; Ah'd been away, mysel, to other parts, but I'd never been there. So I decided I would go tae Blairgowrie at the berry time. He was goin to the berry pickin.

Now, Gothens in these days was a great place because all the Travellers from all over came tae the Gothens at Blairgowrie.* The Gothens—it's all sown out by Forestry now. There was a moor about a mile long between Meikleour and Blairgowrie. There's a great big moor, and that moor was left open for the travellin people all summer long. But not in the winter months; they wasnae allowed in there in the winter months. And that's where they came in the hundreds, wi their ponies an their donkeys an their dogs an their tents, and they swapped and they dealed and they picked berries. An they went intae Blairgowrie, and they left [free] a special place known in Blairgowrie as the Well Meadow. Now that Well Meadow today is a great car park, but in that day it was left out for the Travellers only. That was the Travellers' meetin place in town—but not to stay. Not to stay. So they could drive in there wi their ponies, loosen the horses oot, tie the horse to the wheel of their cart. You would walk, and there the carts were settin in the Well Meadow like that, with their shafts up in the air. The shafts in the air—dozens of them! Some wi governor's carts, we called them, ye know, and some wi flat carts, some wi four-wheelers, all the shafts sittin up like a forest, an all the horses tied tae the wheels.

JN: [Laughs.]

And then [*slaps hand to leg*] they were swappin and dealin and spittin in each other's hand,* and then—[*slaps hand again to simulate a deal being done*]— And everyone had mufflers: hankies around their neck. They was the dealin men. And then the local dealers in the village, they would come oot, because Blairgowrie had pigmen, fruit men, coal merchants, and they all used horses, ponies, for their work in the town. All they would see were the Travellers there, and they would go oot and have a deal wi them, you know what I mean? They would stand in their wee groups and corners, swappin and dealin horses by the dozens; donkeys, dozens o them!

And that was the weekend. That was Saturday, all day on Saturday, and sometimes Sunday. Then Monday, they were all goin back. They drove home that night. There they used tae come along the road, dozens after dozens after dozens of all these horses. Some boys—maybe some boys drivin, their father lyin drunk on the floor, their mother drunk, and them drivin on, and some of the lassies drivin these horses, you know? Tryin tae pass each other on the road and see who's the fastest one: wee Shetlands, big old farm horses, fat ones, thin ones.

JN: [Laughs.]

And they all drove home, loosed their horses oot, then tethered them out, and then they kindled their fires. Then they gathered in groups round the fires. Maybe they started swappin again, maybe they brought a bottle of whiskey back with em. And all these tents!

JN: Is that where you learned a lot of your songs?

I haird a lot o songs roond the fires, the campfire. I learned "The Harbor o Dundee," "The Factory Girl"—oh, these were great popular songs.* "The Marlin Green." All these kind o songs were sung round the fires. Well, that's where I collected a lot of material, and stories forbyes.

(87DW04 @ 05:23.)

§4.7. TRAVELS IN THE NORTH AND EAST OF SCOTLAND

*JN: I was wondering if you travelled up this way as well?**

Not since I got married. Just as a young boy on my own, collectin stories and travellin up to Inverness, aroond Elgin, down into Fraserburgh, down intae Macduff, and round all the wee towns. And meetin the Aberdeenshire travelling folk.

JN: Would you take this route?

Yes, I took this route up to Pitlochrie and right over. Up to Inverness. Aberdeen, Elgin, Forres, right down to Fraserburgh, down to Peterhead.[13]

∾

JN: Were you travelling with your horse and cart when you came this way?

No, just on my own, just as a young man on my own. Just nothing but a pocket-knife an ma coat.

JN: Would you be going on foot, then?

---

13. Some additional conversation about this period of Duncan's life is presented in a section of its own at §4.8.

On foot, yeah. I didn't even have a bicycle. I never got a lift very often, very seldom. I wasn't interested in lifts, I just wantit tae walk.

JN: So how long would it take you to go over this way, over the summit?

Oh, maybe a week from Perth to Inverness. Just walk along the way till it got dark. And then I always had a bob or two tae buy a bit o food, ye know?[14] And then, eh, find shelter for the night, somewhere tae sleep, just on my own. And if you found a travelling family, you probly stayed the night wi them, ye know? And they asked you what direction you were takin, and they told you where you would find more travelling people. They give you accommodation for the night and some food. That's all you needed. Shelter for the night. Maybe you slept in their tents or whatever they had tae offer you for tae sleep in. And then they give ye some breakfast and inquired where you were goin. And, "Well, if you go tae such an such a place, you'll find a cousin o mine, an uncle o mine, or an auntie o mine. Say hello! I havenae seen them for a few months. And if you're on your journey, they'll make you welcome." Ye know?

You carried the message. You'd tell them you'll see them maybe at Blairgowrie or see them at the berry pickin. Probly you never met the person you were lookin for, but you met someone else!

It was a wonderful way tae go, a wonderful way to travel. And, eh, I would stay a while in Aberdeen, and then I would go back intae Fife and meet a lot o Fife Travellers there, around Rosyth, Dunfermline, down tae Burntisland, all around. And then back intae Dumbarton, around tae Balloch, up Loch Lomond, over the Rest and Be Thankful,* see my parents, stay there for another month, and then take off again.

JN: Would all this be during the summer time?

Ah, sometimes in the wintertime too. I remember travellin up the coast from Aberdeen to Ellon. It's about forty-five mile, an it's the coast road all the way. An it was late at night an I cuidnae find a place tae shelter. But there was a corn stack, an I just lay beside the corn stack.[15] An in the morning my two legs were just completely dead frae cold. It tuik me about half an hour tae get the circulation back in ma legs before I could stand up. It was really cold! That was in the month of January. I had tae sleep behind the corn stack, ye know? An the corn stack was built so good, so tight, I cuidnae crawl intae it tae find shelter.

JN: Could you pull something over you to keep warm?

---

14. "A bob or two": a shilling or two, with twelve pence to the shilling.
15. "Corn stack": in Scotland, a stack of oats or other grain, on stalks.

I had nothing. Just ma coat. I just went tae the side away from the wind an curled in behind the stack for shelter.

(86DW26 @ 30:20 and @ 33:25.)

§4.8. WORKING IN FRASERBURGH AND ABERDEEN, WHERE YOU COULD SQUAT IN EMPTY HOUSES

I took a job for a few months tae get some food in Fraserburgh.[16] I was workin in Maconochie's soup factory,* for makin the tinned soup, ye know? And there I met some residential travelling folk who had stayed in houses in Fraserburgh, and they pointed out to me where I would find more travelling folk around Inverness, around Elgin. An they gave me directions. An I stayed there workin for three months. And I moved intae Aberdeen and searched for residential travelling folk in the town. I was out to search for people that were not only travelling folk, but were travelling folk what had settled down in the houses in Aberdeen.

At that time, back in the forties, old houses was going a dime a dozen in Aberdeen.* It was what you call the squatter's rights. If there's an empty house, ye could just walk in as a squatter. And because the houses were so scarce, any old house that was left uninhabited for any length o time, the travelling folk just walked in and took over. The police would come and check an take your name. And then they would leave you there to stay as long as you liked until it was condemned and knocked down. And then, if they knocked it down while you were still in it, they had to find you another place tae stay. So that's why a lot of people like Bessie Whyte and many of the Travellers got council houses today in Aberdeen and in the other towns. They started off as squatters, you know? So once you were in a squatter's house an it was condemned, an it was to be knocked full down tae make way for buildin other houses, then the Council had a right to establish—to give you somewhere else to stay. So the best way to get a house was tae take up an old squatter's house, an then stay in it till it was knocked down, and then they had to rehouse you somewhere else in any town. So that's happened to Stanley Robertson's family, and also a lot of families in Aberdeenshire that Ah'd known as a young man.

Then I started workin in Aberdeen with a minister who had a wood contractin business.* I spent eighteen months with him there in Old Aberdeen. An I got to know all the travelling people that were resident in Aberdeen, and I met some wonderful people.

And then Ah left again and went on ma travels again.

(86DW26 @ 31:01.)

---

16. "Fraserburgh": Duncan regularly pronounces the name as "Frasersburuh."

§4.9. SONG OF LOVE AND LOSS, "THE MARLIN GREEN,"* WITH RECOLLECTIONS OF OLD DUNDEE AND THE TIME HE SPENT THERE MENDING CHINA

♪♫

This is one of my favorites. I sung this in many places all over, many different places. It's one of my favorites because it tells a good story. [*Sings:*]

1   Oh here I am, a stranger, just newly home from sea.
And my ship, it lies in anchor in the harbor o Dundee.
Your face, it is the fairest, dear, that ever I have seen.
Oh fair you maid, would you walk with me, down by the Marlin
    Green?

2   Oh, with kind—[*pauses*]—with kind—eh . . . [*resumes singing:*]
with a roguish smile upon her face she answered me and said,
"Kind sir, I'd love to walk with you, but you know, I am afraid.
For the paths, they are so slippery, and the night so cold and keen.
It wuid not do for me to fall down by the Marlin Green."

3   So with kindly words and promises along with me she went.
We rambled here, we rambled there, until our time we spent,
and I fear that maid had many a fall down by the Marlin Green.

4   So when my time for sailin came from the harbor o Dundee,
I left a poor young maiden for to weep to poverty.
To slightly love an sail away is neither straight nor clean,
so never do what I once done down by the Marlin Green.

5   So as I lay on my bed one night when ma weary watch was done,
I dreamt I was the father of a darling baby son.
And I saw its mother, too, right plainly to be seen,
an she was crying bitterly down by the Marlin Green.

6   So when my ship returns again to the harbor o Dundee,
I'll search the town all up and down till my darling I do see.
I will ask her to forgive me for the rogue that I had been,
and we will make it up again down by the Marlin Green.

The Marlin Green

verse 1

Oh here I am a stran - ger, just new - ly home - from sea.

And my ship, it lies in an - chor in the - har - bor o Dun - dee.

Your face, it is the fair - est, dear, that ev - er I have seen.

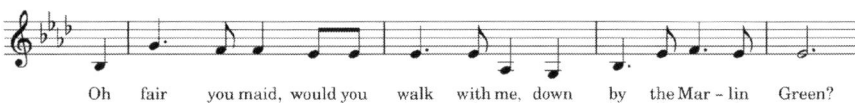

Oh fair you maid, would you walk with me, down by the Mar - lin Green?

Wonderful story. Tells a good story.

JN: Whose song is that, Duncan?

Oh, all the travelling folks sing that. Yeah, everybody knows that song. The Marlin Green* still exists to this day in Dundee; it's a walk along the beach. The Marlin Green—it's along by the Tay Bridge, that real old bridge, and it's a green on the bay. And it's a big place for lovers walkin, on the Marlin Green, ye know, at Dundee. It still exists to this day. They never changed it in any way, from the early days of the sailing ships til this day. The Marlin Green's still the same place.

JN: That's good, because things have changed so much in Dundee.

Yeah. But the Marlin Green has never changed. The old Overgate is gone.* The Overgate was a great place. The Overgate was a big aul street that ran along quayside, and there were the street markets all week long, and luttle secondhand shops, and men with luttle fires cookin peas an chips an mussels an whelks, along the old Overgate, back in the forties. Ah stayed in North Tay Street for three month. I was stayin in Dundee an I squatted in an old house for a while.

Because during the war, any house that was empty, you could go in and break the door down, bust the door, get yourself a bed, police come and tuik your name, and that was all. You're squatters. Because houses were scarce, and empty houses you could walk in. Squatter's rights, ye called it. But you had to stay for three months, you cuidnae just go in there for a week or a night. Ah had to stay for three months.

JN: Once you were there for three months, without being shifted—?

It was your own, you could keep it.

JN: The house was yours?

The house was yours. And, eh, many people got good houses from that time, off of squatters in the houses. Once ye was three months in it, it was yer own. Ye didnae pay any rent when ye were squattin it in. After three months, it was your own house. But these houses were condemned. Then they knocked em down. But before they knocked em down, they had tae [help you] house shift, tae find a place for ye.

Maybe you were wantin tae settle down, like the Camerons an a lot o people who squatted in the {Kelbies}, I remember, a long time ago. Squatters in many houses in Dundee an all the big cities—Aberdeen, Dundee, Glasga—they said, "We're fed up travelling. We're goin tae go settle down for a while." And now these people in the second generation have grown up wi good council houses. Gardens an everything ye need, ye know? All from the squatter's house.

JN: Could you have kept that house in Dundee?

No, I cuidnae. I only went there for the winter months. I would never have stayed in Dundee. I mean, I was single. I wasnae married, I was single. But I used tae be in the Overgate, at nighttime. . . . When was that? Nineteen forty-six, forty-seven. An there I enjoyed myself wi the stalls an the secondhand shops. An, eh, life was very easy for me, because I was mendin Delft at the time. Pottery. I went around houses mendin broken plates and any kind of antique vases or anything. An I had a bow drill—a drill with clasps—an broken plates an things.

JN: You put clasps in them?

Yeah, clasps. You drilled holes in them with a bow drill.

JN: Into the plates?

Intae the plates. If you had an antique plate from your mother, it was worth about two an six, or five bob, to get it mendit. Old heirlooms. Like a vase you had at was a heirloom, an it fell on the floor and broke an it needed mended—well, I had a bow drill, a homemade bow drill made o leather, an a drill in the middle. An you pulled back the bow and druv a luttle drill in the middle, an it drilled a hole intae the plate.

The plate was cracked across the middle. Like this, here, I'll show you.[17] Say that was a plate, and it was cracked across the middle, right? Broken in three pieces. Now I would take my bow and hold it between my two knees, like this. An this is a homemade bow made of leather: bended wood, like a bow an arrow. Then there was a luttle drill twisted across in the middle o the bow. An you jist put the luttle drill in the middle of where you wantit to put a hole, an you pulled the bow back an forward, an this spun the drill around an drilled the wee hole. An then you have luttle clasps. Ye drilled two holes between each other,[18] an you shoved one clasp in there, one on that [other] side, pressed it doon wi yer finger, an that held the plate in place. Or a juig, ye ken? A milk juig. But it had tae be something that ye appreciated. Ye wouldnae do it for *usin* fir soup or onything like that. A wall plate.[19] A family heirloom.

Well, that was what I done in Dundee. I done that for three months. I made myself a few pound. [*Laughs.*] I made living money off it, ye know? I made money fir my pictures,[20] money fir my smokes. Enough to get by. That was taught tae me by an old potter. I spent some time wi him, an old man called Joe Hendry. He taught me how tae do it. An the clasps were cheap to buy. Spring clasps. Once one was placed intae a hole, it would never move; it held the broken bits in place.

(87DW13 @ 40:12.)

---

17. "I'll show you": here Duncan demonstrates how to mend a plate, improvising props out of several twigs and a flat scrap of wood.

18. "Between each other": that is, opposite each other.

19. "A wall plate": that is, a decorated china plate or bowl of the kind that householders might display on the wall of their kitchen or dining room.

20. "Money for my pictures": that is, for picture shows, or movies.

§4.10. BOTHY DAYS AT KIRRIEMUIR,
WHERE A GAFFER WAS CIGARETTE CRAZY

JN: Duncan, you're a good singer of bothy ballads, right?*

Well, I'm not a guid singer. I wouldnae say a guid singer. Ye see, because these people around the bothies, they werenae classed as good singers. It was their source of entertainment. I mean, if you were a good singer, then you had no need tae be there in the first place workin wi the horses, because there was more things for you to do! So I dinnae class myself as a good singer in any way. To keep the tradition alive is my ambition. I'm na worried about the quality o the singin; it's the quality of the story within the song or the bothy ballad.

Now, the days of the bothy ballad were like the days of the West. In a farm like this size,[21] I would say back maybe, say, fifty year ago, there would be about ten men on this place, young men, and they all lived up in the bothies* around the place, ye know. They made their own food. They stole eggs. They boiled potatoes. And durin the weekends, when they had nothing tae do, they got together and they had a few bottles of beer and they had a singsong. And they played the old melodeon, ye know. And they sang songs, and they made up a story about the farmer. Dirty stories, good stories, bad stories. It was the same in every place, especially in the county of Angus, where the farms is large, maybe say three thousand acres. Maybe there were fifty men on a place. You had the foreman. You had the second foreman. You had the second horseman, first horseman, third horseman, down the line. You had the orra man.[22] You had—down to the bothy boy, the youngest chap on the farm. And if you were the youngest chap on the farm, then every dirty job and all the tricks was played on you.

∾

But Ah had a funny experience. Ah worked with the thrashin mill,[23] way back [in] 1941. I was very young at the time. So I had the privilege of being in the late bothy days. And Ah went to the bothy up in Angus in a place called Kir-riemuir,* for the first time, and it was durin the potato planting session, ye see. And the fairmer—old Willie Mitchell was his name, an he had a squeak in his

---

21. "Like this size": Duncan is referring to Kincraigie Farm, the farm of moderate size where this interview took place. "Money for my pictures": that is, for picture shows, or movies.

22. The orra man, also known as the orra loon, was a hired hand who did odd jobs, especially at a farm. See the *DSL*, s.v. "orra" (adj. and n.), sense 2 (2).

23. "The thrashin mill": that is, the threshing machine, the successor to the flail and the ancestor of the modern combine harvester.

voice. He was hurt durin the 1914 War an he had a silver tube in his neck and he cuidnae speak. When he spoke, he spoke with a squeak, ye know?[24]

Ah said, "All right, Mr. Mitchell, Ah'll do that." I was only sixteen, ye know. After my travels I was looking for some work, and they put me in the bothy. It was a big—bunk beds, ye know, Jack, in the bothy. Five beds, an you picked your own bed. Two black blankets, that's all you got. A couple o black blankets an a pillow. Maybe it was smelly. Maybe the pillow had never been washed for weeks, you know. They slept with their socks on and everything. You just stretched oot and went tae sleep, and up in the morning at six o'clock. Twelve o'clock was lunch time, break time, and you come back to the bothy tae make a cup of tea, if you had any tea to make. If you didnae have any tea, you got a handful of oatmeal and you put it in a cup and you stirred water in it and some salt, and that was all you got.

But Ah came back, Holly, at twelve o'clock. I swear on my mother's grave, if Ah'm telling you a lie may I never smoke that cigarette.[25] Here was the gaffer, and he was doon on the fireside, and he's rakin around a fire as big as that [gestures toward the hearth], and he's rakin around the ashes, ye know. He's rakin the ashes. An he was the foreman!

Ah came in at about ten to twelve. We had one hour for dinner. I was workin the horse, a big white horse Ah had, and I was driving tatties out to the people to plant them in the fields. And, eh, he's in, down on his fingers. I thought he was tryin to kindle the fire, ye know. Ah smoked Woodbines in these days,* Jack, Woodbine. For ten Woodbine was four pence. I would buy fags before I would buy food. I'm still the same way yet. Noo, this is a good story, you listen tae this.

Ah came in, and there he's in the fireside, the gaffer, the head o the house. He was above us, and he's rakin around the ashes wi his fingers in the fire. And I said, "What's the problem, Tom?" Tom was his name, Tom Jeffries. I says, "Tom, what's—?"

"Don't talk tae me!" he said. "Don't talk tae me! They're here. They're in there, and I'm lookin for them."

I said, "What're you lookin for?"

He says, "They're in there somewhere." He says, "I'm goin off my head. They're in there. I'll get one yet."

I says, "What's the problem?"

He says, "They're in there. There must be one with a wee taste on it. Must be one that size," he said. "Don't talk to me now till I get one. After I get one, you'll be all right."

---

24. Here Duncan imitates what Mitchell's high-pitched voice sounded like; the result is next to incomprehensible.

25. "May I never smoke that cigarette": the reference is to a cigarette that Duncan has just lit.

What he was looking for, Jack, he was going crazy for fag ends. And he got one, a Woodbine that size [*gestures with a thumb and finger*], and he put it in his mooth.

Now, I swear on my mother's grave, Mary, I won't tell you a lie. I had about six Woodbine in a packet. They were cheap cigarettes. Woodbine. Ah said, "Is that what—?" He luiked at me, an it was as if I had produced Aladdin's Cave in front o his face. An his eyes lighted, and he became a changed man.

He says, "Don't, no, don't tell me." He said, "You have something."

I said, "Luik." I says, "Ah've got Woodbines."

"You, Woodbine!" he said. And I gave him one and he took one long drag. [*Takes a long breath as if inhaling.*] "Oh God," he said, "you've saved my life! From now on," he said, "you'll never need tae worry again about dirty jobs. You're my pal, you're my friend!" He was the gaffer. He was cigarette crazy! Mad on cigarettes. And oncet he had a Woodbine—

"Here, take a couple," I says. "I'll split them wi ye. I'll split them wi ye," I said. "You go halfers an I'll go halfers."

I only stayed there, Marie, for about three weeks, an he was sad to see me go, ye know. I was his social security. He was crazy on fags, mad on fags, Jack. And that's a true story. I swear on my mother's grave it's true. He was a nice big chap. He was only about thirty-three years old, but he was addicted to fags, you know?

JN: You can't get more addicted than that.

No, ye cuidnae get no closer than that tae cigarettes. He didnae drink, though, an he could fight like guns. Nobody would speak tae him. He was the hardest man in the world. I'll tell you what he could do. If he had a horse he could put it to his knees, see? A raging horse, a horse that wouldnae reverse. You back it in the cart. You know, we had fifteen horses on that place at the time, and the horse was a wee bit fresh in the morning. He could het that horse jist a chop in the forehead wi his hand like that [*claps hands sharply*], right on the forehead. He damn near put it to its knees. The most powerful man you ever saw.

(86DW30 @ 00:21 and @ 05:39, with video 86V01.)

§4.11. BOTHY SONG, "BOGIE'S BONNIE BELLE"*

[*Speaking to an audience at the Glenfarg Folk Club:*] We must never forget wir heritage, where it really began. It all began in the bothy days, when they had no television, no radio, nothing. And all we had to do was just make up our own songs, make up our own tunes, an compose as much as possible. All we had [was] an old melodeon to play some tunes an play music. An these were the days of great Scottish invention. Some of these great, fine Scottish ballads were born: told about someone, or some happening, or some story. For this young girl here* I'd like to sing a well-known ballad, it's well known to everybody; it's called "Bogie's Bonnie Belle." [*Sings:*]

♪♫

1   Oh as I gang doon by Huntly toon
     my intentions they were to fee,*
     and I fell in wi Bogie,
     and him I did agree.

2   Now Bogie he had a braw dochter
     and her name was Isabel.[26]
     She was the flooer o his hairt,
     the lily o the dell.

3   So one night as Belle she went walkin
     oh doon by Bogieside,
     an she come and speired to me,
     oh would I be her guide.

4   Now shortly three months has gane by
     and this Belle she gaes wan an pale.
     The roses left her bonny cheeks
     And she began to fail.

5   Then nine month has gone and past
     and this Belle she gien birth tae a son,
     and Bogie he did send for me
     to see what should be done.

6   For syne I promised I would marry Belle
     and Belle promised she would marry me.
     But Bogie said I was nae match for Belle
     nor Belle nae match for me.
     So he sent me packin doon the road
     withoot a penny o my fee.[27]

_____

26. Isabel: pronounced "Eye-zabel."

27. These last two lines of the stanza ("So he sent me packin. . . .") are sung to the same tune as is used for the first two lines. Here and elsewhere, Duncan's concept of the musical strophe is a flexible one.

Bogie's Bonnie Belle

verse 1

Oh as I — gang doon — by Hun - tly Toon,

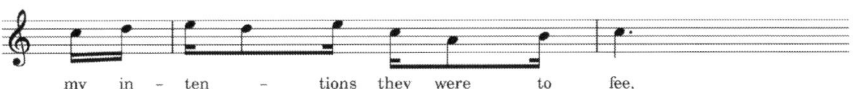

my in - ten - tions they were to fee,

and I fell in — wi Bo — gie,

and him I did a - gree.

7   Now Belle she got married tae a tinker lad
     wha lived in Huntly toon.
     Wi tilly pans an paraffin lamps[28]
     she hawked the country roon.

8   Oh maybe she got a better lad,
     for it's hard for me tae tell.
     But never you dae tae nae bonnie lass
     what I done to Bogie's Belle.

Now that was just a bothy ballad. An there are many, many wonderful versions o that story. There's dozens of versions o "Bogie's Bonnie Belle."

(86DW43 @ 1:17:53; spoken introduction from 84GF02 @ 31:40.)

---

28. "Tilly pans": skillets or saucepans; "paraffin lamps": kerosene lanterns.

§4.12. BOTHY STORY, "THE LAD WHO KNEW NO FEAR"

♪♫

You see, when all the men got together, in the bothy days—the foreman, the grieve, the gaffer, the cattleman, an the shepherd—they probly all were single men an they stayed in the bothy.

Noo, the youngest one in the bothy, Jack, would always take the brunt o all the arguments. They made fun wi him, ye know? They tormented the life out o him. Just say there was an apprentice takin his job for the first time; sent him for "tartan paint" an all these things.[29] So Jack was the brunt o all the fun, just pullin his leg. They never really hurt him in any way.

So they said, "Jack," they said, "Saturday, you're coming wi us tae the toon."

Jack says, "What am Ah goin to do in the toon?" He says, "Ah'll stay home here."

They says, "Come on wi us, you're a big young man. Jist come on tae the pub an have a drink."

He says, "Ah never had a drink in ma life."

"Well," he says, "you're comin wi us tonight. Suppose we have to carry ye, you're comin."

Jack was about eighteen, nineteen—youngest man in the bothy. Now if they took a shortcut down from the farm,[30] they had to pass through a footpath through the local cemetery, see? So the five o them walkit doon through the farm. It wasnae far, maybe, say, half a mile. An they walked the path through the cemetery, and beside the path where they were walkin was a new grave, see? And they said tae each other—cattleman, he says—"Ah, there must be somebody gettin buried here."

So they walked down tae the pub and had a good drink. An then the foreman says, "Man," he says, "it shouldnae be time tae be gaein hame."[31] He says, "Well, come on, Ah'll tell ye what we'll dae." (And Jack, you see, he's well on; he's had a good drink for the first time.) He said, eh, "Come on, we'll slip awa and leave him. We'll go to the grave," he says, "and Ah'll get doon in the grave, and Ah'll give him a frecht." (A "frecht," they called it, meanin a fright.)

So Jack missed them away. And he says to himsel, "Oh," he says, "the boys must have wandered home. Ah'd better go tae, myself."

Noo when they dug the grave, they left the sand the next mornin up on top o the grave, an the old gravedigger stuck his spade in fir tae cover up the body next morning. So the rest o the boys hid behind tombstones, an the foreman got doon intae the grave, close to the path. And they haird Jack comin whustlin up

---

29. "Tartan paint": "tartan" is the Scots term for patterned cloth woven into bands with multiple colors. North Americans generally refer to the same fabric as "plaid." Tartan paint is hard to find!

30. "Farm": regularly pronounced "farrum," as is usual in Scots, with an epenthetic vowel.

31. "It shouldnae be time tae be gaein hame": that is, "Too bad, but it's just about time to be going home."

Figure 4.3 Williamson at Nether Largie South, a Neolithic chambered tomb in Kilmartin Glen, Argyll, 1988. Williamson once spent the night there, in an incident reminiscent of his story about a young bothy worker who felt no fear. Photo by Dorothy Leese.

the path. And he waited till Jeck was comin level wi the graveyard, and he says, "Ohhh God, I'm cau-auld, I'm cau-auld! Ohhh, I'm cauld! Ohhh, I'm cau-auld!"

Jeck stopped, an he looked intae the grave. And he [the foreman] laid down when he seen this; he stayed in the grave. Jack said, "Nae wonder you're cauld, man," he says. "They forgot to pit any muck on ye!" An he tuik his spade and he fulled the grave to the top. "That'll keep you warm!"[32] he said. "That'll keep you warm!"

JN: [Laughs.]

---

32. "Warm": regularly pronounced "warrum," with an epenthetic vowel.

And he walked hame. His mates had tae run an dig him out. He says, "Nae wonder you're cauld. They never put any muck on youse!" [*Laughs.*] He didnae get any fright; didnae fright down too much.

JN: That's good, Duncan, that's good! There's a folktale that's kind of like that, "The lad who didn't know what fear was."* Things like that start happening to him, and he's totally unconcerned. He didn't know what fear was.

Didnae know what fear was, no.

JN: So that's a bothy story.

That's a bothy story, yeah. I was told that as a bothy story.

JN: Because it's about the bothy. Are any others of your stories bothy stories, you'd say?

Ach, well, they dinnae call them stories, they'd just call em wee cracks, ye ken? Short cracks. They'd call em short cracks. Och, there must have been many funny happenins that took place when they were at crofts and farms, ye know? But the youngest one in the bothy—it was just for boredom's sake they tormented the young man. Ye know what I mean? They tormented the young man just for boredom's sake.

(87DW14 @ 32:39.)

§4.13. ON THE RHYTHM OF THE WORK YEAR

JN: Duncan, when you were working out here at Loch Fyne, would you first go out and work the shellfish?

Yeah. We would go out for the shellfish on March to April. Then if the spring was guid, then we'd get the big spring tides, ye see? And then in May and June we'd get the turnip thinnin. Thinnin the turnips on wir knees.

JN: Whereabouts was that?

Around Argyll. Around Lochgilphead an down in Kintyre. There's a lot o farms grew a lot o turnips for feedin the cattle in the wintertime. And these turnips, we thinned them by hand, on wir knees. We got so much per hundred yards for thinnin the turnips. I'd go from one farm to another, thinnin turnips in the summertime. When the turnips was finished, we'd go back tae the shellfish for a luttle while, till the berries were ready, then we'd make wir way all back wi the ponies, back over the hills again to the berries. When the berries were finished, we'd go up tae the potatoes in Crieff. We'd come back tae Crieff for the potato pickin. From Blairgowrie it was a couple o days' journey.

(88DW07 @ 17:49.)

§4.14. LIFTING POTATOES IN CRIEFF

You see, when we were at Crieff at the tatties, on an evening at the tatties in Crieff, we'd all get roond the fire and kindle a big bonfire, and we would sing, and have a drink, and play pipes an that. You haird so many songs and sings— everyone took a turn round the fire, singin. Lassies would sing, and laddies would sing, ye know.

JN: Was it like Blairgowrie in that way?

No, it was jist all Traivellers. Just gatherin tatties, ye ken, they came for the tattie season. Farmer says—in a big field, when you've put up your tents, "Pick my tatties for me," and you stayed there till the tatties was finished, ye know? Well, he was a tattie merchant called Sandy Bain, and he had aboot five hundred acres o tatties. That's a lot o pickin, for five hundred acres. Well, see, for a squad, you would need at least thirty-five people, forty people tae the dreel,[33] you know, a bit in front o each other, pickin the tatties, ye know. Puttin them in baskets. And the tractor came along and you emptied them into bogies and drove them off tae the farm. Well, I was drivin a tractor, ye see? There were seven of us drivin tractors. They needed seven tractors because they hired fields in different farms through the district. They bought fields frae other farmers. He was the merchant. Six weeks is what we used tae get, six weeks o tatties.

JN: Six weeks. How would you get paid for that, Duncan?

We got paid every night. Half past four, he come down the dreel wi his envelopes, with everybody's pay in it. And he had no names on them. And if you were workin, he'd hand you an envelope, on your bit, before the last dreel. He come down—you picked the last dreel at nighttime, and went behind the digger.[34] When the dreel was lifted, he'd walk down and everyone's standin a

---

33. "The dreel": that is, the drill, the row of plants sown on the top of a ridge between two furrows. See the *OED*, s.v. "drill" (noun), sense 4.

34. "The digger": the machine that dug out the soil to free the potatoes for harvesting by hand.

little bit—the measurement was twelve yards. Everybody's ten to twelve yards [apart]. So twelve people would lift a hundred and forty-four yards. So of the two hundred or three hundred yards o dreel, you would need twenty-four people for that dreel, see what I mean? Twelve yards was the standard rate; you cuidnae give anyone over twelve yards.

JN: Was there an overseer there?

The gaffer, the farm gaffer. He'd walk up an down, pickin up any potatoes left and flingin them in the cart, but he wouldnae give you any orders. He'd just see that you kept your back goin, you know, keep up. Because when the digger went doon the one dreel, when the one dreel was lifted, he come up the field single and went doon another one. He come up empty and came down full, diggin the one way all the time. You never got much peace to sit on your back. You were workin down all the time. It's a hard job, workin potatoes.

JN: It's hard work.

Hard work. One pound fifty a day. One pound fifty, fae eight o'clock till half past four, half an hour break for dinner.

JN: Did they give you the dinner?

No, you had tae make your own dinner. Make your own tea an all. You got nothin, all you got was thirty shillins a day. They gave you nothing. You had tae use your own cars to get tae the field, suppose it was five mile away, see? Because he bought fields o tatties from different fairmers from the district. And we'd say, "We'll go tae such an such a place today." When one farm was finished we'd move on to the next farm. We stayed in the same place, but we driv away our cars to the fields.

(87DW14 @ 53:42.)

§4.15. A POLICEMAN BAFFLED AT CRIEFF

♪♫

So we had a wonderful experience. We came in—we were all gathered together at the potato pickin session in Crieff. There were about fifteen families in the one field, ye know? All pickin potatoes for money. An the police used tae come in an check up tae be sure who was all there, ye know?[35] He just wanted to know how many families.

He came in and he took his book down. There were five John Townsleys, there were six Duncan Williamsons, there were six Jimmy Williamsons, ye know what I mean? See, "What's your name?" "Duncan Williamson." "What's your name?" "Duncan Williamson." "What's your name?" "Dun—." Nephews, cousins, we had all the same name! "What's your name?" "John Townsley." (My mother was a Townsley, ye see?) "What's your name?" "Jimmy Williamson." "Jimmy Williamson." "Jimmy Williamson." "Jimmy Williamson." Uncle, grandson, nephew, all wi the same name!

The poliss was baffled. He put his book back in his pocket, sayin, "Ah cannae deal with this!" [*General laughter.*]

The problem was, if one was stopped by the police drivin a car—"What's your name?" "Jimmy Williamson." "OK, you're Jimmy Williamson." But if some other poor Jimmy Williamson was stopped: "You were stopped by the police." "Na me, I was na stopped by the police." "What's your name?" "Jimmy Williamson." It's a bit confusing, ye know? But the age gets them.[36] That's the only thing, the age gets them.

(86DW41 @ 1:07:05.)

§4.16. ON WORKING ALONGSIDE IRISH IMMIGRANT LABORERS

You see, many o the Travellers, like mysel, worked among the Irishmen. And the Irishmen—they took jobs. There were many Irishmen, Jack, on farms. There were potato squads come [from] Ireland tae gather the early potatoes in Ayrshire. And the Travellers worked wi the Irish immigrant workers comin in. And they came there for six months a year, and the Travellers stayed beside them, drank wi them, sang wi them. And the Irish used to treat those people equal wi theirsel. In fact, they married among them. Some of the Irishmen [who] married some of the Traveller lassies never went back. Some of these migrant workers—Irish, young Irish lads—married into travelling families. I know two or three who married intae them; they're my age noo. But they came here tae lift potatoes. Young Paddy O'Donnell,* he came. He was only about eighteen, and he married one o the lassie Reids, and he's still among the travellin people yet. Now he's a grandfather. And he came here an eighteen-year-old from Ireland to gather tatties in Ayrshire.

---

35. "The police": that is, the policeman. The emphasis of the word is on the first syllable, as is frequently heard in Scots.

36. "The age gets them": that is, their respective ages distinguish them.

JN: Do you think a fair number of songs came in with them?

They brought their songs wi them; they're travelling people. And the Travellers learned them off the Irish; that's where they learned some o them. The first place I haird "Glen Swilly"* was in the Shira Glen, when I was up bringin up a message to my father,[37] and an old man was singin it, and I learned it off him. I heard it two or three times from him and I got interested in it cause I liked the song.

(87DW13 @ 09:55.)

§4.17. IRISH SONG, "THE FLOWER OF SWEET STRABANE"*

JN: Well, Duncan, would you do one thing for me and for everyone here?

Yeah; anything you like!

JN: Could you sing that song that you were just starting? [Sings:] "If I—"

[*DW sings, taking up the song:*] Was the King of Ireland.

JN: I've been wanting to hear that for weeks.

Yes, right. You're goin tae have it. It's not well known. I was very proud of this, because I was working in the Shira Glen,* back in the forties. [*Sings:*]

♪♫

1   Oh if I was the king of Ireland, and all things at my will,
     I'd roam through recortations[38] in comfort to find still.
     The comfort I would seek the most, as you will understand
     is to win the heart of Martha, the flower of sweet Ireland.

2   Oh if I had my lovely Martha here, or away in Inchaion,[39]
     or in some lonely valley in the wild woods of Tyrone,
     I'd all endoover for to try, and sure to gain my plan,
     for to win the heart of Martha, the flower of sweet Strabane.

---

37. "Bringin up a message": bringing some kind of provision. This would have been in the 1940s; see the Commentary on §4.17.

38. "I'd roam through recortations": cf. "I'd roam for recreation," the line as it reads in other versions of the song that are in print.

39. "In Inchaion": the name is "Innisown" in other versions.

3 Oh her cheeks they are so rosy red, her neck is like a swan,
and o'er her lily-white shoulders her hair of brown hangs down.
She is the loveliest creature, I'm sure you'll understand.
She is my lovely Martha, the flower of sweet Strabane.

4 Oh if I had my lovely Martha here, or away in Inchaion,
or in some lonely valley in the wild woods of Tyrone,
I'd all endoover for to try, and sure to gain me plan,[40]
for to win the heart of Martha, the flower of sweet Strabane.

The Flower of Sweet Strabane
verse 2

Oh if I had my love-ly Mar-tha here, or a-away in In-chai-on,

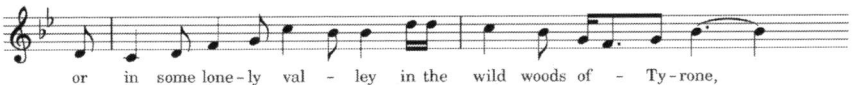

or in some lone-ly val-ley in the wild woods of – Ty-rone,

I'd all en-doo-ver for to try, and sure to gain my plan,

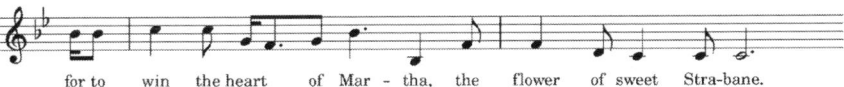

for to win the heart of Mar-tha, the flower of sweet Stra-bane.

That's a very old Irish tune, ye know what I mean?

JN: Yes, yes.

I like Irish ballads a lot. They tell such a wonderful story, and that's what makes them so important.

(88DW05 @ 04:21.)

---

40. Printed versions read, "I work my whole endeavor / and I'd seek to work my plan."

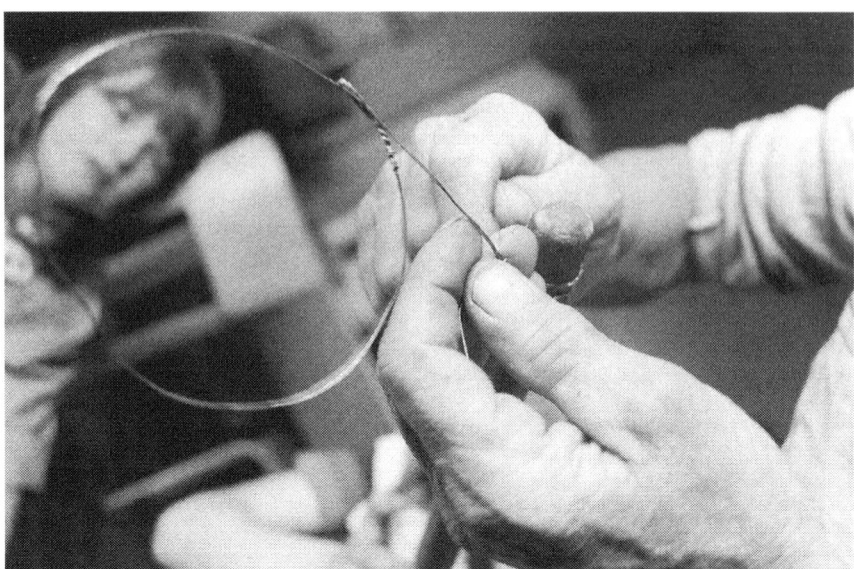

Figure 4.4 Williamson showing how to make a snare, Kincraigie Farm Cottage, close by Strathmiglo, Fife, 1986. Photo by Leonard Yarensky.

Figure 4.5 Pointing out where to set a rabbit snare, back of Kincraigie Farm Cottage, 1986. Photo by Leonard Yarensky.

§4.18. HOW TO SNARE RABBITS, SALMON, AND LOBSTERS, AND ON PEARL FISHING IN SUMMER*

Well, ye see, mostly up here,[41] instead of settin em [the snares] on the moor, the rabbit catchers put pins on em to hold it, to keep them sittin up like that in the fields. But Ah just usually hang em to a hole in the fence from over that side, which I'll demonstrate tae you. And then during the nighttime the rabbit comes thinkin that the hole is still the same hole that he used to pop through. He goes through there, an instead o goin through the hole, he's into the net, an then there's no escape for him. But I don't set them out in the moors an the fields here because o the sheep. The sheep might go get their feet in them, or their tongues caught in them, an the cattle can get their tongues caught in em. So Ah set them in sheltery places where no animals can get to, like under hedges an close up to the fence, which I'll show you up in the hill here an you'll see how it's done. Or in a dike, ye know, looping through a hole in a dike. That's easiest, so the sheep or the cattle cannae get their tongue in em.

JN: So the rabbit's the only thing—

The rabbit's the only thing I'll get. Or a pheasant; the pheasant will go through the same place. Oh, I've had a few pheasants! Or a hare, a brown hare.—So, there's your snare.

Now what we used tae do when we went tae poach the salmon: the salmon, he would lie under a bush with its tail going like this [*mimics a gently waving tail*], and we would go down quietly, open wide a snare and drop it down like this, and we would jist gradually pit it over his tail till it comes up to here [*gestures*], till it gets past the tail, and then—[*mimics pulling the snare tight*]. The salmon always hides his head under a bush or something.

Now when we went to fish for crabs an lobsters, the idea was, we tuik another piece of wire and we would hang a piece o meat behind it. So we dropped this down, an the lobster came up an he put his nipper through tae catch the bait and pulled it into his feedin pouch, an that was how we trapped the lobster.[42]

You search for lobsters. You throw out some meat behind stones. You find a place where there are lobsters about, because you can see where they're scrapin

---

41. This recording was made in the open air, on the hillside back of Kincraigie Farm Cottage. At the point in the interview where the transcription begins, Duncan is pointing out the best places to set out snares for rabbits. See Figures 4.4 and 4.5.
42. Omitted here are detailed instructions on how to position the snare and the bait to trap the lobster.

in the sand where they're under the rocks, you see? Cause when the lobster crawls below a rock he flings out some sand, just like a rabbit. An you know he's there, so you throw down some bait to advertise them out from behind the rock. Then you lower this. Ah have caught them in dozens.

JN: Where do you go to get lobsters?

To the west coast. Plenty o lobsters doon there, anywhere along the shore, by the deep rocks. When the tide goes out, it leaves about four foot o water, you see? You use a juig to see through the water. What we call a juig. A metal one. You cut off the bottom. You put a piece o glass in the bottom, and then you luik through the glass.

   You use these for huntin for pearls, too. Same thing we use for huntin for pearls, freshwater pearls. There're a lot of pearls in the River Tay, and then the Earn and the Spey and all these rivers in Scotland. There're very precious pearls, guid pearls. Oh, there's a shop here; a chap, a non-Traveller, sold one pearl for £3000! It's still in Perth, in Cairncross jewelry shop,[43] up for show. The boy wouldnae sell it after he bought it from the fisherman.

JN: What do you call the viewer that you use for the pearls or the lobsters?

A pearl juig. Jist a pearl juig. You cut a piece of glass round, an then you got a candle for proper candle wax, and then you put wax around the bottom, and you cuid put it in a stream of runnin water, and you can see as clear as daylight right tae the bottom o the water. A can or a tin, or a plastic pail, or somethin like this. [*Goes to get a tin can to demonstrate.*] So we cut off the bottom, leavin a space about an inch from the edge tae hold wir glass on. An then we get a piece o glass the same shape as that there. Thin glass. Face of a clock or anything would do; the glass of a common clock, that's the best ye can get. An ye put it on here, with putty or candle grease, candle wax. An you can put this in the water, an then you can see anything: you can see little creatures right in the bottom o the water.

LY: Like a glass-bottom boat.

You get addicted to pearl fishin, you know? You can't stop it; it's like a drug. You might open, say, a hundred shell and get nothing, and you might just open one—

_____

43. The reference is to Cairncross of Perth Jewellers, St. John Street, downtown Perth.

JN: Then it's like the jackpot at Las Vegas. You keep putting your coins in, and you never know when you'll be a millionaire!

You've got many different rivers. You fish this river today, an you'll fish another river tomorrow. There's the Spey, the Tay, the Earn, the Ettrick, an all these others. They've all got good pearl in them. But some places ye have tae go up to the waist. You dinnae get them very much in the shallows. You've got to get tae the deep streams, the deep-runnin streams. But ye cannae see nothin in a deep-runnin stream, so you've got to get a pearl juig.

And you have what ye call a pearl stick. A long stick, you see? An you split the stick just like you're makin a clothes peg. The mussel lies flat, so you just come doon on the top an you press the split stick onto the mussel, and ye turn it round and squeeze an pick it up, and there's yir mussel caught in the split. And you'll carry a bag. We wouldnae open the pearls when we'd got them. We'd fish all day till the bag was full, and then we'd go out on the bank an we'd let wir legs dry off and then we'd open the pearls, an we'd turnabout openin them: "See, there's one, you try that one an I'll try this one."

JN: Did you ever find any good pearls yourself?

Ah never did get ony big ones. I got wee seeds, ye know? Wee things up in Aberdeenshire, in the Don and the Dee, back in the forties. Sandy, my cousin, he got a few. But you must get a good dry summer. If the burn is in spate, you cannae get to the deep parts, and the good big streams is the ones you want to get the pearl in.

Oh, there's a lot of them [Travellers] up away at it right now, up from Perth, from the caravan site.[44] This is a good summer for the Tay. The Tay's lower this year than it's been for many, many years. Oh, they're all off pearl fishin in the evenings an the nights an everything. A car will go up there wi maybe ten, fifteen, an they'll just walk intae the river with their pearl sticks an their juigs, an they'll fish there until dark at night.

(86DW09 @ 03:20 and @ 09:36.)

---

44. "From the caravan site": Duncan's reference is to the Double Dykes caravan site overlooking the River Almond, across the River Tay from Old Scone. Duncan's close friend Big Willie MacPhee kept his caravan there for many years.

§4.19. HARASSED BY THE POLICE WHEN HIS WIFE WAS IN HOSPITAL

♪♫

I remember I was camped off of an old road wi ma horse an cart. An one of our luttle boys was in the hospital. John, the youngest one, in Edinburgh. And [Polly][45] went off to Edinburgh tae see the baby in the hospital, on the train. And Ah put up the tent, and that was when the police came. Two of them. They says, "You'll have to move on."

Ah says, "Ah cannae move. My wife's in Edinburgh an my baby's in the hospital."

"You'll move," he says. "I'll give you an hour," he says, "tae be on the road."

I says, "I'll no be goin on the road."

"Well," he says, "you'll be in the back o that car. And," he says, "that's another thing. These horses are runnin untied in the road. They're vicious animals."

"Away, for God's sake," I said.

JN: [Laughs.]

"What do you think—?" I says to Edith,[46] I says: "Go an show that polissman, baby, how wicked the horse is." She went and she catched the horse's tail, and she went between the horse's legs and come back the other side. I said: "You call that vicious?"

Now he had a wee bit o ribbon on his chest; a wee bit o ribbon, ye know? He says, "Look. Don't try an tell *me* about horses." He says, "I know too much about horses."

I said, "Where did you learn about your horse trade?"

He said: "The army," he says. "What do you think?"

Ah says, "The army? That's funny," Ah said. "Because in the D-Day division o the battle of Dunkirk," I says, "there were plenty o tanks and guns and boats. But," I says, "I never seen any horses."

"You'll be on the road tonight," he says.

He came back just as it was gettin dark. And he went around my car. He said, "If you stay here, I'm going to charge you for campin. And if ye go on the road I'm goin to charge you for lights.[47] Now," he said, "that's for you."

"Well," Ah said, "I'm stayin here." An I stayed there one night an had to move on in the morning.

---

45. Duncan said "Linda" by mistake, and I have corrected the slip. The reference is to Duncan's first wife Jeannie Townsley, who went by the nickname "Polly."

46. "Edith": Duncan's oldest daughter from his marriage to Jeannie Townsley.

47. "Charge you for lights": that is, cite you for not having proper headlights or tail lights.

JN: Did they fine you for that, Duncan?

No, I got away with it. For one night only, one night. I had to wait there till she [Polly] come back, come back off the train. I wasnae goin away to leave her. If she came back to that camp, where the hell was she goin tae find me that night? Not for the sake o the police; Ah told them that.

(87DW11 @ 51:38.)

§4.20. HARASSED IN A VILLAGE OUTSIDE CUPAR

♫

JN: What are other stories of people being moved or being shifted?

Oh, they were fightin them all the time before this "no-harassment" started.* Comin through to pull you out o bed at ten o'clock. They tuik me an ma two sons intae Cupar. They held us all night in jail. They lifted every single one over fifteen years of age; put us all in jail.

JN: Whereabouts was this?

Outside of Cupar. I was in a caravan on the roadside, a place called Burnturk.[48] I can take you an show you the place. An old right-o-way road. It went through from one end of the village to the other, but there was nobody on the road. It was just an old right-o-way road. There were six of us there, on the verge of the back road. There was no through traffic on it, you could walk through it. And they came at nighttime. Four carloads of them. Four vanloads o police. They thought they were goin tae have a battle or fight or something! They lifted a cousin of mine, they lifted two other men that was there, and they lifted me and my two sons. Took us intae Cupar, held us overnight, took us to the court in the mornin. And they fined each individual ten pound each. Now they fined me thirty pounds for three [people], for one caravan. And they fined the other people that was there ten pound each. I was fined three times because Ah had three—everybody over fifteen had to be fined, even though they were only stayin in the one caravan. Me and my two sons, fined ten pound each. I was payin thirty pound for staying one night.

JN: Did you have the money?

---

48. "Burnturk": Coaltown of Burnturk, a small village on a side road between the towns of Cupar and Ladybank, Fife.

Ah, some good you were if you didnae have the money! They wouldnae have given you time to pay. If you didnae settle the day, you got no time to pay.[49]

(87DW11 @ 53:41.)

§4.21. THIRTY DAYS IN JAIL IN PERTH

♪♫

I'll give you an example of this having no time tae pay. I got thirty days for breakin a boy's jaw in Perth.*

JN: How's that, Duncan?

Thirty days in Perth, in a jail.

JN: What for?

For hittin a miner. A miner, yeah. He comes out tae the tent one night, when there's a lot of us campin oot in the tent. An there's none of us drinkin these days, we're just young men. I mean, I never had a pint of beer till I was thirty-seven. I was thirty-seven before I ever tasted my first drink in my life.

JN: You're kidding!

No, it's the truth. I swear on my mother's grave.

JN: You expect me to believe that, Duncan?

I swear on my mother's grave I'm telling you the truth. And anyone will tell you, I never had a glass of beer till I was thirty-seven years old. That's the truth.

JN: What about all your campfires and all?

Never touched any drink.

JN: Never touched a drink. Not a drop?

Not a drop. Ah've got three sons an four girls, and neither of them smokes or drinks. Not one o them. One o the boys has never been inside a pub in his lifetime.

---

49. "You got no time to pay": that is, they took you straight to jail.

JN: And your father? Would he—?

Oh, my father took a wee drink. He took a wee drink when he could afford it, ye know? But I never touched beer. So we were all there an we were sittin around the fire talkin. It was bow tents they had. An he comes down. A young man in his thirties. An he starts cussin an swearin an challengin us for a fight, ye know; nothing else. Callin us all names and this and that. I said, "Look, get away and to your bed! We don't want nothin to do with ye. You're causin trouble here."

He says, "Can you put me to a bed?"

I says, "Look, I don't want trouble in any way." And the rest o them, Old Sandy Cameron, and old Andy—he's dead now, old Sandy's dead—a few other travelling people—didnae want any trouble at all. He said, "Come here and put me to a bed!" But Ah didn't know what he was goin to dae. He had a piece of iron in his hand, a piece o plat iron in his hand,[50] and Ah didnae know this. About a foot and a half bar, iron bar. And I walked—it was gettin kind o dark. And he het me there [*gestures to his head*], an he split me right doon there.

JN: Right in the middle of your head?

Right there! I've still got the scar there.

JN: Is that the one, right over the eye?

Right over the eye. And I het him, an I broke his jaw in three bits. And he lay there for a long while, and some of the other people picked him up and walked him up to the village. Left him there. And he was tuik by ambulance to Edinburgh, an he lay in Edinburgh for, eh, three weeks.

I walked down to {- - -} an the doctor broke a needle, and he says to me, "I wonder how he split you," he says, "because your skin is very tough," he says to me.

JN: [Laughs.]

I've got two stitches in there, the split there. I was lifted. Ah got thirty days in Perth. No fine. See, if you're a Traveller in Scotland, you dinnae get no time to pay cause you had no registered address, ye see. Nowadays if you live in a caravan, say, that's your address. "Caravan #2." You can say: "Well, your honor, can I have time to pay?" He'll say: "Well, three weeks to pay off, two pound a week," or somethin like that. But not in my time. They wouldnae even gie me the choice. Thirty days.

---

50. "Plat iron": sheet iron.

They come an arrested me the next day. They came to the camp and says, "Look, you, come on! You've been charged," they said. "The boy's in hospital."

Ah said, "The boy struck me with a piece o iron."

They said, "What's with that?"

I said, "I was only defendin myself."

"Why did you not call us?" he says. What they said tae me—when he split me, I should have went an got my eye stitched and then walked up to the police and charged him. That's what they said to me. They said, "If you'd have got your eye stitched and walked up to the police and charged *him*," he said, "he'd have been fined. He wouldnae have been lyin in hospital with a broken jaw. And," he said, "you wouldnae have been in jail."

JN: Well, Duncan, what happened when you were called up before the magistrate then? Do you remember?

Yeah. The prosecutor first of all said, "You're charged with hittin a man an breakin his jaw, for disturbin the peace." I mean, how were we disturbin the peace? We weren't interferin with nobody.

JN: Did you tell them the story?

I told them! They wouldnae listen to me. The prosecutor wouldnae listen to me. And the prosecutor first of all said I was drunk!

JN: And were any witnesses called?

The Travellers had all vanished the next day, packed up an left. They thought the boy was going to die in hospital; they didnae want tae be involved in it. They had tae wire his jaw up. It was just my word against his. And his word was tuik; he was a miner, an he had a home up in the village.

JN: So it was thirty days.

Thirty days.

JN: Did you have family at that time?

My little boy was lyin in the hospital at Edinburgh! I cuidnae even know was he dead or alive—John, the youngest one! And Ah spent thirty days and nights. He was in hospital for nine months, you see.

JN: I see. And how did you find your wife Jeannie again?

Oh, she stayed in the one place till I come back. The police cuidnae move her on as long as I was in jail. So she still stayed in that same place where I was lifted, she stayed in that place the whole time. Her mother was beside her, so she wasnae too bad off with the kids. That's the only time in my life I got thirty days.

(87DW11 @ 55:27.)

§4.22. DEALING IN SCRAP IN FIFE

JN: Duncan, tell us a bit about the scrap. Where do you come up with scrap metal?

Farms, builders—eh, construction works, and, eh, joiners, plumbers. An people buildin houses, people knockin down houses, people sellin houses. And people who wants to clean up some junk around the place, ye know? Scrap iron, bits of brass, wire and cable. Then you clean it and make it sellable.

LW: The Traveller can see through the junk to the possibilities of it.

I use a van. It tuik me half a day to clean up an old-fashioned freezer, but I didnae charge anything for takin it away cause I cuid see by lookin at it that I cuid get something out o it.

JN: How do you sort through the junk?

You've got iron, you've got steel, you have metal, you've stainless steel, you've got copper, you've got brass, you've got lead, you've got aluminium, and you've got zinc, you've got cast aluminium, an you've got pewter, an you've got tin. All these metals. Some people, they havenae a clue! But the Travellers, being metalworkers—I know every type o metal that you cuid find. Any kind o metal. I know just tae luik at it what it really is.

JN: And what do you do with it then, once you've sorted it out?

Take it tae a scrap merchant. The main thing about the scrap merchant is—the local people like you, goin into a scrap merchant's place, you'll say, "Och, I'm no givin this away, I'll put it in my old bogie or my van, I'll take it in myself." Now that man in the scrap store *knows* you as a novice in the game, an he's never goin tae give *you* what he gives *me*, you understand? I'm a dealer. He knows that I know the value of it, so that if he doesnae pay me what I want, I'll take it tae someone else. You were just goin to give it tae me to get rid of this stuff.

Now I was standing one day in a storeroom, waitin for the store tae open because it was closed for lunch. In comes a man. He said tae me, "Is the store closed?"

"Yes, it's closed."

"When does it open?" he says.

I said, "It opens at one o'clock."

He said, eh, "I need to empty my car," he says. "This bogie."

Now I luiked in his bogie. There were three copper tanks, there were four or five car radios, some car batteries, an a lot o brass an piping. I said tae him, "If you're in a hurry, I'll buy it from you."

He said, "I'd rather sell it myself than sell it to you. I'll just wait."

I said, "I'll give you £10 for it, then you can go fir your lunch." I offered him £10. He said, "If you're going to give me £10 for it, I'll probly get more when they open the store."

Ah was there first, and Ah sold my stuff. And he come in wi his car an bogie, and he put it on the scales all together, an there were two copper tanks, some lead, some brass, some copper wire. An he put it on the scale; he put it all together. He never separated—he put it all together. All the metals, he put them on the scale. And the boy weighed it along, and he sat and said, "Three pounds."

"Thank you very much." He walked away, happy as a lark. [*General laughter.*]

If that had been me, I'd have given him fifteen for it!

JN: How long does it take you to "eye" a load of metal like that?

Oh, jist about fifteen seconds.

(86DW13 @ 56:30.)

§4.23. HOW TO SELL A STONE TO A SCRAP MERCHANT

♫

JN: There's a funny story you were telling me one time, but I didn't get all of it, Duncan. It was about when you were dealing with scrap in Fife. And it was about a merchant who kept coming by, and he'd be paying you for a certain amount of scrap. And then finally one day he came, he said—

Oh, that was the rock, yeah! [*Laughs.*] That was a great funny story.

See, when we were collectin scrap wi wir ponies, we went well out in the country, ye see. Cause the farther you get out in the country, the easier it was to get scrap, ye know, scrap iron. So we would phone him up, and he'd come wi his lorry an pick it up, an he'd jist say, "How much d'you thinks's there?"

Ah would say, "A couple of tons, maybe thirty hundred."

An he was a good judge, he jist judged it. An he would pay ye.

So there was a great big stone beside the camp where we were stayin. So we used tae heap the scrap roon the stone, ye see, to make it look bigger. And the first two or three times he'd come, he didnae pay much attention, you see. So, cast metal, if it was good and heavy, is *heavy*, you know; it has a lot o bulk. So we were lookin to get a couple heavy casts from one farmer, ye know, and we broke it up and thought we'd build it roon the stone once more. An we built it roon the stone, an he came out, an he said, "What do you think is there, boys?"

And I said—oh, I said: "Maybe a couple o ton, anyway."

He said, "I'll pay you for—I'll pay you," he says, "for two ton. I know metal's heavy." So we loaded it on his lorry. He looked at it a minute and says, "You'd better give me a lift wi this stone, because I've bought it two or three times already!"

JN: [Laughs, together with DW.]

"I've bought this stone two or three times already," he says. "You'd better give me a lift for it in the lorry. That stone'll weigh two ton!"

JN: [Still laughing.] That's good, that's good, Duncan. Did that really happen?

That took place, that's true. Yeah, that's true, yeah.

CN: He had a good sense of humor. *

That's true, yeah!

JN: I heard that sometimes the merchants would ask for a pile to be moved before they'd pay for it.

Yeah, but we didnae move the pile. We built it around the stone. He bought the stone two times since the last time he came!

(87DW14 @ 27:33.)

Chapter 5

COURTSHIP, MARRIAGE, AND RAISING CHILDREN

§5.1. SONG OF FULFILLED LOVE, "BANKS OF RED ROSES"*

[DW sings spontaneously in the midst of a ceilidh. Others sing along.]

♪♫

1   When I was a wee thing I was easily led astray.
Before I would work I would rather sport and play,
before I would work I would rather sport and play,
wi my Johnny on the banks o red roses.

2   So he tuik out his tune box,[1] he played tae me a tune,
he tuik out his tune box, he played tae me a tune,
he tuik out his tune box, and I did whist a tune,[2]
I said, "Johnny, oh my Johnny, dinnae leave me!"

3   He said, "Jeannie my lassie, how you been guid tae me!
Oh Jeannie my lassie, oh would ye marry me?
We'll settle doon for life and we'll hae bairnies three,
we'll come roamin on the banks o red roses."

4   So we settled doon fir life and married we did be,
and sure as God did help us, for we did hae bairnies three.
And sure as God did help us, an we did hae bairnies three,
we come roamin on the banks o red roses.

---

1. "Tune box": pronounced "tunin box," with an extra syllable, here and elsewhere. The reference is probably to a harmonica ("mouthie"), though a melodeon or similar instrument might be meant.
2. "Whist a tune": the sense is evidently "whistle (or hum) a tune."

5   For the years have gone past, that noo I'm all gone gray,
     but never gien a thought tae Jeannie and me.
     I never gien a thought tae Jeannie and o me,
     we've been happy on the banks o red roses.

6   But the years have gone past, but noo I'm all gone gray,
     but I turned to my Jeannie an tae her I did say,
     I turned to my Jeannie and tae her I did say,
     "Come, we'll go walkin on the banks o red roses."

Banks of Red Roses

verse 2

So he   tuik   out his tune   box, he   played tae me   a tune,

he   tuik   out   his   tune   box   he   played tae   me   a   tune,

he   tuik   out   his   tune   box,   and   I   did whist   a   tune,

I   said,   "John-ny,   oh   my   John-ny,   din - nae   leave   me!"

(84DW04 @ 1:27:39.)

§5.2. SONG OF UNREQUITED LOVE, "LAMBS IN THE GREEN FIELD"*

This is the one I like better than any one. [*Sings:*]

1   Oh, the lambs in the green field, they sport and they play.
     How many strawberries grows in the salt sea?
     How many strawberries grows in the salt sea?
     How many ships sail in the forest?

2   Oh, the first time I spied her she was in the church stan,[3]
       gold ring on her finger and a book in her hand.
       And I said, "My wee lassie, I could still be your man,
       though you're going to be wed to another."

3   And the next time I spied her was on her weddin day.
       With a coach and her bridegroom to the church she did stray.
       And me, like a fool, I had nothing to say.
       She was going to be wed to another.

4   "Oh, stop," said the bridegroom, "may I have one word?
       Would you venture your life on the point of my sword?
       You have lost your wee lassie, you've been courting too slow.
       Now she's goin to be wed to another."

5   Oh, dig me my grave, you may dig it so deep.
       You may cover me over with boulders so steep.
       You may lay me right doon and I'll have my last sleep,
       and maybe in time I'll forget her.

Lambs in the Green Field

verse 3

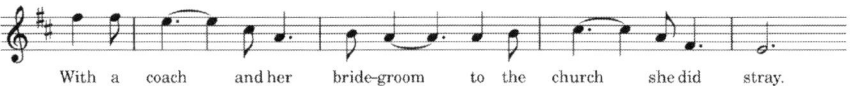

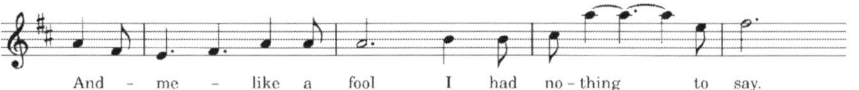

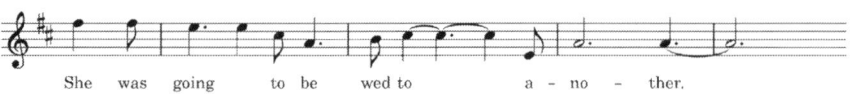

---

3. "Stan": this might be a clipped form of "standin," though what one finds in printed versions of
the song is "church stand."

That's "Lambs in the Green Field." But when Ah sing it, Ah sing it in a higher tone. But Ah just wanted you tae have the words.

JN: Well, the tune is beautiful as well. It sounded beautiful to me, Duncan. It's good in the lower key. Is that one of your family's songs?

Yeah, my family sung it all the time. Big Willy MacPhee and all the Travellers—a lot o the Travellers sings that. It's well known among the Travellers, that song.

JN: Yeah. That's a good one, thank you. That's terrific.

(87DW12 @ 53:48.)

§5.3. SONG IN CANT, "MY WEE MAGGIE,"* WITH STORY OF AN ELOPEMENT

♪♫

Before you go tae Campbeltown, there's a big campin place by the beach known as Tangy. Now, back in the time after the 1914 War, there's a glen goin up the hillside known as Tangy Glen, an at the top o the glen there used tae be an old miller and his brother, an they kept the mill. An auld meal mill, for makin meal. And they were awful good tae the travellin folk. They gien them bags o meal and flour, an they kept a cow for milk.

Figure 5.1 The mill at Tangy Glen, Kintyre, to which Travellers used to elope, as recounted in Williamson's song "My Wee Maggie." Photo © West of Scotland Archaeology Service, licensor www.scran.ac.uk.

The old sister died, but the two brothers kept the mill goin. One o them was kindae blind, my father told me. Noo, my mother was born in Muasdale; that's no far from Tangy Glen. My father was born in Tangy Glen. So the Travellers used tae go up the glen, pitch their tents in the glen, and then they'd go up tae the old mill and get a bag o flour, and they got a bag o oatmeal, and they'd get some milk, you know, from the two auld brothers, who were real kindly auld souls. They liked the Travellers.

Noo, they had a barn that they kept full of straw, and that barn was always left open. And this was like Gretna Green, this barn!* It was a Gretna Green for the Travellers in Kintyre, right. Whenever a young couple would run away, the first place they made was up the glen. They knew, the first thing, they'd go and they would get in the barn and make love, spend all the night and have their sex, and that ways they'd wed. They spent one night together in the barn. The next mornin they'd go to the old farm and get some tea for breakfast.

Now in bygone days in Tangy, the old fellas—as you know, they didnae have any fridges, but they had this great big pantry outside, covered with gauze nettin, to keep the meat cool. And they always left this open for the Travellers to help theirselves. Noo, the Travellers wasnae greedy. They would open the pantry and they would take a wee bit, and they would go to the shed and take some of these potatoes at the shed, but they wouldnae rob him. They would take a wee bit, you know? They loved these old brothers very much, and no Traveller would ever do one thing o harm to these two old brothers. No way! Noo, the old men knew this. As long as they kept in with the Travellers, they [the Travellers] would never steal from them. They would take a wee bit o meat from the pantry, they would take some potatoes, and they would be gone the next day, see? And they [the brothers] would give them some tea. Two auld brothers they were.

So anyhow, the story goes that Johnny's father an mother were camped there,[4] and so was Maggie. Maggie stayed with Johnny 'oght she died,[5] poor soul. She had a big family, but she died when she was in her late forties, I think, and Johnny was left a widower. So the two families that night were camped beside each other. And then—Johnny would be aboot eighteen, Maggie maybe aboot sixteen or seventeen—and then they were gone! Somebody said, "Maggie and Johnny's run awa!" See, they run away. Well, that was a natural thing that did happen in these days.

So the auld Traveller men—and they'd probably had a bottle of whisky between them that night, you see—sat aroond the fire, and they made this song up, about Johnny and Maggie, see? And this was it. [*Sings:*][6]

---

4. "Johnny's father and mother": the reference is to Duncan's relative Johnny Townsley and his parents, as Duncan later specifies.
5. "'Oght she died": that is, "until she died."
6. See the Commentary for discussion of the use of cant in this song.

> Oh my wee Maggie's a-humphin a-proochin,
> a bun wood sprachin,* my wee Maggie.

1   Oh Johnnie wi his burl and Maggie wi her can,
    up the glen tae the aul blin man,
    up the glen to the aul blin man,
    fir tae get their tea in the mornin.

2   Johnnie says tae Maggie, "Oh come intae the shed.
    I will shake the strae and you can make the bed,
    for this is the place where yer mither she was wed,
    and we'll bing doon the glen in the mornin."

See, her father and mother *before* her run away and spent their honeymoon in the shed. "So," he says, "this is the place where your mother, she was wed." [*Resumes singing:*]

> "Oh this is the place where yer mother she was wed,
> And we'll gang doon the glen in the mornin."

3   Oh Johnnie says tae Maggie, "There haben in the chaet,
    the kinchens they are hungry an they cannae wait.
    Thee can bing a haben and we'll bing doon the chaet,
    an we'll bing tae wir naiskel in the mornin."
      Oh my wee Maggie's a-humphin a-proochin,
      a bun wood sprachin, my wee Maggie.

4   So Johnnie wi his burl an Maggie wi the can,
    doon the glen fae the aul blin man,
    doon the glen tae the aul blin man,
    an back tae yer mother in the mornin.

This is what they made up roond the fireside. [*Laughs.*] It was great fun!

JN: That's good! [Laughs.] Does anyone sing that besides you, Duncan?

No, not anybody, no. My father used tae sing it all the time. All these people are all dead now. The people who wrote the song, the people the song was about—all dead. They're all dead an gone.

JN: Could that song be sung in front of the people it was about?

My Wee Maggie

refrain and verse 1

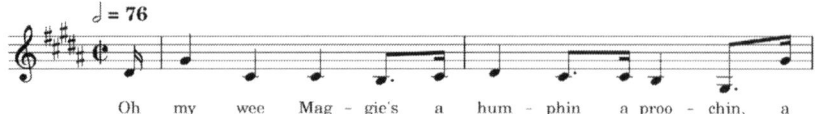

Oh   my   wee   Mag - gie's   a   hum - phin   a proo - chin,   a

bun   wood   spra - chin,   my   wee   Maggie.

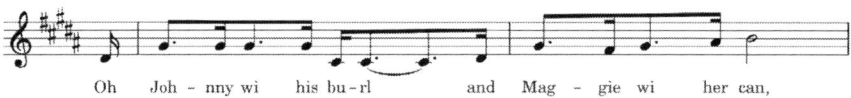

Oh   Joh - nny wi   his bu - rl   and   Mag - gie wi   her can,

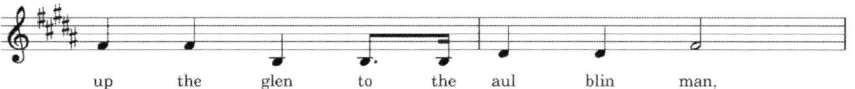

up   the   glen   to   the   aul   blin   man,

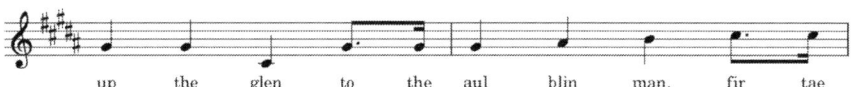

up   the   glen   to   the   aul   blin   man,   fir   tae

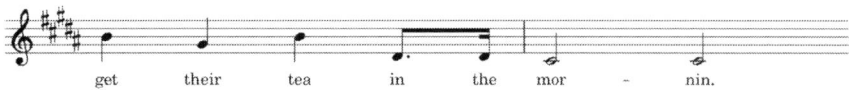

get   their   tea   in   the   mor - nin.

Oh, yes. They wouldnae take nae insult or anything. There's nae nicknames made in it,[7] and no nothing, ye see what I mean? And very rarely young people today would know who Johnnie and Maggie was except people my age, see what I mean?

JN: Right, right.

---

7. "There's nae nicknames in it": on nicknames and their potential use as insults, see §7.6, with Commentary.

If you sing it to a group of young Travellers, they would say, "Och, that's just a fun song." I mean, they wouldnae understand who Johnnie and Maggie was. But Johnny was my mother's cousin, and Maggie was my mother's cousin. Townsleys.

(87DW12 @ 1:20:50.)

§5.4. ON RUNAWAY MARRIAGES, "MY WEE MAGGIE," AND DUNCAN'S OWN MARRIAGE

It really did work, Jack. It really did work! This was what it was all about. An it worked with both families. But—[*Sings a few words of "My Wee Maggie," concluding with some laughter.*][8] It was my mother's cousin, "Monkey John." He was ugly, ye see, but he stayed wi her all his life.

JN: How did you learn the song itself?

The song was made while they were gone. It was kept within the family circle, you see. [*Sings a bit more of the song:*]

> So there's haben in the cheerie, I'll bing ye tae the chaet,
> you can eat the haben an we can fick the chaet.
> Doon tae my naiskell, my naiskell you will meet,
> then we'll bing doon the cheerie in the morgen.
>   My wee Maggie's a-humphin a-proochin,
>   a bun wood sprachin, my wee Maggie.

So instead o the mother an father givin presents tae the runaways as a marriage, the runaways, who spent the night away on the farm, had to bring back somethin in the morning to celebrate their weddin. They had to bring back milk an potatoes, and maybe some meat an some foodstuffs. They didnae get any presents. That was always the way. I mean, if *your* daughter or son was gettin married, you'd give them presents, but in runaway families it was always the other way around. The runaways would bring back the presents, and bring back maybe some tobacca for father, and some potatoes and some meat for mother that they'd collected while they were away on their honeymoon. That one night away, and then they were accepted as good people! [*Laughs.*] It's true!

---

8. What Duncan sings here is the chorus and the first two stanzas of the song as given in §5.3, with the exception that in the last line of stanza 2, he sings, "bing doon the chourie" instead of "bing doon the glen."

It was really good, you know. It was crazy, but it was really good, ye know? It's a different culture, and it's wonderful if you learn these things, ye know? When you think today that so much money is—I mean, your daughter or your son gettin married, an you spend a fortune on the church weddin and all these things. Think about these poor people—the young couple run away happy an together, an said, "I hope your daddy didnae go send your brothers after me," and, "We'll have fun tonight, an we'll sleep together, and we'll try an get some food, and we'll bring it back tomornin an we'll be accepted." And then there was a family reunion and celebration, and they cuiked the things that the young couple brung back, an there was a get-together, an they were wed for life! And that was a wonderful thing, ye know what I mean?

JN: Uh-huh.

It's hard to believe, but it was true. [*Laughing.*] My mother done it, you know? Ah never done it; I didnae do it. Things were gettin more modern in my time, ye know?

My wife an I, we got married in Glasgow, in the Register's office. We were comin along in the mornin, an we had about—she had two dozen flowers an Ah had two dozen flowers. Wood flowers we made wirself.[9] "Luik," I said, "We'll get married at 11 o'clock. Seven an six tae get married.[10] We'll have to get the seven an six first. Now you take that side o the street an I'll take this side o the street."

All: [Laughter and exclamations of surprise.]

She ended up with fifteen shillings, and I had fifteen shillings. She sold her flowers quicker than me. She was a beautiful lassie, she was only sixteen, an she was expectin at the time. So we sold the flowers. She sold hers, I sold mine. We walked to the Register's an got married, an then the two of us went an had a cup o tea an we walked home; got some messages and walked home. And that was the weddin. [*Laughs.*]

JN: Did you go back to your own homes?

Back to her mother. We stayed wi her mother. Ah stayed with her mother for two years and travelled all over Glasgowside and Perthshire as a young man. Stayed with her mother, cause her mother was my auntie. She [Duncan's wife

---

9. "Wood flowers we made wirself": Travellers commonly used to pick up a bit of change or food by hawking "flowers" that they had whittled out of a piece of wood, normally an elderberry stalk; see §3.9 and Figure 5.2.

10. "Seven an six": seven shillings and sixpence, the cost of a marriage license in those days.

Figure 5.2 Williamson demonstrating how to make wooden flowers at a fair held at Traquair House, the Borders, 1988. Photo by the author.

Jeannie] was my cousin, an her brothers, two of them, were my pals. My young brother married the younger sister, years later. Jimmy, he married my wife's sister Leah. So he came along an stayed wi *me*, after he married her sister. He fell in love with the younger sister. So we all stayed together in one family collection, ye know?[11] We camped all together; we were horsiemen, we spent wir life with horses. We travelled through Argyll an through Perthshire, Angus, Ayrshire, thinnin turnips, doin all the seasonal work together. It was a far-flung communion. We stuck together all these lifes, till my wife died.

(88DW09 @ 1:01:45.)

§5.5. A PONY, A BOY, AND A GOOSE

♪♫

I had a beautiful pony one time. An I went down tae the west coast of Argyll, an I met this lady who was a laird's wife. An because I left the pony standing in the street by himself an I walked to the shop for cigarettes, when she come out, she had a great car, and there was my horse standing in the middle of the street by itself; needed no one to look after it.

---

11. Omitted here is a passage where Duncan gives a more complete account of his mutually supportive relations with his in-laws during these years.

And when Ah come out, she said to me, "That's a beautiful, quiet pony you have there."

I said, "It is, my dear."

[She] said, "Why is it so kind and quiet?"

"Well," I says, "it's because of the children. The children treat it as it was their pet." And Ah said, "They love it, and that's why it's so quiet."

"Well," she said, "luik, I have two little boys at home and I have three ponies. But they're terrified of the ponies. They won't go near them."

I said, "Do you want your children to have a pony, or do the children want a pony?"

"Well," she said, "I was born and raised with ponies, and I want my sons to look after their ponies too, as well as me."

"Well," I said, "I'll tell you what we'll do. I'll fetch my pony up, and," I said, "if your son is interested in my pony, and likes it because it's quiet and kind, I'll sell it to ye on one condition: if the son likes the pony."

Now this is a true story, Jack. So I hadn't far to go, about five miles. So the next day, I druv up with the pony an cart and I came to the big house, and there was the lady wi her two little boys. I took the harness off the pony and I laid it round the front door of the house, an took the little boy and I put it on the horse's back. An the little boy was terrified! He was screamin wi fright. So I told the lady, "Luik," I said, "I wouldn't give you my pony," I says, "suppose you gave me all the money in the world for it."

She says, "Why?"

I says, "That little child is terrified of that pony."

And then they ran away across from the door of the house in tears. And what came hoppin around the end but a big goose! You know a goose? And he ran round and he put his arms around the goose, and he sat there cryin. And Ah turned around and I told her, "Luik," I says, "don't buy your son a pony. Let him play with his goose as long as he wants to."

And she thanked me very much for this. I says, "Luik, don't give him a pony, because you're givin him something that he didn't really want."

That little boy loved that goose more than his mother had set out for him.

(86DW14 @ 32:42.)

§5.6. THE PHEASANT AND THE GAMEKEEPER

♪♫

My father would kill us if we broke a bird's egg. You know, he would kill us. And, eh, we would take gulls' eggs tae eat. You know, seagulls' eggs along the shoreside, or wild ducks' eggs, or pheasants' eggs. If they were fresh we would take them to eat, but only on one condition, that we needed tae eat them. "Well," Father would say, "the bird will go off and lay again." But if they were—if she'd sat on them for a couple o days and they were kind of touched, he would say, "Leave them, let them sit, don't touch them."

JN: What do you think about shooting or hunting for pleasure?

Well, I don't believe in shootin or huntin for pleasure. We would never do this. This is a thing that should never happen. People should only kill if it was to eat. That's all. We'll only do it, we kill for eat. We'll no shoot or hunt for pleasure, no way in this world. We only kill tae eat, you know, a fish, or a rabbit, or a pheasant.

Ah had a wonderful experience one time. Ah was down here east o Fife, just above St. Andrews, and Ah had ma pony an ma family and children, an we came to the side o this wood. An I put up my tent for the nighttime. And then along came the gamekeeper the next morning.

Now, during the night, right beside oor fire, where I kindled the fire, was a pheasant's nest. And she was sittin deep on the nest. Now, Ah moved the fire away from the bird, because you can pet her when she sets. You know, she—you can touch it. When she's deep sittin, she won't move, a pheasant. So, I was tellin ye, the next morning, along comes the gamekeeper and the police. And he comes in and he says, "How long have you been stayin here?"

Ah said, "Well, I'm just stayin here for a few days."

"Well," he said, "the gamekeeper has been complainin to me."

I said, "What was he complainin about?"

It was a sergeant from St. Andrews. He said, "You know, there're a lot of birds nestin along here this time of year. A lot of pheasants is nesting." And he said, "There're probably children," he said, "will probably destroy some of the birds' eggs."

Ah said, "Do you think so, sergeant?" And the game, he said,[12] "Of course," he says, "you know what children are."

"Well," I says, "come here. Come here beside my fire and look there beside ye." Beside where I was sittin havin a cup of tea, there beside the fireplace was a pheasant, deep sittin in its nest. And there was my children out playin in the roadside. Ah said, "Luik, Ah've been here nearly two days, and that pheasant has been settin there these two days." And I said, "My children knows it's there, and they're forbidden to ever even put their finger near it."

And the sergeant said, "Do you think I could touch it? Because I've haird o this, that you can touch a pheasant while it's deep settin."

Ah said, "Go ahead, sergeant, touch it."

---

12. "And the game, he said": Duncan refers to the gamekeeper as "the game."

So the sergeant walked down an he put his hand across its back, an the pheasant never moved. An he said to the gamekeeper, he says, "Is this the people you were tellin me about were goin tae destroy your pheasants?"

And the game, he said, "Well," he said, "I think I better shift it."

And the sergeant said, "No, you won't." He said, "Leave it. Let it stay." He said, "I don't think these people interfere with it."

Neither we did! We packed up the next day an walked away an left the pheasant to its own place, ye know? An this made the sergeant—he was very happy about this, you know, the sergeant from St. Andrews.

So it jist goes to show you the Traveller children would never touch a pheasant, nothin like that, no. But if that had been a fresh hen who had just laid eggs, she would fly away. And the children said,[13] "Daddy, here's some eggs." We would break one, if it was fresh, we would use them. But if they weren't fresh we'd say, "Well, just leave that alone, she'll come back."

That's the way it's always been among the travelling folk. Always been the same way. So the children would have been taught from childhood tae respect other things, ye know. So they got their education, maybe not from teachin in schools, but they got it just the same.

(86DW14 @ 55:08.)

§5.7. ON TRAVELLER CHILDREN WHO WERE LIFTED BY THE AUTHORITIES

JN: Duncan, I'm interested in the Traveller children who were taken away from their parents and sent into the industrial schools. Did that happen to any of your own relations, or to people you knew?

I had two cousins of mine—my son-in-law's mother was one o them—but when they came fourteen, they had tae let them go.[14] They cuidnae keep em any longer. They just naturally come back. But when they come back, they were—they were brainwashed. They didnae know what tae do. They could do nothing for theirselves. Now these children had to be reared up with their mother and father.[15] They would know how to work, they could probly make baskets, they could know how to hawk, they would do everything. But here was a young girl, fourteen years of age, comin from a school which she'd been in

---

13. "The children said": that is, the children would have said.

14. "They had tae let them go": that is, the authorities had to release the children after they turned fourteen. The children were then free to return to their families, if they knew where to find them.

15. "Had to be reared up with": that is, "needed to have been reared up with."

as a child. She knew nothing. She was jist one from the other side o the street, that was all. Far better she'd have been left.[16]

Big Willie MacPhee had two sisters was tuik as children. One o them married a policeman and disappeared; never came back tae the travellin way of life at all. An the government finally realized they were doin more harm than good tae the child itself. They were deprivin it from its parents. They were deprivin it of meetin an playin with other children and learnin the things that Travellers should learn. And what was the child goin to do to go intae service? Because nobody wantit a tinker girl tae work as a maid, even so if she was brought up in a Home.[17] See what Ah mean? She could never be trustit: "Oh, she's just one o the travelling people," even so supposin she's brought up in a Home, ye know? Nobody wantit them in their home. She came from a Home School, she came from a poor family an nobody wantit her. What was the poor child goin to do? The same thing with the men, with the boys. So then they realized finally that they were better tae leave them alone, schoolin or no schoolin. Let them get their own schoolin from nature! That was the idea.

(86DW23 @ 11:45.)

§5.8. HOW TRAVELLER CHILDREN LEARN ABOUT SEX, BIRTH, AND DEATH

They [Traveller children] learn about sex and about birth and everything else through stories, after a certain age.

JN: How? How would that happen?

It's told to them through stories. It's quite simple. They tell them about the animals havin babies, ye know? Ah take my children with me tae see lambs gettin born, ye know what I mean? Ah take my children with me tae see calves gettin born. An I take them with me tae the cattle tae see the bull jumpin the cow, and they know what matin's all about. They know about a cat wi kittens, and Betsy's always worried about her dog havin pups, and she's lookin for a—she says, "Why doesn't my dog get a husbant?" She knows all about it, and she's only nine. But in a nice, gentle kind o way, ye know?

JN: You can do that on the farm, bringing them around to see the animals. But how about through stories?

---

16. "Far better she'd have been left": left to her own parents, that is.
17. "A Home": an orphanage to which children who had been taken away from their parents would be sent.

Figure 5.3 "This one's not for snaring." Duncan's daughter Betsy holding her pet rabbit, back of Kincraigie Farm Cottage, 1986. Photo by Leonard Yarensky.

It's the same, it's the same around the fireside. I mean, they don't just go forward an say, "Luik, this happened that way." They give them a little sideline, jist tae tell it tenderly around the fireside. And then they leave the rest tae the children's imagination, to the story.

HT: Did you have any animals with you when you travelled?

Yeah, I had a goose, dogs, an cats. We had plenty o animals around. And every day you saw baby pheasants, baby rabbits. And the dog had pups right in the campin site. Sometimes the dog had kittens in wir bed among the children.[18] I mean, our bitch came in and had puppies at wir feet in the bed. "Leave her alone! Don't touch her. Just pull the blankets back an let her lie there. Don't interfere." And she licked them an cleaned them. They saw the creation, you know? They knew where it come from. This was the idea. This was classed as children's education, ye know?

And I had a wonderful experience one time. I was out in a place outside o Crief, an we had a little bitch, she was a King Charles spaniel, ye know? And, eh, she had puppies, an they all died. Every single one [that] was born. The children waited an they watched, an they said, "When is she goin tae have babies now, Daddy?" I said, "Maybe tomorrow, maybe the next day." Every one

---

18. "The dog had kittens": Duncan probably means puppies. But maybe he is thinking of cats and their kittens, as well? Or of dogs and kittens sleeping together?

Figure 5.4 Williamson greeting a Highland cow in a field near the head of Loch Fyne, 1988. Photo by the author.

died, and the children was so sad. Ah took the little puppies and disposed o them, ye know? And they were terrible sad. But the little bitch went off and she was gone. And she came back, and the amazing thing was—I swear, Jack, on my mother's grave, this is true!—she brought three baby rabbits back with her.

HT: Oh!

Young baby rabbits, just newborn. And she carried them in and she put them beside herself and they suckled her as if they were puppies.

JN: Wonderful.

An the children loved them. And I said, "Luik, darlings, we can't take them with us. We'll wait till they're old enough." And we were there workin at the potatoes, ye know? And then when they were big enough tae run around, we set them free. And Ah think that was the most magic experience that any child could ever have, to see the puppies die, an see the mother goin out and bringin in—. So someday they might have a child of their own that dies, maybe they could never have another one, and it would be nice if they could go an take someone else's child and bring it up, ye know? See, this is education at a level 'at's beyond understanding, Jack, you understand?

JN: Uh-huh.

So they said, "Daddy, what did she do?" She lost her babies and she brought back a rabbit, which is no kin of her own. Right? So maybe my daughter, when she grows up, could maybe bring a wee black child up as her own an say, "Well, if my wee bitch done it, what's good enough for her is good enough for me." You understand what I mean? This is the idea among the travelling people. This is the main idea, tae teach children to do things on their own. And as you say, how could you learn about sex, and how could you learn about creation as children? I mean, we kept ponies. We kept stallions. And the stallion mounted a pony, and we just said, "Well, they're mating." "And when will they have their babies, Daddy?" "Oh, a few—." I mean, they never saw actual sex in the fact between parents, ye know, but we let them see animals do it as much as possible. I mean, in a kindly way. And then it probly dawned on them in their own idea that people does the same thing.

(86DW24 @ 43:08.)

§5.9. ON THE SPECIAL CARE GIVEN TO CHILDREN WITH DOWN SYNDROME

The Travellers reared up mongrel children, ye know.[19] And they loved these children especially, because they thought it was the work of God, that God had given them this. God said, "Look, if you cannae take care of this child, you're not capable of takin care of anythin else."

You know, they loved these children more dearly than anything in this world. I mean, you're not given a mongrel child just because that you are a parent. You're given this child tae show that you're capable of takin care of the child. The next one might be right as rain. But why? You are judged by what you can do. So don't feel sorry if you're born with a deprived child, ye know what I mean? This is no accident.

JN: What brings it about, then, the mongoloid child?

God gives it tae you to prove to the people that they are capable of takin care of this person. But there never was a travelling people who had a mongrel child who didnae love it and respect it more than any other child in the world. Because, they said, "God has given us this tae try us, tae justify that we are capable." And if we can take care of this one, who is not able to take care of hisself, then what good would we do for children who are perfect?" D'ye understand?

---

19. "Mongrel children": that is, mongoloid children; children with Down syndrome.

That's the way they looked at it. And even the people who are not friends to it, who have no relation to it, will love it more than the natural Traveller itself. Because they want to get a little affection from God and say, "Look, it could've been me that had it instead o you." And they love it an kiss it and love it as if God will say, "Look, if you could dae that, to love this one, then you have no need for one of your own."[20] D'ye understand?

Well, maybe that was wrong. But it worked! It worked wi the travelling folk. God said, "You shall go forward and you shall create in your likeness and you shall produce a specimen of your own body and take care o it in any form, what else is it gonnae be." And if he gives you something to test your superiority, then you should love it an respect it.

But the Travellers had a different idea, what they called a "taen-awa."* They believed that God had given them a good baby, but they had tae prove that they were capable of lookin after the baby, so he gave them something who was not the actual child, but a taen-awa. He taen-awa their ain one and give them a mongrel. See? They take away their own good child and left them this in his place, to show that they could take care of this mongrel child who was wrong in the head or something, you know what I mean? Then they will gift it with the prospects that they could have many children and be capable of lookin after them. Many, many more!

(84DW01 @ 1:02:28.)

§5.10. ON DEATH, AGING, AND REMEMBRANCE

JN: What about death? What about when one of the people were sick, or dying, or had died? Would the children be shut off from that at all?

Well, when someone died or someone was sick, the most important thing for a sick person is to get children round the bedside. I mean, they've got an incurable disease, an they know they're goin to die. And the children always come and visit.

You see, with us travelling people, Jack, no one is disembanded.[21] We don't send wir old people to homes in any way. It's impossible. We jist cannot do it. Old uncles and aunties stays with the family till they're ready for the grave. We just can't put wir old people away to a home and then forget about them. We just could not do it. It's one thing we cannae do. And when they get old,

---

20. "You have no need for one of your own": that is, "there is no need for you to be tested by having a child of your own who is born with a disability."

21. "Disembanded": what Duncan evidently means is that no one is cut off from the band, from the extended family.

we appreciate them more, and when they get old and they get sick, we still love them and take care of them.

And even supposin somebody's grandmother, or—I loved my Granny more than I loved anything in the earth. And she was a wonderful storyteller, ye know, and she got old. I walked with her. I went round the houses with her. She tuik me around the doors with her when she was young. And then I grew up. I loved her stories and I loved her from my heart, my mother's mother.

She said to me, "You know, someday I'm goin tae get old." And she says, "I'm goin away to another land and I'll be gone from you forevermore."

I says, "Granny, you cannae go and leave me!"

"Well," she says, "someday I'll have to leave you. But," she said, "I'm leavin myself with ye. I'm leavin ma stories and I'm leavin ma songs. An when you tell my stories an sing my songs, I'll be with you, not in body, but in spirit," ye know? And it's the same wi all the Travellers. I mean, Granny is still with me today. She's not gone. If I tell Granny's story, she's just luikin over my shoulder to see that I'm still there, ye know, cause I'm tellin the story the way she told it.

DC: But when she was actually dying, were you there?

No, we werenae allowed to go when she was actually dyin. But I was at her funeral, and I sat beside her when she was ill, ye know. But we werenae allowed to stay around when she was dyin. My Granny died when she was ninety-six, ye know? And she was a wonderful lady.

(86DW24 @ 48:35.)

§5.11. ON TRAVELLERS WHO WERE GIVEN THE CHILDREN OF SETTLED PEOPLE TO RAISE

HT: There are legends about Gypsies who would take children away. Do the settled people around here ever accuse the Travellers of—

No, Holly, no. That used tae be an old legend. The idea was that the travelling people loved their children so much—an the children o the Gypsies, of course—the way the travelling people saw it, a child is *their* child: every child is their child, even if they've never saw it before. And they hate tae see children hurt or anything happenin tae children. And this belief came to be known among the settled community, and they said, "Luik, these people loves children sae much, they'll take your babies away." This was the legend, ye know. But they never stole babies in any way.

HT: Was there ever a case that a settled woman had a child she didn't want, and she might, uh—

Yeah. I had a particular case that ma auntie—a auntie of mine, she's dead now, God rest her soul—was in a place outside of Glasgow, beside a big hospital, wi a campsite there called Hairmyres Hospital,[22] an we used tae camp there wi our ponies. An this woman stayed in a hut, an she had five children. And, eh, she came over an she said tae my auntie, she says, "Luik," she says, "would ye like tae have another—?" And my old auntie—all her family's grown up, in fact she reared up some o her grandchildren. She [the settled woman] says, "How about takin little Graeme?" A little boy, Graeme.

She tuik Graeme with her, an she brought Graeme up as her own. An she had him with her till he was fifteen, an he never saw his mother again. And he grew up among the travelling family, and then he married a travellin girl, and he's a good Traveller today. But he was *given*, not taken.

HD: Would there have been situations where a mother wasn't married, and she was going to have a baby—

It never went through any authority or any law, ye know? It was just talked between the mother and the Traveller. Ah know many cases where the local people hawkin the houses tuik children *given* tae them. The position was, "Ye must not report it to law, you must not tell on me. You're goin tae give me your child, you don't want it an I'll take it, an I'll take good care of it, nothing will happen tae it." An that was it! "If he wants tae come back an see ye when he grows up, good enough." But [that's] the slightest possibility. "You have no more responsibility once you gien it to me." An Ah knew many situations like this.

My other little aunt in Aberfeldy—she's dead now wi all her nieces and nephews—tuik a luttle child given tae her by a young woman. And grandfather just loved him more than his own family, and he taught him tae play the bagpipes. He became a great piper today. He lived wi the travelling folk and he respected em.

They never tuik them, though. I mean, they never *stole* them. They [the children] were given to them.

(86DW41 @ 23:00.)

---

22. "Hairmyres Hospital": the reference is to a campsite close by University Hospital Hairmyres, a district general hospital in East Kilbride, south of Glasgow.

§5.12. STORY, "THE BOY AND THE HORN SPOON"

♪♫

I'll tell you a story that happened a long time ago to a travelling family in the west coast. You've never heard this story.[23]

This travelling family had a lot of family, a lot o little children. They had one every year. There's a great house down near Skipness in Argyll where you take the ferry to the Isle of Arran. And this shippin magnate an his wife, called Wolf, had—in fact, the shippin business is still in the same family yet. And, eh, this old woman used tae come to the lady's doorway every day hawkin her baskets and scrubbers. An she had all these little children, ye know? An Mrs. Wolf had never had a child in her life. And lo and behold, she respected the old woman, she gave her clothes, she gave her food and some money, ye know?

And one day the old woman came an she had another baby. In fact she had one on her back, a year old, and one jist about three days old, on her bosom.

Then she said, "Oh, Mrs. Williamson, you have another baby again."

She says, "Yes."

She says, "Why are you so lucky? Husband and I been tryin for years to have children and we can't have any. And you simply have all the luck." She said, "Would you come in a moment?"

So she take her in and she gave her a glass o wine, an she sat up, and then the husband came in. An she says, "Look, husband and I has made up wir mind. Would you give us one of your children, especially a young one? And we'll take care of it."

These people were rich! They owned the estate! And they owned the shipping business in Greenock.[24] She said, "Would you give us this little child?" This was about 1804 I'm talkin about. "Would you give us this little child?" Well it was only three months old—three days, I'm sorry, three days auld.

So she said, "I'll have to see my husband."

"Of course," she said, "it'll be reared up and it'll want for nothing. And, eh, we'll give you some money."

"Well," she said, "I'll have to talk it over with my husband."

So they camped along the shore from the estate in Skipness, and, eh, they talked it over, and, "Well," says the husband, "look, you got bangs o Williamsons of your ain,"[25] he says. "If the woman wants the wee baby, give it tae her, because I'm sure you have plenty." And they had about nine.

---

23. Another recording of Williamson telling this story is transcribed in Braid, *Scottish Traveller Tales*, 34–37. That version differs from the present one in many details.

24. "Greenock": the town at the south bank of the River Clyde that was formerly a major center for the shipbuilding industry and for maritime trade linking Scotland with North America and the world.

25. "Bangs o Williamsons": lots of Williamsons. See the *SND*, s.v. "bang," n.²: "a crowd."

Figure 5.5 A collection of horn spoons of the kind once commonly made by Travellers. Photo © Arran Heritage Museum, Isle of Arran, Scotland.

So that night both o them walked along. And they gave Mrs. Wolf the baby. An they were highly delighted, and they gave them some money and said, "Look, we'll rear him up as wir own son; now ye can forget about it. Everything we own will be left to him in days to come." So that went well.

And the travelling man's wife said, "We won't bother you anymore. We'll never mention it. You'll always {put him atall?} in any way."

So days gaen by an the little boy grew up. And Mr. Wolf loved the little boy as his own son, and so did the lady, and they brought him up.

Now there's a large estate—there was two farms on the estate; Ah worked on the farm, the same estate. An when the little boy became aboot five year old, his father bought him a silver Labrador dog for company. And they used tae like walkin around the estate at nighttime. He has the little boy by the hand, and the dog grew up, and the boy loved the little dog.

So one evening they went walkin, on a beautiful summer's evening, and, eh, the dog run out tae play in the moor. And it brought back an old cow horn in its mouth. And the gentleman said to the dog, "What have you got there, boy?" And the dog stood an it dropped the horn. An the little boy walked over and he picked the horn up. "Oh," he says, "Daddy! Luik, Daddy! Luik what Dog has brought back." He said, "A cow's horn!" He says, "Wouldn't this make a beautiful spoon?"

An the gentleman just stood and smiled. And he says, "Of course, it's in your blood." But he says: "In your blood it will remain."

Even as a child, he had an idea that the horn would make a horn spoon, ye know? He never knew the horn spoon; it was in his blood. He says, "Daddy, wouldn't it make a beautiful horn spoon?"

And that man grew up; he inherited his father's business, his father's estate, and he was a Traveller. And the travelling people forgot about him altogether. But there was a woman, about five or six year later; the lady told the story to a travelling woman. And that's how Ah come to know it. And that was a relation of my own.

LW: And that was one of the traditional crafts of the travelling people.

The traditional craft was makin horn spoons. They collectit all the horn spoons,[26] you see? The little boy, he was three days old, but it was in his blood, ye see? He says, "Daddy, wouldn't that make a beautiful horn spoon?"

LW: You can't get away from it, in other words.

You can't get away from it, ye see what I mean? And that's the way it was then.

(86DW41 @ 30:11.)

---

26. "They collectit all the horn spoons": that is, they collected cow horns to make horn spoons from them.

Chapter 6

FOOD AND HEALTH, DRINK AND CONVIVIALITY

§6.1. ON CLEANLINESS AND FOOD PREPARATION

JN: I'm curious about food, you know, when you were young? And how you cooked, and who did the cooking, and so on.

Mother done all the cooking. Father helped sometimes. But ye see, food—when I was young as a Traveller child, not anymore today—today they do all their cookin on electric stoves an gas cookers an all these things. The Traveller folk are very particular about their cookin habits. They are very particular about their cookin habits. I mean, Av've been in houses of nontravelling folk in some o the towns and some o the villages in Scotland, like the big cities, that Travellers would barely have a cup o tea in some o these places.

JN: Why is that?

The Travellers is very clean about what they do. I mean, I saw people—nontravelling people, in Perth, in Hunter's Crescent,[1] when I looked in there for a visit—I saw women puttin their underclothes in the sink, and washin their dishes in the same sink, an all these kinds o thing. I mean, the travelling folk wouldnae do that. No, no, no, no, no, no, no, no, no! That was taboo; that was taboo for the Travellers. And you got a name about yourself. People wouldn't even get a cup of tea off you.

And they were very particular about their eatin habits. They only bought food for one day. If they had money, they bought it for one day. Nothing was kept. The only thing that was kept was tea an sugar, so they could make a cup o

---

1. By the 1970s and 1980s, Hunter Crescent in Perth, whose construction dates back to the 1930s, had become one of the most notorious housing developments in Scotland, known for its squalor.

tea anytime they wantit. That was the only thing that was kept. But everything was eaten as they got it.

JN: What about oatmeal? Would you have that on hand?

Yeah, we always had oatmeal. But as far as any other kind o meats or breads, or any kind o cheese or butter or jams, they only bought enough that they could use in one day.

JN: Even when they were settled, in the wintertime?

Even when they were settled.

JN: Why is that, Duncan?

As far as the travellin people were concerned, every day took care of itself. They only lived an ate for one day at a time. Nothing was kept for the next day; nothing at all. Nothing was bought for the next day.

JN: Does that mean your mother had to get the day's food—

Every day, every day. Every day she went out and she brought it back with her. She bought something; she traded for something, ye know. Maybe she traded a basket or a tin juig or a ladle or a strainer or something for potatoes an fish an herrin and oatmeal flour. She was the provider, the food provider, when we were young. But nowadays, these days are all gone. Young women now go tae the supermarket with their car and they buy as much as does em for a week.

JN: And they'll just keep it on hand just like the settled—?

Keep it on hand just like the locals, like the non-Travellers.

JN: Well, did she bring it home, after she went to the houses or the store? And what would she do then to get your food for you?

The first thing, she'd come back, and we were hungry and . . .²—make a scone or make a bannock by the fire, and then make some tea for us. See, we got our first meal. And then when we went off tae play, she put on the pot an made a pot o soup. A pot o herrin an tatties for us, ye know? Tatties an herrin was a great meal, all in one pot. You put the tatties in the pot, you scraped em and

---

2. There is a short break in the recording here as the tape reverses direction.

washed em clean, and then put a dozen herrin in the top an boiled the herrin an tatties together. The herrin didnae break up wi the tatties, they just cuiked tae the top o the tatties. You waited till the tatties was near boiled, then you put the herrin in, then you brought them tae boil. We really loved the tatties and herring. It's a great meal. Well, someday she'd make tatties an herring; somedays she'd make soup. We used a lot o soup at one time. She made soup most every day o the week, when she could afford tae make it. An she made a lot o porridge.

JN: What kind of soups?

Vegetables; other things. Potatoes an leeks an vegetables. We got plenty o meat from the butcher's at that time because it was cheap tae buy; you could afford it. The butchers didnae have any fridges, in these days, and they cuidnae keep it long, ye know? And the same with the grocer's store. They got in these big hams, ye know? She used tae get these big ham ends. They couldae keep them, ye see, and they just gave them all at the weekend. These shops only bought enough for tae keep them for a week. Same with the butchers.

JN: So would she just buy it real cheap, or would they give it to her?

They would give it tae her because it was no use. Mother had good friends. They would give it tae her.

JN: So she had to be friends with them, she had to get along well with them?

Yeah. And if any other Travellers came intae the district and they went hawkin the doors, often they [the villagers] would say: "Och no, we don't want none from you, we'll get what we need frae Betsy." You know, Betsy was well known from Inveraray to Lochgilphead. And on a Monday she would maybe walk to Inveraray, and on a Tuesday she'd maybe walk tae Minard, and on a Wednesday she'd maybe go round the village of Furnace. Maybe on a Thursday she'd go back to Inveraray again. She'd always take some o the boys with her, carryin the bundles on their backs an carryin the hawkin material. Some of the girls would go with her for company, ye know? Probly she had a baby in her oxters, ye know?

JN: But she'd never go on her own?

Never on her own, no, unless she was goin tae the village where we stayed. It was a small village. It was less than a quarter mile tae the school from where we stayed in the woodland, the forest—the Duke of Argyll's estate. Big woodland, like what you've got here.[3] All oak trees.

(87DW11 @ 42:34.)

§6.2. LIVING ON SHELLFISH IN THE SUMMERS

We loved this, when we could go off in the spring as children, cause we were *free* then. We could do what we liked; no need tae go to any more school for the day. Go on the beach an collect shellfish an cuik shellfish to our hearts' content.

These times were very bad for us because we were very poor, an we were always hungry. That was the only thing. We cuid never get enough food. We were always healthy an strong enough, but we didnae have enough food tae eat, being sae many of us, ye see? We were all right when my father got a job, when he went tae work an got some money, but there were some hard days in between, when we didnae have enough tae eat. But we would always have time tae eat by the shoreside. Ah cuid live off the shore. Ah cuid put ye on an island and could live on the shore an never need nothing else. I wouldnae even need salt; I cuid make my own salt.

JN: What would you live on?

Shellfish. Every kind o shellfish. All I would need was some matches, just tae kindle a fire. I mean you can cuik shellfish, ye can bake shellfish, ye can smoke them, ye can do anything you want wi shellfish. Ye can make your own salt.

HH: How did you make the salt?

You boil salt water an you boil it dry. An you pull it out again an you boil it dry. Till lo an behold, when you boil it for about five or six times, you're left with about that much o salt [*gestures*] in the bottom o the pan, an you just scrape it off an you can use it on your shellfish. Some people think that shellfish, because they live in the salt sea—but they still need salt on them. If you want to cuik them right, you need to put salt on shellfish.

I mean, you've got mussels, you've got cockles, you've got crabs, you've got garrochans, you've got clabbydoos, you've got limpets, an you've got all these wonderful foods. You need nothing else. An they're a source o protein, ye can live all your life off it. An there's many ways you can cuik them. You can roast them on the fire, ye can boil them, ye can smoke them, ye can eat cockles as

---

3. "What you've got here": this recording was made at a house outside Ithaca, New York, where the surrounding hillsides were thickly wooded.

they are from the shoreside. Eat them raw, just like oysters. An ye get oysters, ye get clams, an ye have crabs; I mean, this is real good food!

GP: *Are there greens and wild vegetables you can eat?*

Yeah. You can pick them. We had a lot o herbs that we could eat. An you've got dulse, what ye call sea lettuce. Dulse. It's beautiful tae eat. It's a kind o sea lettuce. It just grows like a lettuce, but the leaves are red, an ye pull them. They grow under the sea. You've got to wait for the tide tae go out, though. And they grow on the rocks. Great things to eat. The Irish is very fond o it, an so is the Japanese. They put it in the soup an they savor soup with it.

Oh yeah, ye can live off the shore, there's nae problem. You never need tae be hungry if you're close tae the sea; it's when you're *inland* that there's a problem. So when I left home, just I travelled on. If I was ever hungry, I just stopped by the shoreside an kindled a fire and went an cuiked myself a meal o shellfish, till I got a job an bought some food.

JN: *Did you keep along the shore?*

Yeah, you can follow the coastline all the way. Follow the shoreside.

JN: *Were there roads?*

Sometimes roads an sometimes not. When the road tuik too lang a bend, ye just kept on the shoreside till ye hit the road again. I mean, Ah carried nothing with me, just a coat.

(86DW06 @ 36:12.)

§6.3. FOODS THAT MIGHT BE HAD FROM TIME TO TIME

JN: *I want to go back to what we were talking about before, Duncan. You say your father would help out, but your mother would do the cooking?*

She done all the cookin, yeah. He would help; he was a good cook, too. My father was a cook in the Black Watch; he cooked in the army.

JN: *But he wouldn't cook at home, normally?*

He would make tea, aye. He would make tea. He would maybe cut things for her and help oot when she was busy. But he could do anything. He was as good a cook as she was, but she done the most o the bakin. She'd make pancakes an scones an bannocks an that, ye know?

JN: What other foods would you eat? What were your favorite foods at home?

The favorite food we used tae get—it wasn't very palatable to some people, because people would think it was rotten, but we loved it. We used tae get a lot o what you call "braxy." Braxy was cured mutton, saltit mutton. And when any sheep died in the hills, by some disease or by storm or something, they never buried it. They used tae skin it tae get the skin off, an then they'd put these dead animals in barrels. An they barreled them, with salt, for about six months. Then they took them out and they hung them out to dry. And they made this kind o hardtack with it, ye know? Mutton. And it was always salted. And we used to roast them in the fire; roast it.

JN: What would you do to get rid of the salt flavor?

Well, we used tae steep it in the river for about a couple o days if you were goin tae make soup with it. You had tae steep it in the river to get some o the salt off. You could eat it roastit over the fire, but it was over salty. You cuid cook it on an open flame. It was a dry hardtack, with legs an necks an sides an limbs, an—

JN: Well, that's probably what everybody used to eat lots of, a hundred, two hundred years ago.

They ate lots of it. Farmers ate it, Travellers ate it, the farmers lived on it. There was plenty o braxy. There are a few bits of braxy to be gotten yet, in the back Highlands o Argyllshire, ye know, if you get tae the right place.

And sometimes my mother would get a bit o venison, if they shot a deer or something—some of the farmers, when they had deer in the corn eatin the corn, they would shoot them. If they shot a big stag in the cornfields, it would be too much for them, cause there was no way of keepin it. They cuidnae save it, ye see? They just gave it away tae everybody. I remember if my mother was lucky enough tae be there with the farmer at the time they shot that deer, she would maybe get a couple of stone o venison,[4] ye see? Well, that would be cuiked right away.

And we ate a lot o salmon. Pots full o salmon. That's one thing we never wantit for, we had plenty o salmon.

(87DW11 @ 1:09:57.)

---

4. "A couple of stone of venison": that is, about twenty-five or thirty pounds.

§6.4. ON MOVING FROM PLACE TO PLACE,
TAKING ALONG VERY LITTLE

JN: So is this where your pony would have to start?*

This is where the ponies were shod, for this was the worst pull for the pony, up the hill.

JN: You'd have to do your own shoeing at this point, right? What kind of tools would you have for that?

You had a claw hammer for the nails, so they'd last on his feet, and a cutting knife for paring his hoofs, and some nails, and some spare shoes. That's all you needed for cold shoeing.

JN: You'd pick up some spare shoes from the blacksmith?

Whatever seemed to fit best. But you had to heat it, maybe add a luttle—take out weight a luttle, to suit your horse's foot, you know? We would do it wirselves. We all had an extra set o shoes, so if we lost one, we'd nail one back on, ye know? And some of the travelling people got really good at it. Big Willy MacPhee, he was one of the best blacksmiths among all o the Travellers. That's why they still call him a blacksmith today, ye know? He did a lot of shoein for other Travellers.

JN: So, what would you be carrying, maybe, coming out of—

You carried your sticks for your tent, your children's clothes an clothes for yourself and your wife, your bedclothes, your cookin utensils, and some of your tools for shoeing your horses, an whatever possessions you had that you fancied, ye know what I mean? Extra cloth, extra boots for the kids, clothes for the kids. Canvas covers for the tent.

JN: Just enough for a bow tent?

Just enough for a bow tent, yeah. If it was a big family, you had a bigger bow tent; a small family, you had a smaller bow tent, ye know?

JN: You kept the boughs [the sticks for the tent]?

You carried the boughs with you. You cut longer ones for the bigger tent. You could take them with you [all the way back] to Cupar, or you could cut them along the way. You'd keep the whole canvas all year round.

∾

I'll show you up here where we used to stay on the beach.[5] Lovely for the kids. You looked forward to it. The boys could fish the loch and the girls could play at the shoreside, ye know.

JN: How much food would you have with you for a family?

Well, you always kept plenty o tea an sugar. That was the main thing. You never run out, you had a tin of tea and a tin o sugar, and you could stop an make a cup o tea anyplace when you felt like a tea. And maybe you'd saved a loaf of bread for the kids, or something, ye know what I mean? Then you just shopped gradually as you went, ye know? Just bought a few things and—you just bought enough for the day, and to eat for the next morning.

JN: So you would have that much with you if you could?

Yeah, if you could. If you could afford it, yeah.

JN: What about gathering food along the way? You couldn't get much up here, could you?

No, you cuidnae get nothing here on the way, you'd have tae go hungry before you came tae the next village. But maybe the wife would sell a couple o baskets and go tae the shop an buy some messages, an we'd go out to the end o the town and kindle a fire an boil the kettle, ye know? A handful of sticks tae make a fire, and the old snottum stuck in, the kettle hung on it, ye know?

People didnae pay so much attention tae the travelling folk. We were well known, but they didnae pay so much attention.

(88DW07 @ 35:59, @ 37:57, and @ 40:17.)

---

5. "The beach": our car is approaching a small freshwater loch situated just west of the pass at Rest and Be Thankful.

§6.5. TAKE ONLY WHAT YOU NEED

♪♫

I remember one time we went to a river. We travelled across this hill, Jack. It takes a shortcut from Minard. Nine mile over the hill will take you to a place called Kilmichael Glassary, where my father used tae work.* Now if you went round the road, it took you two days.

Father would pitch his tent in the middle o the hill for the night. And there was a river ran through there, and it wasnae watched by any fish watchers because fish watchers were farther down near Lochgilphead an farther up near—what's the place noo? near Ford. Now that's really the River Add, but it's the hill river. There're salmon come up there by the dozens, and it was a dry summer, an these pools were full o salmon.

So Father pitches his tent. Noo, he says, "Boys, get one for the pot, 'at's all, cause we only need one for the pot." And he said, "Anyone as needs two can catch it."[6]

So we went down. The burn was dry, and you waded in tae the waist with a huik and a stick, and there was no bother, there were dozens in the pool. But we got one, put it in the pot, made a nice supper of salmon.

And George an me, my brother—he was two year older than me—we went down to the burn, and we caught another two. And you tell the beatin we got! He near killed us. "Didnae Ah told you," he says, "killin these wee creatures, wee fish—they'd better be left alone!" He says, "We had wir supper; we tuik what God give us and we had wirs. Why didnae you leave them? Maybe some other poor soul wouldnae get that, an would maybe need it worse than us." And he says, "You'll carry them all your way on your back." He says, "I'll clean them, an I'll salt them. But," he says, "you'll carry them, both of youse, tae the next campin ground, on your back!"

Well, we carried those two fish all day on wir back. And he cuiked them that night when we were on to the next place. And he said, "Let that be a lesson to you. Take what you need tae eat, but leave the rest!"

(87DW04 @ 1:29:10.)

---

6. "Anyone as needs two can catch it": what is implied is, "If anyone else needs the other fish, it will still be there for them to catch."

§6.6. ON CULINARY TABOOS

JN: Do you know any other taboos, Duncan? Things that you just shouldn't do? You said something about mushrooms.

Oh, mushrooms, yes. 'At's one thing that Travellers won't eat is mushrooms. See, accordin to Travellers, mushrooms is devil's food. Ye see, devils used the mushrooms tae feed his imps in hell, accordin to Traveller legend. Nothing else will grow in hell; nothing else will grow in the dark. I mean, mushrooms mostly come out at night; nighttime is the time they grow, at nighttime in the dark. Well, even in the story, ye get "Jack and the Devil's Purse,"* that story about when Jack was off to hell, the devil gave him mushrooms to feed the imps while he was gone.

JN: Is that right? That's imps' food, eh?

That's imps' food, yeah. So that's why Travellers don't like imps' food. Not for fear of poison or nothing; it's nae a fear of poison.

JN: Do they gather them from the earth?

You can gather them wild, they're wild mushrooms. Horse mushrooms, they call them in Scotland. But no Traveller touches them. The local people does.

JN: I mean, do the devils or their imps get them from the earth, or do they just grow them underneath?

They grow them in hell. They're a fungus. See, they're neither fruit nor vegetable; they're a fungus. And that's what the Travellers believe—that's the taboos.

And it's the same with veal. They won't eat veal. The Travellers will go tae the jail before they'd eat a piece o veal. No, I've never met a Traveller who'd—the idea, it's like—see, a veal calf is a newborn calf. It never gets tae suck from its mother, never tastes its mother's milk. And it's just tuik away, then, an killed for food. And they don't believe that should happen. Every animal that's born should have a chance in life to grow up. They don't mind animals havin a while on earth, and growin up to be a young calf or something; it's had a while on earth, and it's had its mother's milk, and grew up.

JN: Will they eat lamb?

Aye, they'll eat lambs, but lambs never goes to veal. No, you see, lambs is allowed to have their mother's milk and grow up with their mother. And when they leave their mother they're fattened up, and then they go off to the butcher. That's good. That's all right. But no way: veal they won't eat. No way, veal or mushrooms. I don't know a Traveller who'd eat either veal or mushrooms.

JN: Just those two things?

These two things. They'll eat anything else, but no veal or mushrooms. Some of em won't eat shellfish; no, some of the Travellers will nae eat shellfish. I don't know why. It's not that there's any taboo attached tae shellfish. They probably dinnae even like it. Maybe they think it's no clean enough: the sewage has gone in the tides or something like that. But along the west coast, all Travellers eat shellfish. Some of them lived on it! But in the northeast, like the Whytes and some of the other people there, they'd laugh at you if you said they should eat the shellfish.

(87DW04 @ 1:21:25.)

§6.7. HOW TO MAKE TINKER'S TEA

JN: Duncan, if you were by the campfire and wanted to make a good pot of tea, how would you go about it?[7]

Well, same as I'm doin now. Put the kettle on tae boil on the fire till the water comes a-boil, and then measure a good handful of tea wi your hand, let it boil it for a couple of seconds or a minute. I put in about, eh, half an ounce to aboot three pints o water. Then the milk goes in the kettle—it's off the boil now—of course this is boiled over the fire, you know, on the snottum, hangin over an open flame round the campfire. And the milk goes in the kettle, an then the sugar goes in along with it. The sugar goes in forbyes, intae the kettle, about two tablespoonfuls o sugar goes in there. An give em a good stir. And this was done on the ground outside the front o the tent. An everybody gathered around and picked up a cup, and they tuik a cup in their hand an got it straight from the kettle. Straight from the kettle. [*Pours tea.*]

I hope you enjoy that cup o tea! 'At's the way we've done all the years. All the days o my life I never had it in any other way, till I met Linda, till Linda started makin it in a teapot.

(86DW18 @ 22:15.)

---

7. This part of this interview was recorded while Duncan was fixing a pot of tea to serve to our group at Kincraigie Farm Cottage, Fife.

§6.8. HUMOROUS TALE, "THE FIRST TEA IN SCOTLAND"*

♪♫

Ye know, there's a funny story: the first tea that ever come tae Scotland. This young chap, a Scottish chap, went to India, ye know? And that's when tea was only grown in India, long time ago. Of course, they had tea in China long before that, but this was from India. And he sent his mother back a big parcel o tea on a sailing boat, ye know? And he was lucky; he came home for a visit. And she said, "Son, I'm glad that you've come back." She never saw him for over a year. "Maybe," she said, "I should make you some of that tea."

"OK, Mother," he said, "I would love a cup of tea; I would love some tea."

So she goes and she puts on the pot, and she flings two handfuls o oatmeal in the pot and then two handfuls o tea, and she brings it a-boil, ye know? And she mixes it up wi a spoon, you see? And there's a mixture atween porridge an oatmeal an tea. She puts it on a plate. She says, "How'd you like your tea?"

He says [*laughs*], "Mother, I don't like it *that* way!"

She had no clue how to do it! So he showed her how to make tea. Porridge and tea; two handfuls o tea and two handfuls of oatmeal! She stirred it up with a spoon; she says, "And how is that, how do you like your tea?" [*Laughter all around. Linda serves us tea and coffee.*]

(86DW41 @ 37:45.)

§6.9. JOKE, "THE SMOKED KIPPER"

Ye know, there was two fish sittin on a fishmonger's window.[8] And one was a sea trout, and one was a kipper. And they were sittin in the windae, and they watched the people passin by the street. And they said tae each other—there was bills up all around the place about people smokin, ye know. And the sea trout says to the kipper, "What do you think," he said, "about smokin?"

"Well," he said, "there's nothing wrong with smokin," he said. "It cured me!"

All: [*Laughter all around.*]

(86DW12 @ 1:01:55.)

---

8. Duncan told this joke when lighting up a cigarette during an interview in the sitting room of Kincraigie Farm Cottage.

Figure 6.1 Williamson lighting up a fag, Kincraigie Farm Cottage, 1986. Photo by Leonard Yarensky.

§6.10. ON TREATMENTS FOR CUTS AND ABRASIONS

JN: Duncan, I didn't understand what you were saying just now about using cork for healing a horse. How would that happen?

Well, if a horse was caught in barbed wire or had rolled on a piece of glass, or it had wet harness—you know, sometimes we had tae yoke the horses wi the harnesses wet cause they were lyin outside all night. An then they got chaffed, an then they got sore backs or sore shoulders. So we used tae always collect the corks off the beach, off the nets, the fishermen's floats. Cork. And if we cuidnae find them, we got the small corks off the medicine bottles till we had a handful. Then we burned them black in the fire till they were like charcoal. And then we mixed them with—goose grease was the best, goose fat. Or went to the butcher and got a ham skin, an scraped the raw tallow off the ham skin and mixed it wi the burnt cork an salt, and put it in a tin and then mixed it up. And that was the greatest thing for any kind o cuts an bruises on animals.

For humans too. We used it on fingers an nails and all. And there were hawks in your fingers, ye know?[9] Hawks, we used tae have hawks in wir hands. And it was a great, great, great cure for everything.

(86DW18 @ 00:38.)

---

9. "Hawks in your fingers": cracks. See Robinson, s.v. "hack," sense 3: "a crack or chap in the skin caused by cold or frost." Hawks might be caused by long exposure of the hands in cold water, as might occur when a person was collecting whelks.

§6.11. OTHER HOME CURES

JN: What did you take with you when you set out from home?

Nothing. Just a coat on me. Just what I had on my back, that was all.

JN: Did you take anything at all?

Not one single thing. Just a coat and a pocketknife an some matches. That was all ye needed, nothing else.

JN: What about a knapsack or bag?

No bag, no knapsack, nothing. When I came sixteen an then travelled through the north o Scotland, I used tae carry a bag with a spare shirt in it. When I was thirteen till fifteen, I never carried one single thing. Slept under a tree, slept under a bush, an just felt—I was really free! It was a feeling o freedom. You had nobody tell ye nothing. You heard birds whustling, an you cuid do anything ye wanted.

☙

JN: How would you keep your matches dry?

In a wee bottle, a little aspirin bottle. We always kept wir matches dry. There was one time, rain—I was soaked tae the skin! Been walkin till water was runnin out o me! I cuidnae hae been any wetter if I had walked out intae the sea. Ye get really heavy rain in Argyll. Everything was wet! Completely soaked. Ye never felt sorry for yirsel because ye knew you'd be gettin dry sometime, ye know? Then you'd kindle a big fire by the shoreside with driftwood an just stand by it, wi all this steam risin up, you know? Probably wasnae guid for you, but Ah was enjoyin it.

JN: Did you get sick?

No, I never got sick. I only was sick oncet in ma life, when I was aboot twenty-six. Ah tuik, eh, pneumonia. An I didn't go tae the doctor, an when the doctor did come and tuik me tae the hospital, I was [already] recoverin from pneumonia. I was gettin better on my own.

MJ: When you were still at home with your parents, was the doctor called on?

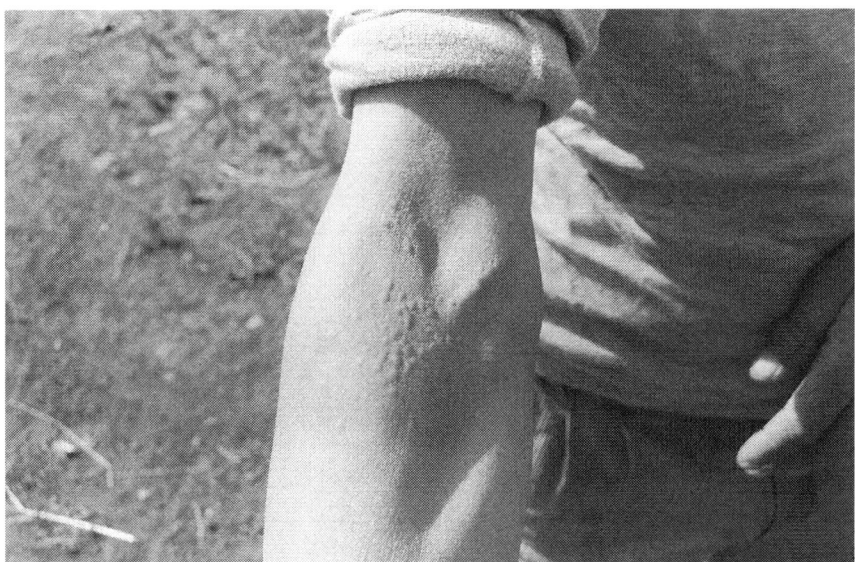

Figure 6.2 Williamson's cure for arthritis. Nettle welts bring an infusion of blood to the elbow, relieving the pain. Kincraigie Farm Cottage, 1986. Photo by Leonard Yarensky.

No. Not very often. I remember ma sister fallin an cuttin her foot. A large cut in her foot, terrible. An my father just tuik up an he got a needle an a piece o thread an he stitched it himsel. He just put the stitches in himsel with a piece o thread. An my mother had all her own cures. Cures of every description.

JN: Did you use anything like antiseptic?

No, nothin like that. We used salt. Salt for every purpose, every poisonous thing, it was just salt. She used salt for making salt poultices. An tobacca, that was another great thing. Tobacca leaf on poisonous cuts. A leaf o tobacca was the greatest thing for cures, for poultices an for sore fingers an things like that. An then foxgloves. You know foxgloves? We call them "monkey thumbles." You put them on a sore finger an tied them up with a thread, an ye kept them on till they rotted away. Till it melted, till it completely disintegrated on your finger. An it cleaned everything away frae it. Cleaned it completely. That's where the word "thumble" came from; puttin them on your fingers. Monkey thumbles. In bygone times they used them for whuttles in your finger,[10] an gettin a thorn in your finger, or maybe a bad nail or something.

---

10. "Whuttles": sores. Cf. the *DSL*, s.v. "whuttle," n², also spelled "whittle": "Reduced or altered forms of Eng. *whitlow*, an abscess round the finger-nail."

HT: Did you use comfrey?

They used a lot o herbs; they used their own kind o herbs. They picked a lot o the herbs; they used them for different things. Ma grandmother used tae make her own nettle brew for arthritis.* When Linda was away in the States, I tuik arthritis[11] in my elbow an I cuidnae hold a pen to write her a letter. My hand was stiff. So I blistered it up wi nettles. Healing blisters. An today there's not one single bit o pain left. It's all gone.

HT: I think I know why that works. It's like when a horse has something wrong with the tendon: there's no blood supply, so you blister the horse. It brings blood to the area.

We used tae blister the horses. We used tae blister them with this stuff—what dae ye call it? We bought it in the chemist's shop. Turpentine. We blistered its ligaments if it got a sore fetlock or anything, for sore tendons or a twisted ankle or something. It took the hair off and the hair come back in white again. Hair turned white from the blister.

❧

HT: What would you do if a horse had really cracked hooves?

We tuik them tae the seashore, for the soft muck, an kept them in the salt ground as much as possible. 'At's the only thing for cracks. An we used tae stop the cracks wi clay, the white clay by the shoreside, an that really helped them. I mean, I used tae pare his feet for corns. We had wir own cures for everything under the sun for horses. I filed their teeth, pulled their teeth, ye know? An I shod them.

I even shod my horse's feet oncet with a rubber tube, because I cuidnae get any shoes. I was up at a place called the Rest and Be Thankful, way up the other side o Loch Lomond, an the horse lost two shoes that night on the hill comin over. Ye cuidnae take a horse on the road in its bare feet. So I found an old rubber tube of an old car by the roadside, an I made two rubber boots from the tube an put them on my horse's feet. An that done me till I went to Balloch,[12] tae the blacksmith's shop. If I *had* some shoes I cuid a done it mysel, but I was completely run out o shoes.

LY: Did you put them on with nails?

---

11. "Arthritis": Duncan regularly pronounced the word as "arthuritis," with an epenthetic vowel.
12. "Balloch": village overlooking the southern shore of Loch Lomond.

No, I used rubber bands. I put splits in the rubber an put a tie on it an pulled it tight. Rubber pads on the horse's feet. I walked that horse for about thirty-six miles wi these pads on his feet till I come tae the blacksmith's shop. An the blacksmith said, "That's a wonderful thing tae do. You'd never have got here [otherwise]." Because the roads in these days across the west coast, they were just chips an tar, ye know?

(86DW06 @ 40:00, @ 41:18, and @ 48:30.)

§6.12. SOME ADDITIONAL CURES, AND ON SELF-HELP IN MEDICAL EMERGENCIES

If you've got anyone in your family that suffers from dermatitis, you take up a goat an you tie the goat up, an you feed the goat on nettles, when they're in bloom. Nothing else for one week. The goat will eat them if it gets nothing else. And then you drink the goat's milk. Forevermore your skin disease will disappear. Forevermore! You will never have it again providin you drink the goat's milk, tie up the goat, feed it nettles—but nothing else!—till the nettles gets in the goat's milk. And then when you drink it, you're clean forevermore. It takes, say, a couple of pints within a week. It'll never trouble you again, never in all your years. And that is true, really true.

So these old people had many cures.* Especially when children had whoopin cough, you know? Whoopin cough is terrible. I nearly lost my youngest brother with whooping cough. He near died with whooping cough. My mother used tae say, "Run down tae the river and guddle me a trout!"[13] You know, a little troot, a wee troot about that size [gestures], in the river. Easy caught, you know. When they're under a stone I used to get them, guddle them under a stone.

"Bring it back alive, don't kill it!" She'd put it in my brother's mouth, right? Six month old. Put it in his mouth and hold it there, and the trout would gasp for breath till it died. And when the trout died, the whoopin cough was gone. Just kept the trout's mouth in his mouth and kept it there till it died. When the trout died, no more whoopin cough. Whoopin cough was gone! It maybe took the trout three minutes out o water to die. And then, never again! In a couple of days it was gone.

CE: Why is that?

---

13. "Guddle me a trout": that is, "Wade into the stream, catch a trout with your hands, and bring it to me."

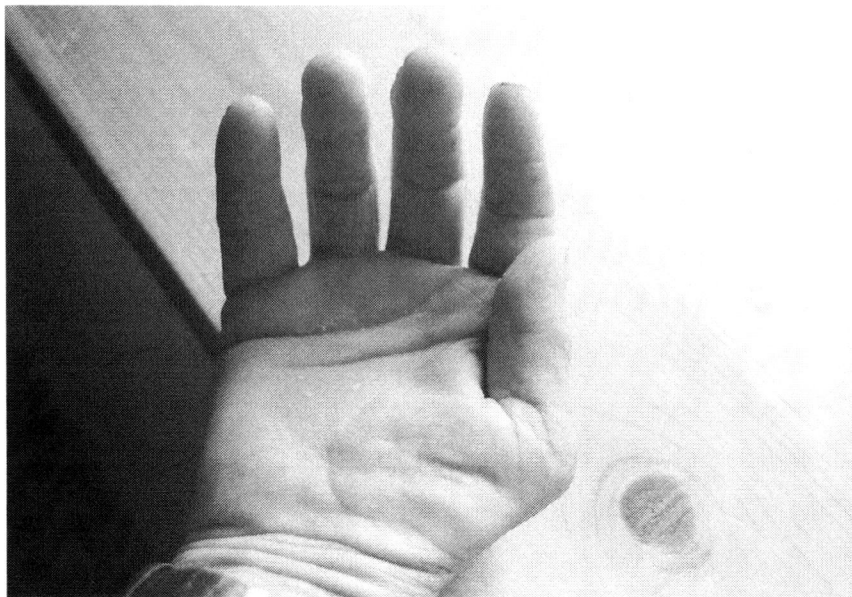

Figure 6.3 Williamson's right hand, showing where a bone is missing as the result of an injury suffered in his teens, Kincraigie Farm Cottage, 1986. Photo by Leonard Yarensky.

I could never explain it; I don't know. I don't know. That's true, 'at's true. I never lost my younger brother Jimmy. He stays in Cupar right now, and he's younger than me. But that's true.

CE: Is it any kind of a fish, or just a trout?

Just a trout. Just put the gaspin trout in the children's mouth. The same thing works for bed-wetting. Any child who wet the bed, you took a mouse—skin and all, tail, everything. You put it in a little pot, you brought the mouse a-boil, and you give the child a drink of the mousey water. No more bed-wettin! It's true! I swear on my mother's grave, I wouldnae lie to ye. You boil the mouse—head, tail, everything—in the water, in a luttle pan. Don't tell the child. Boil the mouse, give the child a drink o the water. No mair bed-wetting!

DC: Did the child know that the mouse—?

The child does not. Once the child knows, it doesnae work anymore. The child is not tae know.

HT: What about herbs, different herbs?

Oh, we had all the kinds of herbs in the world.* We used some of these herbs for many different things, ye know? They made their own cures. They had many wonderful things.

CE: Did they have something for cuts?

They had tobacca, salt, and these herbs. They had docken leaves, they had every kind o stuff you can remember. Salt was the most important thing; it always was used, you know, used in all cuts. The most important thing among the travelling people was salt. A luttle bag o salt. A child got a cut, in goes the salt.

You know, I remember my luttle sister Jeannie; she got a terrible cut in the foot. Cause we ran with wir bare feet as children, ye know. It was just half the foot, across the center. She ran back to her daddy, and he tuik it and he stuffed it full o salt; then he got a needle and thread and he sewed it up himself.

Now, take that hand for me, for instance [*showing a scar on one palm*]. There was a bone was cut from there. Look, see that bone was cut out o there. That was mended by my brother wi a piece o wire. That finger was paralyzed; that one [*pointing to one of his fingers*] was paralyzed. The bone was cut out of there, and he mended that wi a clip o wire, tae keep it together, ye know? And, eh, finally it came back,[14] after all these years. And look: see the hole in there?[15] The bone was cut out o there.

(86DW41 @ 45:13.)

§6.13. HOW JOCK WILLIAMSON DEALT WITH SNAKEBITE

♪♫

The way we luik at it—take for instance an adder or a poisonous snake. You walk off the roadway and ye come there to a snake. I mean, you're invadin his property! He never comes near you! And if you walk to a wasp's nest, you're lookin for trouble; you're intendin to get stung. It's your own fault! You should leave them alone. Well, that's the way with the travelling people.

Ah've never known a travelling child to be bit with a snake in their lifetime. Ma father was bit with a snake oncet, an it was his own fault. He was cuttin willows for makin baskets, and the grass was kind o long, an he was puttin his hand down and cuttin them as close to the ground as he could. An lo and behold, there was an adder there, an he put his finger too close tae the adder,

---

14. "Finally it came back": that is, either the finger's mobility came back or its sense of touch did, or both.

15. "See the hole in there": Duncan calls attention to a hollow pit in his palm, as is shown in Figure 6.3.

an he got bit. But he didnae kill the adder. And he had a knife that could hae cut the adder in just—head off in seconds! So he tuik the knife and just split the finger, tied a piece of tight string round it, and just sucked it an spat out the blood. In a couple o hours it was OK. But he never killed the snake. He never said, "You dirty thing, I'll kill you for bitin my finger!" He never touched it. He let it crawl away.

They taught you many wonderful things as a child, ye know?

(86DW23 @ 04:24.)

§6.14. DRINKING SONG, "JOHNNY YOU'RE A ROVER"*

♪♫

Did you ever hear "Johnny You're a Rover"?

JN: I don't know that song, no.

I've never done "Johnny" for ye yet? It's one o my favorites! If you're makin a collection, you must never leave this out, because this was a drunkin song for the old travellin men,[16] when they really got drunk. And this was their favorite, and women an all. And it goes like this. [*Sings:*]

1   Oh Johnny, you're a rover,
     I may meet you drunk and sober.
     Johnny, you're a young man forbye.
     If I had it in my power,
     with you I'd spend my hour.
     Oh among the shady bower,
     my darlin, first I met.

2   There be millers, brewers, and bakers,
     and candlesticks and shoemakers,
     and every kind of countrymen forbye.
     But if I had it in my power,
     with you I'd spend my hour.
     Oh beneath that shady bower,
     My darlin, first I met.

---

16. "A drunkin song": a drinking song, or, perhaps, a song that tended to be sung when people were far along in drink.

3   Oh Johnny, you're a rover,
    I may meet you drunk and sober.
    Oh Johnny, you're a young man forbye.
    If I had it in my power,
    with you I'd spend my hour.
    Oh among the shady bower,
    my darling, first I met.

Johnny You're a Rover

verse 3

JN: *That's good, Duncan! I've never heard that before. I don't think that's in any songbook.*

No, you won't get that in any songbook, no. "Johnny You're a Rover," yeah. That's what it's called: "Johnny You're a Rover." [*Sings again:*]

    Oh Johnny, you're a rover,
    I may meet you drunk or sober.

She said, she said:
    There be millers, brewers, and bakers,
    and journeymen and shoemakers,
    and every kind of countrymen forbye—

Figure 6.4 A gathering of friends outside Kincraigie Farm Cottage, 1986. From left to right: Duncan, Thomas, and Betsy Williamson; Betsy and Bryce Whyte; Linda Williamson. Photo by Leonard Yarensky.

I mean, she would choose him from everybody.

JN: [Laughs.]

Millers, brewers, bakers, and journeymen, shoemakers—but she didnae want nobody but Johnny. See what I mean? It's a good wee song.

JN: "My darling, first I met?"

"My darling, first I met," aye.

JN: That is, the first love that I met?

The first love that she met, right. The first one she met.

JN: Right. But she doesn't have him now?

She said she chose him from millers, brewers, and bakers, an journeymen and shoemakers, and every kind of countrymen forbye. But she said, "If I only had one hour, if only I had the power"—but she didnae have him.

JN: She doesn't have the power; so they are separated?

No, she doesnae—he was away. [*Sings:*]

> If I only had the power
> with you to spend one hour.
> Oh beneath the shady bower,
> my darlin, first I met.

He must have went and left her. And that's what she was singin about him.

(87DW13 @ 1:23:39.)

§6.15. DRINKING SONG, "NANCY WHISKY"*

[*Sings spontaneously, in the midst of a ceilidh:*]

♪♫

1   Oh as I gang doon tae Glesga City,
     a Nancy Whisky I chanced tae see,
     oh whisky whisky, Nancy Whisky,
     Ah'm sure she was the ruin o me.

2   For I been drunk an I been sober,
     many's a drink that I did hae,
     but whisky whisky, Nancy Whisky,
     the dearest friend I ever did hae.

3   Noo I am a weaver, a Calton weaver,
     I am a member of the weavin trade,
     but whisky whisky, Nancy Whisky,
     was the dearest friend I ever made.

4   Noo I been drunk an I been sober,
     many's the drink that I did hae,
     but Nancy Nancy, Whisky Nancy,
     it's a-ruined you, it's a-ruined me.

5   So I'm goin back to my Calton weavin,
     I bid goodbye to the drinkin trade.
     for whisky whisky, Nancy Whisky,
     sure she was the ruin o me.

Figure 6.5 Ceilidh at the Williamsons: what life is all about. Duncan, his children Thomas and Betsy, and Betsy Whyte, 1984. Photo by the author.

6   Oh whisky whisky, Nancy Whisky
    Whisky whisky Nancy oh
    oh whisky whisky, Nancy Whisky
    it's a-ruined me, it's a-ruined you.

7   So I'm goin back to my Calton weavin,
    I'm goin back to my weavin trade,
    I bid goodbye tae Nancy Whisky
    the dearest friend I ever made.

Nancy Whisky

verse 1

Oh as   I gang doon tae Gles-ga Ci-ty, a   Nan – cy – Whi – sky I chanced tae see,

oh   whi – sky   whi – sky   Nan – cy   Whi – sky,   Ah'm   sure she was   the ruin o   me.

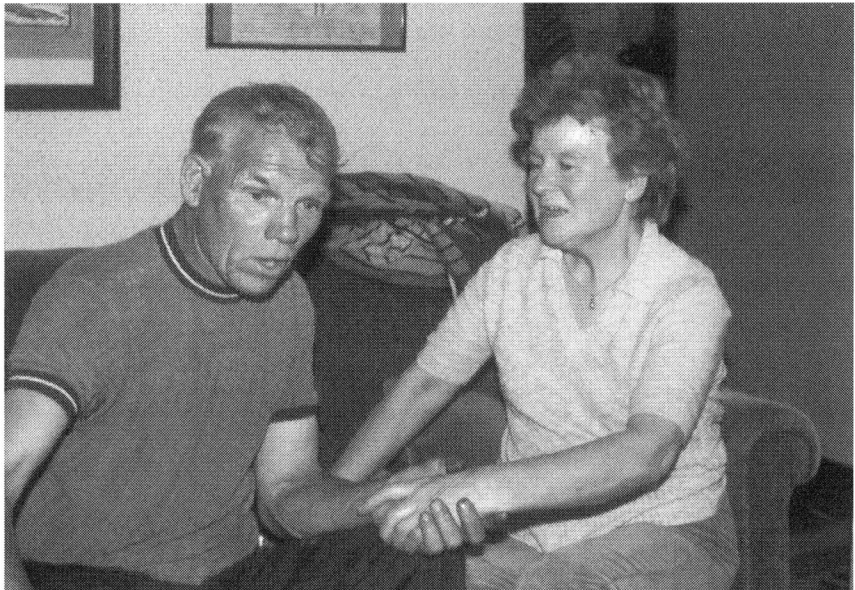

Figure 6.6 Williamson singing to Betsy Whyte while clasping her hand, Kincraigie Farm Cottage, 1984. Photo by the author.

That was a song called "Nancy Whisky," which the Glasgow people always sing. It tells a story that a man was so much in love with whisky that he left everything, just became a member of the Whisky Clan.* [*General laughter.*]

(84DW04 @ 31:42; closing comment from 86DW44 @ 03:22.)

§6.16. TRADITIONAL WISDOM: "IT'S A PUIR SONG WITHOUT A DRINK" AND "LET GOD PROVIDE TOMORROW"

I think it's time for a wee song before we eat. [*Takes a drink.*] They say, "It's a puir song without a drink, it's a puir drink without a song." Aye! [*General laughter.*] That's what they believe. You see, the travelling people, if they ever got a chance tae get together and have a singsong or a ceilidh, "Let's have it, because tomorrow we may die. Tomorrow we might never see each other again."

HT: Uh-hmm.

"Let's enjoy this part o the moment, because tomorrow's another day." And these people, they only lived for one day. Nothing else for them. It's very unlucky tae say, "I'm goin to do this tomorrow." Never say it! They wouldnae say, "I'm goin someplace tomorrow." That was taboo. They would leave that till tomorrow came. They said, "Tomorrow is another day," and if they got any food, they would eat it all in one settin and they would say, "Well, let God provide tomorrow." And sure enough, something always turned up. They didnae provide for a rainy day; nothing was left over, ye see. "Tomorrow will take care of itself." This was the law of the land among the travellin community, an it seemed to work for them.

(86DW41 @ 51:03.)

§6.17. OWN SONG, "WHEN THE YELLOW IS ON THE BROOM"*

[*Sings spontaneously in the midst of a ceilidh, directly to Betsy Whyte, who sings along softly:*]

♪♫

1   Oh come sit beside me, Maggie lass,
     I hate to see ye gloom.
     For I will take you from this place
     when the yellow is on the broom.

2   When the Angus hills are free o snaw
     and the swallow he's on the zoom,
     I will take you far away
     when the yellow is on the broom.

3   Oh we'll tae Loch Leven's bonnie glens
     or tae the River Spey,
     where I can pearl fish,[17] my love,
     and there my pipes I'll play.

4   So it's put a smile upon your face,
     I hate tae see you gloom.
     I will take you from this place
     when the yellow is on the broom.

(84DW04 @ 23:41.)

---

17. "Pearl fish": Duncan pronounces "pearl" with an epenthetic vowel, so that it sounds like "peril." Cf. the notes on "farm" and "warm" in §4.12 and on "arthritis" in §6.11.

When the Yellow Is on the Broom

verse 4

So   it's   put   a   smile   u - pon   your face

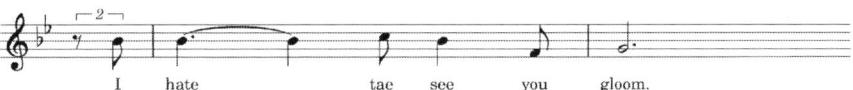

I   hate   tae   see   you   gloom.

I   will   take   you   from   this   place

when   the   yel - low   is   on   the   broom.

Chapter 7

MUSIC AND THE FLOW OF LIFE

§7.1. TRAVELLERS' SONG, "COME AA YE PERTHSHIRE FOLK"*

♪♫

This is the best Travellers' song that ever was in the world.

BW: I'll tell you!

[DW sings; LW sings along with him, and BW does so intermittently:]

1   Oh it's come it's aa ye Perthshire folk,
    ye folk that I ken weel,
    and it's if ony sorrow that ye have
    for me it you may feel.

2   Oh many's a cauld, cauld bed I had[1]
    gaain through the frost and snow.
    There wasnae one tae pity me
    or one tae wish me weel.
    Till the heavens above, my tender love,
    till the fortune turns a wheel.

3   Say "Willie dear, oh Willie dear,
    oh don't you go to sea!
    Oh Willie do not leave me
    A sailor for tae be.
    Oh with your jacket made of canvas

---

1. "A cauld, cauld bed I had": Duncan's usual wording for this line is "many's a cauld, cauld fet I had"—that is, many a cold foot, as in stanza 7 below.

Come Aa Ye Perthshire Folk

verse 3

Say Will - ie dear, oh Will-ie dear, oh don't you go to sea! Oh

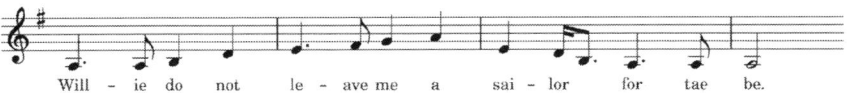

Will - ie do not le - ave me a sai - lor for tae be.

Oh with your jac-ket made of can - vas and your coat - of na - vy blue, and it's

ev - ery port that you'll come to you will have sweet-hearts of true.

and your coat of navy blue,
and it's every port that you'll come to
you will have sweethearts of true.

4   "You will have sweethearts of true, my dear,
    with no girl for to haunt your mind,
    but you'll never forget old Perthshire
    and the girl that you left behind.

5   "I'll cut off my bonny yellow hair,
    men's clothing I'll put on,
    and I will be a waitin maid
    on the ship that you sail upon."

6   "Your fingers are too slender, dear,
    your body is too small.
    You could never be a waitin maid
    on the ship that I sail upon."

7 Oh many's the cauld cauld fet I had
   gaain through the frost and snow.
   There wasnae one tae pity me
   or one tae wish me weel.
   Till the heavens above, my tender love,
   till the fortune turns the wheel.

D'you remember that?

BW: Aye, aye.

How long is it since you heard that? Must be years ago, Bessie.

BW: I ken it, but. . . .

[DW repeats a bit of the song over a lot of cross talk that chiefly concerns how old the song is:]

With your jacket made of canvas
and your coat of navy blue,
and it's every port that you'll come to
you will have sweethearts of true.

You will have sweethearts of true, my dear,
no girl for to haunt—

LW: Was it before World War I?

This is *afore* 1914, *afore* the First World War. [*Sings again:*]

You will have sweethearts of true, my dear,
no girl for to haunt your mind,
but you'll never forget old Perthshire
and the girl that you left behind.

Listen, that was the Perthshire milishee![2] The Perthshire milishee joined up long afore the 1914 War. We're talkin about afore the Boer War.

JN: What makes that such a good song in your mind?

---

2. "Milishee": Duncan's pronunciation of "militia." His reference is to the Royal Perthshire Militia, an army unit active during the eighteenth and nineteenth centuries.

Figure 7.1 Williamson playing the tin whistle outside Kincraigie Farm Cottage, 1984, welcoming me to my first recording session with him. Photo by the author.

Because it was a favorite by the travelling folk. And they maintained that it was only known to them. That was *their* song, and they sung it and it had a lovely tune. Everyone sung it round the campfires.

Campfires at that time were—I mean, Ah travelled round the campfires from 1945 til 1962. Round all the campfires, an Ah listened tae all the old songs an the old travellin folk. And I wantit to collect old ballads an odd bits and pieces an collect bits o songs and stuff, try an build all these stories together, because I haird so many stories that were told tae me when I was young were *ballads*, an Ah wantit tae learn everything, John. They were half sung and half told. Depends on the condition o the people when they were doin it, like here!

JN: [Laughs.]
BW: That's right.

Know what I mean? Depends on the condition. If the beverage was good, the song was puir. If the beverage was puir, the song was good! D'ye understand? But anyway, it was a fantastic way of communication. They had only one way o communication. That was by song an music. Well, they didnae know music,[3] but they had their *own idea* o music.

---

3. "They didnae know music": that is, they did not read sheet music, for they lacked formal musical training.

BW: Traveller music.
JN: They knew music, right!

It was *their* music. An you believe me, there were good singers, good pipers, and good storytellers among them. They had their own tradition, and they lived in their little world, apart from the world outside. When they got together the outside world was gone. They were in their own world. They lived within theirself. They didnae need—they only needed to go outside in the world when they needed a quarter o tea or a bit o tobacco.

BW: That's right.

When they came back, they come back to their own world again. The world of non-Travellers was forgotten when they had a dram and they had everything they needed.

BW: When they were dealing with the country hantle,⁴ they werenae themselves, they weren't as honest. They just said anything at aa to please the country hantle.

That's true! That was true!

BW: But when they come back together, they were real people *again.*

(84DW04 @ 58:14.)

§7.2. "DOWN IN YONDER BUSHES,"* A FAVORITE SONG OF TRAVELLER WOMEN

♪♫

But this one—whenever I would drink wi them, they used tae go crazy aboot it.⁵ Ah've seen them cryin after they sung the song. Ah don't know why, what made them cry. Ah've never seen nothing like it. My mother—Ah don't know what made them so sad, what reason it was. Whether it was the feelings in the song, or something to do with theirsel, Ah don't know. [*Sings:*]

1   Oh, down in yonder bushes I heard a fine song.
     It was sung by a fair maid whose voice was so clear,

---

4. "The country hantle": a term used by travelling people for settled people who live in rural areas, as distinguished from the "scaldies" or "flatties" living in cities or towns.
5. "They used to go crazy about it": Duncan is referring to Traveller women and their songs.

sayin, "What would I give tonight if my true love he passed by, two cheeks like red roses, two rollin dark eyes.

2   "Oh the people of this country, they're rude and they're wild.
    The people of this country says I'm going with a child.
    I'll defy them, I'll deny them, like a bird in yonder tree.
    And the more my love jilts me the prouder I will be."

Down in Yonder Bushes
verse 2

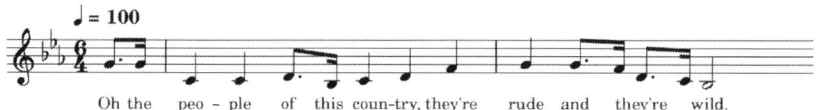

Oh the peo – ple of this coun-try, they're rude and they're wild.

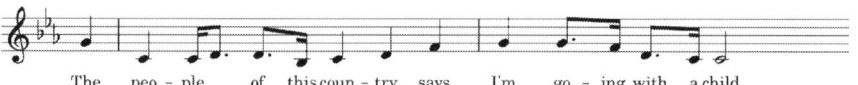

The peo – ple of this coun – try says I'm go – ing with a child.

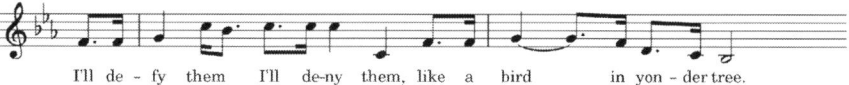

I'll de – fy them I'll de-ny them, like a bird in yon – der tree.

And the more my love jilts me the prou – der I will be.

Ah've seen them sittin, singin that, an cryin to theirselves aboot it, without anything to drink, you know? Ah don't know what made em cry about it; there's nothing in it tae make them cry. Whether it was their own personal feelings or not, Ah don't know. Well, that's true. My mother's song.

JN: Was there more to it, Duncan?

Ah never haird any more of it, no. Ah cuidnae tell you any more of it. There might have been more to it than that, but that was all the bits that they would sing. They never got through it. They were half-brokenhearted afore they finished it, so they never halfway got through it, but the reason for it Ah don't know. Maybe their own personal feelings, or something about it.

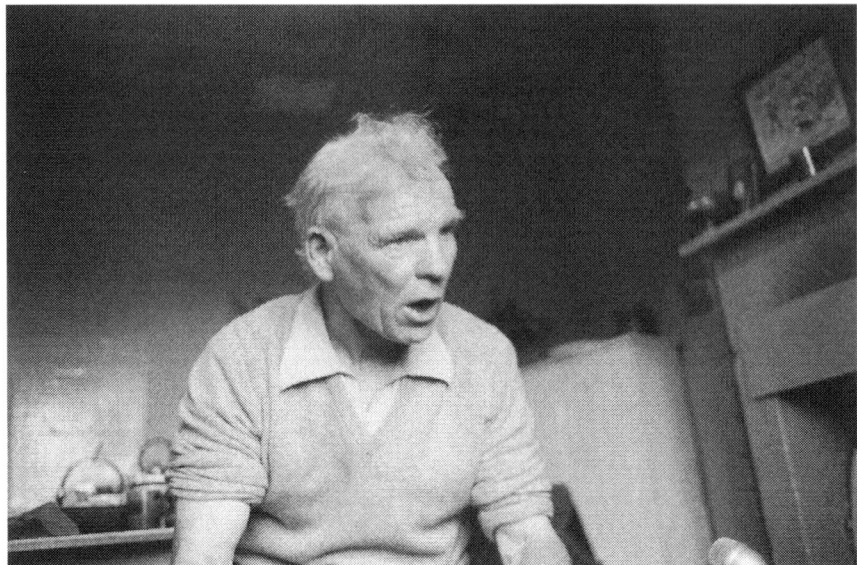

Figure 7.2 Singing a big ballad, Kincraigie Farm Cottage, 1986. Photo by Leonard Yarensky.

JN: I wonder where the woman is in this song.

Ah don't know where the woman is. It doesnae tell you where the woman was.

JN: "The people of this country—"

"The people of this country, they are rude an they are wild—"

JN: It sounds as though she's from somewhere else.

She cuid be from somewhere else. [*Recites or sings:*]

> "The people of this country says I'm going with a child.
> But I will defy them, I'll deny them, like a bird in yonder tree.
> And the more my love jilts me, the prouder I will be."

Ah don't know why or what it meant. That's all I know.

JN: Can the men sing it as well?

No. No, I never—no, the men never sung it. Just the women sung it.

JN: Well—good, Duncan, good. That's what I wanted to hear from you, because again, I don't think that's in any book.

I've never heard many people singin it except for the Traveller women singin it.

(87DW14 @ 16:36.)

§7.3. BROADSIDE BALLAD, "THE FACTORY GIRL,"*
WITH TALK ABOUT SOME FAVORITE SONGS

[*DW sings:*]

♪♫

1   Oh as I went out a-walking one fine summer's mornin,
and the birds in the bushes did warble and sing,
gay laddies and lassies and couples went sportin,
going down to the fact'ry, their work to begin.

2   I spied one amongst them more fairer than any,
her cheeks like the red rose that none could impel,[6]
and her skin like the lily that grows in the valley,
and she but a hardworking factory girl.

3   I stepped up to her more closely to view her,
and on me she cast such a look of disdain.
Saying, "Young man, have manners and do not come near me.
Although I'm a poor girl, I think it no shame."

4   "Young maid, I adore thee, it's not to incore thee.[7]
Oh grant me one promise—where do you dwell?"
"Oh I am an orphan with no relation,
and forbyes I'm a hardworking factory girl."

5   "I have land, I have houses all adorned with ivy,
I have gold in my pocket and silver as well,
and if you'll come with me a lady I'll make you,
and no more you'll be heedin your factory bell."

---

6. "None could impel": a phrase with the apparent sense "none could compare."

7. "Not to incore you": a phrase with the apparent sense "not to cause you shame or embarrassment."

6 "Kind sir, please go leave me, kind sir, please don't grieve me.
   Go marry a lady, and may you do well!
   For I am an orphan with no relation,
   now I hear like the sound of my factory bell."

7 With that she has turned and with less she has left me.
   Oh for her sake I'll go wander away,
   and down in some valley where no one shall know me,
   I'll mourn for the sake of my poor fact'ry girl.

The Factory Girl

verse 7

With that she has turned and with less she has left me.

Oh for her sake I'll go wan - der a - way, and

down in some val - ley where no one shall know me, I'll

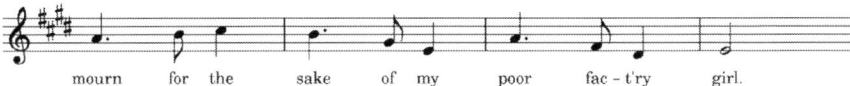

mourn for the sake of my poor fac - t'ry girl.

That's a good story. That's got a good wee story in it. So these were the kind o things that appeal tae me, ye know what I mean? And I used tae ask for it now and again when I was in the campfires. "Do you know such and such, do you know this one, know that one," ye know?

JN: Did other Travellers know that song?

Yeah, a few Travellers knew it, yeah, yeah. It was well known among the Travellers.

JN: I wonder what kind of a song it is, where it comes from. Nineteenth century?

It could be, right, early nineteenth century. When the girls worked in the fact'ries, you know. Yeah, early nineteenth century, I would think. If it's going to be a century I would think it'd be that time. But it was well known among the Travellers. Some non-Travellers too know it.

JN: [Hums.] It's a familiar tune.

It's got a tune 'at's familiar to "The Road and the Miles to Dundee."* 'At's the tune. See—[*sings, to much the same tune:*]

> And then, with the Howe of Strathmartin behind me
> the spires of the toon I could clearly see.
> And boldly I kissed the sweet lips o the lassie,
> and bid her farewell on the roads to Dundee.

Same tune, same tune.

JN: That's a favorite in the northeast, isn't it? You don't sing that particular one, do you, Duncan?

No, I never bother with that one, no.

JN: Just "The Factory Girl"?

Ah sing "The Factory Girl." It's a better story than "The Roads and the Miles to Dundee." A better story.

JN: I think so. A little more to it.

Yeah, it's got more to it.

JN: There's not much to "The Road to Dundee." It's pretty light.

It's pretty light and he just, eh—he meets her, an he walks wi her an he kisses her an says goodbye tae her, ye know. There's nothing to it. But this, when he says, "Oh, for her sake I'll go wander away, down in some valley where no one'll know me," and he'll mourn for the sake of his fact'ry girl—I mean, he really liked her! And he was rich! He had land and houses adorned with ivy. He had everything! But he wanted this wee factory girl, you see. He really wanted her, and he meant it.

JN: But she didn't know that he really did.

She thought he was just teasin her, ye know? She says, "Sir, please—please sir, go and leave me, please sir, do not grieve me. Go marry a lady, and may ye do well." She wanted—You see, you want to marry someone like yourself. She thought he was just havin her on because she's a poor fac'try girl. I like the story line of it, that's why Ah've kept it among some of my songs. I liked the story line of it.

❧

Only thing that had interest for me: if it had a good story line an I liked it, I would follae it up to try an find mair bits o it tae try an make it complete. And try an get a better version of it. But if it didnae have any feelings tae me, if it didnae *dae* nothing tae me, I wasnae interested wi it. Ye know what I mean? I liked "The Harbor o Dundee," and I liked "The Factory Girl," and I liked, eh, "Peggy Gordon."* These kind o songs—ye know, I liked them kind o songs. Some other ones I liked. I liked the old ballads, ye know what I mean?

(87DW14 @ 1:02:28 and @ 1:13:00.)

§7.4. ON COMMUNAL SONG COMPOSITION AMONG THE TRAVELLERS

They had their funny songs, they had their serious songs, an they had their love songs, an they had their stories, an they had everything. An they done things for different occasions, ye know?

JN: Yeah.

Somebody would start with a funny song. I'll tell you one thing the Travellers used tae do. They would start off and they would make up a line. And somebody else would make another line. Somebody around the fire would make another line in the same song. And they followed it an followed it an followed it tae see how far they could take it. Oh, ten, fifteen, twenty verses. And then the last man tae add the last verse was the best man of them all.

Noo I was tellin this to, eh, the old professor from Turkey,* who had come to visit Linda and I. I was tellin him this. He says to me, "You know, in Turkey, we have competitions for that. A group of people gets together on a stage, an a lot of people in a hall, and one man gets up. And you make something out of your mind—[he] starts a song or a recitation of some kind. Another man jumps up on the stage and he carries on. The first one jumps doon. The second

Figure 7.3 Playing the Jew's harp, Auchtermuchty, Fife, 1986. Photo by Leonard Yarensky.

one does a bit. A third one jumps up, and the third one jumps doon. And it goes on like that, you see, anything for two hours at a time, to see how far they can really go. And," he said, "the last man onstage wins the competition." Now this was told tae me about Turkey. The [Scottish] Travellers done this all the time round the campfires.

JN: Were you present at any sessions when people made songs or plays like this?

I remember em makin funny stories and tales aboot other Travellers roond the fire, you see what I mean? And, eh, dirty ones, filthy ones, serious ones, funny ones, ye know what I mean?

JN: Yeah.

We used tae do them all the time. Some people say a line, and then the next tae be up would say another line, say another two verses. He could say as much as he wantit, but when he cuidnae go any further, somebody else in the group would have tae take over, ye see what I mean? Well, if you had nothing to say, they'd pass on tae the next one.

   But these auld things are all gone now. There's naebody doin that anymore. But there were never—they were never sung—it was only for the evening.*

(87DW12 @ 1:15:38.)

§7.5. SONG IN CANT, "BIG JIMMY DRUMMOND"*

🎵

JN: Duncan, do you ever sing "Jimmy Drummond"?

Yeah, Ah sing some bits. But there's not really much tae "Jimmy Drummond."
[*Sings:*]

1   Oh my name is Big Jimmy Drummond,
     my name I will never deny.

[*Starts over:*] My name—Ah, no. I get—what tune is—? [*Hums a bit.*] "My name
I will never deny." [*Resumes singing, starting in on a new verse:*]

2   Oh whenever you dae bing a-chorin[8]
     you're better tae bing by yoursel.
     Ye can moolie the gannies in dozens
     and there's naebody there fir to tell.

3   Tonight I am in a cauld stardy,
     tonight I'm-a in a cauld quod.
     My mort and ma kinchens are scattered
     and I dinnae jan where I may be.

4   So if you dae bing a-chorin,
     you're better tae bing by yoursel.
     Ye can moolie the gannies in dozens,
     and there's naebody there fir to tell.

Noo Jimmy Drummond: when my brother Jock was a young lad, he stayed
along with Jimmy Drummond in Arran. And him and Jimmy Drummond—
Jock left home when he was fourteen. And on his first trip he went to Arran
with old Uncle Duncan, my mother's brother; they went to Arran. And there
they came to see Jimmy Drummond.

   Big Jimmy Drummond, he was middle-aged at that time. And the story
aboot Jimmy Drummond was, Jimmy Drummond cuidnae stand to see any
child hungry. If the Travellers had no meat for their kids, Jimmy Drummond
would go an he would steal hens, and he would steal onything. He'd steal fish

---

8. The cant vocabulary in this song is meant to be impenetrable except to those in the know. "Bing
a-chorin" means "go out stealing." "Moolie the gannies" means "kill the hens." A "stardy" is a jail
cell, and so is a "quod." "My mort and ma kinchens" are "my wife and my children."

Big Jimmy Drummond

verse 2

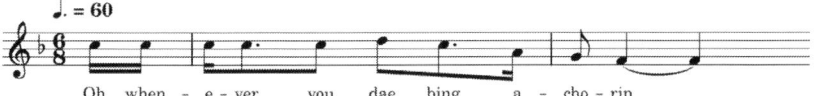

Oh when - e - ver   you   dae   bing   a - cho - rin

you're   bet - ter   tae   bing   by - your - sel.

Ye   can   moo - lie   the   gan - nies   in   do - zens

and   there's   nae - bo - dy   there   fir   to   tell.

at the rivers; he was a great salmon poacher. And he was a kind of Traveller Robin Hood among the Traivellers. And if it was his last penny he had in his pocket, he would give it tae you.

And one man went round tae him one night, he said—that man, he said—he took sheep in Arran, ye know, lambs and all[9]—he said, "Man, your weans is hungry. Come wi me. Ah'll get some meat for your weans tonight," he says, "when it gets dark."

And there was a big henhouse near the fairum, full o hens. Those days they used tae keep hens out in the fields in these wee bit huts. And Jimmy and him went doon, an they broke into the henhouse, and they killed about six or seven hens. And, eh, this man took a fright because he feared the police'd come the next mornin.

An the police did come. By that time, Jimmy had buried the hens in the ground in his tent, you know, buried them in under the ground. But the man, he squealed on Jimmy. He crowed. "I didnae want tae go, but," he says, "I had tae go wi him because I was kind o feared o him."

Jimmy was arrested and he got thirty days. And he [the other man] got free, so he flit from Arran the next day. Yeah, Jimmy—big Jimmy Drummond, yeah.

JN: So he wasn't just a legend? He was a real—?

---

9. "He took sheep in Arran": that is, he stole sheep for food.

Figure 7.4 Travellers' bow tent, Isle of Arran, 1984. Big Jimmy Drummond was camping on Arran when lifted for stealing hens. Photo by the author.

No! Brother Jock was campin with him. Jimmy Drummond was nae legend. Jock is seventy-five now, and he would be—see, he was fifteen. That was sixty years ago. Jimmy would maybe have been in his forties. Jimmy, if he would be alive today, would come up for his hundredth birthday. That's the truth, because Jock sat here and told me the story. The Travellers think it's unlucky to sing it. The Travellers will rarely sing it, because Big Jimmy was well respected among the travelling people, an he got the thirty days. The police shifted his wife away cause of him stealin those hens. So she had to wander, hersel and the kids, while he was lying in jail. Thirty days he got in Greenock, and he didnae even know where his wife was, you see? And he made up the song while he was lyin in jail.

JN: So it's his own song?

His own song. He made it up hissel. He made it himsel about himsel. He said [*sings:*]

> If ever you dae bing a-chorin,
> you're better to bing by yoursel.

I mean, there will be naebody to tell on you.

JN: Right. [Laughs.]

If you're goin stealin, go by yourself, because you've nobody to tell on you! Well, that's a true story.

(87DW12 @ 35:20.)

§7.6. OWN SONG, "THE NICKNAMES"*

♪♫

JN: So he [Jimmy Drummond] was a songwriter. Were a lot of the travelling people songwriters?

Well, they kind of made things up, just for fun.

JN: Nothing that they'd ever trouble about?

No, they'd never trouble about, no. No. They made songs about each other, and everyone else, you know.

JN: Usually with a bit of a dig in them?

Oh, aye, sometimes wi a dig in them, yeah. Oh, aye, sometimes they had a bit dig in them. You see, the thing was, families always made songs about other families, and other families made songs about *that* family, you see?

JN: Right, right. [Laughs.]

And we sung them all the time. But Ah made a song about them all, "The Nicknames," and Ah played it to them.* But it was in fun, they took it in fun. I mean, Ah played it roond the fire, and they heard their own nicknames on the tape. I said, "What do you think of this song?" [*Sings:*]

1   Oh there's Gravits and there's Spotties,
     there's Pigs doon fae the glens,
     there's Hardfish from Argyllshire
     and there's some they call the Hens.
         And me-doo-diddum-doo, me-doo-diddum-day,
         me-doo-diddum doo-diddum dandy oh!

2   Oh on and on these nicknames go
     from one unto the other.
     But who am I to talk
     with a Treacle for a mother!

> Oh ma ring-ding-doo, ma ring-ding-doo,
> ma ring-ding-ma-diddle tae ma dandy oh!

3   Oh there's Breids-an-Milk from Aberdeen,
    there's Scroggies from the North,
    and there's the Dandies
    with their big mouths!
> With my ring-ding-doo, my ring-ding-doo,
> my ring-ding-ma-diddle tae ma dandy oh!

4   Oh on and on these nicknames go
    from the old unto the young.
    I think it would be better
    fir me tae hold my tongue!
> With my ring-ding-doo, my ring-ding-doo,
> my ring-ding-ma-diddle tae ma dandy oh!

The Nicknames

verse 4

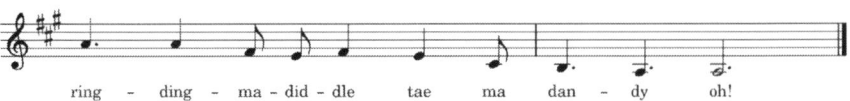

And on and on it went, you know. It was really funny! So when Ah mentioned my own mother's nickname, and the hardfish, and the, eh—you see, the John-stones was the pigs, and then there were the hens, the green hens, you know?

There were the hedgehogs, there was the bigmouths, there was the Scroggies. The breid-an-milk, we called them.

JN: *The Scroggies?*

The Scroggies, aye, the Stewarts. The Stewarts; the Scroggies.

JN: *What does that mean, now, Scroggies?*

The Scroggies is—some of the islands where the Stewarts stayed in, there was no trees, there were just wee bushes. Well, a small bush is a scrog. So we called them Scroggies, because they lived among the small bushes, you see?

Now we had good fun. I had good fun. They never took any offense at it, you know? Ah wasnae carin a damn whether they did or no! I was young and strong, I wouldnae have cared about none o them. I mean, some o them, if they wasnae pleased, there's not much you could dae about it. You ken what I mean? Not much to dae about it. But they all took it in fun.

JN: *Was anyone ever offended by one of your songs?*

No, no way, no. Never got anyone offended. Whether they said it behind my back or no—but they never said it tae my face! [*Laughs.*]

(87DW12 @ 39:43.)

§7.7. TRAVELLERS' STORY AND SONG, "THE SHANGHAI BALLAD"*

♪♫

I remember a funny experience I had when I left home. I was just about sixteen, ye know? An in these bygone times there was a very lot of ceilidhs and singsongs among the Travellers. If you knew the right places tae go ye could have it every day in the week, in different parts, in different families.

So I was landit at this campsite. Ah knew some of the people. Well, they knew my people, and Ah was made welcome, as I was tellin ye. You're always welcome wi strangers tae your fireside. There's nobody gets turned away from a fireside—it's the rule—by a Traveller at all. And, eh, I was sittin there an had a cup o tea, listenin. She says tae me, an old woman—she pit some coal from the fire in her pipe, ye know. We're all sittin on the ground. She says, "Och, ye're sittin tae ma feet. You're na bein nobody," she says tae me. "Whaur d'ye come frae?"

"Oh, Ah come up from Argyll," I said.

"Oh aye," she says. "Doon Argyllshire country. Can ye tell us a wee story or sing a wee sang or somethin?"

So I wasnae bashful in any way. I say, "I'll tell ye a story." An I started tae tell one o my father's tales which was a story tae me, but as far as she was concerned was not a story at all. It was a traditional ballad. Ah did not know it was a ballad. Ah was about seventeen, eighteen before I knew what ballads were. They were all told tae me as stories. They were stories. Ah was tellin the story about the Shanghai ballad, ye know, about the Traveller boy gettin took away, gettin shanghaied onto the boat.

HT: I never heard that one.

So the prisoner got put into the—eh, it's during the Spanish invasion, when Britain was fightin against the Spaniards, you know? And the press-gang were out on the streets.

And they picked up this young Traveller boy, young Traveller man. And he was put aboard the sailin ship to fight against the Spaniards. Queen Elizabeth was givin orders to press men to go out on the streets and towns and pick up everybody they could find, young men, and put them aboard the ship. Shanghai them and put them aboard the ship. And the boat was captured, and he was threwn in prison in Spain. An the only company he had was a little sparra on the window, ye know?

HT: Right.

And the sparra was flying back an forward through the bars, ye know? There was no glass in these days, just bars. And it built a little nest in the side o the window. And this was the only company he had. And the sparra used tae sit there and sing. And he [the prisoner] was visualizin from the song that the sparra was telling him not to worry; someday he would be free. And he composed the traditional ballad himself of the sparra's song. And sure enough, years later, about two years later, he was set free and he came back home, and naturally, he joined his travellin family. And he carried with him his own homemade song, and he sang it around the campfires.

But Ah was telling it as a story. So the old woman said, "Excuse me a minute, laddie," she said. "Man, that's no a story. 'At's guid enough," she says, "but that's a sang. That's a sang," she said. "That's a Traiveller sang."

"Oh," I said, "is it?" I said, "I'm sorry."

"Oh, no, dinnae be sorry, laddie," she said. "I'm glad that ye ken the story."

Ah said, "Could ye sing me a wee bit of it, then?"

"Well, I'm nae muckle a singer," she said, "ye ken." And she fulled her pipe. "But I'll gie ye a wee bit o it. But I'll only gae ye the wee bit verse where he watched the bird," she said. [*Sings:*]

1   Oh up in the window of my cell,
    a sparra built his nest.
    And as he hopped from bar to bar
    thus was he sore oppressed.
    And as he hop from bar to bar
    Ah'm sure he seemed to say:
    Cheer up your hairt, my bonny lad,
    some day you will be free.

2   For to see those young and strappin men
    reduced to skin an bone,
    for to see those young and strappin men
    would bring salt tears from a stone.
    With a ring and chain around their legs
    'tached to a ball of lead,
    you could hear them saying, it's from their hearts
    and wishin they were dead.

The Shanghai Ballad

verse 1

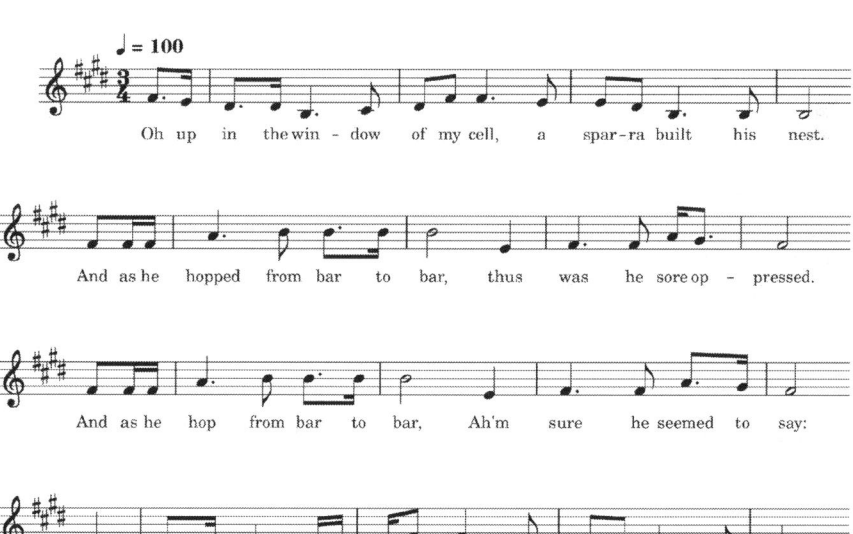

That's the song from "The Shanghai Ballad."

(86DW19 @ 48:44.)

§7.8. TALK ABOUT "THE SHANGHAI BALLAD" AND
SONGS SUNG AS FRAGMENTS

JN: Your father was a singer sometimes, right?

When he had a drink he would sing a wee bit.

JN: And your mother, would she sing as well?

Not so much.[10] My mother liked to diddle at nighttime. She liked mouth music. She used tae sing "Bundle an Go."* She used to diddle; her favorite tune was "Bundle and Go." She was never much of a singer. She would sing wee bits o things, ye ken? Wee bits an pieces.

JN: Would your father sing whole songs?

He would mostly just tell you a ballad, an he would sing you a wee piece in the middle of it. His favorite was "The Shanghai Ballad." He told me the story, but I've never haird nobody singin it.*

JN: He didn't sing any part of it?

He sung one part.[11]

ॐ

He told you the story, and then he said, "The little sparrow came tae the window." And then he said, "The sparrow sung—he thought he heard the sparrow singin." He always sung the sparra's song, and it went:
   [*Sings the same two stanzas of the "Shanghai Ballad" that are given before.*] And then he would tell the rest o the story. But Ah never heard him singin any more o that song. Only that part. And he told you the story that he [the prisoner] lay there, an he watched the birds hatchin, and he watched them flyin away. And when they flew off, he says to hissel, "I wish Ah could fly off jist the same." And then he was set free! As if the bird had told him, "When my song is finished an my young ones fly away, you will be free." And so he was set free, and he come back. He came back to Scotland an he told this story. And

---

10. "Not so much": see §7.2, however, for a song that Duncan associated with his mother, "Down in Yonder Bushes."

11. Here Duncan summarizes the story of "The Shanghai Ballad," much as in §7.7, while also talking about another song that Duncan's father sang only in part, telling the rest as a story. This was a cantefable about the last man hung for sheep stealing in Scotland.

Figure 7.5 Mimicking the calls of a mavis, or thrush, during a recording session in the woods outside Ithaca, New York, 1997. The origins of music are in nature. Williamson grew up in the woods outside Furnace, Argyll, and knew the song or call of every bird in that region. Photo by the author.

he composed the song in his cell, in his head, watchin the sparra flyin through the window. And that's away back, oh, it would be round the sixteenth century.

(87DW04 @ 31:00 and @ 34:15.)

§7.9. MIMICKING BIRDCALLS

JN: Alan, do you want to come over here and listen? I think you'll like this; it's something for you especially.

[*DW speaks to Alan:*] You cuidnae show me a way wi your fingers that Ah cuidnae whustle. Any way at all. [*Demonstrates a few trial whistles.*] We used tae sit in the forest and imitate the birds in the mornin.*

JN: Is that the trick to it: how you hold your fingers?

How you hold your fingers. If you listen to the birds in the mornin, you've got the dawn chorus and all the birds. An you picked out one that was louder than the rest, and you'd try tae imitate it, you know? This was the mavis, the mavis[12]:

---

12. "The mavis": also known as the thrush.

Figure 7.6 Mimicking another bird's calls, Ithaca, 1997. Photo by the author.

[Whistles the varied cries of the mavis.]
And then you were listenin in the mornin—coming over the moors, an you'd
hear:
[Whistles the rising cry of the curlew.]
—The caralews would be callin tae one another.[13] We called them "whaups";
they'd call them "caralews." With the long legs and the beaks that—.[14] We were
up in the moor:
[Whistles the cries of various birds including curlews and fieldfares.]
This was the fieldfares, the Scandinavian fieldfares. They came in during the
spring, and, eh, they used to go like this. Funny, funny noises they make:
[Whistles the cry of the fieldfare.]
Funny, funny noises they made, Scandinavian fieldfares. But I like the mavis
the best. *[Imitates the cry of the mavis again.]* Then you had the skylarks.
[Whistles the cry of the skylark rising.]
Up an up an up an up an up an up! Skylarks disappear in the air. Its noise gets
weaker and weaker as it climbs high. It goes like this:
[Whistles the cry of the skylark on the ground.]
Then they would go in. *[Laughs.]* Oh, we used tae do these—Ah've never done
these birdcalls for years an years an years!

---

13. "Caralews": Duncan's pronunciation of "curlews."
14. Duncan was about to say "and the beaks that curve downward" or words to that effect, but
broke off in midsentence.

Figure 7.7 Playing the mouthie, or harmonica, Auchtermuchty, Fife, 1986. Photo by Leonard Yarensky.

JN: That's good, Duncan! Those are terrific.

We used to make these birdcalls all the time. It was easier when your fingers was thin, ye ken? When you were young it was nae problem. We used tae listen to them all the time in the forest in the nighttime. The mavis would sit in the high trees, sittin up there from four in the evening till about eight o'clock at night, a beautiful noise. We used tae set under the trees imitatin them, tryin tae whistle back to them. It was guid fun. I loved tae hear the caralews on the moor, when it takes off an he goes *garacle-garcle-garcle-garcle* [*mimicking the sound of the curlew, using just his vocal cords this time.*] He glides, ye know? You'd hear him fading away as he goes, then you'd hear one comin in close. Beautiful sound, the caralew. I used tae do a lot of these but my fingers are gettin too thick for it.

JN: Did anyone teach you how to do this?

No, I just learnt it myself. Naebody teached ye. Naebody teached ye.

(87DW11 @ 1:03:10.)

Figure 7.8 Traveller piper playing his pipes for tourists by the roadside in Glen Coe, Scottish Highlands, while dressed for the part. The touring map of Scotland used by the author in the 1980s featured this photo on its cover, with no information on the piper's identity or the date. Williamson recognized the man as John Townsley, a relative on his mother's side.

§7.10. ON SKILLED PIPERS AMONG THE TRAVELLERS

I'll tell you one thing. There's some damn good players among them. An you know, Ah had a great friend who oncet was a pipe major. He owned a great shop in Glasgow: was Donald MacLeod.* He was the greatest piper in the world, and he won medals at the Highland Games. An Ah walked in tae Donald's shop, and I knew Donald MacLeod well, and you can take this as fact. And Ah come to Donald and I said, "What dae you think of the travelling folk, Donal, as pipers?"

"Well," he says, "I'll tell you something." This is Donald MacLeod, God rest his soul in heaven. Now you can record this, you can tell this, you can write about it, and you can say it anywhere in the world and not be ashamed to admit it. He said, "I'll tell you something, my friend," he said. "I've been at the Highland meetings and I've been to Highland Games," he said, "and I've haird some good pipers. But," he said, "I have haird some better travellin pipers."

That's the truth! [Pipers] who never even knew a word of music in their life!* That's Donald MacLeod told me that in Glasgow in his shop, in his tartan shop in 1962. Donald MacLeod shook hands with me an I sat wi him in his shop, and he said, "I've haird some better Traveller pipers than was at the Games."

An I'll tell you who was with me was Big Willie MacPhee.[15]

(84DW01 @ 49:09.)

§7.11. OWN SONG, "MY OLD HORSE AND CART"*

♪♫

I know Len and Jeppy would like to hear it[16]; it's a wonderful story. It tells a true story of the travelling people. Once you have this, you've got something 'at's unique among the travelling people, because I wrote this myself, for the travelling people. I used the tune from Robbie Burns,* but the words are all my own. An it tells a true story, because sometimes travellin people are very poor, an they travel wi their ponies around the land. An some days they came up to the smitty, and the horse had lost a shoe and they cuidnae afford new shoes, so they told the smithy man to put a secondhand shoe on the horses. This, Jack, is a wonderful story. It's a wee bit sad, but it's true.

JN: Did it happen to you?

It happened to me, and it happened to the whole world! It was life among the travelling people! And they love it because it tells a story of times that are gone. It can never come again; it can never happen anymore. It's the story of the past of the travelling people. And it's so wonderful, it makes you feel so sad that these people who were the primitive savages of Scotland—now their way of life is gone. Listen to this. [*Sings:*]

---

15. "Big Willie MacPhee": Duncan regarded him as one of the finest pipers of his generation, as well as someone who could confirm the truth of this account..

16. Duncan is addressing Len and Jeppy Yarensky now that the other participants in this particular ceilidh have gone home. He is a bit far along in drink, at this late hour, and I believe he sang the song from the heart.

1   Oh the summertime is come again
     and it surely breaks my heart,
     when I think on the happy days I spent
     with my old horse and cart.
     The roads they werenae lang for him
     nor yet too lang for me.
     It's on the road we used to go,
     oh, my old horse an me.

2   Fraem Aberdeen to Gallowa
     we tramped the country wide.
     Frae Edinburgh doon tae Stranraer
     and roon the banks o Clyde.
     The roads, they were nae lang for him,
     nor yet too lang for me.
     It's on the road we used to go,
     oh, my old horse and me.

3   Oh many's a time in a winter's night
     he stood tied to a tree.
     We'd no a bite to give to him,
     nor no a bite for me.
     With a wee bit cover across his back
     to shelter him from the snow,
     an I know it's in the morning
     on the road we'd have to go.

4   Oh many's a time upon the road
     my horse, he cast a shoe.
     Up tae the smitty I would gang,
     to the smitty man I knew.
     "I cannot buy a new shoe,"
     to the smitty man, I'd say:
      "Oh put me on an auld one,
     Ah'm sure it will have to dae."

5   Noo those happy days they're gone and past,
     I've bought a motor car.
     Sure, I go drivin on the roads,
     Ah'm sure I travel far.
     I drive past all those places,

but I'll come to you and I'll say:
"I'll never be as happy as I was
with my old horse and me."

(87DW08 @ 1:11:13.)

My Old Horse and Cart

verse 2

Fraem A - ber-deen tae Gal - lo-wa we tramped the coun - try wide.

Frae E - din-burgh doon tae Stran-raer and roon the banks o Clyde.

The roads, they were nae lang for him, nor yet too lang for me.

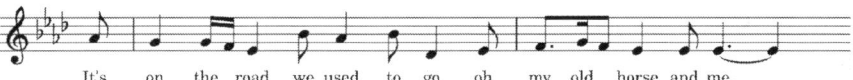

It's on the road we used to go, oh, my old horse and me.

Chapter 8

THE HOW AND WHY OF STORYTELLING

§8.1. THE STORY OF GRANNY'S PURSE*

♫

After Ah left home at the age of sixteen, I worked for two [years] as a dry stone builder. And I was collectin tales which are in my silkie book* which were told to me by nontravelling folk. Not Travellers at all, just the local crofters an builders an fishermen in these stories. And Ah started to travel at the age o sixteen. I travelled all over, but my main ambition was to find as many tales—Ah had an obsession in stories of all descriptions.

And Ah still tell these stories today. They never change. The same stories are still alive, and it gives me a great privilege tae tell the stories about people who are dead, because in our family tradition, wir travelling people never dies. Well, I mean, the body dies, but the spirit disn't die. Because when Ah tell a story of a man who had told me the story, Ah can visualize him in ma memory, still there, still the same person, still alive, tellin me the story. Every single word Ah'm repeatin as if he was jist sendin me a phone message through his memory tae me at the present moment. Now, how can I find him dead? How could someone be dead when he could sit there beside me an say to me, "Tell my story"? And I'll tell his story tonight that he told me thirty years ago, and I visualize him sittin there by the fireside.

I can visualize my Granny settin there with a wee bit pipe in her mouth. You know, she smoked the pipe, this wee clay pipe. She smoked a wee clay pipe, and she'd sit there, and she'd say, "Now," she said, "son, I'll tell ye a wee tale." Because Granny was a wonderful woman. She was very old when she died. And we used tae go for two pennysworth o tobacco to her. You know, a pennysworth in these days was a lot, but not like anything now. She used to put it in her pipe, and she had this wee clay pipe, an she'd just set there, and I'd say, "Granny, tell us a story."

Now there's a wonderful experience I would like you tae hear. This is something you'll never hear in a million years.

Now, my grandmother was very old, an she stayed with us for many, many years. And in those old and bygone days, they never carried a purse or a hand-bag. They had a belt around their waist, like my belt here, and on the side they kept a pocket, like a holster for holdin a gun. They made this theirself. And it was a large pocket—and they put shell buttons on it—made of tartan. And they put it on their belt. They took it off at nighttime when they went to sleep, round their skirt or their kilt or whatever they wore. And Granny used tae say to me, "Put your hand in the pocket and give me a penny and go for some tobacco," or whatever she needed. And when we came back, we said, "Granny, tell us a story," for goin for a message for her.

"Well," she says, "I'll go an look in my pocket an see. I'll get ye a story." And she would tell us a story from her pocket, ye see? And accordin to us little children, all the stories were in Granny's pocket, right?

So one day, ma sister Jeannie and me, who was aboot two years younger than me, we came up, and there, in Granny's part [of the tent], she fell asleep on her bed.[1] It was jist grass, a grass bed, ye know, of heather an grass. But she took off her belt and her pocket, and she placed it aside her, Holly. So, ma sister Jeannie and me pulled back the flap, an there was grandmother lyin—just a bundle o wrinkles, ye know; she was just that size, ye know. A wrinkled old woman, jist like one o those old Indian women you see. And there was the pocket on the floor. Just a airthen floor polished hard, hard dry airth. We said, "Come on!" We tuik the pocket, an we tuik it behind a tree, and we opened it up, luikin for stories, see? [*General laughter.*]

Now I'll tell you what was in the pocket. There were thumbles. There were pieces o thread, pieces of pipe, bits of tobacco, ha'pennies, verdegris ha'pennies, pennies, thrupenny pieces, bits o thread, needles, buttons. Not one single story could we see in the pocket! [*More laughter.*] We never touched nothing. We looked in, we put it back, closed it with a button. There were no zips in these days. We walked in. She was still asleep. We placed it doon by her side. We went out to play in the hillside, you know, climbin the trees and quarries an these things. Then we came back about four o'clock. Granny was up. She was just nae very tall; she was only four foot two high an she must've had eight great sons who fought in the—she lost two sons in the First World War. Great big sons she had, and her husband was a piper. He died the day I was born, 1928.

So anyhow, Granny says, "Come here." And she—intae her pocket, you know, and she took oot a couple o pennies, an she said, "Run down to the village an get me a bit tobacco for my pipe," you know? We ran down to the village, tobacco for her pipe, ye know? Now Granny's quarters was private. Nobody was allowed in there except a storytellin session. But it wasnae small, it was

---

1. Here Williamson points to a diagram he has made depicting his family's large, compound win-ter tent with its separate sleeping compartments, one of which was for his grandmother.

big, you know, bigger than this room. An she had her bed, an she had her wee bit o clothes, and she had everything she needed, and all these luttle things in the corner. She was ma mother's mother, an we loved her dearly.

So we ran down, my sister Jeannie an I, and we got a penny's—Now, in these bygone days, they had these what you call bogie rolls o tobacca. And it was a long roll of tobacca, round a wheel. And the old man in the local shop would pull a wee bit, and cut a wee bit, and if it was too much long for the people who bought the tobacco, he'd take another wee bit off, and he'd fling the wee piece he cut off in a drawer. And Granny would say, "Go and buy all the wee bits that he'd cut off," you see. So I'd go tae the old shopkeeper and say, "Give me a penny's worth of tobacco for Granny"—a poke—and he would pick out half a dozen o the wee bits and put them in. "Take it up to grandmother," and he'd twist it round like that. We run up and said, "Granny, here's your tobacco." And she would full her pipe, ye know, and she'd puff away at this wee scraped bit.

"Granny," I said, "tell us a story now." That's all we had. No radio, television; we wanted a story. Because she's travelled all over Scotland, ye know?

"Well," she says, "I'll tell you something. I'll see what's in the pocket." She said, "I'll see if there's a story left." (Now, she had told us many stories. Ah still tell her stories today. Ah mean, "The Laird and The Crane"* you heard last night was one of her favorite stories.) She opened the pocket. She had it on her when we come back, cause the first thing the old travelling women did was, when they got up from bed, they put on their shoes, and then they put their pocket on their waist. She opened the button; pearl buttons on it, ye know; made of tartan. It was about that size, that broad, and that long [gestures], and it held all these things, ye know. She opened the pocket. An she turned round, and I swear on my mother's grave, I won't tell you a lie. She said, "Look, children," she said, "I'm sorry. I can't tell you any more stories." (Now she was asleep, she was definitely asleep when we stole her pocket. We put it back, we never touched nothing.) She says, "Somebody opened ma pocket, and all the stories escaped."

All: [Some laughter amid some exclamations of dismay.]

I swear on my dear mother's grave if I'm tellin you a lie, I swear on my mother's grave.

CE: Oh, no! I bet you felt terrible.

She says, "Every story has escaped." And frae that day on, my grandmother had never told us one single more story. Now, that is the God's honest truth.

CE: Oh, my!

Figure 8.1 The storyteller's eyes tell a story. The storyteller himself is transformed from his ordinary self into something more nearly otherworldly—"the broonie," as his friends used to say, only half in jest. Auchtermuchty, Fife, 1986. Photo by Leonard Yarensky.

On my mother's grave I swear. From that day on, my Granny had never told us one single more story, because we tuik her pocket while she was asleep and luiked at it behind a tree and opened it.

CE: Didn't you feel terrible?

I felt horrible! We destroyed the nicest thing we ever had in wir life. But we were never—

CE: You were just curious.

We were just curious. I was about nine, an Jeannie, ma sister, was aboot seven, two years younger than me. And we'd never done anything wrong. This is the first time that we'd ever got a luik in Granny's purse. This is what happened. And from—I was nine. She never told us another story, and she was ninety-five when she died.

(86DW04 @ 02:23.)

§8.2. OLD JOHNNY MACDONALD THE STORYTELLER*

JN: Duncan, I wanted to ask you about another person you learned a lot of stories from. This is Old Johnny MacDonald.

"Auld Toots," we called him.

JN: Would you tell me who he was?

Old Johnny MacDonald was in the 1914 War, and he'd been disabled in the war. He had never married in his life, an he went with two walkin sticks cause he was cripple. He had a pension from the army. Now, he had many relations, but he stayed with Travellers, and he was a great storyteller. And he got his keep and he got his bed for takin care o the children while the people was out workin.

JN: Right.

And he took care of the horses, an he went an fed the horses, even though he had two sticks. And at nighttime he was a great storyteller. Old Johnny Mac-Donald. He never married in his life, never had a wife in his life, an he died when he was aboot seventy-five years old. And if Johnny was around, people would take him along wi them for the sake of watchin the kids. He was a great man for children. They called him "Toot-toots," or "Toot," or "Toots." He used to bend down on his two staffs, and he was the engine, and all the children would hang on tae his coattails, and they'd make a train!

JN: [Laughs.]

And the more children he got wi him, the better. And he'd go, "Toot-toot, toot-toot! Here we go!"—on his two staffs. And he would play wi these kids, he would tell them stories, an if you wanted anyone tae care—he was what you'd call a babysitter. Right. Well, he got his meals, he got his food, and he got his bed, and everyone loved Old Johnny MacDonald.

And when nighttime—when the men come back from their work, sat down—"Tell us a story, Johnny." Ah mean, Ah travelled two and a half mile among snow, tae there above my knees [*gestures*], for one story! For tobacca for his pipe.[2] He was a great man to smoke, he liked his tobacco. He was fond of tobacco, and, eh—if you had anything, any possession on ye—a good belt, he loved a good belt, or a good pocketknife—"You gie me that, and I'll tell ye

---

2. "For tobacca for his pipe": that is, Duncan went for tobacco for Johnny in exchange for Johnny's telling him a story.

Figure 8.2 The storyteller's eyes, close up, Auchtermuchty, Fife, 1986. Photo by Leonard Yarensky.

a good story." Ye know what I mean? He was a wonderful old man, yeah, Old Johnny MacDonald.

JN: Can you think of any particular stories you learned from him?

Aye, he told many stories; he told hundreds o stories. He could—you see, he travelled among the Travellers, and he collectit stories. He cuidnae read or write, but he was like me, and hears everything. He had haird stories—"Did ye ever hear this one, Johnny?" He spent time among the Stewarts, he camped among the Whytes in Aberdeenshire, he spent time in Argyllshire among the Townsleys and Williamsons, he spent time in Glasgow among the Reids and the Camerons and the MacPhees. And he cried tae all their stories,[3] and he told their stories over again. Ye see what I mean?

JN: Right, right. Can you think of any specific ones you tell that you learned from him?

There's some there in my books I learned from him. Some of the stories in Penguin are told by him. "La Mer la Moocht" is one o his stories, and "The Happy Man's Shirt."* That's where I heard it the first time, was Old Johnny.

(87DW13 @ 49:36.)

---

3. "He cried to all their stories": that is, he listened intently to their stories.

Figure 8.3 Williamson telling a story while his son Thomas listens, Kincraigie Farm Cottage, 1986. Photo by Leonard Yarensky.

§8.3. ANOTHER REMARKABLE STORYTELLER, JOHNNY TOWNSLEY

Johnny Townsley; they called him "Monkey John."* He's dead now, God rest his soul. He was a dear old friend o mine. That was the man that sat wi me an my cousin an my brother from ten o'clock at night till six o'clock in the mornin an told us stories the whole night through, nonstop. He told us stories about his family, he told us stories about the 1914 War, he told us stories of when he was a child, he told us stories—we made more tea, smoked more cigarettes, some more tea. Six o'clock in the mornin, he was still goin, under this big bush, with a firecan under the tree. A place called Burntisland*; that's no far [from] where Sir Patrick Spens went doon. And he told stories nonstop fae ten o'clock at night till six o'clock in the mornin, Old Johnny Townsley. He was one of my informants I got many stories from. And, eh, I kept in wi him after that, and I lairned many stories from him, ye know?

JN: So you travelled with him?

I travelled with him, aye. He was a great basketmaker. His wife died an left him with two boys, an the boys grew up, and, eh, they went off an got married. And he kept his own wee camp, and he would stay along with Travellers because he liked to get his wee bits of stuff hurled in a cart, ye see? So I'd say, "Come on, Johnny, come along wi me for a while." And I would carry his bundle for him, and his tent, and his bits o things that he needit, and he would pitch his tent beside us, and he would do his own shoppin an make his own tea. An he was a good company at nighttime, just a good entertainer. And he would make his baskets and he'd go off an sell em. Well, he came along and would maybe stay with me for a week, and then he'd move off and stay with some other family, see what I mean?

(87DW12 @ 1:18:28.)

§8.4. ON STORIES AND THEIR EDUCATIONAL VALUE, AND ON TELLING THEM IN THE SCHOOLS

Well, you see, stories were our life, Jack, because we had nothing else. Cause we were very, very poor, and tae have a large family an a tent in these long winter evenings, have maybe, say, ten–twelve children—what were ye goin to do wi them? We had no radio, no television, no nothing. On the long, cold winter nights sittin around the fire, you needed some entertainment tae keep the children quiet. So Father would say, "I'll tell you a story."

Now the reason these stories were told to the travelling children was not actually just as a form of entertainment. These stories was also learned tae teach and educate the children, because they were stories of everything they need to be taught.

I mean, you had Jack Tales.* Jack was a hero. Jack was a underdog. Sometimes he was a rogue, but he was always good. And it doesn't matter what his name was, he was always Jack! Father wanted sons tae grow up like Jack. Then there was stories of princesses an that for the girls. There were animal tales, talkin animal tales, for the young children, which taught them to live and learn animals of nature and to love and respect nature, and love an respect animals of all kinds.

So this is what the children was taught. I mean, my children—Ah've told stories—they jist *love* animals. Everything that crawls, moves, or jumps is to them something nice an something to appreciate. I mean, they wouldnae hurt a fly. If they find a spider in the house, they'll carry it an take it outside. This is what were taught. And on the roadways, when we travelled along the roadways in these bygone days, we weren't even allowed tae pull a flower. It was a sin an a disgrace tae pull one single flower, or even hurt a butterfly on the way. This was something tae be respected. And that was the education that was taught to the travelling children. I mean, they were taught from nature. They were natural as the hare.

And, eh, they had all these wonderful stories when the children were small. And when the younger children went tae sleep, then the older children joined in tae the Travellers' own stories, like for grownups. And oncet a child came thirteen, let it be a girl or boy, if the parents didn't mind, then they could set around the fireside and listen to these tales, which were educational to them forbyes.

An Ah haird many, many stories as a child. An ma interest grew as I got older. An I started travelling all over Scotland, and everywhere my ambition was tae collect all these wonderful tales. And after many years collectin stories, someone said to me—especially from the School of Scottish Studies, like Alan Bruford and Hamish Henderson—"What's going tae happen tae all your stories when you're gone? You're no goin tae be roaming around *all* the days o your life."

I said, "I know that."

"So, why don't you try and put them in book form, so that someone you've never met can read some of your stories?" So I thought it was a wonderful idea. So we started publishin these stories in book form so someone who I had never met could read these stories.

But ma main ambition is tae go around the schools an meet the children, an find out what kind of material the children are getting in *their* day an age, apart from material that I got in *my* time an age. So I try my best to bring them back to my life, when I was a child, and also tae find out the kind o material that they're gettin right now, like television an radio an all these videos an things, what exactly they mean to a child, and then I compare that with *my* childhood. And I make a report for the Arts Council at the end o the year. And also I search out tae find, at this day an age, young children, especially in the schools, could they give me a version of any old story that they could tell me? Something they were told from their grandmother, or their uncle or auntie. And then tae see if this story that they have told me has got anything tae do with any o the tales that I have haird.

So, in Islay, in this school in Islay, one little boy about five years old stuid up, and I asked him up and he told me a story, just a short story. And I had haird many versions of that story in Aberdeenshire, in Argyllshire, and in many other wonderful places. An it told a story about a man with his dog: a piper, goin intae this cave in the rock face during the nighttime for a shelter. He saw a light there, and he walked in wi his bagpipes, an he had his dog with him. An the dog came out but [with just] one piece o hair on the dog. But the piper never came out.[4] Now we find that story in Argyll, we find it in Aberdeenshire, Invernesshire, but that was the only time that I ever had the chance to hear it from a non-Traveller child. So it goes to show ye that there's still a little tradition goin on among the young ones coming up, which is a wonderful thing.

---

4. Several tape-recorded variants of this story, as told in either Gaelic or English, can be heard via Tobar an Dualchais through a search for "The piper's cave."

JN: So you do some collecting as well as telling?

All in my head. I don't write nothing down. I don't use books or pencils or nothing. I compose an write songs of the travellin folk, and, eh, I need to write *them* down, because I'll maybe have tae pass on a copy to them for to learn the song. But I never write no stories down. I always collect them in my head.

Up here [*pointing to his head*] I've got over three thousand tales, all in their own little boxes. And when Ah want to tell a story, I just tune onto that story, and that story will not get mixed up with any other story. Ah pick the story, like you goin up there and pickin a tape from the wall and puttin it on. Nothing can interfere with that story. The pictures in that story just come floatin into your mind, one after the other, till the story is completely finished. An then it goes back on the shelf for the next time. And the more you tell it, there's no more changes in it. You see the pictures in that story completely, and that story remains fixed in your mind.

JN: So it's more like a video than a tape recording, in a way? What is it, the images more or the words, that hold—?

The pictures, mostly. The images comin into your mind. I try my best to bring the listeners—to get them to *see* what they're listenin to, and put their mind into the story themselves. That's why I get so many wonderful pictures from schools.

JN: What is this you do with pictures in the schools, Duncan?

When I go to the schools, I tell some stories to the children. Different stories for different classes. And I have a competition in schools, and I get the certificates made in Edinburgh tellin em that they've won first prize, second or third prize, for the picture of the story they've haird. An they get a prize and a certificate signed by me tellin them they've won a prize. Now they must draw a scene from the story as they see it in their mind. And you believe me, I have many wonderful pictures!* I must have over eight hundred at the present moment. And not only pictures, but stories forbyes. If they don't want to draw a picture, then they'll write me a story. But the story—they must make it up themselves. I don't want anything from television; I just want some period in their life where something took place that happened.

(86DW14 @ 09:16.)

§8.5. MORE ON STORIES AS A FORM OF EDUCATION

MJ: I wondered about the children's stories, whether you used those stories to teach the children things that you believed?

That's what it all was about, sweetheart. That's what the stories were about. Because, I mean, Jack was the Jack tale. And suppose his name was Tom, Dick, or Harry, it was always Jack. And Daddy wantit the son to grow up like Jack, you know? In some of the stories, Jack was a lazy layabout. Sometimes he was a hero. He was a great strong man, like Jack the Giant Killer. And there's hundreds and thousands of stories about Jack. But Daddy always wanted his son tae grow up like Jack. And Jack always come out best at the end, ye know? He never was a failure. And this is how the Jack stories were.

Now, there were stories about—for the little children, the kindergarten type, ye know—always about talkin animals. And the idea of these animal tales among the children was that when the children grew up, they would be kind to animals. There's not one Traveller child I have ever known in my lifetime has ever hurt an animal in their lifetime. In no way. They wouldn't even hurt a fly. If Tommy sees a spider crawlin about on our floor—sometimes they comes in out o the cold—he says, "Daddy, there's a spider, don't hurt him, just pick him up an put him outside," ye know? They wouldn't hurt a butterfly. And that's the truth, because they were taught so many animal tales when they were children. I think it's a nice way tae grow up, ye know? To respect life in all forms. And that was the idea of these stories that was told tae them.

(86DW23 @ 02:40.)

§8.6. STORIES TEACH YOU LESSONS YOU WILL ALWAYS REMEMBER

As children there were many codes to live by. There were many do's and not-do's,* ye know what I mean? You can do this but not do that. Noo, when it comes tae stories—stories, as I tell you, was a matter o teachin.

Ye see, when Jack had problems, in his story—when your father was tellin you a Jack tale—well, he also told you how Jack got out of his problem. Well, if you were to listen tae the stories, you could get out o the problems the way Jack got out o his problem. To *think*: "What do I do next?" You see what I mean? And these stories was tellt for teachin you.

In your life, your father'd say when you got out intae the world, "You are just a Jack." That's what he was in the story. You got out there in this strange world, you don't know nobody. You go to another country, you don't know nobody. What did Jack do when he went intae another country? He had to make his

Figure 8.4 At home at Kincraigie Farm Cottage, with children's illustrations of his stories set out on the mantel. Photo by Leonard Yarensky.

way just same as you. He had tae find friends; he had tae find food; he had tae meet new people; he had problems in his journeys, in his travels. An he had to cope with them. So that's what you've got to do when you go out in this world. You see, you'll have your problems. You may not cope with them the way Jack done, but you have to *think* about it.

JN: Did your father ever make that connection for you, or is this your own?

No, our father told us that, in the story. That was your teachin. That's the reason these stories was told tae you in the first place, tae teach you things, ye know? Teach you. He knew, you see—[take] you yourself. Someday you'll have a problem when Alan grows up.[5] Tellin him something, it's in one ear an oot the other! You know, they won't pick it up so quick. But when you sat—when they sat down in a company of old Travellers, and [they] told their story, you would listen. Because it also was a story with a bit of entertainment in it, and they knew you would listen tae the story and lairn the teaching from the story, when you wouldn't listen to the teacher by him tellin you these things.

So that's what stories were for. And animal stories for children were the most important for the wee ones. How tae look after a wee animal. Because they believe that if children can be good to animals, then they'll grow up tae be good people. See what I mean? Because that's where it all starts: little creatures,

---

5. "When Alan grows up": the reference is to the author's four-year-old son.

you know? Boys are taught not to throw stones at birds or hurt little creatures. Only kill a rabbit or something if you need it tae eat, or kill a fish.

(87DW04 @ 1:26:40.)

§8.7. EVERYONE IS A STORYTELLER

HT: I don't think of myself as a storyteller.

Darling, *everyone* is a storyteller. Listen, OK, look at it this way. Say you went out and you're drivin your car and you got in a small accident. You reversed into someone, and somebody's upset. And when you went back home to your daddy and mammy and you're tellin them what happened: you were tellin them a story, weren't you?

HT: Uh-huh, yeah.

Everybody's a storyteller at heart. A long story is only a larger extension of a short story. You could go there today and you could walk into the village,[6] and you could reverse your car into someone, an they'll break your light. Or you could meet someone you never know.

HT: Yeah, I can imagine that.

A story happens from the minute you wake up in the mornin till you go to bed at night. Everything is a story. It's a story you being *here*.

HT: Yeah! I wonder, Duncan, do you think a lot of these traditional stories that you tell actually came from—just like that, from somebody having an experience?

That's true. That's what the minstrels done a long time ago. They walked in away begging with a bag on their back, and they sang their experiences tae the castle for food as an entertainment. And then, lo and behold, it became a story. All these wonderful ballads you can hear today were performed by the minstrels a long time ago as just a collection of what happened in their day-to-day experiences. They spent an overnight with someone. They says, "My son has been lost at sea. My wife is so—my daughter is so upset." [*Sings a phrase of a favorite song:*]

> "It's seven long years"—*

---

6. "The village": that is, the nearby village of Strathmiglo, Fife.

The minstrels wrote that, you see. They made it. They were great composers although they had little knowledge of music. They added the tunes; they done the words first. And then they jist—anything that came intae their head is a tune, like what Ah do. Anything that fits the words is a tune. Suppose it's been a mixture of nine different tunes in one moment. That's what the minstrels done. And they collectit stories and they collected anything, any kind o material. And then when they came tae this laird's castle, they stayed three and five and six weeks at a time, entertainin the guests in the castle.

HT: Uh-huh.

There were jugglers, tumblers, ye know, and there were club throwers and all these things. And then, late at night, there were the storytellers. There were the singers and there were minstrels, and they told a story.

(86DW29 @ 39:40.)

§8.8. ON TELLING STORIES IN THE DIALECT IN WHICH YOU HEARD THEM

♪♫

I thought, for tomorrow, I would tell Ross's story "A Bag o Salt" at the competition.*

JN: Ross Noble's?

Yeah. I promised him I would. He said, "Will ye tell my story at the competition this year?" Ah said, "I will." He tells my stories, so it's good for me tae tell—and Ah'll explain how I got it from.

JN: How is that "his" story?

He told it tae me. Cause I never knew it till he told me. I never read it of a book. Where Ross got it, I don't know, but he told it tae me sittin in his car, an that is oral tradition. It has been passed on from him tae me. See, it's not read in a book. That's what you call oral tradition. It's really good. And I'm telling Ross's story tomorrow. But in *my way*, not his way. It has to be my way. The theme of the story, I will not change nothing, but probly the words an the tongue will probly change. Cause I'll probly tell it in Aberdeenshire tongue. I might tell it in a Buchan tongue, or I might tell it in the West Highland tongue. It only depends on the audience I've got.

JN: Can you change it just like that?

Yeah, sure. I can talk many, many different accents when I feel like it. When I tell a Highland tale, I tell it . . .[7] Aberdeenshire story, Aberdeenshire tongue. Buchan story, Buchan tongue. See what I mean? Gaelche story, Gaelche tongue.[8] Border story, the Border tongue. Cause Ah've been around and Ah've spent my life with these people, an I know how they speak. I know how they talk. . . .[9] "Now I would like to tell you about this tale, especially told to me a long time ago, and by my grandmother, and it's a wonderful story." See, this is the idea. I'm not tryin tae copy the folk. I'm jist tryin tae tell the story the way it was told tae me, Jack. This is the idea.

JN: Right. Exactly.

To get the actual effect: what it was like tae hear the story for the first time. And it's magical when you hear the effect o the story as it was told for the first time, ye know?

JN: So do you think about that time when you first learned the story yourself, when you're telling the tale? Like tomorrow, if you're telling this story—

I am there where I haird it first. I'm back where I begun. I just reverse myself an go back to where I heard it. Everything comes as clean—the picture is as pure as crystal, from the very first day that I heard the tale.

(86DW29 @ 43:58.)

§8.9. THE STORYTELLER'S WHOLE BODY TALKS:
"THE SILENCE WAGER"*

Old Patrick an his old wife Bridget, they lived in a little Irish farm in the hills of Connemara, nae much bigger than a croft. They kept a couple o cows an a couple o calves, and they sold the calves in the wintertime, an they had hens an a couple o goats. But they lived up in the hillside, it was aboot three or four

---

7. There is a short break in the recording here as the tape reverses direction. Duncan was evidently about to say "in Highland tongue."

8. "Gaelche": this appears to be Duncan's term for a story told in the Scottish Gaeltacht: that is, the part of Scotland historically associated with the use of Gaelic as a first language.

9. Here Duncan gives two examples of northeast dialect, not transcribed here, followed by the following example in the lilting tones of West Highland speech.

hundred feet above sea level. And they had tae walk doon the hillside every day for the water. Noo this was always a source of an argument: who was going tae go fir the water. And the argument never stopped.

So one day they got a visit fae the priest. And they were busy arguin away as usual, who was going tae go fir the water. She says, "Patrick, it's your turn." He says, "Bridget, I went the last time. It's your turn!"—when the priest arrived.

The priest he says, "What's goin on here?"

He says, "You know the problem. We're always arguing who's goin tae go fir the water. Bridget never takes her turn. She depends on me all the time tae go fir the water."

"Well," the priest said, "this cannae go on. You'll have tae settle a pact between youse."

"Well," he says, "what do you mean?"

"Well," he said, "can youse no come to an agreement of some kind?"

"Well," he said, "what do you think?"

"Well," said the priest, "can you sing?"

"No really," he said. "We dinnae sing very much."

"Can you whistle?"

"Ach, no," he said. "We dinnae whistle very much."

"Well," he says, "you must do something!"

"Och, aye," he says. "Bridget and me, we do the mouth music sometimes."

"Well," says the priest, "I'll tell what we'll do wi ye. We'll set a challenge between youse. And youse'll do a diddle on the mouth music, and," he says, "them that stops first, it disnae matter what you're doin, workin, anything," he says, "you must keep goin on the same tune. And the one that gives up first," he said, "that's the one that goes to the water for a full year."

So Patrick and Bridget thought that was a good idea. "Now," he said, "use any tune you like, any tune you like."[10]

So then after the priest left they started. Bridget started:[11]

A rúm di doodle dúm dideley dóodle dum
di dóoden dadden dídden dadden dúm di doodle
dúm di doodle dúm di doodle dídeley doodle dúm,
a rúm di doodle déedle dadden dóoden dadden dóo—

She went and stirred up a bowl for makin the pancakes and the scones:

---

10. The tune that Duncan employs when diddling the main part of this story is "The Old Beggar Man," a favorite among Irish musicians in particular.

11. The following notations are only a rough guide to Duncan's diddling, which presents a challenge to any transcriber since the pace is just about as rapid as possible. Stressed syllables are marked with an acute accent.

> Ha rúm da doodle déedan daddan dóodan daddan dóo,
> a dóodan deedan déedan daddan dóodan daddan dóo,
> rum ba dóodan daddan dóodan daddan déedan daddan dóo—

She's up there at the table:

> A rúm di doodle dúm di doodle dóodle dadden dóo,
> a dóoden dadden dóoden dadden déeden dadden dóo,
> a dóoden dadden dóoden dadden, dóoden dadden dóo—

Patrick's fixing his pipe [*picking up the pace:*]

> Úm da doodle dóodle dadden dóoden dadden dóo,
> a dóoden dadden dóoden dadden dóoden dadden dóo,
> um dóoden da, dóoden da, dóoden dadden dóo—

She says, "Patrick, a mist's coming down, you have to go and get the calves in."
Patrick says, "Right."

> A dúm da doodle déedle daddle dóodle dadden dóo—

He's running through the hills, "Where are these—"

> A dúm da doodle déedle dadden dóoden dadden dóo—

"Where are these calves?"

> A dúm da doodle déedle dadden dóoden dooden dóo—

He wandered doon the hillside:

> A rúm da doodle déedle deeden déeden dadden dóo,
> a déeden dad, dóoden dad, déeden dadden dóo,
> rum da déeden daddan déeden daddan dóoden dadden dóo—

Bridget, she's telling him—"I'd better get these cows back to home and milk
my cows":

> A díddle doodle déedle dadden dóoden dadden dóo,
> a dóoden daddan dóoden dad—

Feeding the hens [*still picking up the pace:*]

> a dóoden daddan déeden daddan dóoden dadden dóo,
> a dóoden daddan déeden daddan déeden dadden dóo,
> rúm diddle dóoden dadden déeden deeden dóo,
> a rúm a doodle déedle dadden dóodle doo—

Now Patrick, he got lost in the hillside looking for his calves, but he's still going on:

> A rúm di doodle déedle daddle dóodle dooden dóo—

A mist came down:

> A rúm di doodle déedle daddle—

"There they is, *ssshhh!* Come on, home ye go—get on wi' youse!"

> Úm da doodle déedle dadden dóoden dadden dóo—

"Where in the hell am I? I'm lost; I cannae see a thing!"

> A rúm a doodle déedle dadden dóoden dadden dóo—

So he saw a light, and he wandered up to the light. He saw a light an a woman sittin milkin a coo:

> Úm da doodle déedle diddle déeden dadden dóo,
> a dóoden dadden déeden dadden dóoden dadden dóo,
> a díng a dooden dádden, dóoden dadden dóo—

He says, "Woman, can you help me? I'm lost!"

> A dúm da doodle déedle dadden dóoden dadden dóo—

She said, "You're no lost, you're home, and you stopped diddling. You go fir the water!"

> Úm da doodle dídden dadden dóoden dadden dóo!

JN: Duncan, that was terrific. Fantastic! That's a good one. And what was that again that you said, that you got that story from Crieff?

Aye, I got it from an old Irishman. An old Irishman at the tatties. They come here for the tatties, the tattie picking time. They come for the tattie picking every year.

(87DW15 @ 23:57.)

Figure 8.5 The storyteller's whole body contributes to the tale. Telling "The Silence Wager" near Ithaca, New York, 1987. Photos by the author. The first photo: the tale begins.

Figure 8.6 Stirring a bowl.

Figure 8.7 Patrick fixing his pipe.

Figure 8.8 Milking the cow.

Figure 8.9 Feeding the hens.

Figure 8.10 Still milking.

Figure 8.11 Tale's end.   **Figure 8.12** A moment after tale's end.

§8.10. BEDTIME STORY, "THE SKELETONS AND THE TINKER"*

♪♫

JN: Duncan, I have a request for you. It's for this lad over here, this boy with the tartan shirt. He's been making a little pile of precious things over here. He'd like one story, and then—whsst!—off to bed, all right? Carole, would you like it to be any special kind of story?

CN: A ghost story.

JN: It has to be a ghost story? A ghost story, right.

Alan, all these people have come tonight to visit you because you're a wonderful little boy, and your daddy is Jack Niles, and your Uncle Duncan has come all the way from Scotland tae see you, and it's just about bedtime, and you are goin to hear a ghost story. Well, it's not actually about ghosts, but skeletons is as close to ghosts as ye can get. All right? [*General laughter; someone says, "Better!"*]

So, then, oncet upon a time, a long time ago in Scotland, there was an old travelling man and his old travelling wife. And they had travelled far, and they had two little boys, just like you. And they travelled through Scotland, pushin a luttle handcart because they didn't have a pony or they didn't have a car, they didnae have nothing. An he said to his old wife, he said, "We'll make wir way to a luttle campin ground. We have been there for many years before." He said, "There we'll pitch wir tent, and we'll make some tea for the children, and," he said, "it will be all right tonight."

They were very happy. They were primitive people that needed very little. So they pushed on their way and soon they came to the camping ground. They put down there, and he said to her, "After we put up the tent," he said, "we'll need to get some firewood for the fire." But they looked all around, and there was no firewood tae be seen. They were not that close to the seaside, because sometimes by the seaside you can get driftwood, but this was a luttle place far from the seaside. So he put up his tent, and he said, "I need tae have a fire."

Then he luiked up an he saw a great big wall along the way, and he saw some trees behind the wall. All the parts of the trees were dead and rotten. He said to his wife, he said, "Look. You pull some grass tae make a nice bed for the children, an I'll climb up the wall and get some sticks for the fire. I can reach these sticks because I'll stand on the wall." But he didn't know that behind the wall was a graveyard.

So she said, "OK, you do that, and I'll make the bed for the children." Because they were very tired, they had travelled far that day.

So then the man went up to the wall, an he climbed up on the wall, and he started breakin the sticks, which were of holly. Holly trees behind the graveyard. And then he haird—"*Clickety-clock, clickety-clack, clickety-click*"—in the graveyard![12] An he looked over, and there were three skeletons, and they were fightin each other. With their skinny legs, an their faces, and—markin the ground between each other—three skeletons fightin in the graveyard. Two to one! [*General laughter.*] The two of them was tryin to beat the youngest one, who was smaller than the three.

"By God," said the travelling man, "this is no fair!" "Two to one!" he said. "My father and mother taught me it's not fair, not fair!" [*More laughter.*]

So he spat on his hands [*claps hands and imitates spitting on them*], and he broke a bit of holly from the hedge, and he jumpit down intae the graveyard. And the three skeletons were busy battlin away; they were beatin up the youngest one. He said, "Hey you!" to the skeletons. [*More laughter.*] "This is not fair! Two tae one is not fair!" And he tuik a piece o the holly and he went into battle. An he battled the two big fellows, and he broke their legs and he scattered their bones and he scattered their arms, and he—heads fell in different directions. And then the young one stuid up, and he said, "Thank you very much!"

An then a wonderful thing happened. A little mist came up from the graveyard, and there lay the other skeletons, legs there, hands there, heads there. But

---

12. Here one of the musicians in the room starts making a *clickety clack* sound in the background, using a wooden puppet with jointed legs to "dance" the beat on a flat board.

the youngest one, he stuid up, and he became the form of a beautiful young man. An he stuid there and he says, "Old man," he said, "that was wonderful what you done."

He said, "I done nothing." He said, "In my life, you know, among the travelling people, two to one is not fair." He said, "I only helped out," he said, "tae see that you didnae get beat. Ah tuik your part. Two to two's fair."

And the young man said, "You don't know nothing," he said. "You see these two fellows lyin there? They were my two brothers. And," he said, "they killed me for my money, because my father loved me dearly and I was the youngest of the family." And he said, "They killed me for my money, but before they could get my money," he said, "I hid it where they would never find it, after our parents died. Now," he said, "I could not rest because I never had a chance to save myself. Both of them beat me and battered me to death. Oh," but he said, "they were hung for my killing, but I could not rest in peace. But now," he said, "I can rest in peace, because you have come to help me. And now my soul will rest in peace."

"But you won't go unrewarded," he said, "because I have a great present for you." He said, "Old man, you go back tonight where you're camping in that luttle field, and go back about half a mile, and then you'll come to a great pine tree that leads up to my farm. That's been sold to someone else now, but," he said, "when you go up tae the pine tree, take two steps forward, an you'll come to a draw well. Go down intae the draw well, as it's dry, and in the very bottom stone," he said, "you'll pull it out, and you'll find all my fortunes." He said, "I hid them there from my brothers. They tried tae make me tell where it was, but I wouldn't tell them, so they killed me, and they were hung for killing me. But," he said, "I could not rest because I never had a chance, because they beat me two to one. But now I can rest in peace. But you go back tonight," he said, "an there you will find my fortune. It's yours forevermore."

And then the skeleton was gone. The graveyard was quiet; the bones disappeared, an the old man rubbed his head an he said, "Was I—did I fall asleep in here?" And he luiked up at the wall, and he saw the trees, and he had the good stick in his hand, an he said, "It must have took place."

So he gathered a few sticks and went back to his wife an the campfire, an he kindled up a fire, an his wife made some supper for the children, and they went off tae bed. But he cuid not rest. He said, "Is that story really true? I must prove tae myself if it really took place." And he said, "I'm going for a walk."

She said, "Don't leave me here! I'm afraid," she said, "wi the children, because body snatchers might come along."*

He said, "Don't worry about body snatchers; they'll not bother you."

He walked back about a mile, an then he came to a big pine tree. An he walked up tae the pine tree, ten steps from the farm road, and sure enough, he came to a draw well. And he luiked in the draw well. It was dry, there was no water in it. So he climbed down the draw well tae the last stone, and he pulled the last stone out, and he found an old box. And it was full of gold pieces! He said, "I never been asleep; I never been dreamin. I really did meet two skeletons in the graveyard!"

And he tuik all this old money and he tuik it home to his wife. He did not tell her one single thing. He wrapped it up, and he put it in his little handcart, and he travelled on the next day. They packed up the tents, and he put the box in the bottom of his little handcart, and they travelled on throughout the village. An he walked on, an he said to his wife, he said, "I never made any baskets for you today; you've nothing to sell."

"Well," she said, "how are we going to have food? How are you going to keep your children? You're a lazy man!" she said. "I wish I'd never married you in the first place!"

Well, they walked up, and there were a sign "For Sale." A great mansion house was for sale in the village. He looked and he said, "Ah," he said, "I think that would do me." [*Laughter.*]

She says, "What do you mean?" She says, "A house? In the village, among all these people?" She says, "That would cost thousands of pounds."

He said, "Well, I'm tired of wandering. I'm tired of roaming, and," he said, "my children needs to go tae school."

She said, "Look, stop tellin these stories. Why didn't you make something for me tae sell tae get some food for the children?"

He said, "I'm goin to buy that house."

"You?" she said. "Buy that house?" She said, "You're crazy!"

He said, "No, I'm not crazy."

So he walked in an he bought that beautiful house, and he put his children tae school, an he lived happy all his life. And these big boys grew up, and they went to college and they became wonderful men. But they never knew that they had tae give thanks to a skeleton who their daddy had defended in a cemetery, a long time ago.

JN: [*Speaking in joking fashion:*] And that's a true story.

And that's a true story. [*Laughter and applause.*]
[*Speaking to Alan:*] Did you like that story?

AN: *Yeah.*

Any questions? [*Speaking to the group:*] Any questions you'd like tae ask? What do you think took place in that graveyard? What do you think? Did that really take place, or did that really happen? What do you think, Alan? Was it true? [*General laughter.*] It wasn't true??? How was it not true?

AN: Because, because—skeletons aren't real.

Because skeletons don't die; only human beings die. But skeletons can come back again! You've never heard the story of the dancing skeleton? How about Grayskull? He's a skeleton. Grayskull's a skeleton. You love Grayskull, don't you?*

AN: No. Grayskull's only got a face like a skeleton.

Oh, he's got a *face* like a skeleton. But he's still a skeleton, isn't he?

AN: Un-unh.

He doesn't have a body like a skeleton. Well, you feel my ribs. I'm just like a skeleton. [*Laughter.*] Feel my ribs. Ah'm just a skeleton!

AN: [Laughing.] No, you're not.

OK, off to bed!

JN: Thank you, Duncan! Good night, Alan.

(87DW08 @ 25:58.)

Chapter 9

SCENES FROM A VANISHED WORLD

§9.1. A VISIT TO THE HIGHLAND FOLK MUSEUM

Duncan Williamson was not just a compelling storyteller and an authoritative interpreter of traditional Scottish songs. He was also a creative songwriter, and he was tireless in collecting all manner of lore from the people he met. After decades of camping alongside other Travellers and "having a crack" with people of different breeds,* by the time I met him he had become a font of information regarding the older lifeways of the Scottish travelling people.

Duncan's knowledge of the different regional cultures of Scotland was exceptional. As a child he had travelled with his parents and siblings each summer in the West Highlands, and he spent many summers of his adult life on the road as well. In his more far-flung travels, in the years before he ever took a seat in a plane to visit other parts of the world, he journeyed to Aberdeenshire and other districts in the north and to Dumfries and Galloway in the southwest, while the rhythms of the year regularly brought him from his winter quarters in central or eastern Scotland to his boyhood home in Argyll and back.

To draw on his deep reservoirs of knowledge relating to the Travellers' older way of life, on August 6, 1986, I drove Williamson from his home near Strathmiglo, Fife, to the open-air Highland Folk Museum,* which at that time was located at Kingussie, a few miles south of Aviemore in the north central region of Scotland. Accompanying the two of us were my wife Carole and our young son Alan, while a group of five UREP volunteers accompanied us in a second vehicle. We spent much of that day visiting the Museum's exhibits relating to the Scottish Travellers, with Duncan acting as our informal docent. Special events took place during the day: piping demonstrations, craft demonstrations, and athletic events, including tossing the caber.

Among the Museum's exhibits, side by side with examples of Traveller-made baskets, tinware, horn spoons, scrubbers, and other handcrafted items,

235

Figure 9.1 Helen Beccard Niles at a farm near Flemington, New Jersey, ca. 1948.
Photo by Walter Niles.

were archival photographs documenting Travellers' lifeways during the earlier
decades of the twentieth century. This was a time when camping was generally
permitted on unused ground in Scotland as long as the campers remained law
abiding. The campsites served as staging points for seasonal farmwork or for
the hawking of wares from door to door. The photographers are for the most
part nameless, as are most of the Travellers who are depicted. Some photos of
this kind were made into souvenir postcards sold here and there as records of
a former way of life that was rapidly being superseded.[1]

What follows in the main part of this chapter is a transcription of Duncan
Williamson's tape-recorded comments on certain of these archival photographs. His comments, though brief, were of special value since he was so fully
conversant with the types of scenes that the anonymous photographers had
captured years before. As he remarked to me with a laugh at one point, "See,
it's like readin a book if you know what ye're doin."

Since Williamson's remarks were made impromptu, in two different sessions,
in the midst of many comings and goings, there is a stop-and-start quality to
the following transcriptions that I have not tried to edit away. I have also added
some remarks of my own, whether between square brackets or in supplemen-
tary paragraphs. The photos on which Williamson comments are available for
consultation at the Highland Folk Museum, and duplicates of some of them
are archived at other research centers, including the Elphinstone Institute,

---

1. For an example of such a postcard, see Figure 2.2.

Aberdeen, and the School of Scottish Studies photo archive at the University of Edinburgh. The transcriptions that follow are highly selective, for Williamson commented on many photographs that are not represented here.

As for the sketches featured in the following pages (Figures 9.2 to 9.10), they are line drawings made in 1991 by my mother, Helen Beccard Niles,* modeled after a select number of these archival photos. She produced her drawings in a manner that faithfully represented each scene while also allowing room for the exercise of artistic judgment. This combination of accuracy and artistic freedom is what I was hoping for. Where one of her drawings departs noticeably from the photo that was her model, my Commentary draws attention to this fact. No such differences should stand in the way of one's understanding of Williamson's comments on the photographs on which the drawings are based.

PART 1. FROM THE COLLECTIONS OF THE HIGHLAND FOLK MUSEUM

§9.2. OLD TRAVELLING MAN, CHILD, AND HORSE CART

Figure 9.2 Old travelling man, child, and horse cart. Line drawing by HBN, 1991, based on Highland Folk Museum photo HF2/12/ca.

JN: What are these photos, Duncan? What are we looking at here [pointing to one of the photos on the wall]?

We're looking at a Traveller's encampment here. This one would go back tae about—would take you round to about 1914, this one here. I would think that's about 1914, that one.

JN: How can you tell?

I know by the state of the land, the state of the cart, an the pot, ye know.

JN: Mm-hmm. So it's an early twentieth-century photograph.

This is the oldest picture here. That's the oldest one.

(86DW27 @ 01:32 and @ 04:36.)

Additional comment by JN:

The artist has chosen not to depict two additional children who are visible in the photo on which the drawing is based. The effect of this choice is to focus the viewer's attention on the relationship between the old man and the child, who might well be the old man's granddaughter. To judge from the size of the cooking pot, a fairly large family has set up camp. The cart in the background would normally have been drawn by a horse. If a horse was lacking, family members would have pulled the cart themselves.

§9.3. TWO TRAVELLER FAMILIES CAMPING TOGETHER

Figure 9.3 Two Traveller families camping together. Line drawing by HBN, 1991, based on Highland Folk Museum photo HF 2/11/cb.

Here we have another family get-together. Just two nights—[*corrects himself*]—one night's stay with two tents. Two different families have met and they've come together. Probly relations. They've put the two tents together just for company's sake.

JN: How can you tell that there are two different families there?

Ah can tell there are two different families because there are two different types o tent, you see? This [*in the foreground*] is a different type of tent from that one over there [*in the middle ground*]. No family builds a tent the same way, like no bird builds a nest the same way.

JN: [Laughing.] I see.

(86DW27 @ 06:05.)

Additional comment by JN:
The artist has made no attempt to depict a clothesline, extending to the left in the original photo, on which some clothes have been left hanging out to dry.

§9.4. BOY ASLEEP ON HANDBARROW

Figure 9.4 Boy asleep on handbarrow. Line drawing by HBN, 1991, based on Highland Folk Museum photo HF2/12/da.

Now this is a handcart, Jack. This is a handbarrow, and you know, they made that from old bicycle wheels or anything they had.

JN: A handbarrow.

A handbarrow, right.

◌

This is a winter scene here. He's carryin his camp sticks [*referring to the father, who is not shown in the photo*]. The baby is asleep. This is the camp cover [*pointing to the bundle of canvas at the boy's feet*]. These are the sticks for the tent [*tied to either shaft*], which tells me that he [the father] has more children, he has more children there than this one. This is probably the youngest. Because he has two sets of sticks, meanin he needs two tents. An he has a big kettle, meanin he has a large family. So the mother and father is not in the scene. This [the handcart] is probably made from an old, an old—the wheels is probably from an old invalid carriage, ye know, an invalid chair. And he has put an axle through them and made this little handcart. He'll probably pull this himself.

(86DW27 @ 09:15 and 1:10:35.)

Additional comment by JN:
In the photo on which this drawing is based, the cart is parked beside a fence next to some woods. The artist has omitted the fence and the woods, with their wintry aspect. Not visible in the drawing, but discernible in the photograph on which it is based, is a rod tucked in alongside the wooden sticks. This appears to be the shaft of a snottum, the iron rod with a crook from which a pot or kettle could be hung.

§9.5. TRAVELLER WOMAN OUT HAWKING WITH HER CHILD

Figure 9.5 Woman out hawking goods with her child. Line drawing by HBN, 1991, based on Highland Folk Museum photo HF2/11/aa.

This is a young woman here. She's been out hawkin all day an she's got a baby under her oxter,[2] here, and she's got a bundle on her back. She's been out hawkin. She's just comin home from her day's hawkin.

JN: How can you tell that she's coming home now?

She's coming home because she's got the bundle there all tied up, and she's got the baby well wrapped up, meaning that she's coming home. She's been out hawkin all day and she's coming home.

∾

DC: You said you knew she was coming home because the bundle is all wrapped up. You mean when she was selling things, the bundle would be open or something?

Yeah, well, she's collected what she's got for the day. She's probably food and old clothes in here. And it's tied up and she's walkin. She's coming home with her bundle. She's a beautiful young woman, I'll tell you that.

DC: Would some of the things that she made [that is, that she was carrying] be traded?

She has probably been out hawking tin or baskets or something, and she's packed her bundle for the day coming home.

DC: So sometimes they would get goods in return?

They would exchange, the barter system, yeah.

(86DW27 @ 03:14 and 04:10.)

---

2. "A baby under her oxter": that is, a baby in her arms.

§9.6. TRAVELLER FAMILY ON THE ROAD, WITH PIPES

Figure 9.6 Family of Travellers on the road, with pipes and pushchair. Line drawing by HBN, 1991, based on Highland Folk Museum photo HF 2/12/ba.

And this is a family on the road. They don't have a pony. And this is the mother, father, son and wife, an grandson again. This is probly his mother here [*pointing to the older woman in a shawl*]. This is his wife [*pointing to the woman carrying the child in her arms*]. He's a piper. That's probably either his son or his daughter. He [*that is, the son or son-in-law, the younger man who is pushing the pram*] also plays. He's a piper like his dad. His pipes are packed up on his little perambulator here. That's all the dwellings in there,[3] and there's the canvas [*pointing to the white bundle of cloth*]. They're not carryin any sticks wi them for their tents, so it means it's summertime. It's summertime. They're on their move. You see?

---

3. "That's all the dwellings in there": that is, the family is carrying only one part of the canvas that, in winter, would cover a large tent with multiple sleeping compartments. The people are traveling light.

Just a baby carriage, and these carriages carried a good bit weight. And he's probably got blankets in there, and maybe some cooking utensils.

JN: Mm-hmm.

(86DW27 @ 09:23 and 1:10:07.)

§9.7. TRAVELLER PIPER IN HIGHLAND DRESS

Figure 9.7 Traveller piper in Highland dress. Line drawing by HBN, 1991, based on Highland Folk Museum photo HF2/10/da.

This is a piper, here. He probly has his pipin dress on. He's probly goin off tae play somewhere, at some Games or something. He's probly goin off tae the Games.

JN: He's got his tent in the background, right?

Yeah, but he's probly going off to the Games, tae play at the Games here [*that is, to a Highland Games taking place nearby*].

(86DW27 @ 1:11:03.)

Additional comment by JN:

Both Traveller and non-Traveller pipers have long competed in the Highland Games that take place here and there in Scotland during the summer months. Substantial monetary prizes can be won in some of the Games, along with significant prestige. Pipers generally dress for the occasion, since a judge's impression of their performance can be influenced by their dress and bearing. John Stewart (1870–1955), the father of Belle Stewart's husband Alex, as described by the musicologist Peter Cooke ("The Music of Scottish Travellers" 215), "acquired a considerable reputation as a competing piper, winning a gold medal for pibroch in 1912, and was for a time a member of the pipe band of the Duke of Atholl's Highlanders." As for Alex Stewart himself, he and his close friend Willy MacPhee used to pipe for tourists up the glens during the summer months, dressed for the part. The unidentified piper of Figure 9.7 looks to be the same man as the well-dressed piper featured in an archival photograph facing p. 179 of Timothy Neat's book *The Summer Walkers*. The man in that scene is identified as "Robert Stewart, Aberdeenshire, 1930s."

§9.8. OLD WOMAN, MAN, AND CHILD SEATED BY A FIRE

Figure 9.8 Old woman, man, and child seated by an open fire. Line drawing by HBN, 1991, based on Highland Folk Museum photo HF2/12/ab.

This is the old lady with the tartan shawl here. There's the shawl. These silver skiffers,* they call them, went through the shawl there when she had a baby on her back. That was a traditional way for carryin a child, when they got older, on their back.

(86DW27 @ 10:03.)

Additional comment by JN:
Duncan took this woman to be the same person as the woman with a shawl shown in Figure 9.6. Included in the original photograph on which Figure 9.8 is based is a fourth figure, standing just behind the three shown here. This is a mustached male with cap and neckerchief. The artist's revision of the scene concentrates the viewer's gaze on three people representative of three successive generations: grandmother, son and father, and grandchild. In addition, in the original photo, a kettle is attached to a chain hanging from a tripod, while the fire is located slightly behind the people rather than in front. The artist's changes make for a cozier ensemble.

§9.9. TRAVELLER FAMILY HAVING TEA BY THEIR FIRE

Figure 9.9 Family of Travellers seated at their fireside. Line drawing by HBN, 1991, based on a photo by Angus Stewart in the archives of the School of Scottish Studies, Edinburgh.

Comment by JN:
Since Williamson did not have an opportunity to comment on this image, I will add a few words myself. It is summertime. The father has set up a bow tent close by some woods where firewood ("sticks") would have been available. His wife, whose face is partly obscured by the older boy's dark head of hair, is seated to his right, while clustered closer to the fire are the couple's four children, three boys to the left and a girl to the right. In the original photo (though not in this drawing), a fifth boy, wearing a cap, can be seen in the foreground. Overhanging the fire is a snottum, driven into the ground at an angle so that a kettle could be suspended from the crook. One of the boys holds a mug for tea, another mug has been set down by the fire, and a third mug sits on the ground in front of the girl. The camp has probably been set up for only a night or two.

PART 2. A PAIR OF IMAGES FROM
THE GENTLEMAN REPORT

Helen Beccard Niles made the following illustration (Figure 9.10) on the basis of a photograph included in a government report known to the Williamsons as "the Gentleman Report" (that is, Gentleman and Swift, *Scotland's Travelling People: Problems and Solutions*, 1971). In October of 1987, when Duncan was my guest for a week outside Ithaca, New York, I tape-recorded his comments on a number of photographs included in the Gentleman Report. This proved to be a remarkable experience. Not only was he familiar with most of the camping sites shown in the photos, but he also knew, by name, who certain of the people in the photographs were; he could provide information on their family relations; and he recognized the style of tent they customarily built, among other details relating to these scenes.

Duncan's comments on two of the photographs included in the Gentleman Report are transcribed here.

§9.10. INTERIOR OF A GELLY, CAMPBELTOWN, 1969

Figure 9.10 Interior of a gelly owned by Travellers from Campbeltown, Kintyre. Line drawing by HBN, 1991, based on a photo in Gentleman and Swift, *Scotland's Travelling People* (Plate III, bottom).

Here's another cousin of my mother's, here.[4] This is Geordie Townsley [*the man seated to the left rear*]. This is Campbeltown, doon near Tangy Glen. Now he made that fire—[*pointing to the square firebox*]—see, he's got the fire tidy there. He's got a tin under the fire tae keep it, to keep any sparks.

JN: To catch sparks and ashes.

To catch ashes. He's got—he made this chimney. He made that elbow himself once. And that's a big tent. 'At is a big tent. And that's his wife [*pointing to the woman seated at center rear*].

JN: What would you call this type of tent?

That's a big gelly. That gelly there will hold about—oh, well, Geordie, he's . . . "Tap," we call him, because he used tae wear tap shoes when he played the pipes. We call him "Tap" for a nickname. "Tap Shoes," we call him. That's Geordie. This is his wife, an his wife is a cousin o my mother—that's Geordie Townsley. He's one of the last—oldest Townsleys left in Campbeltown, now.

JN: Is he still living?

Aye, he's still living, yeah. But all his family's grown up. And his wife's still living. I saw Geordie aboot—when did I see him last? I went to a funeral in Campbeltown; it's only been a couple o years ago.

JN: Is there anything special about this tent?

Just the tent—it's a large gelly. Well maintained, well done. Anybody could live in there. When that fire was red at nighttime, the chimney was hot. It was really warm in there.*

JN: You were inside, then?

Ah've been in that tent, yeah.

(87DW11 @ 07:51.)

---

4. "A cousin of my mother's": Duncan's mother was a Townsley, and members of her family regularly camped at Campbeltown, where Duncan visited on occasion.

§9.11. INTERIOR OF A MOTOR CARAVAN OWNED BY TRAVELLERS

Figure 9.11 Interior of a motor caravan owned by a Traveller family from Lanarkshire. From Gentleman and Swift, *Scotland's Travelling People* (Plate III, top). Used by permission.

JN: Let me read you what Hugh Gentleman says at the top of the page here. He says, looking at these two pictures[5]: "Some Traveller caravans are very comfortable and have high standards of interior fittings and finish, as in this one in Lanarkshire in 1970." Then he says about the interior of the Townsley's tent: "In contrast to the comfortable and well-maintained caravan, life in a tent such as this one in Argyll in 1969 is very cramped and unsatisfactory with the homemade stove as the main source of heating and cooking."

If it came to a choice, if I had the choice of living there, I'd prefer that one anytime [*taps the picture showing the interior of the Townsleys' gelly*].

JN: Why is that, Duncan?

That's more comfortable than that [*the motor caravan*]. That's just for show [*that is, the motor caravan is for show*]. 'At's only a box with wheels. It luiks nice, but there's mair comfort in that tent than what you've got in there.

---

5. "He says, looking at these two pictures": the two photos are printed at the top and bottom of plate III of the Gentleman report, between pp. 68–69. The quotation is from the captions at the top of the page.

JN: Why is that, Duncan?

Because this tent is longer, ye can walk about, ye can invite people tae sit in the tent, but that caravan is just for show. That's old Betsy MacDonald's caravan, and that thing cost—oh, that thing would cost thousands o pounds. And it's just a dead weight to pull along. Well, that thing weighed aboot two ton. It luiked nice inside, with all the brass fittins an all, but to live in there—they just bought that for show.

JN: So you would prefer the tent. Do you think you'd be more comfortable there?

I'd be more comfortable in here, yeah. If I had a choice tae live in any o these two places, I would stay in there [*taps photo of gelly.*]

JN: Well, do you think it would be more cramped in the tent or in the caravan?

It'd be more cramped in here [*pointing to the motor caravan*]. When three or four folks sits in there, there's nae room for naebody.

JN: But you could invite any number of people—

Any number. You could have a dozen people sittin in there [*in the gelly*], yeah. You could have a good ceilidh in there by the fire.

(87DW11 @ 09:06.)

Chapter 10

WEBSPINNER

The Book, the Poem, and the Man

---

§10.1. ON THIS BOOK AND ITS POTENTIAL VALUE

The present book has gone through a series of metamorphoses in the course of its making. In the 1980s, when I began work on this project, it was one piece of a larger program of research involving the oral traditions of Britain, Ireland, and North America, with a focus on Scotland in particular. Duncan Williamson proved to be a standout performer, and it did not take me long to realize that a book centered on him would be a granite foundation for that wider program of research. Books written prior to that time by scholars for whom I had a high regard had demonstrated the value of studies that took as their subject a single gifted tradition bearer,* highlighting that person's repertory in the context of his or her life story, and I appreciated the potential value of a study of Williamson undertaken along comparable lines. Moreover, I had little doubt that a study of that kind would honor not just one individual storyteller, but also the Scottish Travellers whose collective experience Williamson was able to articulate in a manner than extended back decades and centuries into the past. By extension, the book would be expressive of the rich cultural heritage of the Scottish people as a whole. That was an aspect of the project that especially appealed to me, for I had come to know Scotland as a land shaped by its people's enormous resourcefulness and resilience, often in the face of sharp adversity. Williamson and other Travellers whom I encountered possessed those qualities of resourcefulness and resilience to an exceptional degree.

In the 1990s, as I continued with this program of research, my attention shifted somewhat to engage with the dynamics of oral narrative across the board. I began to think of Williamson not just as a gifted Scottish tradition bearer, but also as a prime example of human beings as the one hominid that tells stories, and that indeed dwells in a reality that is shaped by the stories that people tell. Drawing on both my Scottish fieldwork and my training as a medievalist and comparatist, I argued in my 1999 book *Homo Narrans* that it is the counterfactual potential of oral narrative—the ability to tell beautiful lies, often set in landscapes that do not literally exist—that offers human beings the prospect of shaping the world that we inhabit, doing so to a far greater extent than any other creature has ever done. Through our ability to invent stories that take place in imagined scenarios, we humans do not just inhabit the world that we live in. We also have the power to use the resources of our imagination to shape ourselves, our societies, and the external world into new forms that have never existed before.

In practical terms, however, this dimension of my research did not go far to advance my projected book on Duncan Williamson. In fact, it retarded progress on it somewhat by diverting my thoughts and energies elsewhere, even if those other directions were closely related. In the meantime, the ground on which I had stood had shifted. This happened first of all in Scotland, chiefly as the result of a rift between Duncan and Linda Williamson that left me somewhat at a loss on how to proceed, seeing that my project depended on collaborations with both of them. But the ground beneath me in North America had shifted as well, as I moved from the West Coast to the Upper Midwest to take up a new academic post with correspondingly new challenges and responsibilities.

The force that eventually turned my energies back to this project, once I had retired from university teaching in 2011, was chiefly guilt: the advance of time and the corresponding encroachment of guilt. I became aware that I would not sleep well unless I did a better job of repaying Duncan Williamson for the hours he so generously spent with me in the 1980s. Younger generations and future generations too, I felt, deserved to hear Williamson's voice more fully, more robustly, and in a more integrative way than was possible by other means. Guilt, in my experience, is not just a pain that gnaws at one's insides. It can also be an ethical force if it induces one to engage with matters that call for redress. So I came back to this book project as one that would serve the double purpose of honoring a remarkable storyteller and balancing the ledgers.

Now that the book is done, I can see it with new eyes. For one thing, it has become Williamson's book more than originally foreseen, for its main substance consists entirely of his own words. As for my own words, they are confined chiefly to its periphery—the initial chapter, the present concluding chapter, and the separate Commentary—where I present information and offer critical perspectives that establish wider horizons for Williamson's songs, stories, and reflections.

More importantly, it is only now that I can fully appreciate the three features of the book that constitute its main achievements, in my eyes.

First and most obviously, the book presents a mediated self-portrait of a remarkable individual tradition bearer, someone whose intelligence and creativity was matched by his personal charisma. Although the impression of Duncan Williamson that is conveyed through the present pages is necessarily a selective one, the book is still, I believe, of a value at least equal to comparable portraits of individual tradition bearers that have seen print in the past. Its worth is enhanced by the fact that the excerpts are all directly based on tape-recorded interviews and represent Williamson's exact words and phrasing, without any refashioning on my part except for the omission of an occasional word, phrase, or passage for the sake of economy. Also contributing to the value of this study is that far from being a stereotypical representative of the "folk," Williamson was a cosmopolitan individual whose character was shaped by his interactions with people from all walks of life. At the same time, he retained a firm sense of who he was in his roots as a Traveller. It seems that in some ways, his voice is the voice of all Scotland, not just that of a member of a persecuted minority. A value-added feature of this book, as it is published now in the present century, is that many of the recordings upon which these printed selections are based can be heard on the searchable Scottish Voices website available through the University of Wisconsin Digital Collections Center. This is not an outcome that could have been foreseen when I first undertook my fieldwork. Williamson thus emerges here in his true character as a man of words—a living voice, not just a source of written transcriptions—and thus as a person who can serve as a prime example of what in *Homo Narrans* I call the "strong" tradition bearer. This is the person, whether a man or a woman, who not only inherits or safeguards an oral tradition but also carries it forward in new forms into the future.

A second achievement of the book resides in its ethnographic dimension. Williamson's anecdotes and reflections command attention not just for their own sake as colorful specimens of the storyteller's art but also because they provide an entry point for understanding the traditional lifeways of the travelling people of Scotland as practiced up to at least the middle decades of the twentieth century. One can learn much here about the particulars of the semi-nomadic way of life of that group of people—funerals, weddings, childbirth, trades and skills, food and medicine, interpersonal conflicts, conflicts with the police, and the like, including such sidelights as how to snare rabbits or lobsters or how to make tinker's tea—with all this information conveyed to the reader not through dry academic prose, but rather through the warm and authoritative voice of a man who lived the life about which he speaks. The book likewise offers manifold insights into the role of music and oral art forms among the Scottish Travellers of Williamson's generation, with numerous examples chosen out to illustrate those performative practices. Of added interest is that most of the passages featured in the book have no published parallels elsewhere of which I know, or only remote ones. While the book is far from constituting an ethnography of the Scottish travelling people of the present day—the tools of a social scientist would be required for that task—its anecdotal contents, relating chiefly to what is now a vanished way of life, have a value to which statistics could never aspire.

The third of the book's main achievements draws us into the realm of psychology, mentality, and values. In selection after selection featured here, Williamson gives expression to a worldview that transcends his individuality or that of any other single person. The worldview in which one is immersed, as soon as one starts hearing Williamson's voice, encompasses and transcends every topic that is introduced here seriatim, whatever interest that topic may have in its own right. And Williamson's worldview stands out in sharp contrast, I believe, to that of most persons born into today's technologically advanced, materially rich, but often morally rudderless societies. This is a topic worth developing in a section of its own.

§10.2. ON WILLIAMSON'S WORLDVIEW

By definition, worldview is a collective phenomenon, one that normally only crystallizes among a group of people over the course of generations. Although I am reluctant to generalize about people and their mindsets across the board, I have no doubt that Williamson was more than a remarkable individual. He was also an informal spokesman for a worldview that was shared widely among the Scottish travelling people of his generation. This worldview, moreover, was rooted in a past whose depths cannot be sounded, for it is an aspect of the evolution of human society itself as a system based on cooperation and mutual support.

In brief, what I am speaking of is the contrast between nonmaterialistic, group-oriented values versus the individualism and commercialism that are taken for granted among many if not most persons living in technologically advanced societies today. If one prefers, one can think of this contrast in terms of the replacement of what the Gaelic storyteller Donald Morrison speaks of as the Clan System by what Morrison terms the Capitalist System.[1] Without laboring those terms, whose relevance to Williamson's situation could be disputed, it is inconceivable to me that human societies evolved as successful entities through cutthroat competition alone, let alone through the kind of fear that is generated when one individual or group attempts to assert authority over

---

1. See Cregeen, "Donald Morrison," 175–76. Morrison was born in the year 1885 on the Isle of Mull in the Inner Hebrides.

others through acts or threats of violence, thus only succeeding in strewing their paths with hatred and resentment. On the contrary, successful societies could only have come about when groups of people conducted their relations with one another in accord with an ethos of mutual toleration, respect, and support. For the most part, the members of such early groups (like the Scottish Travellers of recent times) would have been related to one another by multiple interlocking ties of kinship, as well as by such factors as a common physical environment (with its rigors), shared technologies and crafts, shared songs and stories, a common mythology and oral history, and a similar lifestyle. The cooperative ethos of such groups would have encompassed not just the strong and fit but also those individuals, including children and the elderly and infirm, who required special protection or care.

For decades if not centuries, the travelling people of Scotland have routinely been spoken of as being disadvantaged and deprived, and this is the light in which they are often still viewed today. What is seldom realized is that many of those same Travellers have looked down upon *settled* people as being disadvantaged or deprived, if not worse, on account of their skewed system of values. Betsy Whyte put this matter succinctly in *The Yellow on the Broom* (151) when recalling an incident that shocked her when she was a child. After an unpleasant encounter with a farm woman who had made herself literally sick with spite and greed over a lost inheritance, Betsy exclaimed to her mother, "Oh, Mammie, they are all mad, those country hantle!" To which her mother replied, "Haven't I told you a thousand times, lassie, that they are nearly all mad?"

Throughout her two books of memory and reflection, Whyte gave clear expression to her personal worldview,* always in the context of her identity as one of Scotland's travelling people. What this identity meant to her in practical terms is that she felt at home among people who loved to laugh; who put their children at the center of their lives; and who respected the weak, the disabled, the elderly, the orphaned, and the outcast and freely welcomed them into the family circle.[2] She was drawn to people, like Duncan, who put freedom, leisure time, and conviviality near the top of their scale of values and who regarded wage slavery with contempt, even while those same people were habituated to hard work on their own terms. Correspondingly, she took a keen delight in living in the open air, in the beauty of the natural world, and in the proximity of animals whether domestic or wild. And she sympathized with those people who openly grieved and shed tears when calling to mind their dead parents or other loved ones. People who lived by values other than these, especially if they were selfish to the point of never being satisfied no matter how much they acquired, she viewed with an amalgam of suspicion, fear, and distaste

---

2. Note what Williamson has to say in §5.9 and §5.10 about the care of children and the elderly and in other chapters of this book about the extended family as the ultimate caregiver.

Figure 10.1 Betsy Whyte, Auchtermuchty, Fife, 1986. Photo by Leonard Yarensky.

that was hard to conceal. That attitudes like these were bedrock elements of the Travellers' collective worldview is confirmed by everything that Duncan Williamson had to say to me, on top of what I have learned by talking with other Travellers or reading their published works.

This is scarcely to say that Williamson or other Travellers of his generation lived lives of elevated spiritual detachment. On the contrary, they were perfectly at home in the material world into which they were born; indeed, they swam in it like fish.[3] Moreover, their sense of practicalities was so well developed as to enable them to stay relatively comfortable, drawing often on very meager resources, in a northern climate and topography whose potential rigors need

---

3. Note those parts of chapter 4, "Making a Living," that illustrate the skill sets on which Travellers relied while leading their seminomadic life.

no emphasis. One could even call those people masters of the material world that they inhabited, as shown by their ability to make use of the resources of nature as a chief basis of their livelihood (birch or willow wands, hazel or oak or elderberry sticks, fallen antlers, heather, reeds, grasses, salmon, rabbits, berries, and the like). Dealing in scrap—a trade requiring technical knowledge, physical strength, and pragmatic skills that should not be underestimated—has long been another of the means of livelihood of Traveller men.[4] But this is very far from calling those people materialistic. On the contrary, the key to the equilibrium of their traditional way of life, before it was constricted by statutes to the point of becoming untenable, was the ability to make do with just enough food and other provisions for the current day. As for the next day, they let it take care of itself, confident that their pragmatism and resourcefulness—and, with their extended families, their solidarity as a group—would see them through. It mattered to them to know that in case of outright need, the support of a larger kin group was always close to hand.

As far as I can tell, Williamson's worldview remained basically unaltered throughout his life. This is because it was so well suited to his "society within the society": this group of seminomadic people who lived out their lives in proximity to settled people who liked to think of themselves as "the Scots," without any qualification of that term, and who tended to regard Travellers as no better than social deviants. Williamson never lost his philosophical and psychological equilibrium even while maintaining close relations with well-educated people coming from very different backgrounds. Those other people included his second wife Linda, who embraced much of his mindset as her own. Moreover, even though Williamson resided between the four walls of a house during the later years of his life, he never became "scaldified," to use a term that I picked up from Stanley Robertson, the celebrated Aberdeenshire spokesman for Traveller traditions. That is to say, Williamson was never tempted to adopt the value system of those people who lived cooped up in houses year round—the "scaldies," as some Travellers called them—and whose souls, in the eyes of some, had been petrified by a mindset of consumerism, consumption, and greed.

Moreover, I suggest, Williamson remained confident in his worldview because he knew that his personal experiences, while unique to him, typified those of a large number of other people of his social class. It therefore makes sense to think of his life in terms of cultural geography,* something that Donald Smith has argued to be a definitive element of Scottish storytelling in general. A great number of Williamson's stories are firmly set in the topography of Scotland. This is true whether one think of the lochs and hills of Argyll in the west, or of the agricultural belt encircling the urban center of Aberdeen in

---

4. See §4.22 and §4.23 for stories about scrap dealing, an aspect of Traveller existence that is often undervalued.

the northeast, or of the rambling farmlands, woods, streams, and hills of Fife or of Angus or Perthshire in east central Scotland. Moreover, Williamson's stories call up images of specific places on the Scottish landscape, whether or not those same places are recognizable today: the old mill at Tangy Glen to which young Traveller couples used to elope; the quayside at Furnace with its upturned boats; the hillsides above Loch Fyne, with their woods, knowes, deer, hayfields, heather, stone dikes, and drains; the derelict houses in Aberdeen or Dundee where Williamson squatted when a young man; the jail in Cupar, Fife, where he once spent thirty days; or the campfires in the potato fields near Crieff where he and other Travellers would swap stories and songs far into the night.

When one takes into account, as well, the diachronic dimension that pertains to these places[5]—their anchorage in the stream of time, as marked by the passing of generations—one can discern the outlines of a Scottish social history that extends well back into the past. Pertaining to these same images, as well, is an ethical dimension that Williamson articulated in one tale after another. Among the elements of this ethos were respect for the land; respect for the animals and other creatures (both wild and domestic, both visible and invisible) that were known or thought to dwell on that land, often in close interchange with humans; and a kindly regard for children, the elderly, the disabled, and the needy. The physical topography that is evoked through Williamson's songs and stories is thus at the same time an ecological map with a moral compass.

There is thus some justification for approaching Williamson not just as a gifted tradition bearer and a consummate performer but also as a representative of larger aspects of the cultural heritage of Scotland and, by extension, of the world. If a claim along such lines should strike one as absurdly grandiose, though I do not think it is, then it is enough to say that Williamson's personal worldview was expressive of that of a significant subset of Scottish society: that of the seminomadic Travellers of his day, whose history and heritage extend further back in time, perhaps, than is usually imagined.

§10.3. RECITATION, "WEBSPINNER"

Near the beginning of this book, I remarked that I would have something to say at this point about the book's title. Doing so requires introducing a recitation by Williamson that we both thoroughly enjoyed. Although a slight piece like this can easily be disregarded when set amid Williamson's big ballads and internationally known wonder tales, I believe it hits close to his identity as a man and a storyteller.

---

5. This diachronic dimension is most clearly manifest in chapter 2, "Those Who Went Before," and chapter 9, "Scenes from a Vanished World," though it informs the whole of the present book.

Figure 10.2 At home, having just finished a story, Kincraigie Farm Cottage, 1986. Photo by Leonard Yarensky.

Recitations,* although easy to overlook as an oral art form, are a time-honored means by which a raconteur can entertain a live audience. In Scotland they often enliven ceilidhs and other festive occasions, especially when liquid refreshments are flowing. The basis of a recitation is a rhymed narrative poem, one that is generally droll in content. Some such poems are innocent and might be performed at any social event including church soirees, while others fall off the bawdy end of the spectrum.

Williamson's favorite recitation during the years when I recorded him was one that he called "Webspinner." The protagonist of this mock heroic poem, Webspinner by name, is of course a spider—a humanized one, as in all animal fables. The spider's antagonist, a bluebottle fly, is a large fly with obnoxious habits and a buzz that can drive you mad. The third actor in this minidrama is a broom-wielding housewife, the spider's perennial nemesis. To put the poem's narrative content into a nutshell, the resourceful Webspinner is the victor in an epic combat waged against the upper-crust fly, only to fall victim to a sad fate in the end. Whether Duncan saw the spider Webspinner—an "underground" character of low degree, and yet of strong arm and potent craft—as his own comic alter ego is not for me to say.

In any event, here is the poem as Williamson recited it to members of my research team at his and Linda's cottage near Strathmiglo, Fife, in July of 1986:

♪♫

1   He was a miser old
and he came of low degree,
his body was large and his legs were thin
an he kept bad company.

2   His house was seven stories high
by the corner of the street.
It always had a dirty look
when other homes were neat.

3   The day was hot, the chase was poor,
the night came on apace,
when a burly baron of a bluebottle
he came ridin from the chase.

4   Says he, "I'll ask for lodgings
at the first house I come to."
Like that, the gate o Webspinner
came suddenly in view.

5   Oh, loud was the knock the Baron gave,
Webspinner he came with glee.
He said, "Come in, come in, kind sir," he said,
"and pass the night with me."
Like that they sprang upon each other
and they fought quite furiously.

6   Now the Baron, he was a swordsman,
a swordsman of renown,
but the spider, he had the strongest arm
and he kept the Baron down.

7   Then out he took a little cord
from a pocket by his side
and with manys a cruel an crafty knot
his hands and feet he tied.

8   Then he went about his house
arranging dish an platter

and doin all his work of care
as if nothing was the matter.

9   Then he seized on poor Bluebottle,
that strong and burly man,
and step by step and step by step
the "hoist him up!" began.

10 And step by step and step by step
he went with weary tread,
but when he reached his parlor door
poor Bluebottle, he was dead.

11 Then a lady came that way
with a long and cruel brush,
which she raised above her carefully
Webspinner's house to crush.

12 Now, that wicked churn[6] who all his life
had looked for such a day,
he passed through a trap door in the wall
and took hisself away.

13 As where he went, no one can tell,
it was said in underground,
an he died a miserable death,
and his body ne'er was found.

(86DW03 @ 1:00:22.)

When Williamson recited this poem to me on a different occasion,* it ended
in the same manner as here: with Duncan breaking into an infectious grin
while his audience—at that time consisting of myself alone—joined in with
appreciative laughter.

Williamson did not tell me where he learned this poem. Since I had not
come across it before, I speculated that he had either picked it up from a poetic
miscellany during his schoolyears or had possibly composed it himself. Thanks
to the digital revolution in library science, I have now discovered that what
Williamson's "Webspinner" represents is his streamlined version of a poem
composed by the nineteenth-century English poet Mary Howitt,* whose poems

---

6. "Wicked churn": the original poem reads "wicked churl."

THE TRUE

STORY OF WEB-SPINNER.

WEB-SPINNER was a miser old,
    Who came of low degree ;
His body was large, his legs were thin,
    And he kept bad company.
His visage had the evil look
    Of a black felon grim ;
To all the country he was known,
    But none spoke well of him.
His house was seven stories high,
    In a corner of the street ;

Figure 10.3 The first page of Mary Howitt's poem "Webspinner," as illustrated by Hector Giacomelli. From Howitt's book *Sketches of Natural History* (1873). Courtesy of the Baldwin Library of Historical Children's Literature, George A. Smathers Libraries, University of Florida.

about animals once circulated widely on both sides of the Atlantic even if they are little known today.[7]

There is no doubt, then, that Williamson first memorized this poem when at school in the village of Furnace,[8] retooling it in his own fashion either then or in the course of time. Much the same process of memorization accompanied by retooling may account for the composition of at least two, and perhaps four, other items in his repertory during the period when I recorded him. One

---

7. Howitt's droll poem "The Spider and the Fly" is an exception, in that it remains well known.
8. In reviewing my tapes, I see now that on my tape 86DW03, in a session that took place when I was not present, Williamson remarks that he was awarded the Dux medal at his school in Furnace for his outstanding performance of this poem.

indisputable example is his re-creation of Thomas Campbell's poem "Lord
Ullin's Daughter"* (first published in 1809, beginning "A chieftain to the Highlands came"). Another is his reworking of Henry Wadsworth Longfellow's
poem "The Wreck of the Hesperus"* (first published in 1842, beginning "It
was the schooner Hesperus, / That sailed the wintry sea"). Williamson sang his
reworked versions of those poems to tunes that he evidently devised himself.
A similar re-creative process may account for his sung versions of the well-
known historical ballad "Sir Patrick Spens"* as well as the long poem "John
Barleycorn,"* Robert Burns's tribute to whiskey (though in England that poem
is generally taken to be in honor of ale).

§10.4. ON SPIDERS AND SPINNING, AND ON WILLIAMSON THE MAN

The main reason I have put Duncan's recitation of "Webspinner" on display
here, however, has to do with the image of the spider. Williamson himself, of
course, was a webspinner. He devoted much of his adult life to spinning out the
threads of his knowledge and experience into a strong, airy fabric, one that was
compounded of memory and imagination, of truth and of the kind of truth in
lies that is the substance of most good stories. Like a spider spinning out gos-
samer threads from his own anatomy, Williamson fed on his own knowledge
of the world before spinning out the results of this process of internalization
for others to enjoy.

As for the figure of speech whereby telling a story is likened to spinning
yarn, it is an ancient one, well known to ancient Greek and Roman myth-
makers with their tales of Penelope and Arachne. Ever since the time of the
Brothers Grimm, as well, the conjunction of storytelling and the spinning of
wool has been etched into the imagination of people from all over the world.
The yarn-spinning figure of speech is made visible, for example, in European
genre paintings depicting the *Spinnstube*, the spinning room of an old wood-
timbered house. Such paintings, which, thanks to the vogue of the Grimms'
Kinder und Hausmärchen, were especially popular during the period of the
nineteenth-century Industrial Revolution, tend to center on the atavistic image
of an old woman seated at her spinning wheel close by a hearth where children
are gathered around, seemingly entranced by her stories.

Moreover, literary scholars have made much of the thread of metaphorical
associations whereby a writer's labors in composing a text are likened to a
weaver's work in fashioning a textile. After all, our very word "text" is derived
from the past participial form of the Latin verb *texere*, "to weave." In like manner, our word "technology" derives from Greek *téchnē*, meaning "art" or "craft,"
a word that in turn derives from the reconstructed Indo-European root *tek-* or

teks-, meaning "to shape, construct."[9] This same Indo-European root form has likewise been taken to mean "to weave," "to fabricate" (as with a carpenter's ax), or "to make wicker or wattle fabric for mud-covered house walls."[10] My point in introducing this philological diversion is to suggest that the technique by which a storyteller narrates a text has deep linguistic and intellectual affinities not just with the crafts of spinning and weaving but also with the act of constructing a house and, furthermore, with what scientists call the tectonics of the earth.

One reason "Webspinner" seems to me an apt choice as the short title of the present book, then, is that it readily calls to mind the idea of storytelling as a cosmoplastic activity: that is, a world-building one. A related idea is that storytelling is an act akin to a craftsman's construction of a house that one can live in. That is a concept that deserves sustained reflection, I suggest, though I will not labor it here.

Another reason "Webspinner" is an apt title for a tribute to Williamson— though this connection is scarcely an intuitive one—is that members of Williamson's family were well known for their skills in basketmaking. This fact is brought out in chapter 4 of this book, "Making a Living," which includes a transcription of Duncan's story "The Elf and the Basketmaker," a tale that offers a genealogy for the Williamsons' unusual capabilities in this craft. Significantly, in an interview I recorded in 1986, Williamson likens the art of making a basket to a spider's craft in spinning out a web. "Spall" is the term he uses for the grid of interwoven wands that forms a basket's base.[11] Once the spall is made, the basketmaker weaves additional wands round and round it "like a spider's web," in Duncan's words (tape 86DW24). If the basket is initially woven upside down (as it usually is), with the spall at the top and the framework of wands set vertically on or into the ground, then the art of framing a basket could be compared with that of building a bow tent out of bent poles set vertically into the ground, with the difference that the tent requires no tight horizontal interweaving since it is equipped with a cover made of canvas or some other material. Furthermore, weaving a *spall* and weaving a *spell* are two activities that are distinguished from one another by only a single phoneme. Though unrelated in their literal meaning, the two words thus make up what linguists call a minimal pair, so that it would take a fine knife blade to separate them.

Still, I am troubled by the last lines of the poem "Webspinner" as Williamson recited it in mock serious fashion: "an he died a miserable death, and his body

---

9. See *The Oxford Dictionary of English Etymology*, edited by C. T. Onions (Clarendon, 1966), s.v. "text" and "technology."

10. *The American Heritage Dictionary of Indo-European Roots*, revised and edited by Calvert Watkins (Houghton Mifflin, 1985), s.v. *teks-*.

11. See the *Oxford English Dictionary*, 2nd ed, s.v. *spale*, sense 1.3 in the draft online edition of 1993. In basketmaking, a spale is "a thin strip of wood woven to form the cross slat of a wooden basket," or "such strips collectively."

ne'er was found." One would have wanted a better end for the brave protagonist of this poem, the slayer of the obnoxious Baron Bluebottle.

§10.5. TAKING LEAVE OF A FRIEND

I was four thousand miles away when Williamson died, in the year 2007 at the age of seventy-nine. I could not well have attended his funeral in Strathmiglo, Fife, even if I had known about it at the time. I am sorrowed, however, when I reflect upon my inability to be present on that occasion, for I would have wanted to be among those sending Duncan off from the pains and indignities of the present world. And I am aware that, as Linda Williamson has written, "The most important event in Traveller life is death."[12]

I also regret that I could not be of practical help to Duncan during the last years of his life. Those years were not easy ones, as I well understand, for a battery of illnesses took their toll on his aging body despite the energy with which he still occasionally took part in storytelling events both in Scotland and abroad. Thankfully, Linda Williamson—the woman whom, Duncan once confided to me, he was willing to die for, even if he also liked to joke that when she turned fifty, he would trade her in for two twenty-fives—Linda Williamson, as I say, came back to stay with him during his last three months of life, before he was stricken by a heart attack that left him partly paralyzed. This was an act of love and compassion on her part for which he must have felt gratitude to the core of his heart, whether or not he was capable of articulating that feeling to her. Before long, though, his caretakers had little choice but to see that he was hospitalized. This was a fate that Travellers of former generations tended to dread more than death itself, and it is no surprise that he died in the hospital of complications of his stroke within days of being admitted.

The last time I saw Williamson was about ten years before that, when I happened to be in the United Kingdom conducting some unrelated research. It was a cold December afternoon when I managed to track him down at the cottage in Balmullo, Fife, where he then resided. He joked to me about being so chilled in his house that he was burning the furniture, and when I looked around at the sparse furnishings, I was afraid it was no joke.

Later that afternoon I drove him to a nearby shop to pick up a few necessities. The essential items, as those who knew his habits will suspect, were a couple of large bags of coal for his fire, a carton of cigarettes, and a liberal supply of Carlsberg Special Brew. After lingering conversations, I eventually took my leave from him despite the guilt I felt when contemplating the somewhat stark dwelling where he remained on his own. Whether rightly or wrongly, my

---

12. Williamson, "Narrative Singing," 24.

Figure 10.4 Williamson near the village of Furnace, Loch Fyne, walking toward the place by the shore where he was born, 1988. Photo by Dorothy Leese.

guilt was tempered by the knowledge that he had friends and family who were not far off in case of real need. But I was also bitterly aware that the book that I had planned to write based on my recordings from the 1980s was still undone, with my work on it stalled inexplicably in his eyes.

The book is now finished, many years after it was begun. For a long time, as I can see now with hindsight, the fact that Williamson was still alive, slowly drinking and smoking himself to death (as I imagined his situation to be), was an impediment for me, though it was not my business how he conducted his life. What chiefly impeded me was a sense that other things had to fall into place in my own life and work before I could complete this project. But to paraphrase the wisdom of Ecclesiastes, there is a time—a *kairos*, or "right time," as the ancient Greeks used to say—for everything under the sun. It is the right time now to send this book forth, confident that those who loved or admired Duncan, especially the surviving members of his family, will take pleasure in his words as I was able to record them and as I have retrieved them here, simulating Duncan's voice as much as the medium of print allows.

So here's to you, Duncan! For me, you are still alive, just as—to your own way of thinking—you will remain alive as long as at least one of your surviving friends or family members calls you to mind. And if this book is read in future years, then people who never had the pleasure of knowing you face to face may discern your lifelike semblance. If so, then they will have found a rock that they can lean on in a world that is rampant with greed, shallowness, and chicanery.

By now, the messages of your stories have merged with the message of your life: that in a world of threats and obstacles that can seem monstrous in scale, a person who remains resourceful, generous, kind, and courageous—the chiel who is both canny and couthy—will always be the hero of the tale.

COMMENTARY

An asterisk in the main text (*) flags the fact that an entry will be found on that topic in the Commentary, keyed to the main text by chapter and section number (for example, §6.11 for chapter 6, section 11).

CHAPTER 1: WILLIAMSON AND THE TRAVELLERS

§1.1. **The Scottish Travellers, or tinkers.** The travelling people of Scotland are known collectively by a number of different names. The time-honored term "tinkers" was (and is) often shortened to "tinks," whether affectionately or with contempt, as in "dirty tinks." Now that tinsmithing has ceased to be a viable occupation for itinerants, however, to speak of "tinkers" has become not just a potential insult but also an anachronism. An alternative that is occasionally heard is "gaan-aboot people" (literally "people who travel about"). An equivalent phrase in standard English is "the summer walkers," as in the book and film by Timothy Neat that take that phrase as their title. Another name, "nyakin" (also spelled "nyakim" or "nawken" or "naken"), is a cant term used by certain Scottish Travellers to distinguish themselves from the settled population. A handful of writers have favored the name "tinkler-Gypsies," as in Andrew McCormick's book of that title, though at the risk of conflating Travellers with Romani, a group of different ethnicity. Finally, though at the risk of anachronism, a few authors have used the term *caird* or *ceard*, a borrowing into English or Scots from Scottish Gaelic *céard*, denoting a silversmith and, in earlier times, a metalworker patronized by the Gaelic-speaking nobility. Most people today seem content with the term "Travellers," often capitalized (as in the present book) to distinguish this more or less cohesive social group from other people who happen to take to the road, including Romani, vagabonds, tramps, New Age campers, and tourists in their camper vans.

§1.1. **Argyll's Gaelic heritage.** Readers wanting a comprehensive orientation to Argyll's geography, history, and culture are referred to *The Argyll Book*, edited

by Donald Omand, with chapters on special topics including "Oral Tradi-
tions/Folklore of Argyll," by John Shaw and "Gaelic Language and Literature in
Argyll," by Donald E. Meek. With reference to the rich oral heritage of this land
of peninsulas, islands, mountains, and lochs—one of almost limitless physical
beauty—Shaw comments, "Since medieval times Argyll, including the islands
of Mull, Coll, Tiree, Jura, and Islay, has provided evidence of an oral tradition
rivaled only by that which has come to light in the Outer Hebrides" (2006, 213).
The name "Argyll" itself derives from old Gaelic *Airer Goidel* (modern Gaelic
Earra-Ghàidheal), meaning "Coastland of the Gaels."

§1.1. **The foremost of them all?** In the absence of objective criteria for
determining excellence in storytelling, there is no way other than a shouting
match whereby claims regarding the preeminent skills of any one tradition
bearer can be either championed or denied. All the same, it is worth recalling
what Hamish Henderson has to say in his introduction to the Williamsons'
story collection *A Thorn in the King's Foot*, where, already in 1987, he refers to
Duncan as "in many ways possibly the most extraordinary tradition bearer
of the whole Traveller tribe" and then again as "one of the most enormously
gifted folk artists now living" (quotations at 18 and 28). Henderson was not
alone in this assessment. In an obituary published in the Glasgow *Herald* dated
November 9, 2007, Maxwell MacLeod first quotes two other authorities who
characterized Duncan as "uniquely gifted" and as "number one—head and
shoulders above anyone else in his field," before adding his own assessment:
"Indeed, if the Scottish storytelling community had the gift of beatification
it would probably have made Williamson its first saint." In like manner, the
title of the obituary for Williamson published by *The Guardian* on Thursday,
November 22, 2007, was "Traveller acclaimed as Scotland's greatest modern-day
storyteller." David Campbell states without qualification that by the time of his
death, Duncan was "acclaimed as the best-known and best-loved storyteller in
the English-speaking world" (*Traveller in Two Worlds*, 1.253).

§1.1. **"His tapes from the 1960s are now evidently lost."** I once recorded
Duncan reminiscing about the time when he bought a tape recorder and used
it himself around the campfires. Speaking of the late 1960s, he remarked, "See,
Jack, after the festival in Kinross, I [bought] a tape recorder, a wee Phillips reel-
to-reel; they was just comin out on the market then. It went with six batteries.
I was around all the Travellers. I collected everybody under the sun! I wish I
had some o this material: bagpipes, diddlin, chanters, stories, cracks, ceilidhs.
For years! An I kept all these tapes. Batteries was cheap at that time; you got
them six for a pound, ken? I never went among non-Travellers; it was Travellers
all the time I went among. I let them hear theirselves singin. They had never
heard theirselves on tape in their life! Ah played bagpipe tapes back tae front
and made wonderful fun wi them. That chap Willie Cameron, he was one o the

pipers that Ah played back tae front. I said, 'Listen to Willy, he's great!' [*Laughs.*]
Ye ever hear bagpipes played back tae front?" (87DW12 @ 08:10). Duncan went
on to explain that he later gave the tapes to his friend the folklore collector
Helen Fullerton for safekeeping to keep them from being ruined by damp:
"So I packed them all intae a big box, over a hundred, some o them with their
names on them, tellin who they were. I always used tae write on the back whose
names they were." But the box of tapes seems to have gone missing, perhaps
when Fullerton subsequently moved house to Wales.

§1.2. **The Scottish Storytelling Centre in Edinburgh.** In his book *Storytelling Scotland*, Donald Smith surveys the history of storytelling in both Highland and Lowland Scotland with an eye to the collection of oral narratives by
pioneering folklorists. Smith offers an account of the founding of the Scottish
Storytelling Festival in 1989, an event that led in turn to the founding of the
present Scottish Storytelling Centre in Edinburgh in 2006. These events took
place within the sustaining environment of Scottish nationalism at a time
of increasing Scottish political representation within the UK. Even though
Williamson tended to stand aloof from politics, his personal sentiments were
aligned with nationalistic ideals, and his career was buoyed by these developments. The Centre is a thriving theater for the performing arts (for information
on its activities, see https://www.scottishstorytellingcentre.com).

§1.2. **Jimmy Williamson** (b. 1951). In addition to Braid's book *Scottish Travel-
ler Tales*, see also the article "Jimmy Williamson," *Tocher*, vol. 8, no. 56, 2000.
Jimmy's younger brother William Williamson can be heard singing one song,
"The Dowie Dens o Yarrow," on Yates's CD *Travellers' Tales* (vol. 1, track 6).

§1.2. **Linda Williamson** (b. 1949). A native of Wisconsin, Linda completed
her PhD thesis "Narrative Singing among the Scots Travellers" at the University
of Edinburgh in 1985 on the basis of ten years of fieldwork she had undertaken
with thirty-four individual Scottish Travellers. More than anyone else, she was
responsible for drawing Williamson into the public eye as one of Scotland's
premier storytellers and interpreters of traditional song. Born Linda Jane Rast,
in certain publications of the 1970s she goes by the name Linda Headlee, her
married name from her first marriage, which ended in divorce not long after
she met Duncan, whom she married in 1977. To my mind, the three most
important books that she and Duncan brought out on the basis of her recordings of his oral tales are *Fireside Tales of the Traveller Children*, in its expanded
1985 edition as well as the first 1983 edition, which includes annotations that
are absent from the later publications; *The Broonie, Silkies and Fairies* (1985),
with its tales of otherworldly encounters; and the comprehensive anthology *A
Thorn in the King's Foot* (1987). Additional story collections brought out jointly
by Linda and Duncan, some of them published under Duncan's name alone,
are listed in the Selected Bibliography.

§1.2. **Inveraray Castle, Argyll.** The ancestral home of the Duke of Argyll, Chief of Clan Campbell, the present castle (see Figure 2.4) was completed in the mid- to late eighteenth century. Much of its present appearance results from major restorations that were undertaken after fires in 1877 and 1975. Adjoining the castle are woodlands that encompass the forestry hut where Duncan's mother and father lived toward the end of their lives. Helen Fullerton, who died in 2005, has been quoted by David Campbell as saying that she often used to visit the Williamsons there until 1974, after which time she acquired a farm and started teaching as a lecturer at Glasgow University. "Betsy [Duncan's mother] lived in a forestry hut in the back of Inveraray in a beautiful piece of woodland, and in the springtime it was just like a fairy hut because it was covered in bluebells so blue it hurt your eyes. Beside the hut was a little burn, just a teeny stream" (*Traveller in Two Worlds*, 2.50).

§1.2. **The Scottish Folksong Revival.** For different perspectives on the Revival, often with attention to efforts to carry traditional musical idioms forward in innovative ways, see Adam McNaughtan, "The Folk Revival in Scotland"; Ailie Munro, *The Folk Music Revival in Scotland* (1984), reissued in 1996 in a revised and updated edition under the title *The Democratic Muse*; Michael Brocken, *The British Folk Revival, 1944–2002*; Ian A. Olson, "Scottish Contemporary Traditional Music and Song"; Gary West, *Voicing Scotland*; and Owen F. Hand, "The Folk-Song Revival in Scotland." Hand emphasizes the extent to which the Revival was spearheaded by men (including Henderson and MacColl) who were current or former members of the Communist Party of Great Britain or who were otherwise involved in left-wing politics, striving to celebrate working-class culture while dramatizing the needs of persecuted groups, including the Scottish Travellers. Writing in a related vein in her article "Belle Stewart," Sheila Douglas remarks, "The word 'Traveller' became invested in the Folk Revival with all kinds of romantic and fanciful associations, particularly for politically-minded people who wanted to view Travellers as underdogs, shut out from society, harassed and mistreated by settled people" (438). In the present book, the terms "Folksong Revival" and "Storytelling Revival" are capitalized to distinguish these movements, which in Britain are associated with the period from roughly 1950 to the first decades of the twenty-first century, from other revivals of a comparable kind.

§1.2. **Jeannie Robertson** (1908–1975). For a sustained view of this towering figure in twentieth-century Scottish song, see Gower's article "Jeannie Robertson: Portrait of a Traditional Singer" and Porter and Gower's book *Jeannie Robertson*, particularly on the evolution of Robertson's singing style once she became an active participant in public concerts and festivals. Two noteworthy recordings among others that feature her singing are the Prestige/International LP *Scottish Ballads and Folk Songs by Jeannie Robertson* and the 1998 CD *The*

Queen among the Heather. A brief tribute to her storytelling abilities, "Jeannie Robertson as a Storyteller," was published in *Tocher*, vol. 1, no. 6, 1972, with an introduction by Hamish Henderson that is reprinted in Henderson's essay collection *Alias MacAlias* (159–60).

§1.2. **Hamish Henderson** (1919–2002). Henderson's impact on the twentieth-century Scottish Folksong Revival was long-lasting and profound. His life is reviewed in intricate and colorful detail in Neat's two-volume study *Hamish Henderson: A Biography* (2007–2009), while his impact on Scottish nationalist politics is emphasized by Gibson, *The Voice of the People: Hamish Henderson and Scottish Cultural Politics* (2015). A special issue of *Tocher* (vol. 7, no. 43, 1991–1994) consists of a tribute to Henderson and his seminal work as a collector of folksong and other traditional lore. Henderson's reminiscences on his initial collecting experiences in the north of Scotland are presented by Neat, *The Summer Walkers* (65–85), along with about a dozen photos relating to his fieldwork. Most of Henderson's writings on Scottish folksong are comprised in his collection of papers *Alias MacAlias: Writings on Songs, Folk and Literature*. Selections from his field recordings are featured in the two-volume CD release *Hamish Henderson Collects* (2005–2006). I present Henderson's account of his first meeting with Jeannie Robertson, as recorded on my tape 84HH01, at the head of my article "Context and Loss in Scottish Ballad Tradition," rewritten as chapter 6 (146–72) of *Homo Narrans*.

§1.2. **Alan Lomax** (1915–2002). As the most influential American folksong collector of the later twentieth century, Alan Lomax, son of the distinguished folklorist John A. Lomax, Sr., is the subject of an appreciative biography by John F. Szwed: *Alan Lomax: The Man Who Recorded the World* (2010). Lomax conducted fieldwork in Scotland in the early 1950s as part of his efforts to set the study of American folksong within a global field of vision. The entire body of Lomax family materials at the American Folklife Center encompasses more than ten thousand sound recordings, among many other items.

§1.2. **The School of Scottish Studies.** Established in 1951, the School is now folded into the subject area of Celtic and Scottish Studies at the University of Edinburgh. Over the years it has sponsored a wide range of instruction and research devoted to native Scottish traditions, with an emphasis on traditional singing and storytelling practices. Its Archives are a mine of information for studies in ethnology, ethnomusicology, social history, and Scottish oral traditions. For an account of the School's history, see Fenton and Mackay, "A History of Ethnology in Scotland," 56–61. On the scope of the School's Archives, with an overview of the history of collection efforts in Scotland, see Macaulay, "Dipping into the Well." Since 1971, leading examples of holdings from the Archives have been published both in the journal *Tocher* (meaning "dowry" in Gaelic and in Scots, from Scottish Gaelic *tochar*) and through record albums or CDs in the Scottish Tradition series brought out by Greentrax Records, with some twenty-six volumes published to date. Thousands of digitized recordings in the School's Archives have been made available to the public via the website Tobar an Dualchais / Kist o Riches: https://www.tobarandualchais.co.uk/.

§1.2. **Jimmy MacBeath** (1894–1972). A tribute to MacBeath appeared in *Tocher*, vol. 2, no. 12, 1973, and some of his songs are featured on the 1967 Topic LP *Wild Rover No More*. The introductory part of that *Tocher* piece, by Hamish Henderson, is reprinted in Henderson's essay collection *Alias MacAlias* (161–66).

§1.2. **Davie Stewart** (d. 1972). A tribute to Davie Stewart appeared in *Tocher*, vol. 2, no. 15, 1974; the part of that piece that was written by Hamish Henderson is reprinted in *Alias MacAlias* (167–74). Stewart's voice can be heard on a number of anthologies of Scottish folksong dating from the 1950s or 1960s and later, while close to a dozen of his songs are featured in Peter Kennedy's comprehensive anthology *Folksongs of Britain and Ireland*.

§1.2. **Lucy Stewart** (1901–1982). Another of Henderson's "discoveries" from the early 1950s, Lucy Stewart of Fetterangus, Aberdeen, is well known among folksong specialists as a result of fieldwork conducted by the American folklorist Kenneth Goldstein in 1959–1960. Her clear, unpretentious style of unaccompanied singing is heard on Goldstein's 1961 Folkways record album *Lucy Stewart: Traditional Singer from Aberdeenshire, Scotland*. An online tribute has been published by Smithsonian Folkways Recordings: https://folkways .si.edu/lucy-stewart-scottish-ballad-singer/childrens-world/music/article/ smithsonian.

§1.2. **Jane Turriff** (1915–2013). A tribute to this outstanding traditional singer from the northeast of Scotland has taken the form of the 1996 Springthyme CD release *Singin' Is Ma Life*, edited and annotated by Thomas McKean. A niece of Davie Stewart, Jane Turriff was partially disabled because of an injury suffered in childhood. She often sang her songs to her own accompaniment on either accordion or harmonium. A recording session that I conducted with her at her home in Mintlaw in July 1984 is preserved on my tapes 84JT01 and 84JT02.

§1.2. **Belle Stewart** (1906–1997). Not just through her acclaimed performances in folk clubs and festivals and through the record albums that feature her singing, but also through the generous hospitality that she offered to folksong enthusiasts who called on her at her home in the neighborhood of Blairgowrie, Belle Stewart (along with other members of her family) came to epitomize the folksong traditions of Lowland Scotland in the minds of many admirers. A tribute, "The Stewarts of Blair," is featured in *Tocher*, vol. 3, no. 21, 1976, while Sheila Douglas offers a capsule portrait of Belle in her article "Belle Stewart." Two audio releases that foreground her singing are *Belle Stewart: Queen among* *the Heather* (originally issued by Topic Records, 1977) and *The Stewarts of Blair* (originally issued by Topic Records, 1965). She and her husband Alex (or Alec) and other members of her family were likewise outstanding storytellers, some of whose tales are featured in Douglas, *King o the Black Art*, and Bruford and MacDonald, *Scottish Traditional Tales*. My interviews with her are recorded on my tapes 84BS01 to 84BS03 along with 88CE04–05 and 88CE07. Several recordings of her songs or stories can be heard via Scottish Voices and many more via Tobar an Dualchais.

§1.2. **Ewan MacColl and Peggy Seeger.** MacColl (1915–1989), whose name at birth was James Henry Miller, was as well known for his political activism as for his commanding presence on the concert stage, as Ben Harker brings out in his biography *Class Act: The Cultural and Political Life of Ewan MacColl*. MacColl's wife Peggy Seeger (b. 1935), the sister of Mike Seeger and half sister of Pete Seeger, is the subject of Jean R. Freedman's biography *Peggy Seeger: A Life of Music, Love, and Politics*. As an accomplished singer-songwriter and musician, Seeger was both a strong advocate for social change and a stellar interpreter of traditional song. Working as a team, MacColl and Seeger dramatized the value of Travellers' oral culture whether through BBC radio broadcasts, book publications, or live performances.

§1.3. **Gypsies—also known as Romani or Roma—and Scottish Travellers.** Although there is a large scholarly literature on the Romani of Britain, it is tangential to my purposes since the history and culture of that ethnic group are largely distinct from those of Scottish Travellers. Janet Keet-Black, *Gypsies of Britain*, provides a capsule survey up to recent years. Robert Dawson's book *Times Gone* features a wealth of images relating to the travelling peoples of England, Wales, Scotland, and Ireland; see also Dawson's related study *Empty Lands: Aspects of Scottish Traveller Survival* (2007). An overview of Scottish Traveller culture from a musicologist's perspective is offered by Ailie Munro in chapter 6, "The Travelling People," of her book *The Folk Music Revival in Scotland*. See also the account offered by Duncan Williamson in his own words, as edited by Linda Williamson, in the Introduction to *Fireside Tales of the Traveller Children*.

§1.3. **Ireland's Travellers.** There are close connections between the Irish Travellers (or Tinkers, as they have customarily been called) and the travelling people of Scotland, even while the two groups have tended to maintain separate lifestyles and family affiliations. To complicate this picture, some Irish Travellers have settled down in the London metropolitan area. For the situation in Ireland, see Court, *Puck of the Droms*; Gmelch, *The Irish Tinkers*; Gmelch, *Nan*; and most recently Gmelch and Gmelch, *Irish Travellers*. On songs collected from Irish Travellers living in and around London, see Carroll, "Irish Travellers."

§1.3. **Internal strangers.** The concept of the "internal stranger," as articulated by sociologists in Germany and elsewhere going back to the early decades of the twentieth century, goes far to account for the irrational revulsion with which many settled people have viewed Travellers, Gypsies, tinkers, and other seminomadic groups. Since such minorities as these do not share the worldview of the dominant society, they place into question "nearly everything that seems to be unquestionable" to that larger group or may seem to do so (Schutz, "The Stranger," 96). It is hard for outsiders to understand the depth of the psychopathology involved in such attitudes, almost as if the "strangers" in a given society were a tainted class analogous to the group traditionally known as the Untouchables of India (now known as the Scheduled Caste).

§1.3. **Betsy Whyte** (1919–1988). Whyte, whose maiden name was Townsley and who was a Johnstone on her mother's side, grew up in Perthshire. During much of her life she lived with her husband Bryce in the town of Montrose, Angus, on the east coast of Scotland. There is a warm tribute to her in *Tocher*, vol. 3, no. 23, 1976, while other issues of that journal have featured additional examples of her stories, songs, and other lore. I recorded her stories and reflections both at her home in Montrose and at several locations in Fife (see my audio tapes 84BW01 to 84BW03, 86BW01 to 86BW07, and 88BW01 to 88BW06, among others, plus videotapes 86V06 and part of 86V04). Hillers, "Storytelling and the International Folktale in Scotland," 164–65, draws attention to Whyte's stature as a storyteller. Transcriptions of certain of Whyte's *Märchen*-like stories—that is, long complex fairy tales—have been published in Bruford, *Green Man of Knowledge*; Bruford and MacDonald, *Scottish Traditional Tales*; and Philip, *The Penguin Book of Scottish Folktales*. Her clear and expressive voice, with its Perthshire lilt, can be heard via Tobar an Dualchais in over 200 selections and via Scottish Voices in some fifteen audio or video selections.

§1.3. **An occasional ceilidh.** What the term "ceilidh" means to most people in Scotland today is a dance, often featuring live Scottish music (a ceilidh band). To many Scots active in folk singing and storytelling circles in the 1980s, the term denoted an informal social gathering, often held at someone's house, with interactions ranging from gossip and small talk to songs and stories of various kinds. The word is a borrowing from Gaelic *ceilidh*. The older sense of the term among the townships of the Highlands and Islands is summarized as follows by the Scottish poet and social historian Francis Thompson in his book *Crofting Years*: "In older times, the *ceilidh* was . . . the occasion when memories were revived, when the lineage of the folk of the township was re-stated, when the bards and singers were given the chance to freshen up old songs and poetry with yet another airing, and when the young were gradually made aware of their responsibilities to their families and to the community at large; and, not least, when the older folk of the township were taken into the heart of the communal spirit as manifested by the *ceilidh*" (132). The Williamsons' home in the mid-1980s at Kincraigie Farm Cottage, Fife, readily took on the character of a ceilidh house where friends, including children and the elderly, entered into the heart of a communal spirit as urged on by the man of the house, Duncan himself, who acted as informal master of ceremonies.

§1.3. **Stanley Robertson** (1940–2009). A riveting storyteller, an evocative singer, and a mine of information about Travellers' songs and other elements of traditional lore, Robertson was a venturesome intellectual who wrote three plays and seven books. Taking pride in being the nephew of Jeannie Robertson, he strove to carry on her heritage. There is a tribute to him in *Tocher*, vol. 6, no. 40, 1986. Many of his songs and stories can be heard on the Elphinstone Institute double CDs *The College Boy* or *Rum, Scum, Scoosh*. Over one hundred selections in Tobar an Dualchais feature his voice, while over two dozen audio or video recordings of Stanley and other members of his family are available via Scottish Voices. I recorded him on my audio tapes 86SR01 to 86SR07, among others, and on videotape 86V08.

§1.3. **Sheila Douglas** (1932–2013). Douglas's high regard for Traveller tradition bearers, including Belle and Sheila Stewart and other members of their family, came from the heart and was warmly reciprocated. One of her early publications is the folktale anthology *The King o the Black Art* (1987), which features her transcriptions of tales told by the Traveller storytellers John Stewart, Alex (or Alec) Stewart, Belle Stewart, and Willie MacPhee. Scottish singers of many different regions and backgrounds, Travellers among them, are represented in Douglas's two folksong anthologies *The Sang's the Thing* (1992) and *Come Gie's a Sang* (1995). Two recordings of her singing at evening ceilidhs can be heard via Scottish Voices.

§1.3. **Willie MacPhee** (1910–2002). Incorporated into Sheila Douglas's biographical portrait *The Last of the Tinsmiths* are transcriptions of a number of MacPhee's songs, stories, and piping tunes. These are based in part on materials included in a tribute to MacPhee, edited by Douglas, that is featured in *Tocher*, vol. 7, no. 44, 1992. Examples of his stories are included in Bruford and MacDonald, *Scottish Traditional Tales* and Douglas, *King o the Black Art*. During the later years of his life, MacPhee and his wife Bella lived in a motor home in the Double Dykes caravan park on the outskirts of the city of Perth.

§1.3. **Sheila Stewart** (1937–2014). See the note on "Belle Stewart" above; Sheila Stewart can be heard on various recordings that feature the voices of her family members. She recounts many incidents relating to her life as a Traveller in her 2008 storytelling collection *Pilgrims of the Mist*. Sheila became accustomed to singing on the world's stages while still remaining rooted in the traditional way of life of the Scottish Travellers. She was awarded the MBE in 2006 for her services to Scottish traditional music.

§1.3. **Jess Smith** (b. 1948). A native of Perthshire who spent most of her life there and in adjoining districts of Scotland, Jess Smith is the author of two novels in addition to a trio of autobiographical books that tell of her experiences growing up as a Traveller and her struggles adapting to life in settled society. Her animated style of narration differs from the matter-of-fact style that is characteristic of the writings of other Scottish Travellers mentioned in these paragraphs.

§1.3. **The portable reel-to-reel tape recorder.** To survey all the uses that have been made of this technology to document the cultural heritage of travelling people would take us far beyond the scope of the present book. Two fieldworkers in addition to those previously mentioned, however, stand out for the energy and professionalism that they have brought to the recording of Scottish traditions. One of them is the English folksong collector Mike Yates, author of the two-volume CD set *Travellers' Tales: Songs, Stories and Ballads*, based on recordings he made in Scotland in 2001 and 2002. Yates also edited the 2006 print anthology *Traveller's Joy: Songs of English and Scottish Travellers and Gypsies 1965–2005*, based on his fieldwork. A second collector who merits special recognition for his services to Scottish folksong is Peter Shepheard, a founding member of the Traditional Music and Song Society of Scotland (TMSA) and the owner and producer of Springthyme Records. Of special relevance to the present book is his 1987 cassette release *Mary and the Seal and Other Folktales*, which features Duncan Williamson telling a half dozen stories and singing one of his long ballads, "Thomas the Rhymer."

§1.3. **Sociological perspectives on the Gypsies and Travellers of Britain.** A starting point for research in this area is Judith Okely's 1983 book *The Traveller-Gypsies*. A sociologically oriented study with a tighter connection to the present book is Rehfisch and Rehfisch's chapter "Scottish Travellers or Tinkers," based on fieldwork that Farnham Rehfisch undertook with Scottish Travellers in the region of Blairgowrie in the 1950s.

CHAPTER 2: THOSE WHO WENT BEFORE

§2.1. **"At the age of fourteen she married my father."** Duncan's mother's maiden name was Betsy Townsley. His father was John Williamson (also known as "Jock"). It was not unusual for Travellers to marry very young, by settled people's standards, and to take on the role of adults from that time on, if they had not done so already.

§2.1. **The eighth Duke of Argyll.** Duncan's reference is to Niall Diarmid Campbell, who was actually the tenth Duke of Argyll (by Scottish reckoning), not the eighth. Niall was born in 1872, had no siblings, never married, and died childless in 1949. In 1914 he succeeded to the title of Duke, becoming at the same time Honorary Colonel of the 8th Battalion, Argyll and Sutherland Highlanders. Although Duncan Williamson refers to him by the name "Duncan Campbell," the Duke's actual forenames were "Niall Diarmid." It is not impossible, however, that "Duncan" was a nickname of his. In his biographical article "Niall Diarmid, 10th Duke of Argyll," Alastair Campbell of Airds reports that the Duke always wore the kilt when in the Highlands, enjoyed riding a bicycle as his chief mode of transport, was always an excellent host, had keen antiquarian interests, and "was actually a considerable eccentric." One of his noteworthy traits, we are told, was "a strong belief in the parallel world of fairies" (301–2).

§2.2. **"You had an anvil for making tin."** The tinsmith's easily portable anvil or stake—shaped similarly through much of Eurasia, I believe—was an iron stake with a flattened head. The sharper end could either be fitted into a wooden base or knocked into the ground so that the head provided a firm surface for hammering. Tinsmiths characteristically worked while seated on a low stool or cross-legged on the ground, as did itinerant silversmiths, who used a light anvil of the same type.

§2.2. **Muasdale rock cave.** Muasdale is located on the west coast of Kintyre about fifty miles south of Williamson's home village of Furnace. In former years, a cave was not an improbable place for a Traveller child to be born. Certain caves have served as habitations since Mesolithic times, as Leitch and Smith document in their article "Archaeology and Ethnohistory of Cave Dwelling in Scotland." The Scottish coastline is dotted with potentially habitable caves, especially in the western Highlands and Islands where raised beaches have resulted from the changes in sea level that accompanied the melting of ice caps and ice sheets at the end of the last Ice Age.

§2.2. **"She . . . tied its navel and everything herself."** One might compare what Belle Stewart has to say about her own birth in a bow tent: "I wis born in a wee bow tent on the bank of the River Tay on the eighteenth of July, 1906. . . . No doctors, no nurses, nobody, just my aunt, my mother's sister; that was all that was there with her [my mother]" (Bennett, *Scottish Customs*, 4).

§2.2. **"Their names is up on the stone in Argyll."** Duncan's reference is to the memorial cross, standing in the village of Furnace adjacent to the primary school, that commemorates the men of that part of Argyll who died while serving in the military during World Wars I and II. The names "Private A. Townsley" and "Private C. Townsley" are among twenty-one names listed there "in memory of our glorious dead, 1914–1919."

§2.3. **"She cuid not tell the time."** Naturally there were no clocks in tents in earlier days, nor were clocks to be found even in the houses of most settled people until the nineteenth century or later, though wealthy householders might own them. Church bells rang the hour by its quarters, however, and in some towns a town clock marked the minutes. As Betsy Whyte writes of her own childhood, speaking of the summers when the family camped out: "We didn't have a clock. We rarely needed one, preferring just to do everything in God's own time" (*Red Rowans*, 46).

§2.3. **"Shinglin turnips for the farmer."** That is, using a sharp hook (a "huik") to lop off the tops of turnips, or neeps. Travellers often contracted with farmers to do this work in the late fall or early winter, after the turnips were harvested. So—if one wishes to shore up the plausibility of the situation recounted here—there might have been ice on the road at the time when the accidents of which Duncan speaks occurred.

§2.3. **"He wasnae hurt," she says, "was he?"** Readers familiar with Scottish popular beliefs concerning witchcraft, the evil eye, and second sight will recognize what Duncan's mother meant by these words. According to such beliefs, certain persons are endowed with the power of causing harm to others by looking at them with evil intent (the "evil eye") or even just by thinking evil or jealous thoughts of them. (For discussion, see Ross, "Seers and Second Sight," *Folklore of the Scottish Highlands*, 33–62.) The Gaelic term for the evil eye is *buidealaich*, a word that has been englishized as *bootchlach*, as in "to put the bootchlach on someone." Gypsy women and Traveller women, in particular, were often attributed the power of the evil eye, hence householders might variously either fear and avoid them or offer them hospitality to avert their possible malice. Betsy Whyte, for example, was painfully conscious of being endowed with the "gift," as her mother had been as well, and she strove hard to keep her power under wraps. Jeannie Robertson too was aware of having the "gift" and was not happy about it, as Porter and Gower report in their book *Jeannie Robertson*: "I cry it nae gift. I cry it a rotten curse upon us that has it" (29).

§2.4. **"He was sharpenin his razor."** Duncan is alluding to his father's skill as an informal local barber, one whose razor was available not just for shaving but also to remove corns, or heavy callouses, from the feet of people who came to him for this service.

§2.4. **"What we call a frecht."** In Scotland as in other lands with a Celtic heritage, the line between the seen and the unseen worlds is paper thin. The dead or the soon to die can manifest themselves to the living whether or not the living person possesses the power of second sight, though "gifted" persons are more likely than others to have this experience. "Frecht," a word related to standard English "fright" in the sense of terror or apprehension, is the Scots term by which Duncan refers to the apparition of a person who is soon to die. See the *OED*, s.v. *Fright*, sense 2: "Anything that causes terror," a sense of the word that is now obsolete. (For discussion, see Ross, "Seers and Second Sight," *Folklore of the Scottish Highlands*, 33–62; Bennett, "Death Omens," *Scottish Customs*, 204–17.)

§2.6. **The Duke of Argyll used to call on Jock Williamson.** Despite the apparent implausibility of a personal relationship between a leading member of the gentry and a family of impoverished Travellers, relations between these two groups were often more cordial than those between Travellers and villagers or townspeople. As Betsy Whyte writes, "Somehow the gentry seemed to be the only people who had any understanding of us Travellers. In their own way they had many of our own characteristics. Their love of privacy to do what they really wanted to do. Their acute awareness of another human's inner feelings. Their love of freedom to wander at will. Their ability to give without meddling and interfering with our lives" (*Yellow on the Broom*, 162).

§2.6. **"It's the tinkers cuttin the trees."** On a different recording, Duncan makes clear that it was only dead or fallen wood that the family gathered for their fires: "We collected all the sticks and all the stuff that was windblown and the rotten stuff; we kept the wood clean. Windblown branches and windblown trees; we cleaned em all up for the fire" (87DW11 @ 49:07).

§2.6. **"I loved the Duke of Argyll."** For alternative tellings of this story of the Duke's visits to the Williamsons' tent, see Campbell, *Traveller in Two Worlds* (1.17–18) and Neat, *The Summer Walkers*, 169.

§2.6. **"His sporran was full o verdigris."** The sporran is traditionally worn at the belt as a core element of Highland dress, serving the function of a large pocket or, for a woman, a purse. Examples can be seen in Figures 2.1, 7.7, and 9.7. Verdigris is a natural patina that is formed when copper, brass, or bronze (including copper coins) is weathered by exposure to the elements. The Balmoral bonnet of which Duncan speaks is another facet of traditional Highland dress, as are the kilt, high stockings, and brogues.

§2.7. **"Like Thomas the Rhymer."** Duncan's reference is to Thomas of Ercildoun, also known as "True Thomas," the legendary seer famed for having been taken away by the fairies for seven years, after which he received the gift of prophesy. Duncan was a masterful singer of the ballad "Thomas the Rhymer" (Child no. 37; Roud no. 219), some of whose words he had perhaps picked up from print, and he told stories about Thomas's accomplishments as a seer, as well; see in particular Williamson, *Thorn in the King's Foot*, 252–57. Available in Scottish Voices are two recordings (one audio and one video) of Williamson singing the ballad and telling about its protagonist.

§2.11. **"He was an umbrella mender."** Like mending tinware, baskets, or china, mending umbrellas was a traditional Traveller trade. The cant term for a person who pursued this craft is "mushfeeker," a term used by Williamson in *The Horsieman* (65, 275).

§2.11. **"Grandfather had went and made the biggest mistake of his life."** This story is told with similar specifics in Williamson, *The Horsieman* (65–66).

§2.12. **"My grandfather had his tent apart away, and his gelly."** The gelly (also spelled "gailie," "geily," or "galley") was a long winter tent with either a hearth or a firebox in its central space. In her book *Pilgrims of the Mist*, Sheila Stewart characterizes the gelly as simply "two bow tents put together" (137), but there could be more to it than that. If a firebox was built into the interior, as is shown in my Figure 9.10, then a stovepipe conducted smoke out through the roof. Otherwise a hole, perhaps lined with tin, was left in the roof so that the rising smoke could escape. Willie Williamson evidently maintained both a gelly and one or more unheated storage tents. A photo reproduced at p. 51 of Douglas's study "Narrative in Traveller Scotland" shows Duncan Williamson and his oldest son Jimmy fashioning the framework of a gelly near Cupar, Fife, in 1980, while sketches of three different types of tents used by Travellers (the bow tent, the gelly, and the barrakit) are among the illustrations included in Williamson, *The Horsieman* (between pp. 116 and 117).

§2.14. **The snottum.** This tool—also spelled "snottem" or "snottam"—is an iron rod with its upper end bent into a crook. Travellers drove the rod into the ground at an angle so that the crook could be used to suspend a pot or kettle over an open fire. See Figure 9.9 for a line drawing showing its use. The snottum could also be used to drive holes into the ground to secure stakes or poles. In addition, like a wooden staff but heavier, the snottum could serve as a weapon, as we see, for example, in a comical scene in Betsy Whyte's *Yellow on the Broom*, where, feigning madness in order to scare off some intruders, Betsy's father pulls a snottum from the ground and threatens to use it to kill "all the redcoats that's in the glen" (83).

§2.17. **The Clearances.** The reference is to the notorious period of Scottish history when, beginning not long after the defeat of the Jacobite army by English military forces in 1746 and continuing intermittently for the next hundred years, many tenants in the Highlands and islands were forced to leave their homes and lands, often to make way for a new economy based largely on sheep pastoralism and industrial-scale weaving. There is a lively debate among current historians as to what extent the Clearances were a brutal act of deracination; to what extent they were a product of misguided efforts to improve the lot of those Highlanders who stayed in place; and to what extent they were a product of social and economic developments that were transforming the Highlands, to the detriment of many native Highlanders, regardless of these other factors.

§2.19. **"They threw in a cup—a tin cup—and a piece of bread and a coin."** This information was apparently communicated to Duncan by his mother. In Neat's chapter "Duncan Williamson" (247–48), Duncan is quoted to much the same effect; moreover, he identifies the person who was buried in this manner as his mother's uncle Geordie Townsley, from Campbeltown. Elsewhere Neat paraphrases the words of a Traveller from Ross-shire, Alec John Williamson (no direct relation to Duncan), as follows: "In the old days a Traveller would be buried with a hammer in the coffin, a silver sixpence and a candle. These were for the hereafter. 'Knock on the door with the hammer, pay the ferryman with the sixpence, and light your way with a candle'" (*The Summer Walkers*, 155).

§2.19. **"Yeah, pipes were valuable."** This could be quite an understatement. When Betsy Whyte writes about her Uncle Jimmy, who was a fine piper, she remarks that his bagpipes "were his only earthly treasure—of course I mean things, not people" (*Red Rowans*, 63).

§2.19. **"And the old woman's jewelry was put on her."** Compare Betsy Whyte's comments about funerary customs among Scottish Travellers, as reported by Bennett, *Scottish Customs*, 291–93. Whyte confirms that while most of a dead person's personal possessions would be burned, a woman's jewelry might accompany her into the grave: "Oh well, we burned everything personal. All the clothes, bedding, everything that belonged. We still do, but we dinnae burn furniture, anybody can get the furniture. But we burn everything else, even if it's worth a lot of money—like jewellery an things like that. Provided the dead person hasn't given it to somebody when they're alive, or promised it tae them, then it jist goes wi the rest intae the fire or intae the grave wi them" (291).

§2.19. **"They'll have drinks together."** Although one would not want to generalize about Travellers' behavior across the board, this statement may involve some understatement on Williamson's part. Worth quoting in this connection are Betsy Whyte's remarks concerning the funeral of one of her cousins, a young woman of nineteen years old who died tragically three days after giving birth to a baby girl: "Elsie was buried in Little Dunkeld. Hundreds of travelling people attended the funeral. Many of them stayed over and most of them got drunk that night, and the next and the next night. They stayed until their money was done then, after prolonged sentimental farewells, went off to their own camping places" (*Red Rowans*, 58).

§2.20. **How much land does a man need?** The title of this section of the chapter is indebted not just to Duncan's closing comment ("'At's all the land I need") but also to a brilliant short story by Leo Tolstoy that takes that question as its title.

§2.20. **"He owned Crarae Estate."** This estate adjoins the shore of Loch Fyne less than a mile north of the village of Minart. Crarae Garden, with its Himalayan-style plantings that were brought back from India by a former owner, is now owned by the National Trust of Scotland.

§2.20. **"A wee bit of ground in the cemetery for my baby."** No one can say how many Scottish Travellers lie in unmarked paupers' graves located either within a cemetery's grounds or nearby. If within the grounds, they would be separate from graves marked by headstones or family mausoleums. Sandy Stewart, for example, relates that his maternal grandfather Donald Reid, a well-known craftsman, was given a great communal sendoff after his death but then was buried in an unmarked grave (Leitch, *Book of Sandy Stewart*, xii). See, too, Figure 2.5, showing Williamson standing at his mother's unmarked grave in the cemetery at the village of Minard. Social distinctions that were operative in life, with Travellers living almost invisibly on the outskirts of settlements, were thus replicated after death.

CHAPTER 3: A CHILDHOOD IN ARGYLL

§3.1. **"He brought up sixteen children."** It was not unusual for the married couples of Williamson's parents' generation to have a large number of children, not all of whom survived. Betsy Whyte, for instance, reports that her mother had fourteen brothers (*Red Rowans and Wild Honey*, 94). This would have made for fourteen uncles for Betsy on her mother's side alone. If one also takes into account those uncles' wives and extended families, then this was no small support group. In general, as John Shaw has remarked, "Traveller society places a strong emphasis on kinship groups, which promote mutual support to their members, provide wide contacts, and serve as an effective 'multiconduit system' of transmission for their traditions" ("Storytellers in Scotland," 29).

§3.1. **"Then my father come an he beat me."** It is easy to misunderstand what is meant by this matter-of-fact statement. Corporal punishment of male children was routine in Scotland in the time of Duncan's childhood, whether in school or at home, and Duncan makes mention of it a number of times in these pages. Its basis was the belief that when a child experiences pain, he will always remember to avoid the behavior that brought about that pain, as happens with a hand burned accidently at the fire. Physical punishment meted out in the home was administered by the father, not by the mother, more likely as a juridical act than as an act of passion. As for Duncan's father, he would have been aware that Travellers were a vulnerable sector of society. If children born to Traveller parents were found to be ungovernable at school and undisciplined at home, then local authorities had the power to take them away from their parents, in an expression of state authority that was deeply feared and resented.

§3.1. **"We were persecuted at every turn."** To judge from other Travellers' testimony as well, Duncan is not exaggerating, even if there were notable exceptions. Compare what Betsy Whyte has to say of the time of her childhood: "So we travelling people were judged without knowledge. Every crime, sin, foulness, acts of violence, cruelty, stupidity, and brutish behaviour under the sun was . . . the heritage of all travelling people. Some of this lingers yet in the minds of a minority of people—those without the ability to think for themselves, or to believe what they can see with their own eyes" (*Red Rowans*, 106).

§3.2. **"These lamps hung from the ceilin on pieces o wire."** For discussion of cruisies, which were little domestic oil lamps furnished with a floating wick, see Grant, *Highland Folk Ways*, 182–83, and Stewart, *Crofts and Crofting*, 35. Williamson's father made his cruisies in a different manner from what is described in those sources, however. Duncan describes his father's lamps as follows (with his words paraphrased, rather than quoted verbatim, from my tape 86DW13): "My father used to make his own cruisie. Travellers couldn't afford to buy lamps, so they made their own. My father took a tin can, cut off the top, took soldering iron and put on a spout halfway up the side, drilled holes, and put on a handle. He took cotton and screwed it down into the lamp, then filled the lamp with paraffin oil (that is, kerosene) and lit it. Any tin would do, but a teapot was great." Duncan's father also made portable potato lamps (as paraphrased from the same source): "On a summer night, they took a common whiskey bottle, put a potato on top of the bottle, drilled a hole through the potato, and pushed in a wick. The potato would turn hard and black, but the bottle wouldn't crack because the potato was collecting all the heat. It gave a red glow. This would burn for twenty-four hours on a pint of paraffin oil."

§3.2. **"My father was a tinsmith an a basketmaker."** These were two of the traditional crafts by which Traveller men traditionally pieced together a living. Willie MacPhee, for example, who was Duncan's senior by eighteen years, was a skilled tinsmith. Some tinsmiths were likewise silversmiths, for similar tools were used for both crafts. While men were generally the makers of these wares, women would hawk them around the houses. While on their rounds, the women might collect things that needed mending. Neither tinsmithing nor basketmaking, however, was destined to survive the social and economic changes that transformed mid-twentieth-century Scotland. Once, when Duncan was speaking of the woods near Furnace where he had lived as a child (on my tape 86DW13), he remarked to me that his father had walked off alone into the hills one day and had buried his tinsmithing tools where they would not be found. This was his way of ensuring that no son of his would take up the tinsmith's craft, which had become practically worthless in an era of cheap mass-produced goods.

§3.2. **"You left school at the age of fourteen in these days."** At p. 46 of *The Book of Sandy Stewart*, Leitch discusses the legal requirements for the education of Scottish children at the start of the twentieth century. Children were required to attend school from age four to age fourteen. The Children's Act of 1908 prescribed a minimum school attendance of 200 half days per annum (though I have also heard the figures of 120 days, 202 attendances, or 250 attendances spoken of). As for an early end to the school year, Sandy Stewart remarks, "The earlier we went tae school in the winter, the earlier we got oot again" (33). If the minimum number of required attendances was not met, as confirmed by an official attendance book, then local authorities were empowered to take Traveller children away from their parents and send them off to an industrial school (a kind of reform school). For this reason among others, representatives of the Society for the Prevention of Cruelty to Children were known to Travellers simply as "the Cruelty." Sheila Stewart writes about this topic with some bitterness in her short story "Orphanages," observing that "people in my family, long, long ago, were taken away" (*Pilgrims of the Mist*, 160).

§3.3. **"The big barrakit."** Also known as a barricade, this was a winter tent with room for a fire or a metal firebox in its large central space and, as Duncan's father constructed it, with separate sleeping and dressing compartments for the boys, the girls, and the parents. Each compartment was partitioned off from the others, and if an additional sleeping compartment was wanted, it could be built into the main structure by using additional canvas and sticks. A Traveller named Alexander Reid (1922–1985), as quoted by Leitch, described the barricade as "a good thing—better than some [motor] caravans today. Ye had yer living room, then ye had yer bedrooms. . . . The fire was in the middle o the floor—no drum, tank, or anything like that—a fire on the ground. Then ye had a thing like a big gramiephone horn that went up aneth the roof and drew the reek up" (*The Book of Sandy Stewart*, xxvi).

§3.3. **"You hansel a new baby with silver."** To hansel is to offer a gift or token for good luck, as at the beginning of the New Year or, as in this passage, when first meeting a new baby. On the practice of hanseling a baby, see Margaret Bennett, *Scottish Customs*, 43–46. According to Betsy Whyte (as quoted there), the hansel for a newborn baby was a silver coin, as is consistent with the etymology of the word "hansel" (from "hand silver"). "They would give as much as they could afford—a sixpence, a shilling or a half crown. The more you gave, the more luck to the giver. . . . You had to put it in the baby's hand" (46).

§3.4. **"That was all oak—there were no conifers there."** The old-growth oak forest where Duncan's father pitched his tent was sold off in the 1940s and was subsequently cleared. The Forestry Commission then established a plantation on the grounds, planting chiefly Sitka spruce among other fast-growing conifers. The plantings were so dense that their foliage soon blocked out the light, rendering large parts of the woods practically impenetrable by humans and barren of wildlife.

§3.4. **"Huntin for the hares—rabbits."** Both hares and rabbits were a significant source of food for the Williamsons, as they were for many other people living in rural areas at this time (though not for Betsy Whyte's family, who ate rabbits but not hares; see *Yellow on the Broom*, 85). This was true until 1953, when the myxoma virus was deliberately introduced to the United Kingdom. as a means of causing myxomatosis in rabbits and thereby controlling their numbers. The disease caused rabbits to develop skin lesions, ocular and nasal secretions, and blindness, followed usually by their death. Williamson felt undisguised contempt for those who were responsible for this development, which he viewed as a barbarous act of cruelty to animals. It was likewise an act that struck at the welfare of people who depended in part for their sustenance on the resources of the land.

§3.4. **The Auchindrain Museum.** While a young man, Duncan worked off and on at Auchindrain, a township owned by the Duke of Argyll and located six miles south of Inveraray. See Neat, "Duncan Williamson," 242, on this phase of Williamson's working life. Duncan's mother too worked there from time to time. The last resident of the township moved out in the mid-1960s. Twenty-two acres pertaining to the former township are now the site of the Auchindrain Township Open Air Museum, where restored buildings, agricultural tools, and living history programs illustrate the traditional lifeways of this part of Argyll (see Powell, "Scotland's Open Air Museums," 132–33). A photo of the former township is included in Williamson, *The Horsieman* (after p. 116).

§3.5. **Own song, "Collechan."** As one of Williamson's own compositions, this short lyrical song has no Roud number. Williamson often referred to his father as a bagpiper, as he does toward the end of this excerpt. At a ceilidh I recorded in 1984, for example, he states that when he was a child, "My mother used tae dance wi her feet in the cinders of the fire" in their tent while "Daddy was playin the bagpipes" (86DW34 @ 37:40).

§3.7. **"A great big Pictish stone."** Mid-Argyll is one of the richest archaeo-logical sites of northwest Europe in terms of its multitude of standing stones, stone circles, and megalithic tombs. Only specialists can date these monuments, most of which go back to Bronze Age or Neolithic times. In Scottish popular belief, such stones are readily associated with the Picts, viewed sometimes as mysterious aboriginal inhabitants of Scotland. Duncan liked to think of himself as a descendant of the Picts. This story about his being struck dumb on a Pictish stone is one that may have had an iconic significance for him as singling him out, perhaps, as a person attuned to otherworldly phenomena or otherwise "gifted." (For other versions of the story that are in print, see Williamson, *The Horsieman*, 11–13; Campbell, *Traveller in Two Worlds*, 1.60–61.)

§3.9. **"I could learn nothing at school."** Compare the similar sentiments of Stanley Robertson: "I can say that I gained more knowledge and wisdom from the travelling people's tales than I ever did from any of the schools or colleges that I have attended" (*Exodus to Alford*, 62).

§3.10. **"Were you treated that badly other times when you were a boy?"** Duncan has just been telling us of an incident in his boyhood when his hand was bleeding profusely from a severe cut, and yet when he approached a house-holder to ask for a strip of cloth for a bandage, the man's response was, "Get away, you're spoilin my gravel with your blood."

§3.14. **Cumulative rhyme, "The House That Jack Built."** A version of this rhyme or game was published in Halliwell's *Nursery Rhymes of England* (1843 edition, 222–24), and many other versions have since been printed; see Iona and Peter Opie, *Oxford Dictionary of Nursery Rhymes*, 229–32, with commentary. It is assigned Roud no. 20584 and ATU tale type number 2035. Recordings of Duncan reciting it are on my tapes 86DW29 (with video 86V01), 86CEIL03, and 86DW38 (with video 86V05). Two of these performances (86DW29 and 86V05) can be accessed via Scottish Voices. Available in Tobar an Dualchais is an Aberdeenshire version that Kenneth Goldstein recorded from Jean Stewart, Elizabeth Stewart's mother, in 1959 (track ID 47000).

§3.15. **Children's song, "The Mousie's Wedding to the Frog."** Also known as "Frog He Would A-Wooing Go," among many other titles, this has been a favorite song of young and old since a version of it was first published in 1611 in Thomas Ravenscroft's anthology *Melismata*. Folksong specialists know it as Roud no. 16. For an early nineteenth-century English version (with commentary), see Opie and Opie, *Oxford Dictionary of Nursery Rhymes*, 177–81, and a cluster of Scottish versions is published as a group as Greig-Duncan no. 1669. A version sung by Jeannie Robertson and recorded by Hamish Henderson in 1955 can be heard via Tobar an Dualchais (track ID 29807). An Orkney version recorded by Alan Bruford in 1973 is printed in *Tocher*, vol. 7, nos. 48/49, 1995, pp. 390–91 and can be heard as track 12a of the Scottish Tradition CD *Chokit on a Tattie*. I recorded Duncan singing it on 86DW29 (with video 86V01), 86DW41 (with video 86V05), and 87DW13. The last two of these performances are included in Scottish Voices.

CHAPTER 4: MAKING A LIVING

§4.2. **"Good willows along the other side o Dalmally."** The following conversation was recorded in the summer of 1988 while Duncan and I were travelling by car from Fife to Argyll, accompanied by two UREP volunteers, to visit places that figured importantly in Duncan's childhood. At this point in the recording, we are heading west on the A85 in the direction of Crianlarich. For a map of the route that Duncan used to take by horse and cart along this way during the 1950s, see the front and end flaps of Williamson, *The Horsieman*.

§4.2. **"The next fine place over here on the road, we'll get a stop."** What Williamson had in mind was stopping for a while so that he could cut some willows, then demonstrate how to use them in basketmaking. Once we reached the western shore of Loch Fyne, he made a slipe from a hazel branch and cut and peeled an armful of willows (see Figures 4.1 and 4.2). For a photo of Duncan weaving a basket out of peeled willows, see Shaw, "Storytellers in Scotland," 30.

§4.2. **"The children would help peel the willows with a slipe."** A slipe is a simple handmade tool, cut normally from a hazel sapling, used to strip willows. A person skilled in its use can strip the rind and leaves off a willow wand in a matter of seconds. See the Commentary on §4.2. A video, dating from the summer of 1988, showing Williamson making a slipe and using it to strip a number of willows is available in Scottish Voices.

§4.3. **"Ye'll get the . . . story in Ailie Munro's book."** Duncan is referring to Munro's transcription of a different telling of this story as she recorded it from him in Cupar, Fife, in 1977 (see Munro, *Folk Music Revival in Scotland*, 219–28). Williamson did not care for the style in which Munro transcribed the story for print, with its multiple strings of ellipses. When compared with that version, the version offered here, in a less meticulous style of transcription that is easier to read, illustrates the facility with which Williamson varied the particulars of a tale with each telling. Jimmy Williamson, Duncan's oldest son from his first marriage, has been recorded telling his own version of the same story; see the article on "Jimmy Williamson" in *Tocher*, vol. 8, no. 56, 2000, at 377–80.

§4.4. **"I tried to get all his tales."** The stonemason for whom Duncan worked at this time was Neil MacCallum, a native Gaelic speaker who told him numerous stories rooted in the rich oral traditions of Argyll. Some of these became a core part of Duncan's repertory.

§4.4. **A drystone dike builder.** A drystone dike is a wall built up of stones assembled without mortar, usually capped with half-rounded stones that help to hold the wall in place. By making a point of calling MacCallum a stonemason, Duncan makes clear that skilled work with hammer and chisel was involved in his craft.

§4.4. **"Mother and I were walkin down to Achnagoul one day."** Achnagoul is an old township located about halfway between Auchindrain and Inveraray, just north of the A83. When, in the following section, Duncan speaks of "a shortcut when you left the farm," he means that you could walk back from Achnagoul to his home village of Furnace while bypassing a stretch of the main road.

§4.6. **"An then she ran away wi my brother."** It was Duncan's oldest brother, Sandy, who eloped with young Betsy Townsley. "Granny and Grandfather" are Bett MacColl and Willy Williamson. Sandy and Betsy Williamson subsequently settled in Perthshire and raised their children there. As Duncan goes on to say, his brother Sandy introduced him to the travelling way of life as it was then in Perthshire and in other parts of Scotland where Duncan had never been.

§4.6. **The Gothens at Blairgowrie.** The scene at Blairgowrie during the berry-picking season in the 1940s must have been quite a spectacle for a young man who grew up in a quiet part of Argyll. Hard work in the fields by day was matched by hard drinking—and sometimes fighting—at night, alongside cheerful family get-togethers by the campfires. Hamish Henderson evokes the high spirits of that time in his article "Folk-Songs and Music from the Berryfields of Blair." It was not just Travellers who congregated in the neighborhood of Blairgowrie during the berry season. Settled working-class people (or "flatties") did so as well, flocking in from Dundee and Glasgow and elsewhere during the school holidays to earn a bit of extra cash. The hurly-burly that erupted from this mix of populations was not to everyone's taste.

§4.6. **"Swappin and dealin and spittin in each other's hand."** Duncan came to be skilled at swapping or selling horses or donkeys, as he recounts in *The Horsieman*. Deals were done in cash. Once the terms of a deal were settled, a bit of spit in the hand and a slap of palms sealed it. After that there was no going back.

§4.6. **"These were great popular songs."** The first of the songs Duncan names here, "The Harbor of Dundee"—also known as "The Magdalen Green," "The Maudlin Green," or "The Marlin Green"—is featured at §4.9; the other, "The Factory Girl," at §7.3.

§4.7. **"I was wondering if you travelled up this way as well?"** "Up this way" refers to the present A9 road running north from Perth to Inverness, following the route of an older road that took this same route. The conversations that follow were recorded while travelling by car on the A9 past Pitlochry in the direction of the Highland Folk Museum at Kingussie, in the central Highlands, with Williamson beside me in the front seat.

§4.7. **The Rest and Be Thankful.** This well-known rest point is located at the crest of the road (the current A83) that runs from Loch Long to Loch Fyne. The hairpin turns of the former road leading up to this pass posed a challenge for anyone travelling up it by horse and cart, or indeed by almost any vehicle.

§4.8. **Maconochie's soup factory.** Maconochie's factory in Fraserburgh produced a large quantity of tinned stew during the period from the Boer War to the 1940s and later. The stew was widely used as a ration for British soldiers during World War I.

§4.8. **"Old houses was going a dime a dozen in Aberdeen."** In the early years of World War II, many houses in Aberdeen were vacated on account of the Blitz. Some blocks were destroyed by bombs, while many houses that were scheduled for demolition and replacement were left standing for years. Itinerants like Duncan, who had been excused from military service because of his injured hand, were able to squat there.

§4.8. **"A minister who had a wood contracting business."** The minister was the Reverend Iain Begg, who treated Duncan respectfully and fairly; indeed, a warm friendship developed between the two men. More details about this episode in Duncan's life are recounted in Williamson, *The Horsieman* (146–51) and in Campbell, *Traveller in Two Worlds* (1.190–98).

§4.9. **"The Marlin Green."** Duncan's title for this song refers to a green whose formal name is the Magdalen Green. This is a recreational ground, fronting the River Tay, that is Dundee's oldest city park. The song is usually titled "The Magdalen Green" (Roud no. 2893) and has the alternative title "The Harbor of Dundee." Ten or so recordings of it can be accessed via Tobar an Dualchais, including a version of it sung by Williamson for the ethnomusicologist Peter Cooke in 1978 (track ID 64465). For printed versions by two singers from the region of Dundee (Eck Harley of Fife and Jim Reid of Angus), see Gatherer, *Songs and Ballads of Dundee*, 72–73. Another recording of Duncan singing it is on my tape 86DW40.

§4.9. **"The old Overgate is gone."** Duncan describes this old Dundee street, which is now demolished, as it was in the '40s. Nigel Gatherer characterizes the Overgate as having been "one of the oldest, most colourful, and, at one time, most notorious streets in the town" (*Songs and Ballads of Dundee*, 55). The spicy song "The Overgate" (Roud no. 866) gives an impression of the low-life culture that once thrived there. Hall, "Scottish Tinker's Songs," 59–61, prints a version of that song as sung by Davie Stewart. Many other versions of the song, including performances by Jeannie Robertson, Belle Stewart, and other Scottish Travellers, can be accessed via Tobar an Dualchais. A version that I recorded from the fine traditional singer Charlie Lamb of Dundee is included in Scottish Voices.

§4.10. **Bothy ballads.** These are songs, often composed in a broad rural dialect, that deal with the traditional way of life of farm laborers. Though primarily associated with former days in Aberdeenshire and the rest of the agricultural northeast, they have also been recorded in other parts of Scotland as well as in Northern Ireland. Ian Olson surveys songs of the type in his chapter "Bothy Ballads and Song," while many examples are included in *Ord's Bothy Songs and Ballads* (best consulted in its reissued edition with an introduction by Alexander Fenton). Songs of the type are well represented in the Greentrax CD *Bothy Ballads: Music from the North East*; in John Strachan's album *Songs from Aberdeenshire*; and in Jock Duncan's CD *Ye Shine Whar Ye Stan!* Although bothy songs are usually performed unaccompanied, Jock Duncan's release features deft accompaniments by musicians from the Folk Revival scene.

§4.10. **"They all lived up in the bothies."** Unmarried male farmworkers generally lived in outbuildings, known as bothies, that served as bunkhouses. Overlooking the Williamsons' cottage at Kincraigie Farm, Strathmiglo, were the ruins of a former bothy.

§4.10. **A place called Kirriemuir.** The burgh of Kirriemuir, Angus, is situated in the midst of fertile agricultural land extending to the north of Dundee. The town is the putative setting of "The Ball of Kirriemuir" (Roud no. 4828), a ribald song that MacColl and Seeger characterize as "Scotland's most popular erotic song" (*Till Doomsday*, 209). A group performance of this song to which Williamson, Andrew Douglas, and Betsy Whyte contributed individual stanzas is recorded on my tape 86DW34 (with video 86V04).

§4.10. **"Ah smoked Woodbines in these days."** Duncan's reference is to "Wild Woodbine Cigarettes," a cheap British brand of strong, unfiltered cigarettes. This was Duncan's brand of choice, just as it was among vast numbers of British working-class people at that time and among soldiers during both world wars.

§4.11. **Bothy song, "Bogie's Bonnie Belle."** This noteworthy bothy ballad set in Aberdeenshire (Roud no. 2155; Greig-Duncan no. 1396) is thought to have been composed in the 1840s and to tell the true story of a woman named Isabella Morrison, who bore a child out of wedlock to one of her father's farm servants, James Stephen. If so, then the particulars underlying the song have been worn smooth in the course of its oral transmission. The song's setting, Bogie Water, is a river that runs through Strathbogie to the towns of Rhynie and Huntly. Bogie is a landowner who takes his name from this locale. Versions of the song as performed by Jimmy MacBeath, Stanley Robertson, and other outstanding traditional singers can be heard via Tobar an Dualchais, while a performance by Belle Stewart is on *Songs and Ballads from Perthshire Field Recordings* (track 3). Williamson's version stands out for its tight presentation of the story and for the direct and unaffected manner in which he sings it. While my transcription of Duncan's singing is from tape 86DW43, his spoken introduction is from tape 84GF02, which was recorded at a meeting of the Glenfarg Folk Club in July of 1984. A third recording of Duncan singing it is on my tape 87DW07. There are slight variations of wording from one of his performances to another, as is usual with his songs.

§4.11. **"For this young girl here."** Duncan often liked to single out a single person as the recipient of a song regardless of who else was present in the room. Here, in the setting of a folk club, he directs the song to a visitor from Ireland who, shortly before this, had sung the Irish song "The Mountains of Morne."

§4.11. **"My intentions they were to fee."** To fee with a farmer was to enter upon an agreement to work for him for a set period of time, usually six months. The worker who signed on in this way was provided with his meals and lodging, typically of the simplest kind. At the end of the term, he was given his wages and was free to go elsewhere if he wished. If the farmworker broke his fee, however, then he was paid nothing and might find it difficult to find employment elsewhere. The speaker of the present song, we learn, loses his sweetheart (who then gives birth to a child outside of marriage) and is sent packing "withoot a penny o my fee," with these griefs attributable to a father's misplaced pride in his social standing. In Duncan's version, still, the possibility is left open that Belle's marriage to a tinker has turned out well enough. Typically, when a settled woman chose to marry into the Travellers, her Traveller in-laws would accept her as one of their own even though her own family had ostracized her.

§4.12. **"The lad who didn't know what fear was."** I was alluding to ATU tale type 326, "The Youth Who Wanted to Learn What Fear Is." The gist of this tale type is that a youth who seems to have no sense of fear whatsoever is put to various tests in an attempt to scare him. One common test is spending the night right by a grave, or in it.

§4.16. **Young Paddy O'Donnell.** I do not know who this was. He does not seem to be the same Patrick O'Donnell (or O'Donnel) about whom Williamson reminisces in Campbell, *Traveller in Two Worlds* (1.116–20), and Neat, "Duncan Williamson," 237–40. When Duncan was in his early teens, he worked for that older man for a number of weeks, helping him cut peats and dry them on a hillside at Glen Aray, close by Inveraray.

§4.16. **"The first place I haird 'Glen Swilly.'"** Although Williamson did not sing this song (Roud no. 5087) on this occasion, I recorded it from him another time, at the Glenfarg Folk Club (see §4.11).

§4.17. **Irish song, "The Flower of Sweet Strabane."** This song, also known as "If I Were the King of Ireland" (Roud no. 2745; Greig-Duncan no. 722), is representative of the ones that Duncan learned through his contacts with Irish immigrant workers. It has been recorded with some frequency in Ireland and occasionally in Scotland and North America; Irish versions can be consulted in Huntington and Herrmann, *Sam Henry's Songs of the People*, under no. 224. Peter Kennedy collected it from the Irish street singer Margaret Barry in 1952, as can be heard on track 19 of her CD *I Sang through the Fairs*, while Maurice Fleming recorded it from the young Sheila Stewart, who had strong Irish connections, in 1954 (Tobar an Dualchais, track ID 33032).

§4.17. **"I was working in the Shira Glen."** Glen Shira is located at the northern end of Loch Fyne, to the north of Inveraray. The Shira Dam was completed in 1956 in a major engineering project for which Irish immigrant workers were recruited as navvies, or manual laborers.

§4.18. **On pearl fishing in summer.** Pearl fishing, or gathering potentially pearl-bearing mussels from one of the rivers that run down from the Highlands, was a favorite summer occupation among Traveller men of former generations, particularly in Perthshire. (For discussion, along with photos and personal interviews illustrating this aspect of Scottish social history, see MacLean, "Pearl Fishers"; Neat, "Pearl Fishers," *Summer Walkers*, 105–51.) Betsy Whyte makes frequent mention of pearl fishing in *Yellow on the Broom*. Stanley Robertson writes authoritatively about this art in chapter 2 of his story collection *Reek Roon a Campfire*, remarking, "There wis naething mair relaxing than tae gang pearl-fishing on a fine simmer's nicht wi the ither Traiveller laddies" (8). He regrets, as do many, that the species of pearl-bearing mussels that was prized by people of Williamson's generation is now on the brink of extinction in Scotland as a result of overexploitation. It is now illegal to disturb, take, or kill them, although illegal pearl fishing is not easily eradicated.

§4.20. **"Before this 'no-harassment' started."** Duncan is referring to a policy regarding the nonharassment of Travellers that was instituted by Act of Parliament not long after Duncan and Linda were married in 1977. The police thereafter had no authority to shift Travellers from permitted campsites unless they were breaking the law. As Duncan put it to me, "Don't destroy any property, behave yourself, don't cause any trouble, don't cause any nuisance, an there's nothin the police can do" (87DW11 @ 1:02:32).

§4.21. **"Thirty days for breakin a boy's jaw in Perth."** For another version of this incident, which occurred when Duncan was camping close by a mining operation in Fife, see Campbell, *Traveller in Two Worlds*, 1.239–40.

§4.23. **"He had a good sense of humor."** Carole's comment is on the mark. Readers of this anecdote should understand that Duncan viewed this particular scrap dealer with respect, appreciating the man's straightforward dealings and easygoing manner.

CHAPTER 5: COURTSHIP, MARRIAGE, AND RAISING CHILDREN

5.1. **Song of fulfilled love, "Banks of Red Roses."** This song (Roud no. 603) is a popular one in Scotland, but Williamson's interpretation of it differs from that of other singers. Munro, *The Folksong Revival in Scotland*, 280–92, prints transcriptions of it as sung by Sheila Douglas, Stanley Robertson, Jane Turriff, and Peter Shepheard. See also Belle Stewart's version, as published in MacColl and Seeger, *Travellers' Songs*, no. 72 (pp. 235–37), and Ruby Kelbie's, as heard on track 22 of *Songs and Ballads from Perthshire Field Recordings*. Some ten different versions can be heard via Tobar an Dualchais. In all of these the song takes the form of a grim murder ballad of a familiar Anglo-American type: a man entices a woman to a secluded flowery bank, seduces her, then kills her, leaving her body behind. But there is no murder in Duncan's version, which he sang in an upbeat, impromptu style in the midst of convivial circumstances. The song may have personal meaning for Duncan in that his first wife, who died in 1971 leaving him as a grieving widower with five children, was named Jeannie.

§5.2. **Song of unrequited love, "Lambs in the Green Field."** This beautiful song (Roud no. 154) is fairly well attested in Ireland and Scotland and has been recorded in England as well. Many songs of a similar kind, lamenting a frustrated love affair from the man's perspective, were printed by the broadside press and have circulated in oral tradition under such titles as "I Aince Looed

a Lass" or "The False Bride." Other Traveller singers have been recorded singing it, among them Jeannie Robertson, Lucy Stewart, and Elizabeth Stewart
(as a search of Tobar an Dualchais under "The False Bride" will reveal), and
Duncan's friend Willie MacPhee sang a version that is printed, with tune, in
Douglas, *Last of the Tinsmiths*, 172–73. It is possible that Duncan learned the
song from MacPhee. Douglas notes that MacPhee sang the song in a manner
that "particularly suited Willie's high, lyrical, expressive voice." Another recording of Duncan singing it is on my tape 88DW12.

§5.3. **Song in cant, "My Wee Maggie."** A song from Duncan's family tradition; no Roud number. Other recordings of the song, with differences of detail,
are published by Neat, *Summer Walkers*, 210–12 (text, no music) and in Williamson, *The Horsieman* (best consulted at p. 21 of the 2nd edition; full text with
transcription, no music). My fondness for this song was matched by Duncan's
knowledge that I liked it, considering it a brilliant entry point to Traveller
lifeways and values. I made nine recordings of Duncan singing it and talking
about it on different occasions over a five-year period: see my tapes 84DW03,
84DW05, 86DW11, 86DW18, 86DW30 (with video 86V01), 86DW38 (with
video 86V05), 87DW12, 88DW09, and 88DW11. Each of these performances
is unique, in keeping with the song's improvisatory nature. Recordings of two
of them (86V05 and 87DW12) can be accessed via Scottish Voices.

§5.3. **"This was like Gretna Green, this barn!"** As a parish in Dumfries and
Galloway located just over the Scottish border from England, Gretna Green
was a famous destination for runaway marriages involving English lovers who
were under the age of twenty-one and who wished to marry in defiance of their
parents' will. English law prohibiting such marriages did not apply in Scotland.

§5.3. **"A bun wood sprachin."** The language of "My Wee Maggie" is partially
impenetrable thanks to Duncan's use of cant words whose exact meaning is
hard to discern, though their gist may be clear enough. "Sprachin," as he later
explains, means begging, in the sense of going from house to house to obtain
food or the wherewithal for food. I am not sure what "burl" means here, except
that in a different performance, what Duncan sings at this point is "bundle."
A "can" is a tea can or kettle, often used by Travellers to obtain boiling water
from a householder to make tea. To "bing doon the glen" is to go down the glen.
"Haben" is food, while "bing haben" means "bring food." "Chaet" is a general
term for "thing," perhaps with reference here to an outdoor shed or pantry or its
contents. "Kinchens" are children. "Bing to wir naiskel" means "go to our father."

§5.9. **"What they called a 'taen-awa.'"** What the word "taen-awa" means
literally is "taken away," with reference to a human child taken away by fairies,
who substitute one of their own for it. Duncan's remarks here are suggestive of
some overlap between the powers of God and those of the fairies in northern
belief systems. In popular belief in the Highlands of Scotland, fairies are reputed

to covet human children. They may substitute a changeling for the true child, and the changeling's incessant whining may then make life intolerable for the parents. See the first five items in James MacDougall's collection *Highland Fairy Legends*; or, for an example told in a much more leisurely style, see Duncan's story "The Taen-Awa," in Williamson, *The Broonie, Silkies and Fairies*, 43–65 (1985 edn.), reprinted with different framing matter in Williamson and Williamson, *The King and the Lamp*, 145–62. A recording of Duncan telling it can be heard on the Springthyme cassette *Mary and the Seal*, side 2, track 6.

CHAPTER 6: FOOD AND HEALTH, DRINK AND CONVIVIALITY

§6.4. **"Is this where your pony would have to start?"** At this point in this recording, Duncan and I are heading west by car on the A83 from Ardgarten, on Loch Long, toward Cairndow, on Loch Fyne, approaching the pass known as Rest and Be Thankful. Duncan is reflecting on the days when he used to travel each summer by horse and cart, with his first wife and family, from central or eastern Scotland over to Argyll and back, as he recounts in *The Horsieman*.

§6.5. **"Kilmichael Glassary, where my father used tae work."** Kilmichael Glassary is a parish in Argyllshire that can only be reached by road from Furnace by a circuitous route, hence the reference to a shortcut through the hills. Just two miles from Kilmichael Glassary is the prehistoric stronghold of Dunadd, the chief seat of the Gaels of Scottish Dalriada and one of the most significant archaeological sites in Britain. Duncan's father was a skilled scytheman who used to earn money by cutting hay for farmers during the summer months. This was in addition to such temporary work as cutting bracken, cutting hedges, and digging ditches, as is touched on by Linda Williamson, "Narrative Singing," 303.

§6.6. **"Jack and the Devil's Purse."** See the *Tocher* article "Duncan Williamson," 150–55, for a version of this tale, one that is reprinted in Bruford, *Green Man of Knowledge*, 55–60, and in Williamson, *May the Devil Walk behind Ye!*, 117–32. Duncan tells it on my tape 86DW15 in a version available via Scottish Voices. Although he makes no mention of imps feeding on mushrooms, this was evidently how Duncan envisioned the story.

§6.8. **"The First Tea in Scotland."** Duncan told the present anecdote at a time when there was a tea break in the recording session. The question came up, "How do you like your tea?" That is, "Do you want it with milk, sugar, or both?" Duncan's joke depends in part on a linguistic play. Typically, in Scotland, "tea" is a term not just for the beverage but also for the evening meal.

§6.11. **"Ma grandmother used tae make her own nettle brew for arthritis."** Elsewhere, speaking with reference to his grandmother Bella MacDonald,

Duncan specifies how this brew was made: "My grandmother used tae get a bunch of nettles. She would boil them an strain them through a piece o muslin, an she had this green-bluish water, ye know? She'd put it in a jar and she would put salt in it an she would save it. Her fingers used tae be curled with arthritis, ye know? An then for days it was gone. When she was eighty-four years of age she beat me tae catch a bus! Granny used tae drink this brew twice a day, night an morning" (86DW41 @ 43:00).

§6.12. **"So these old people had many cures."** A miscellany of cures known to Williamson, including the "trout" cure for whooping cough and the "mouse water" cure for bed-wetting, are listed in summary form in Hendry and Stephen's compilation *Scotsgate*, 30; see also Neat, *The Summer Walkers*, 166–69. In *Scotsgate*, as well, is a section headed "The Weatherlore of Duncan Williamson" (27–29) that features his precise observations of nature in its changing seasons.

§6.12. **"We had all the kinds of herbs in the world."** Williamson did not go into specifics with me regarding herbal cures, perhaps because herbalism is largely a woman's domain, while his knowledge of herbs and their uses may have been limited. Plants that figure in the medical lore of the Highlands are listed in Thompson, *Crofting Years*, 122–27, while Beith, *Healing Threads*, surveys that topic from a wide historical perspective.

§6.14. **Drinking song, "Johnny You're a Rover."** Williamson can be heard singing a version of this song on Yates's CD *Travellers' Tales* (vol. 1, track 1), and a transcription of that 2001 recording is included in Yates's book *Traveller's Joy* (no. 29, p. 86). According to Campbell, *Traveller in Two Worlds* (1.44–45), Duncan's grandmother Bett MacColl used to sing this song on the streets in Tarbert, while his mother, too, sang the song while on the road (1.65). The song is not easy to track down, though it has loose analogues in British and Irish tradition. Another recording of Duncan singing it is on my tape 86DW39.

§6.15. **Drinking song, "Nancy Whisky."** Williamson's wording of this song, which is also known as "Nancy's Whisky" or "The Calton Weaver" (Roud no. 883; Greig-Duncan no. 603), was subject to change from one performance to another. As he sang it for me in 1986, for example, it begins as follows:

> As I went doon by Glesgow city
> Nancy Whisky I chanced to smell;
> And I fell in with Nancy Whisky,
> And for seven years with her did dwell.
>
> (86DW44 @ 03:53.)

The song is fairly well known in both England and Scotland, with versions attested both in the broadside press and as recorded from oral tradition. Ord, *Bothy Songs and Ballads*, 372–73, prints a narrative version in ten stanzas, and a similar version was recorded in Oxfordshire in 1952; see Kennedy, *Folksongs of Britain,* no. 279 (p. 611, with notes at p. 629). Recordings by four Scottish singers can be heard via Tobar an Dualchais. One of these versions, as sung by Willie Mitchell of Kintyre, has been published in *Tocher,* vol. 5, no. 31, 1979, pp. 13–15, and can be heard as track 1 of the CD *Hamish Henderson Collects, Volume 2.* Calton, a former borough that is now assimilated into the City of Glasgow, was famous in former years for its weaving industries.

§6.15. **"The Whisky Clan."** The joys and hazards of drink—"the drinkin trade," as it is called in this song—are a staple source of humor not only among Scottish Travellers but throughout Britain and Ireland. On a different date, for example, Duncan repeated a wry joke that he had picked up from an old bothy man in Morayshire: "'I was so drunk last night, Duncan,' he said, 'It's a guid job I had ma car wi me, cause I cuid never have walked home!'" (86DW10 @ 34:02).

§6.17. **Own song, "When the Yellow Is on the Broom."** Williamson wrote this song for Betsy Whyte on the occasion of the publication of her book *Yellow on the Broom.* Other printings of the song are in Neat, "Duncan Williamson," 244–45, and Braid, *Scottish Traveller Tales,* 20–23 (with music). At the ceilidh where I recorded it in July of 1984, Betsy and her husband Bryce were visiting the Williamsons' home outside Strathmiglo. Duncan sang the song directly to Betsy, holding her hand firmly in his (see Figure 6.6). The words of the song are set in the voice of Betsy's father, who is imagined to be addressing Betsy's mother Maggie when she is restless to set out on the road after a winter cooped up in town. Other recordings of Duncan singing it are on my tapes 84DW03, 86BW02, 86DW33 (with video 86V03), and 86DW37 (with video 86V05). On that last recording, Duncan comments that once he has given a song to someone—as with this one, which he gave to Betsy—it's theirs "to do as they feel fit. It's their story. It's not my property anymore, but once I give it tae them, then it's theirs. An I just can't give it tae no one else" (86DW37 @ 49:06).

A different song with very nearly this same title, "The Yellow on the Broom," composed by the songwriter and educator Adam McNaughtan, became the next thing to an anthem in Scottish folk clubs of the 1980s and later. It is included in McNaughtan's 1993 album *Words, Words, Words* (reissued on CD in 2000), and I recorded him singing it during an interview recorded on my tape 86AM01, in a performance included in Scottish Voices.

CHAPTER 7: MUSIC AND THE FLOW OF LIFE

§7.1. **Travellers' song, "Come Aa Ye Perthshire Folk."** This was one of Williamson's mother's favorite songs. It tells of a young Traveller who wishes to join the Royal Navy despite his sweetheart's dismay at that prospect. Another name by which Duncan knew the song is "Cauld Fet" (cold foot or feet). It appears to be a fusion of at least two others. Stanzas 2 and 7 are closely related to a song called "When Fortune Turns Her Wheel" (Roud no. 3798), which was published in seven long stanzas in Ord's *Bothy Songs and Ballads*, 180–81. The remainder of Duncan's song is an offshoot of a popular song type, exemplified by Laws types N8 ("William and Nancy I") and N9 ("The Banks of the Nile"), in which a soldier must leave his sweetheart to fight abroad. She vows to follow him, disguising herself as a man. Another analogue is the song headed "I'll Cut Off My Long Yellow Hair" that Martha Reid sings on track 16 of *Songs and Ballads from Perthshire Field Recordings*. A recording of Duncan singing the song in 2001 is included in Yates's CD *Travellers' Tales* under the title "Fortune Turns the Wheel" (vol. 2, track 11): a somewhat misleading title since a quite different song is known by that same name. Other recordings of Williamson singing it are on my tapes 86BW02, 86DW39, 87DW13, and 88DW02.

§7.2. **"Down in Yonder Bushes."** I know of no other song quite like this short lyric lament. Certain individual lines or couplets, however, are paralleled in other songs of a lyric character, as Yates points out in his commentary on a recording he made of Duncan singing it in 2001 (see Yates's book *Traveller's Joy*, no. 14, p. 60, and his CD *Travellers' Tales*, vol. 1, track 8). See also Linda Williamson, "Narrative Singing," 37–38. A recording of Duncan singing it in 1977, as recorded by Linda Williamson, can be heard via Tobar an Dualchais (track ID 30890). I also recorded him singing it in July of 1984. As he commented then, "Ah remember ma mommy and ma daddy cryin, tears runnin down their cheeks, just for one single song. Heartbroken! My daddy was a big man, six feet tall an a hardworkin man, an he cried. But no sober; when he had a wee drop, like me. . . . I don't think it was actually the words o the song, it was jist the air, the flow o the music that raised an fell, that made them feel so sad" (84DW01 @ 1:24:10).

§7.3. **Broadside ballad, "The Factory Girl."** A favorite of the broadside press, this song (Roud no. 1659) is fairly well attested in oral tradition. A recording that George McIntyre made of Williamson singing it in 1967 (Tobar an Dualchais, track ID 28815) is very much like two of my recordings from about twenty years later (on my tape 86DW16 and, as given here, on 87DW14). For a recording of Williamson singing it in 1991, see Veteran Tapes cassette *Put Another Log on the Fire*, track B3. A recording made by Peter Kennedy of the Irish street singer Margaret Barry singing a short version of it in 1952 can be heard as track 2 of her CD *I Sang through the Fairs*.

§7.3. **"The Road and the Miles to Dundee."** This song (Roud no. 2300) is a favorite in the northeast of Scotland, and a version of it composed in a rather literary style can be found in Ord, *Bothy Songs and Ballads*, 152–53. Two versions, one of them as sung by Belle Stewart, are included in Gatherer, *Songs* *and Ballads of Dundee*, 125–28, and some sixteen versions are represented in Tobar an Dualchais. I recorded Charlie Lamb of Dundee singing it in 1988 to two different tunes (my tape 88CL01), in a fine performance that can be heard via Scottish Voices. When Duncan states that the tune of "The Factory Girl" is "familiar" to that of "The Road and the Miles to Dundee," what he evidently means is that it is "similar" to it (and hence is likely to be familiar).

§7.3. **"Peggy Gordon."** This traditional song of unrequited love (Roud no. 2280) has been recorded with some frequency in Canada as well as Britain. I recorded Duncan singing it twice, on 87DW13 (available on Scottish Voices) and 88DW02.

§7.4. **"The old professor from Turkey."** Duncan is alluding to a professor from Ankara University, Turkey, who was visiting Scotland and invited Duncan to come to Ankara to participate in singing or storytelling events there. Duncan planned to follow up on the invitation but was unable to do so at the time.

§7.4. **"It was only for the evening."** What Duncan means to imply, I believe, is that improvised communal songs of this kind never crystallized into pieces suitable for performance on a stage. Each evening's impromptu entertainments were unique to that occasion.

§7.5. **Song in cant, "Big Jimmy Drummond."** This song (Roud nos. 2157 and 2506) has been published with some frequency in recent years, never in quite the same form, sometimes under the title "The Choring Song." A version collected from travelling people in Perthshire in 1956 is printed in Kennedy, *Folksongs of Britain* (no. 342, p. 768, with notes at p. 795). Performances by several different singers, Jeannie Robertson, are available for listening via Tobar an Dualchais, and Robertson's version is published in Porter and Gower, *Jeannie Robertson* (no. 24, pp. 153–54). Peter Cooke recorded Williamson singing two exceptionally long versions of it in 1978, one in cant and one in ordinary Scots (Tobar an Dualchais track ID 60740 and 60738, respectively). Peter Hall, "Scottish Tinker Songs," prints two versions, one of which, like Williamson's, is set on the Isle of Arran. Textually, Duncan's version is very similar to Willie MacPhee's version as published in MacColl and Seeger, *Travellers' Songs* (no. 97, pp. 295–97) and, with slightly different wording, in Douglas, *The Sang's the Thing*, 148–49. Williamson uses a different tune, however. In stanza 2, when Duncan sings, "And I dinnae jan where I may be," his wording differs from MacPhee's wording "I dinna jan whaur *they* may be," with reference to Jimmy's wife and children. Another recording of Duncan singing it is on my tape 84DW03.

§7.6. **Own song, "The Nicknames."** At 250–51 of his article "Duncan Williamson," Neat presents a different version of this comic song. It includes the following additional stanza:

There's Old Game Befukum
And Old Scabby Kate,
O, yin they call the Hedgehog
And yin they cry the Skate
    With me he riddee doo [etc.].

The song must have been subject to improvisation on the spot. If the use of bynames for particular kin groups of Travellers is a phenomenon that is little known, this may be in part because the use of those names in the presence of those people—or even an oblique allusion to those names—could be taken as an insult. Travellers' use of personal nicknames is addressed by Henderson, "Bynames among the Tinkers," with colorful examples of names that were rarely used face to face except as fighting words. The Travellers' custom of giving pet names to campsites is brought out in Betsy Whyte's and Sheila Stewart's accounts of their early days on the road. A passing reference to such names as cited by Linda Williamson, "Narrative Singing," 305–6, includes "The Hoolit's Neuk" near Dundee, "Two-Penny Moor" near Aberdeen, and "The Hangman's Strip" near Dunfermline.

§7.7. **"Ah played it to em."** Duncan is referring to the time when, during the 1960s, he owned a tape recorder and used it to record other singers and instrumentalists, sometimes playing a joke on those people by replaying the tapes backward. See the Commentary on §1.1, "His tapes from the 1960s are now evidently lost."

§7.7. **Travellers' story and song, "The Shanghai Ballad."** See Linda Williamson, "Narrative Singing," 82–87, for transcription of an interview dating from 1984 when Duncan sang these verses plus a little more of the song, with his reflections. The only other recorded example of this song of which I am aware is a recording, available via Tobar an Dualchais (as track ID 90745), of Sheila Stewart singing "Beneath the Window of My Cell" at the 1978 Kinross Festival. Stewart's performance includes one stanza not sung by Williamson; this is borrowed from a different song tradition, that of the penitent criminal who awaits his death. The closest analogues to the song are Roud no. 8122—a type with only one cited example, an Irish recording dating from 1977—and Roud no. 16638, whose sole attestation is "The Prisoner's Song" as sung by a travelling woman in Aberdeen in 1962 (MacColl and Seeger, *Travellers' Songs*, no. 99, pp. 300–301).

§7.8. **"She used tae sing 'Bundle an Go.'"** That is, she used to diddle this tune, which is a lilting Irish fiddle tune classed as a march or jig. Irish fiddler John Doherty is recorded playing it on Green Linnet GLCD 3077, a reissue of Topic records 12TS 398, based on field recordings made in 1977.

§7.8. **"I've never haird nobody singin it."** What Duncan evidently means is that he never heard anyone—whether his father or anyone else—sing more than the two stanzas given here. The item is thus an example of what is known as a cantefable: a story that is part told, part sung.

§7.9. **"We used tae sit in the forest and imitate the birds in the mornin."** A story of related interest that Duncan liked to tell in the schools is the one he called "Thomas the Thatcher." This tells of an old man who was an expert at thatching, but who let his own roof remain untidy to let birds nest there. As Duncan remarked to me after telling this tale, "You've got too many boys throwin stones at birds an breakin birds' eggs an destroyin nests. We would never do that!" (86DW01 @ 54:58).

§7.10. **Donald MacLeod.** This is evidently Pipe Major Donald MacLeod (1917–1982), who won gold medals in solo piping at the Northern Meeting in Inverness in 1947 and at the Argyllshire Gathering in Oban in 1954.

§7.10. **"Who never even knew a word of music in their life!"** That is, the Traveller pipers admired by Donald MacLeod had never been trained in musical notation; they played by ear.

§7.11. **Own song, "My Old Horse and Cart."** This song, also called "My Old Horse and Me," has been ascribed Roud no. 8112 even though no examples of it are cited apart from a single recording, made by John Howson, of Duncan's singing it in 1991. That performance can be heard as track A3 of the Veteran Tapes cassette *Put Another Log on the Fire*. The words alone (without music) are given in Williamson, *The Horsieman* (206). The song's array of place names drawn from many regions of Scotland has the effect of making it representative of the experience of all Travellers, even while certain of its details are of an autobiographical character. Other recordings of Duncan singing it are on my tapes 86DW10, 86DW16, and 87DW09. There are two versions in Tobar an Dualchis recorded by Linda Williamson in 1976 (track ID 30876 and 110375).

§7.11. **"I used the tune from Robbie Burns."** The tune that Duncan adopted for the song is "Whinny Knowes," an easy one to adapt to practically any song that is composed in "sixteeners": that is, in four phrases of four beats each, with the second and fourth phrases linked by rhyme. Belle Stewart adopted this same tune for her theme song "The Berryfields of Blair" (Roud no. 2154), for which see MacColl and Seeger, *Till Doomsday*, 298–99, or Kennedy, *Folksongs of Britain* (no. 339, p. 765, with notes at p. 794).

CHAPTER 8: THE HOW AND WHY OF STORYTELLING

§8.1. **The story of Granny's purse.** While the impact of this story rests chiefly on its narrative content, with its lessons about steel-willed women and about actions and their consequences, it derives as well from the convincing details with which Duncan develops the tale's physical setting: his father's fireside, his Granny's wee clay pipe, the shell buttons on her tartan purse, her bed of heather and grass, the pennyworth of tobacco. For other versions of the story, see Williamson, *The Horsieman* (7–8), and Campbell, *Traveller in Two Worlds* (1.30–31). Another recording of it is on my tape 87DW01.

§8.1. **"My silkie book."** Duncan is referring to his and Linda's storytelling anthology *The Broonie, Silkies and Fairies* (1985). His silkie tales proved to be especially popular, leading to the Williamsons' later publications *Tales of the Seal People* (1992) and *Land of the Seal People* (2010).

§8.1. **"The Laird and the Crane."** Duncan is referring to a story that he had told the previous day. (For two published versions, see Braid, *Scottish Traveller Tales*, 13–19; Williamson and Williamson, *The Genie and the Fisherman*, 18–20.) It was one of Duncan's favorites, and I recorded him telling it on five different occasions, on audio tapes 86DW02, 86DW31 (with video 86V03), 87DW02, 87DW06, and 88DW13.

§8.2. **Old Johnny MacDonald the storyteller.** Duncan learned a number of his long, internationally known folktales from this Traveller. One example is "The Giant with the Golden Hair of Knowledge" (a version of ATU tale type 461), for which see *Tocher*, vol. 5, no. 33, 1980, pp. 165–83 or *Thorn in the King's Foot*, 36–61. Another is "Jack and the Singin Leaves," in *Thorn in the King's Foot*, 230–43. Williamson can be heard telling versions of these tales on recordings, made by Linda Williamson in 1976, that are available via Tobar an Dualchais (track ID 29904 and 29643, respectively). Duncan's prominence as a source of internationally known folktales is brought out by Hillers, "Storytelling and the International Folktale in Scotland," 160–61. Duncan recalls his encounters with Johnny MacDonald in a recording dating from 1976 that is available via Tobar an Dualchais (track ID 29953).

§8.2. **"La Mer la Moocht"** and **"The Happy Man's Shirt."** For printed versions of Duncan's tellings of these tales, see *Thorn in the King's Foot*, 265–71 and 86–92, respectively.

§8.3. **"They called him 'Monkey John.'"** See the note at §7.6 on Duncan's song "The Nicknames." Johnny Townsley was the person about whose runaway marriage the song "My Wee Maggie" was made (see §5.3 and §5.4).

§8.3. **Burntisland.** A borough on the south coast of Fife. Duncan located the shipwreck in the ballad of "Sir Patrick Spens" close by this borough, as he relates on my tapes 86DW11 and 86DW29. For more on that ballad, see the Commentary on §12.3.

§8.4. **"You had Jack tales."** Tales of this kind take on a wide variety of forms but typically feature a boy or young man named "Jack" who sets out into the world to find his fortune. Such stories are ubiquitous in Duncan's repertory, as they are in those of countless other tale-tellers including the Appalachian storytellers featured in Carl Lindahl's anthology *American Folktales from the*

Collections of the Library of Congress (1.1–158) and in William Bernard McCarthy's prior anthology *Jack in Two Worlds*. A dozen such tales are featured in Williamson's collection *Don't Look Back, Jack!*, along with a short introduction in which Duncan introduces Jack as "a piece of everyman" (xiii). Duncan can likewise be heard reflecting on Jack tales and their hero on Yates's CD *Travellers' Tales* (vol. 1, track 4).

§8.4. **"I have many wonderful pictures!"** Duncan made a point of showing a number of children's illustrations of his stories to members of my 1986 UREP group. He had fitted several of these pictures into recycled picture frames to display them on his mantelpiece, as can be seen in the background of several of the photographs included in this book, including Figures 7.2, 8.3, and 8.4.

§8.6. **"There were many do's and not-do's."** At the point where this transcription begins, Duncan has just been talking about taboos that Travellers taught to their children. These "not-do's" include never harming insects, including moths and butterflies; never pulling flowers that grow by the wayside; and never cutting holly with a knife, although breaking off a branch of a holly tree for Christmas celebrations was permitted. The reason given for this last taboo is that Jesus's side was cut open by a knife.

§8.7. **"It's seven long years. . . . "** Here Duncan sings just the first phrase of the song "The Cruel Grave," one of his favorites. Two recordings of him singing it can be accessed via Tobar an Dualchais under the title "Willie's Lost at Sea" (track ID 64460, dating from 1978, and track ID 65842, dating from 1979), while another is available on the Veteran Tapes cassette *Put Another Log on the Fire* (track B7). A version included at pages 54–56 of Yates's book *Traveller's Joy* can be heard as track 9 on that book's accompanying CD. I recorded Duncan singing this beautiful revenant song on my tapes 84DW02, 86DW07, 86DW36, 86DW38 (available in Scottish Voices), 87DW07, 88DW02, and 88CE02.

§8.8. **"I would tell Ross's story 'A Bag o Salt' at the competition."** The references here are to Ross Noble, who at that time was curator of the Highland Folk Museum, and to a special storytelling session that Duncan was planning to host at the 1986 Auchtermuchty Festival. His subsequent performance of that story, which is commonly known as "Love You More than Salt," is recorded on my tape 86DW31, while a printed version is available in Williamson's folktale anthology *The King and the Lamp*, 40–47.

§8.9. **"The Silence Wager."** At my request, Duncan repeated this humorous tale from a previous telling that same afternoon so that I could photograph his gestures. See Figures 8.5 to 8.12. There is a well-known comic ballad on a closely related theme, "Get Up and Bar the Door" (Child no. 275; Roud no. 115).

§8.10. **"The Skeletons and the Tinker."** Duncan told this bedtime story in October 1987 in the course of a ceilidh at a house that Carole and I were renting outside Ithaca, New York. Taking part in this event were about twenty people affiliated with the Cornell Folk Song Society. As a rule, Duncan did not choose to tell ghost stories or other potentially scary stories to children, so what he told to our son Alan is a droll *skeleton* story with a happy ending. Aware that his larger audience consisted of settled people living in the neighborhood of a university town, he tells a story that equates happiness with owning a house and that ends with mention of children being so fortunate as to attend school and go on to college. For a version of this story as told by Williamson on a different occasion, see Braid, *Scottish Traveller Tales*, 23–31.

§8.10. **"Body snatchers might come along."** Fear of body snatchers was endemic among Scottish Travellers of prior generations, finding frequent expression in cautionary legends known as burker tales. These tell of black-garbed "doctors" who go about by night in their vans attempting to kidnap Travellers to murder them and sell their bodies to anatomy schools. The genre takes its name from sensational kidnappings and murders committed by William Burke, who was executed for his deeds in Edinburgh in 1829. By extension, any would-be kidnapper is a "burker," while what these sinister figures try to do is to "burk" someone. For the most part, Duncan avoided telling potentially disturbing tales of this type, but they hover in the background here. I recorded him telling one such tale on my tape 86DW02, and other tellings are available in Williamson, *Thorn in the King's Foot*, 157–61, and Braid, *Scottish Traveller Tales*, 79–83. A search of Tobar an Dualchais under "burkers" will yield many examples told by different informants over the years.

§8.10. **"You love Grayskull, don't you?"** While Duncan was telling this story, Alan was in a corner of the room playing with some 1970s "He-Man" action figures, one of which had the name "Grayskull." Taking notice of this incidental activity, Duncan recognized Grayskull for who he was and so was able to draw Alan's toy into the closing conversation. To my mind, what Duncan offered us here was not just a bedtime story; it was also a master class in the dynamics of spontaneous interactive storytelling.

CHAPTER 9: SCENES FROM A VANISHED WORLD

§9.1. **People of different breeds.** The term "breed" has been used by some to denote a group of Travellers whose ties of kinship were more or less close, who often camped at the same sites, and who looked after one another's welfare, keeping an eye on one another's children. Indeed, members of the same breed sometimes went so far as to pool their earnings or to adopt an orphaned child or a child whose surviving parent was hard-pressed. Betsy Whyte comments on this phenomenon as follows: "Travelling people liked to marry into their own breed. A breed was usually two or perhaps three names. Our breed was made up of Johnstones, Townsleys, and Reids. . . . Every breed was very distinctive and recognizable, even to non-Travellers who were familiar with them." She adds: "This is no longer the case" (*Red Rowans*, 110).

§9.1. **The open-air Highland Folk Museum.** Located at Kingussie in the Central Highlands of Scotland at the time when this recording was made, the Highland Folk Museum has since been relocated to Newtonmore, about three miles to the south. It was established in 1976 on the basis of material objects donated by Isabel Grant, the author of *Highland Folk Ways*, that were representative of traditional Scottish rural lifeways. Grant took her inspiration from open-air folk museums that had previously been established in Scandinavia. (For discussion, see Powell, "Scotland's Open Air Museums," 127–32.)

§9.1. **Helen Beccard Niles.** A third-generation native of St. Louis, Missouri, Helen Beccard Niles (1903–1994) received her training in the arts in St. Louis before pursuing a career in that field as a teacher and, up to the end of her life, as a painter and printmaker in both naturalistic and abstract styles.

§9.8. **"These silver skiffers."** As Duncan explains, a skiffer—also spelled "skiver" or "skivver"—is a long pin used to tie up a woman's shawl so that the shawl will sit securely on her back and chest. See the *OED*, s.v. "skiver," defined there as "a skewer." According to Belle Stewart, "Some o' them were real fancy, in the shape o' a wee sword or something, like a hatpin but langer. . . . If ye were a weel-aff Travelling woman ye'd be prood o' your skivver and want tae show it aff" (MacColl and Seeger, *Till Doomsday*, 19–20).

§9.10. **"It was really warm in there."** Compare what Sandy Stewart has to say about the warmth of the gelly, or barrakit, where his family lived during the winter months: "Ach, ye wir aaricht, an supposin it wis snow or oniething, ye didnae feel it" (Leitch, *Book of Sandy Stewart*, 8). Stewart called the stovepipe a "vunnel" (like standard English "funnel"), while he characterized the stove itself as a big "bully-beef tin" of the kind that one could find in a town dump: it "was jest an oil tin an they cut it—a round hole in the side an pit a vunnel intae hit" (7). Betsy Whyte confirms that whether heated by a firebox or by an open fire on its earthen floor, the gelly or barrakit "was warm and cozy inside, and as those structures were round-shaped, lots of people could sit round the fire" (*Red Rowans*, 93). A photo at p. 220 of Neat's book *The Summer Walkers* shows the interior of a gelly that Duncan Williamson built for his family at Lochgilphead in 1980, with its firebox and chimney.

CHAPTER 10: WEBSPINNER: THE BOOK, THE POEM, AND THE MAN

§10.1. **Studies that took as their subject a single gifted tradition bearer.** I had been impressed, for example, by Linda Dégh's 1969 book *Folktales and*

Society, which emphasized the role of individual storytellers in their Hungarian communities, as well as by Mark Azadovskii's earlier book *A Siberian Tale Teller*, a portrait of a single tradition bearer (English translation 1974). Dégh's subsequent book *Hungarian Folktales: The Art of Zsusanna Pálko* is an outstanding study of the art of one individual storyteller. Written in a kindred spirit were studies by the folklorist Edward D. Ives on individual singer-composers of the northeastern woodlands of North America, including his 1978 book *Joe Scott: The Woodsman Songmaker*. It was only later that I became familiar with other publications based on the songs or stories of a single gifted tradition bearer, including Joe Neil MacNeil, *Tales until Dawn*; Porter and Gower, *Jeannie Robertson*; Thomas McKean, *Hebridean Song-Maker: Iain MacNeacail*; Lauchie MacLellan, *Brìgh an Òrain = A Story in Every Song*; and Elizabeth Stewart, *Up Yon Wild and Lonely Glen*, to cite only select examples dealing with Scottish tradition.

§10.2. **Whyte gave clear expression to her personal worldview.** An impassioned statement of Whyte's values finds expression toward the end of *Red Rowans*. After first commenting on the terrifying effect of the brazen aggressiveness of Mussolini and Hitler on her consciousness as a young mother at the start of World War II, Betsy eloquently writes:

> What is happening to the world? I wondered. Or rather to the people of the world? What did they want? All that anyone needs is the health to work to pay their way; a comfy bed; couthy friends; love; the gift of sight to fill our hearts, minds, and souls with the unlimited, unending beauty of the world around us. To see the faces of loved ones and friends; people to laugh with . . . and to cry with when sair sorrow comes. The gift of hearing the music of nature alone, never mind the abundance of other music made by gifted men. (166)

The complementary worldview of Duncan Williamson is addressed by Linda Willliamson in her study "What Storytelling Means to a Traveller."

§10.2. **Cultural geography.** As Donald Smith argues in his book *Storytelling Scotland*, one of the great motivations for oral storytelling is "the need for a cultural geography—a desire to place the interaction between environment and history in known locations, and to express the importance of nature within the framework of cultural memory. Land and environment shape the story while stories shape how we see the world of nature. Oral traditions reflect a collective mentality, world view or vision in which nature and the environment play a dynamic rather than a passive role" (5).

§10.3. **Recitations.** For a succinct account of this popular oral genre, see Bethke's article "Recitation." Scottish recitations are often delivered in a broad form of Scots dialect and may rely on in-jokes that only locals are likely to get. As for their formal qualities, many recitations are composed in "fourteeners," an adaptable form that has lent itself well to such well-known American narrative poems as "Casey at the Bat" (by Ernest Lawrence Thayer, 1863–1940) and "The Shooting of Dan McGrew" (by Robert W. Service, 1874–1958). Recitations are often received as anonymous compositions, although someone must once have composed them, while in the American West there are bunkhouse poets, or their imitators, who specialize in the genre.

§10.3. **When Williamson recited this poem to me on a different occasion.** This other performance is recorded on my tape 87DW13; other recordings are on 87DW09 and 88CE02. A recording of Duncan reciting a slightly different version of the poem in 1979, as recorded by Peter Cooke, can be heard on Tobar an Dualchais (track ID 68623). For a record of another performance, see Neat, "Duncan Williamson," 252–54. I also recorded Duncan's daughter Betsy reciting the poem (on my tape 86CEILIDH-01, available via Scottish Voices) in a performance that illustrates the transmission of oral lore from father to daughter.

§10.3. **Mary Howitt** (1799–1888). Howitt's poem "Webspinner" was printed and reprinted various times during the later nineteenth century, for example at pp. 16–22 of Howitt's handsomely illustrated anthology *Sketches of Natural History, or, Songs of Animal Life* (1873). This can be consulted online through the University of Florida Digital Collections of children's books: https://ufdc .ufl.edu/UF00026956/00001.

§10.3. **"Lord Ullin's Daughter."** Williamson sang his reconstructed version of this poem by Thomas Campbell in the apparent belief that the poem had existed as a song, in one form or another, before being written down in a polished literary form. Neat, "Duncan Williamson," 257–58, prints a version of Duncan's re-creation of this poem (text only), taking it as an example of Williamson's bardic capabilities. I recorded Duncan singing his version of this poem, which he misattributed to Robert Burns, on my tape 86DW43, in a performance available via Scottish Voices. Two performances are available via Tobar an Dualchais.

§10.3. **"The Wreck of the Hesperus."** Another poem, this one by Henry Wadsworth Longfellow, whose words Williamson refashioned, setting them to a tune of his own device. He misattributed this poem to Tennyson. I recorded him singing it on my tape 86DW43 and, in a performance available via Scottish Voices, on 87DW13.

§10.3. **"Sir Patrick Spens."** The quasihistorical ballad "Sir Patrick Spens" (Child no. 58; Roud no. 41) is perhaps best known in the form of the long literary version published by Walter Scott in volume 3 of his *Minstrelsy of the Scottish Border* (1803). Although anthologized with some frequency, the song has seldom been recovered from oral tradition. Williamson's version of it is featured in his book *The Horsieman* (222–23). He may well have learned the words from a printed source, perhaps when in school, fitting them to a tune of his own device. When I recorded him singing it, as I did on my audio tapes 84DW03, 84DW05, 86CEIL03, 86DW07, 86DW43, 87DW05, 88DW02, and on videotape 86V01 (in a performance available via Scottish Voices), this was often in concert settings. A recording of Williamson singing it in 1991 can be heard on the Veteran Tapes cassette *Put Another Log on the Fire*, track A7.

§10.3. **"John Barleycorn."** This droll song (Roud nos. 164 and 2141) circulated widely in seventeenth-, eighteenth-, and nineteenth-century broadsides and songsters. Robert Burns's polished literary version dating from 1782 has left a strong mark on the song's later tradition. Where versions have been collected from tradition, chiefly in England, they have probably been picked up at least ultimately from print, while electronically supercharged performances have been recorded by folk or folk-rock bands. One recording of Williamson singing it is included in Yates's 2-volume CD *Travellers' Tales* (vol. 2, track 5), and five others can be accessed via Tobar an Dualchais. I recorded it from Williamson on tapes 84DW03, 84DW05, 86CEIL03, 86DW07, 86DW43 (available via Scottish Voices), 87DW05, and 88DW02.

APPENDIX I:
THESE RECORDINGS AND HOW THEY WERE MADE

The present book is based on tape-recorded interviews that I conducted with Duncan Williamson during the years 1984, 1986, 1987, and 1988, often with the assistance of other persons and at other times on my own.

During an initial round of fieldwork in Scotland in the summer of 1984, I conducted interviews with Hamish Henderson and with certain talented singers or storytellers residing chiefly in Lowland Scotland from Fife to Aberdeen. Duncan Williamson was the person whom I recorded at greatest length. Among the others were Sheila and Andrew Douglas of Scone, Perthshire; Stanley Robertson of Aberdeen, along with members of his immediate family; Belle Stewart of Blairgowrie, Perthshire; Jane Turriff of Mintlaw, Aberdeen; and Betsy and Bryce Whyte of Montrose, Angus.

During the summers of 1986 and 1988, I organized two bipartite University of California Research Expeditions to Scotland. Each expedition consisted of a pair of two-week programs, each of which involved a team of six to eight volunteer participants. In 1986 I arranged to rent a pair of small houses in the town of Auchtermuchty, Fife, at dates that roughly coincided with the Auchtermuchty Festival, an event featuring numerous concerts, ceilidhs, and competitions sponsored by the TMSA. In 1988 I arranged to rent a pair of townhouses in the Royal Burgh of St. Andrews, Fife, at dates that coincided with that year's St. Andrews Highland Games. I chose these locations in part because of their proximity to the places where the Williamsons were then living, so that members of my teams could easily spend time interviewing Duncan while also taking part in local events. During these same weeks, we made a sustained set of recordings of other outstanding singers and storytellers of Traveller background, including Lizzie Higgins of Aberdeen[1]; Stanley Robertson and his daughters Nicole and Gabrielle; Elizabeth Stewart of

---

1. Lizzie Higgins (1929–1993), daughter of the celebrated traditional singer Jeannie Robertson, was a woman of intense inner strength, conscious of having powers as a spiritual warrior. The Musical Traditions double CD *In Memory of Lizzie Higgins 1929–1993* features thirty-four of her songs together with a number of still photos. Also noteworthy is Ailie Munro's article "Lizzie Higgins, and the Oral Transmission of Ten Child Ballads," a study of intergenerational influence and

Fetterangus, Aberdeenshire[2]; and Betsy and Bryce Whyte. We also interviewed singers who were not of Traveller identity but who were standout figures on the Scottish folksong scene, among them Charlie Lamb of Dundee and Adam McNaughtan of Glasgow.

In October of 1987, while my wife Carole was teaching at Cornell University and I was on sabbatical from my teaching duties at the University of California, Berkeley, I interviewed Williamson at some length at a rented house outside Ithaca, New York, where he was our guest for somewhat over a week. Here, during the interstices between events that I had organized where Duncan was the featured performer (and that I likewise recorded), he and I were able to talk for many hours with the tape recorder running, whether by the warmth of a cast-iron stove or, when the weather permitted, seated out of doors under trees that had recently shed their autumn foliage. I took advantage of those tranquil hours to record most of Duncan's active repertory of songs and many of his autobiographical reflections.

All my interviews were recorded on a portable, battery-driven, reversible Uher cassette tape recorder. I was fond of that machine in part because of its real-time capacity of ninety minutes of recording, a time span that often allowed the recording of an interview or a session in its entirety. I used a high-quality external microphone for all recordings. The technical conditions under which the recordings were made were necessarily mixed—sometimes adequate, sometimes far from it—but physical settings that were less than ideal from a studio perspective were conducive to the spontaneity that I valued as a means of gaining insights that tend to be unavailable in formal settings.

Each recording was subsequently logged; that is, its contents were registered in a typed summary keyed to the playback machine's counter numbers. Over the course of time, selective preliminary transcriptions were made, either by me or by student research assistants. I have subsequently made additional transcriptions and have checked the accuracy of all transcriptions against the tapes, making corrections as needed. When contemplating the number of hours of labor involved in that whole process of logging and transcription, I sometimes reflect that conducting a tape-recorded interview is a bit like making a baby. There can be great fun in the doing of it, but then come the long

resistance. I recorded Lizzie's songs and reminiscences at her home in Aberdeen on my audio tapes 86LH01 to 86LH06 and on videotapes 86V07 and part of 86V08.

2. Elizabeth Stewart (b. 1939), a niece of the celebrated traditional singer Lucy Stewart, is an acclaimed singer and keyboard musician from the northeast of Scotland. The Elphinstone Institute double CD *Binnorie: Songs, Ballads, and Tunes*, introduced by Alison McMorland and annotated by Thomas A. McKean, features a large sample of her repertory, while her book *Up Yon Wild and Lonely Glen*, compiled and edited by Alison McMorland, is a comprehensive collection of her songs and autobiographical reflections. I recorded Elizabeth's songs and reflections in St. Andrews on my audio tapes 88ES01 to 88ES10 and in several joint sessions that were videotaped.

years of care! But those responsibilities, too, come with their satisfactions, as any parent or folklorist will tell you.

My collection of Scottish field tapes, now digitized, is housed in the Archive of Folk Culture of the American Folklife Center at the Library of Congress, Washington, DC. The collection includes a number of video recordings that, though they have no place in the present book, help to contextualize my collection of audiotapes through sustained images of performances and their settings and through ambient images of landscapes, houses, fairs, festivals, and so forth. In addition, a small set of audio recordings made on reel-to-reel tapes is housed in the Sound Archives of the School of Scottish Studies at the University of Edinburgh. At the time of writing, thirty-five digitized selections from those recordings have been made available to the public for listening via Tobar an Dualchais, the Archives' web-based platform. Those items feature the voices of Lizzie Higgins and Betsy Whyte.

By the time this book is published, a much larger and more diverse set of selections from my field collection will have been made available to the public at the website Scottish Voices, a publication of the University of Wisconsin Digital Collections Center. There, alongside much else that relates to Scottish music, song, storytelling, festivals, games, and the physical landscape and ecology of Scotland, one can gain access to many of the recordings that are the basis of the present study of a single outstanding tradition bearer, Duncan Williamson.

The original reference numbers for my tape recordings remain in use. If mention is made of tape 87DW09, for example, the reference is to the contents of the ninth tape (09) featuring the voice of Duncan Williamson (DW) that I recorded in the year 1987. When additional numbers follow that designation, they refer to the hour, minute, and second where a particular item can be found on that recording. For example, if a reader comes across a reference to "86DW41 @ 1:08:40," then the item in question begins at the one-hour, eight-minute, forty-second point on the digitized recording.

My recordings from the 1980s represent only a small part of Williamson's total repertory. This was far too capacious for any fieldworker to encompass in its entirety, even in multiple recording sessions taking place in varied circumstances over a period of years. Moreover, Williamson was constantly adding new items to his active repertory while other items slipped into his passive repertory, though still remaining subject to recall with a bit of prompting. What I perceived to be his repertory, of course, was reflective not just of his tastes but also of the contexts in which these recordings were made. Although Williamson enjoyed an occasional risqué song, for example, he never sang songs of an exceptionally bawdy character in the presence of my microphone. After all, many of our recording sessions took place when visitors from abroad were present, as were children or the elderly from time to time; while my own identity as a university professor conducting research, even if of a distinctly pleasurable kind, was of course a major factor in the proceedings. No one was acting in a drunk or disorderly fashion, although if friends were getting together with friends, then the likelihood of drink becoming a factor in the session increased as the evening progressed. So too did the likelihood of someone breaking out in one of the truly raunchy songs that represent, to some, the pride and glory of Scotland.

Williamson was well aware that when the recording equipment was running, he was always "on camera." He was never maudlin, rude, or profane, and his warm and vibrant manner made his visitors from abroad, including me, feel ever welcome and at ease. When off-camera, if he ever moped or swore up and down like a peevy sailor, I cannot say. My impression, though, is that by nature he was more reticent as regards bawdy humor or transgressive subjects than many of the seasoned performers on the Scottish Folk Revival scene have been known to be. And to pursue that last comparison a step further, Williamson had relatively little interest in singing songs of left-wing protest or class conflict, for his thoughts tended to linger elsewhere and he did not wear his politics on his sleeve.

APPENDIX 2:
TRANSCRIBING "ORAL TEXTS" FROM VOICE TO PAGE

Transcriptions of recordings of oral art forms do not make themselves. Rather, someone somewhere has shaped those written records of a performance into a particular form, always doing so in a manner that suits the transcriber's or editor's purpose.

Correspondingly, what is commonly called "oral literature" is neither the one nor the other. That is to say, it is not oral, for what it consists of is not spoken words, but rather black marks printed on a page. Nor is it literature, in the sense of having a close resemblance to a poem or novel written by a well-educated author. Rather, it is a hybrid creation. It is an amalgam of voice and print, of tradition and individual talent. When taking account of the huge body of what is called the world's "oral literature" from Homer's day to the present, including traditional epic poetry, the ballad, the folktale, legends, riddles, jokes, and Native American oral autobiography (among other genres), I like to think of these written forms in terms of "literature of the third domain."

What defines this category of writings is that it is produced neither by a gifted performer using the voice, nor by an educated person working alone with pen and paper or word processor, but rather by the combined efforts of the two. The task facing the transcriber or editor of such works, accordingly, is to serve as midwife to the birth of the text, that is, to nurse the words of oral performance into readable script or print. By definition, literature of the third domain is a collaborative phenomenon, for without the mediating skills of the transcriber/editor, the words of the performer would vanish on the wind.

One of the curiosities of this category of literature is that the role of the midwife is often effaced. The readers of a published example of third-domain literature are sometimes given the impression that a speaker's words have shifted to the page by magic, so that what one is reading is the singer's or storyteller's unmediated voice. Although this kind of sleight of hand can result in a book that is commercially successful (and so publishers have been known to favor it), the method should be resisted in any publication that strives for transparency and accuracy, for it can verge on fraud. Elsewhere, I have discussed this phenomenon in some detail, calling attention to the illusions that can result when authors or publishers sidestep the question of just how a text of "oral literature" is produced.[1]

What I have done in this book is to represent Williamson's words on the page in prose that is both accurate and readable, maintaining fidelity to his Scots language while conveying as much of his expressive style of oral delivery as can be reconciled with the aim of producing a book that will be a pleasure to read.[2] I have avoided quoting long passages of unedited transcriptions in a manner that would only bore or daze the reader. Instead, I have organized the substance of interviews undertaken in a variety of circumstances over a five-year period into a chapter-by-chapter presentation, setting out excerpts in a thematically coherent sequence. Instances of verbal "noise"—cross talk, false starts, interjections such as "eh," "you know," "aye," "yeah," and the like—have most often been edited out while being retained here and there for the sake of fidelity to the character of the interview, for the frequent reiteration of semantically empty words might prove irritating to readers who are not specialists in sociolinguistics. The questions, comments, or exclamations voiced by interviewers (including myself) are freely edited for print, often being omitted entirely when their inclusion would pointlessly interrupt Williamson's exposition of a theme. Researchers who wish to investigate either the precise qualities of Williamson's speech or the interactive dynamics of these recording sessions are invited to listen to the recordings themselves.

There is one fundamental principle that I have observed as scrupulously as if it were the Eleventh Commandment. I have never put words of my own into Williamson's mouth. My chief task while preparing these excerpts for print has been to arrange Williamson's words into a sequence that progresses in a coherent manner through a given topic, and then from one topic to the next. Omissions of individual words and phrases are left unmarked, as can be true of whole verbal paragraphs (though some such omissions are noted), for I have not wanted to leave a trail of ellipses on the page. Nothing of my own has been added to the transcriptions of Williamson's speech, with the exception of brief words of clarification, always set between square brackets to identify them as editorial interventions. Other editorial comments are relegated to the footnotes, if short, or to the Commentary, if more discursive.

A special problem relating to these transcriptions is how to represent Williamson's speech on the page. This is largely a problem in orthography rather than phonetics. What I have aimed for is a pragmatic compromise between

---

1. See my Introduction to the special issue of *Western Folklore* titled "From Word to Print—and Beyond," and my two different studies titled "Orality," one published in *The Cambridge Companion to Textual Scholarship* and the other in *The Oxford Encyclopedia of Literary Theory*.

2. Similar principles of transcription are advocated by Alan Bruford in his review essay "Travellers Tales," along with cautionary remarks about practices that fall short of those guidelines.

close graphic mimicry of his Scottish pronunciation, on the one hand, and conversion of his speech into standard English spellings, on the other. Neither of those two options has struck me as desirable, for the first alternative would fail the test of readability, while the other would insult Williamson's identity as a Scot. What I have offered readers, therefore, is a simulacrum of Williamson's pronunciation as opposed to a linguistically precise representation of it. Williamson's speech was subject to subtle changes depending on whom he was addressing, where, in what circumstances, with what degree of animation, at what stage of drink (if any), and so forth. It is for this reason that I have refrained from normalizing his speech into a standardized representation of Scots, for he switched codes effortlessly and intuitively between the speech of his native Argyll, the broad Lallans Scots of Fife (where he lived for most of his adult life), and language that more closely resembled standard British English or American English. Moreover, as an artful storyteller who was mindful of the individual narrators from whom he first learned his tales, he sometimes mimicked the speech of one or another region of Scotland, including the lilting Highland English of crofters from the western Highlands and the equally distinctive Northeast Scots dialects of Aberdeen or Buchan. He likewise imitated Irish speech on occasion.

The same principles of transcription apply to Williamson's verbal grammar, which in general is simply the grammar of present-day Scots. Examples include such contractions as "didnae" or "couldnae"; such personal pronouns as "wir," "youse," "hisself," and "theirselves"; and the use of double or triple negatives as a means of rhetorical emphasis. Such linguistic features as these go far toward defining the character of his colorful, confident, and highly expressive speech. If inconsistencies remain on these pages (as they manifestly do), I believe the majority of them will be found to be his, not mine.

Cant words—that is, the Travellers' "insider" lexicon—and other nonstandard terms and phrases present a special problem. I have had no wish to clutter a page with linguistic apparatus, and yet the reader has a right to know what every word on the page means. To address this issue, certain words or phrases are glossed at the foot of the page, while the Glossary that is included at the back of the book provides a comprehensive list of words that might cause difficulty. Those readers who wish additional information about particular words can consult standard reference works such as *The Concise Scots Dictionary* edited by Mairi Robinson or the online *Dictionary of the Scots Language*, which is a combined digital version of the ten-volume *Scottish National Dictionary* and the *Dictionary of the Older Scottish Tongue*.

As for the tunes for Duncan's songs, basic musical notations are supplied right by the texts for the convenience of readers who will welcome immediate access to the singer's idea of the tune. My son Alan Niles, in consultation with Linda Williamson, has produced singable notations that should serve most readers' purposes. Specialists in musicology, as well as anyone else who welcomes access to Duncan's voice itself, are encouraged to consult the recordings themselves as published in Scottish Voices and as accessible there through the website's search engine. These will reveal the particulars of Williamson's exposition of a tune from the start of a song to its finish, for the contour of one of his tunes often differs somewhat from strophe to strophe in accord with the rhythm of the words, as is characteristic of the live, informal performance of traditional song.

LIST OF TRANSCRIPTIONS

Only those recordings that figure in the present book are cited. UREP volunteers who took part in one or more of these recording sessions are listed by their initials, as follows.

AS	Andrew Sachar
BC	Barbara Connelly
BE	Barbara Edwards
CE	Caryl Emerson
DC	Donna Chang
DE	David Edwards
DK	David Kotyk
DL	Dorothy Leese
DY	Dianne Yanney
ES	Eugene Schwartz
FM	Fern Moore
GP	Gloria Pasterack
GS	Gene Sharee
HD	Howard Diller
HH	Helen Henderson
HT	Holly Tannen
JY	Jeppy Yarensky
LR	Leslie Reicher
LS	Linda Shue
LSills	Louise Sills
LY	Leonard Yarensky
MJ	Maria Jeffress
MJohn	Mary Johnson
MM	Marion McDow
MW	Malcolm Westcott
RS	Ruth Schwartz

SJ   Sarah Johnson
SLamb   Sheila Lamb
SL   Susan Luntz

84DW01   Recorded by JN on July 13, 1984, in the sitting room of Kincraigie Farm Cottage (the Williamsons' home at the time) near Strathmiglo, Fife. Others present: DW, LW. Selections at §§4.1, 5.9, and 7.10, plus the Commentary on 7.2.

84DW04   Recorded by JN on July 20, 1984, in the sitting room of Kincraigie Farm Cottage near Strathmiglo, Fife. Others present: DW, LW, and their children Betsy and Thomas; Betsy and Bryce Whyte; CN and our son Alan, then one year old. Selections at §§2.6, 3.13, 5.1, 6.15, 6.17, and 7.1.

84GF02   Recorded by JN on July 16, 1984, at the Glenfarg Hotel, near Kinross, district of Perth and Kinross. A recording of an evening's entertainment hosted by the Glenfarg Folk Club. Others present: DW, Sheila Douglas, other Scottish singers and folksong enthusiasts. A selection at §4.11.

86DW03   Recorded by HT on July 21, 1986, in the sitting room of Kincraigie Farm Cottage, near Strathmiglo, Fife. Others present: DW, LW, and their children Betsy and Thomas; three UREP volunteers (CE, DY, SL). Selections at §§2.1, 2.3, 3.1, 3.2, 3.6, 3.8, and 10.3.

86DW04   A continuation of the same session. Selections at §§2.3, 2.4, and 8.1.

86DW06   Recorded by JN on July 22, 1986, in the sitting room of Orchard Cottage, Auchtermuchty, Fife (one of two rental houses used by UREP participants that summer). Others present: DW, HT, and four UREP volunteers (GP, HH, JY, LY). Selections at §§6.2 and 6.11.

86DW09   Recorded by JN on July 23, 1986, at Kincraigie Farm Cottage, near Strathmiglo, Fife, or in that cottage's immediate vicinity. Others present: DW; LW and the Williamsons' children Betsy and Thomas; two UREP volunteers (JY and LY). A selection at §4.18.

86DW12   Recorded by HH on July 24, 1986, at Kincraigie Farm Cottage, near Strathmiglo, Fife. Others present: DW, LW; three additional UREP volunteers (JS, JY, LY); the Williamsons' two children Betsy and Thomas for some of the time. Selections at §§3.9 and 6.9.

86DW13   Recorded by JN on July 27, 1986, at Kincraigie Farm Cottage, near Strathmiglo, Fife. Others present: DW, LW, the Williamsons' children Betsy and Thomas; two UREP volunteers (LY, JY). A selection at §4.22.

86DW14   Recorded by JN on July 28, 1986, at Orchard Cottage, Auchtermuchty, Fife. Others present: DW; HT; six UREP volunteers (CE, HH, JS, JY, LY; later, SL). Selections at §§5.5, 5.6, and 8.4.

86DW18 Recorded by JN on July 31, 1986, at Kincraigie Farm Cottage, near Strathmiglo, Fife. Others present: HT; later, LW and the Williamsons' two children Betsy and Thomas. Selections at §§6.7 and 6.10.

86DW19 Recorded by HT on July 31, 1986, at Kincraigie Farm Cottage, near Strathmiglo, Fife. Others present: DW; JN; later, Duncan's and Linda's son Thomas. Selections at §§2.2 and 7.7.

86DW23 Recorded by JN on August 5, 1986, in the sitting room of Weaver's Cottage, Auchtermuchty, Fife (one of two rental houses used by UREP participants that summer). Others present: DW, HT, seven UREP volunteers (DK, FM, GS, HD, LSills, MJ, RS). Selections at §§5.7, 6.13, and 8.5.

86DW24 Recorded by JN on August 5, 1986, at Weaver's House, Auchtermuchty, Fife. Others present: DW; HT; five UREP volunteers (DC, DK, FM, MJ, RS). Selections at §§5.8 and 5.10.

86DW26 Recorded by JN on August 6, 1986, in a van while en route to the Highland Folk Museum, Kingussie, from Auchtermuchty, Fife. JN was the driver. Others present: DW in the front seat, CN and our son Alan in the back. Selections at §§4.7 and 4.8.

86DW27 Recorded by JN on August 6, 1986, while at the Highland Folk Museum, Kingussie, Highlands Region. Others present: DW; HT, CN, five UREP volunteers (DC, FM, HD, LSills, MJ) from time to time. Selections at §§9.2 to 9.8.

86DW28 Recorded by JN on August 6, 1986, returning by van from Kingussie to Fife. JN was the driver. Others present: DW in the front seat, CN and our son Alan in the back. Selections at §§2.3, 2.8, 2.10, and 2.11.

86DW29 Recorded by JN on August 8, 1986, in the sitting room of Kincraigie Farm Cottage, near Strathmiglo, Fife. Others present: DW, LW, and their children Betsy and Thomas; HT; two UREP volunteers (DK, MJ). Much of this session was recorded simultaneously by DK on video 86V01. Selections at §§3.10, 3.11, 3.12, 3.14, 3.15, 8.7, and 8.8.

86DW30 A continuation of the same session, along with 86V01. A selection at §4.10.

86DW37 Recorded by JN on August 11, 1986, at Weaver's Cottage, Auchtermuchty, Fife. Others present: DW; HT; five UREP volunteers (DC, DK, FM, HD, MJ). Much of this session was recorded concurrently on reel-to-reel tape recorder and by DK on video 86V05. A selection in the Commentary on §6.17.

86DW38 A continuation of the same session, along with 86V05. Selections at §§3.14 and 3.15.

86DW41 Recorded by HT on August 14, 1986, in the sitting room of Kincraigie Farm Cottage, near Strathmiglo, Fife. Others present: DW, LW, five

UREP volunteers (DC, FM, HD, LSills, MJ). Selections at §§2.9, 2.14, 2.15, 2.16, 4.3, 4.15, 5.11, 5.12, 6.8, 6.12, 6.16, plus the Commentary on 6.11.

86DW43 Recorded by HT at Weaver's house, Auchtermuchty, Fife. Others present: DW, JN; three UREP volunteers (DC, LSills, MJ). Parts of this session were recorded concurrently by JN on reel-to-reel tape. A selection at §4.11.

87DW04 Recorded by JN on October 22, 1987, in the sitting room of a house rented by the Niles family that academic year in the woods outside Ithaca, New York. Others present: mostly just DW; CN and our four-year-old son Alan from time to time. Selections at §§2.13, 2.19, 2.20, 3.7, 4.6, 6.5, 6.6, 7.8, and 8.6.

87DW08 Recorded by JN on October 23, 1987, at a ceilidh held in the same house as for 87DW04. Others present: DW; CN and our son Alan; Len and Jeppy Yarensky; and a group of about twenty guests from the region of Ithaca, New York, including some skilled singers and musicians. Selections at §§7.11 and 8.10.

87DW11 Recorded by JN on October 25, 1987, at the same house outside Ithaca, with just DW present for most of the time and CN and our son Alan from time to time. Selections at §§4.19, 4.20, 4.21, 6.1, 6.3, 7.9, 9.10, 9.11, plus the Commentaries on 2.6 and 4.20.

87DW12 A continuation of the same session. Selections at §§2.5, 2.12, 3.5, 5.2, 5.3, 7.4, 7.5, 7.6, 8.3, plus the Commentary on 1.1.

87DW13 A continuation of the same session. Selections at §§3.15, 4.9, 4.16, 6.14, and 8.2.

87DW14 Recorded by JN later that same day in the same setting. Others present: mostly just DW; CN and our son Alan from time to time. Selections at §§2.6, 2.7, 2.17, 2.18, 4.12, 4.14, 4.23, 7.2, and 7.3.

87DW15 Recorded by JN on October 26, 1987, in the same setting. Others present: just DW. A selection at §8.9.

88DW05 Recorded by BC and LR on August 1, 1988 at the Williamsons' home at Lizziewell Farm Cottage, near Ladybank, Fife. Others present: DW, JN; four other UREP volunteers (BE, DE, DL, MJohn). A selection at §4.17.

88DW07 Recorded by JN on August 2, 1988, while en route by car from St. Andrews, Fife, to the villages of Furnace and Minard, Loch Fyne, Argyll, with occasional stops along the way. JN was the driver. Others present: DW, in the front seat of the car; two UREP volunteers (BC, DL) in the back. Selections at §§4.2, 4.13, and 6.4.

88DW09 A continuation of the same session. Selections at §§3.3, 4.4, 4.5, and 5.4.

88DW10   A continuation of the same session while en route by car from Minard to Lochgilphead, Argyll, with occasional stops along the way. A selection at §3.4.

GLOSSARY OF SCOTS WORDS AND TRAVELLERS' CANT

The following Glossary is intended to elucidate any words or terms in the present book that might be found puzzling. Most of these are Scots words, many of which are in common use and are unlikely to give pause. Others are cant terms that are intended to be impenetrable except to those in the know.

A brief note on cant and its use might be welcome here. Travellers' cant is not a separate language. It is best characterized as "a vocabulary of a few hundred words superimposed on Gaelic or English in such a way as to be incomprehensible to outsiders" (Leitch, *Book of Sandy Stewart*, 47, n. 13, citing the linguist David Clement). It is a mode of speech that Travellers used chiefly when in the presence of outsiders—police, for example, or a potentially dangerous stranger—when they wished to disguise their speech. The vocabulary of cant is of diverse origin. Some cant words are borrowed from Romany, the language of Gypsies and a tongue that is itself of complex origins on account of the Gypsies' migrations through much of Eurasia before arriving in the British Isles. Certain other cant words used in the matrix of Scots speech are based on Scottish Gaelic vocabulary. Yet other terms pertain to the time-honored lexicon of underworld or rogue characters or are made-up words perhaps known to only a few persons, or are of unknown origin.

For a more inclusive list of cant words used in Scotland, see Douglas, "Narrative in Traveller Scotland," 55–57. When speaking of the use of cant in practice, Betsy Whyte emphasizes that "one word could have many meanings and could carry the meaning of a whole sentence, depending on the situation and the tone of voice" (*Yellow on the Broom*, 178). Learning the lexicon of cant is thus only the first step to understanding how to speak it. Anyone might pick up a few words, however. When Whyte was a child, she writes, her dog Ricky "knew a lot of words in cant," adding, "I taught him as many as he should know, for it came in useful sometimes" (*Red Rowans*, 15).

a-chorin	stealing (cant)
a-humphin	a cant word of uncertain meaning
a-proochin	a cant word of uncertain meaning

aa	always; all
aaricht	all right
aboot	about
aff	off
afore	before
Ah	I
ain	own
airth, airthen	earth, earthen
airum	arm
an	and
aneth	beneath
aroond	around
'at	that
aul, auld	old
awa	away
bairn, bairnies	child, children
bangs o	lots of
barrakit	large winter tent with partitions and room for a firebox
besom	broom
bills	posters
bing	go; get, bring (cant)
blin	blind
bogie	trailer, cart
bogie roll	twist of tobacco
bothy	bunkhouse; quarters for farm workers
braw	beautiful
braxy	mutton salted from a sheep found dead in the hills
breid	bread
broonie	otherworldly figure resembling a human being
brung	brought
bun wood	bundle of wood (?) (cant)
burkers	people who kidnap and murder Travellers
burl	bundle (?) (cant)
burn (n.)	stream, river
caber	tall pole like a telephone pole
can (n.)	tea can, kettle, jug
cannae	can't
canny	astute, good, kind, fortunate
caralew	curlew
caravan	motor home
cauld	cold
ceilidh	informal get-together with songs, music, and drinks

chaet	thing (cant)
cheerie, chourie	cupboard? (cant)
chiel	lad, fellow
chop (n.)	a punch or blow with the hand
clabbydoo	large mussel found in the region of Loch Fyne
clupped	clipped
come	come, came
coo	cow
couped	overturned
couthy	friendly, sympathetic
crack (n.)	casual talk, an exchange of news or stories
crill	creel
cruiket	crooked
cruisie	old-fashioned oil lamp hung inside a cottage
cry	call
cuddie	carpenter's bench or trestle (literally "donkey")
cuid	could
cuid a	could have
cuidnae	couldn't
cuik	cook
d'ye	do you
dae	do
deek	see; look, look at (cant)
diddle (v.)	sing using only vocables
diddle (n.)	a tune that is diddled
didnae	didn't
dike	stone wall
dinna, dinnae	don't
disnae	doesn't, don't
disn't	doesn't, don't
dochter	daughter
docken	the dock plant
doesnae	doesn't
doon	down
dreel, drill (1)	row of turnips, potatoes, or berries
drill (2)	little iron bar with holes, used to make rivets
driv	drove; driven
drunk (v.)	drank
'e	he
em	them
et	ate
fae, frae	from

fag	cigarette
fairm, fairmer	farm, farmer
faither	father
feared (adj.)	afraid
fee (v.)	sign on with a farmer for a season's work
fee (n.)	wages for a season's work
fet	foot, feet
fick	take, get (cant)
fir	for
flit	moved house, moved camp
flooer	flower
follae	follow
forbye, forbyes	also, besides
frecht	terror, apparition, fright
full; fulled (v.)	fill; filled
gaain, gaan, gaein	going
gadgie	man (cant)
gae	to give
gaes	goes
gaffer	foreman
gaithered	gathered
gane	gone
gang	go; went
gannies	hens, chickens (cant)
garrochans	beds of horse mussel, also known as clabbydoo
gelly	large winter tent with room for a firebox inside
gie; gien	give; gave
give	gave
Glesga, Glasga	Glasgow
gonnae	going to
gramiephone	gramophone
grieve (n.)	foreman
guddle	catch fish with one's hands
guid	good
haben	food (cant)
hadnae	hadn't, didn't have
hae	have
haird	heard
hairt	heart
hame	home
hansel (v.)	offer a gift for good luck
hansel (n.)	something given to an infant for good luck

hantle	people, esp. country folk (cant)
hardfish	salted and dried fish
hawk (v.)	go from house to house with things for sale or trade
hawkin material	goods to barter or sell
hawks (n.)	cuts or cracks in one's hands
hersel	herself
het	hit
hissel, hisself	himself
hit (pron.)	it
hond	hand
hoolit	owl
huik	fishing hook; blade used to top turnips
hurl	wheel someone or something about
intae	into
ither	other
jan	know (cant)
jest, jist	just
juig (1)	jug
juig (2)	metal vessel equipped with glass lens, used for pearl fishing
ken (interj.)	you know
ken (v.)	know
kep	kept
kinchens	children (cant)
kist	chest
knowe	hill
lairn, lairned	learn, learned
lang, langer	long, longer
lift (v.)	gather potatoes
lifted (1)	harvested
lifted (2)	arrested
loon	young man
loss (v.)	to lose
luik	look
luttle	little
ma	my
mair	more
mavis	thrush
mendit	mended
messages	groceries
mither	mother
moolie	kill (cant)
mort	wife (cant)

muck	dirt, earth, mud
muckle	big; much of
mysel	myself
na, no	not
nae	no, not
naebody, naething	nobody, nothing
naiskel	father (cant)
near (adv.)	nearly
neeps	turnips
neuk	nook
nicht	night
nipper	claw
noo	now
nyakin	Traveller (cant)
o	of
oncet	once
ony	any
onything, oniething	anything
oot	out; out of
orra man	hired farmhand
oxter	arm, armpit
pairl	pearl
paraffin lamp	kerosene lamp
peevy	drunk, drunken
pit (v.)	put
plats	places
poliss	policeman
prood	proud
puir	poor
puu'd	pulled
quod	jail (cant)
reek	smoke
roon, roond	around
sae	so
sair	severe, acute
sang (n.)	song
scaldies	low-class town-dwellers
scrog	bush
sellt	sold
set	sit, sat
settin	sitting

shifted	moved along by the police
shinglin turnips	cutting the tops off turnips
shouldnae	shouldn't
simmer	summer
singsong	ceilidh
skiffer	long pin used to tie up a woman's shawl
slipe	cleft hazel branch used to strip willows
smitty	smithy
snore	snort
snottum	metal crook used to hang pots over an open fire
sook	suck, sucked
spall	grid of interwoven wands that forms a basket's base
sparra	sparrow
speired to	asked of
sporran	pouch or purse worn at the waist
sprachin	begging (cant)
stardy	jail (cant)
sticks (1)	branches, firewood, lumber
sticks (2)	poles used as framework for a bow tent
stookin	piling hay into stooks, or stacks
strae	straw
struppit, strupped	striped
stuid	stood
swey	a bar from which a kettle could be swung out over a fire
syne	then; after that
tae	to; too
taen	taken; took
taen-awa	a child who has been taken away by the fairies
tak	take
tatties	potatoes
tea	(1) supper; (2) hot tea
tea can	kettle in which tea is made
tellt, teld	told
theirself, theirsels	themselves
they days	those days
they're	there are, they are
thrashin	threshing
thumbles	thimbles
til	until
tilly pans	saucepans
tinkler	tinker; itinerant tinsmith and peddlarFS

tomornin	in the morning, tomorrow
toon	town
Traiveller	Traveller
tuik	took
twa	two
vunnel	stovepipe
walkit	walked
wasnae	wasn't, weren't
weans	children
wee	little
wee bit	small; a bit
wee puckle	little bit; little patch of
weel	well
weel-aff	well off
werenae	weren't
wha	who
whaups	curlews
whaur	where
whit	what
wholp	blow
whustlin	whistling
whuttles	sores, abscesses
wi	with
windae	window
winnae	will not, won't
wir (v.)	were
wir, wirs	our, ours
wirself	ourselves
wis	was
withoot	without
wonderest	most wonderful
wouldae	would have
wouldnae	wouldn't
wuid	would
wull	will
ye	you
yer, yir	your
yese	you (pl.)
yin	one
yirsel	yourself
youse	you (usually pl.)

SELECTED BIBLIOGRAPHY

BOOKS AND ARTICLES

Abrahams, Roger D. *Everyday Life: A Poetics of Vernacular Practices.* U of Pennsylvania P, 2005.

Azadovskii, M. K. *A Siberian Tale Teller,* translated by James R. Dow. Center for Intercultural Studies in Folklore and Ethnomusicology, 1974. [First published in Helsinki, 1926.]

Beech, John, et al., editors. *Oral Literature and Performance Culture.* John Donald, 2007.

Beith, Mary. *Healing Threads: Traditional Medicines of the Highlands and Islands.* Polygon, 1995. [Reprinted. by Birlinn, 2019.]

Bennett, Margaret. *Scottish Customs from the Cradle to the Grave.* 2nd ed., Birlinn, 2004. [First published by Polygon, 1992.]

Bethke, Robert D. "Recitation." *Folklore: An Encyclopedia of Beliefs, Customs, Tales, Music, and Art,* vol. 2, edited by Thomas A. Green, ABC-CLIO, 1997, pp. 695–98.

Bogucki, Peter. *The Origins of Human Society.* Blackwell, 1999.

Braid, Donald. *Scottish Traveller Tales: Lives Shaped through Stories.* UP of Mississippi, 2002.

Brocken, Michael. *The British Folk Revival, 1944–2002.* Ashgate, 2003.

Bruford, Alan, editor. *The Green Man of Knowledge and Other Scots Traditional Tales.* Aberdeen UP, 1982.

Bruford, Alan. "Travellers' Tales." *Scottish Studies,* vol. 30, 1991, pp. 107–16.

Bruford, Alan, and D. A. MacDonald, editors. *Scottish Traditional Tales.* Polygon, 1994. [With accompanying double CD. Reprinted by Birlinn, 2003.]

Campbell, Alastair. "Niall Diarmid, 10th Duke of Argyll." *History of Clan Campbell,* vol. 3: *From the Restoration to the Present Day.* Edinburgh UP, 2004, pp. 300–303.

Campbell, David. *A Traveller in Two Worlds,* vol. 1: *The Early Life of Scotland's Wandering Bard.* Luath, 2011.

Campbell, David. *A Traveller in Two Worlds,* vol. 2: *The Tinker and the Student.* Luath, 2012.

Carroll, Jim. "Irish Travellers around London." *Folk Music Journal,* vol. 3, no. 1, 1975, pp. 31–40.

Child, Francis James, editor. *The English and Scottish Popular Ballads.* 5 vols. Boston: Houghton, Mifflin, 1882–1898.

Cooke, Peter. "The Music of Scottish Travellers." Beech et al., pp. 213–24.

Court, Artelia. *Puck of the Droms: The Lives and Literature of the Irish Tinkers.* U of California P, 1985.

Cregeen, Eric R. "Donald Morrison: Oral Tradition of Mull." 'Recollections of an Argyllshire
    Drover' and Other West Highland Chronicles, edited by Margaret Bennett, John Donald,
    2004, pp. 163–92. [Reprinted with new notes from Tocher, vol. 3, no. 24, 1976, pp. 289–319.]
Dawson, Robert. Empty Lands: Aspects of Scottish Traveller Survival. Nottingham, UK: privately
    printed, 2007.
Dawson, Robert. Times Gone: Gypsies and Travellers. Alfreton, UK: privately printed, 2007.
Dégh, Linda. Folktales and Society: Story-Telling in a Hungarian Peasant Community, translated
    by Emily M. Schlossberger. Indiana UP, 1969. [First published in Berlin, 1962.]
Dégh, Linda. Hungarian Folktales: The Art of Zsusanna Pálko. UP of Mississippi, 1995.
Douglas, Sheila. "Belle Stewart, 'The Queen Amang the Heather.'" Folk Song: Tradition, Revival,
    and Re-Creation, edited by Ian Russell and David Atkinson, Elphinstone Institute, 2004,
    pp. 431–40.
Douglas, Sheila, editor. Come Gie's a Sang: 73 Traditional Scottish Songs. Hardie Press, 1995.
Douglas, Sheila, editor. The King o the Black Art and Other Folk Tales. Aberdeen UP, 1987.
Douglas, Sheila. Last of the Tinsmiths: The Life of Willie MacPhee. Birlinn, 2006.
Douglas, Sheila. "Narrative in Traveller Scotland." Beech et al., pp. 49–57.
Douglas, Sheila, editor. The Sang's the Thing: Voices from Lowland Scotland. Polygon, 1992.
DSL Online. Dictionaries of the Scots Language, https:/dsl.ac.uk. [An online resource compris-
    ing the 22 volumes of A Dictionary of the Older Scottish Tongue and the Scottish National
    Dictionary, plus the 2005 supplement to the Scottish National Dictionary.]
Fenton, Alexander, and Margaret A. Mackay. "A History of Ethnology in Scotlalnd." An
    Introduction to Scottish Ethnology, edited by Alexander Fenton and Margaret A. Mackay,
    John Donald, 2013, pp. 49–70.
Freedman, Jean R. Peggy Seeger: A Life of Music, Love, and Politics. U of Illinois P, 2017.
Gatherer, Nigel. Songs and Ballads of Dundee. John Donald, 1986.
Gentleman, Hugh, and Susan Swift. Scotland's Travelling People: Problems and Solutions. H.M.S.O.,
    1971.
Gibson, Corey. The Voice of the People: Hamish Henderson and Scottish Cultural Politics.
    Edinburgh UP, 2015.
Gillies, Anne Lorne. Songs of Gaelic Scotland. Birlinn, 2010.
Gmelch, George. The Irish Tinkers: The Urbanization of an Itinerant People. Cummings, 1977.
Gmelch, Sharon. Nan: The Life of an Irish Travelling Woman. Norton, 1986.
Gmelch, Sharon Bohn, and George Gmelch. Irish Travellers: The Unsettled Life. Indiana UP, 2014.
Goffman, Erving. The Presentation of Self in Everyday Life. U of Edinburgh Social Science
    Research Centre, 1956.
Gower, Herschel. "Jeannie Robertson: Portrait of a Traditional Singer." Scottish Studies, vol. 12,
    part 2, 1968, pp. 113–26.
Grant, I. F. Highland Folk Ways. Routledge, 1961.
Hall, Peter A. "Scottish Tinker Songs." Folk Music Journal, vol. 3, no. 1, 1975, pp. 41–62.
Halliwell, James Orchard. Nursery Rhymes of England. 2nd ed., London: John Russell Smith, 1843.
Hand, Owen F. "The Folk-Song Revival in Scotland." Beech et al., pp. 405–11.
Harker, Ben. Class Act: The Cultural and Political Life of Ewan MacColl. Pluto Press, 2007.
Henderson, Hamish. Alias MacAlias: Writings on Songs, Folk and Literature. Polygon, 1992.
    [2nd edition, 2004.]
Henderson, Hamish. "Bynames among the Tinkers." Scottish Studies, vol. 5, 1962, pp. 95–96.
    [Reprinted in Henderson, Alias MacAlias, pp. 231–32.]

Henderson, Hamish. "Folk-Songs and Music from the Berryfields of Blair." Henderson, *Alias MacAlias*, pp. 101–3. [Published originally as the sleeve notes to the record album of that name, 1962.]

Hendry, Ian D., and Graham Stephen, editors. *Scotsgate: Rhymes, Legends and Traditions*. Oliver and Boyd, 1982.

Hillers, Barbara. "Storytelling and the International Folktale in Scotland." Beech et al., pp. 153–70.

Howitt, Mary. *Sketches of Natural History, or, Songs of Animal Life*. London: T. Nelson, 1873.

Huntington, Gale, and Lani Herrmann, editors. *Sam Henry's Songs of the People*. U of Georgia P, 1990.

Ives, Edward D. *Joe Scott: The Woodsman-Songmaker*. U of Illinois P, 1978.

Keet-Black, Janet. *Gypsies of Britain*. Shire Publications, 2013.

Kennedy, Peter, editor. *Folksongs of Britain and Ireland*. Oak Publications, 1975.

Kroeber, Isidore. *Ishi in Two Worlds: A Biography of the Last Wild Indian in North America*. U of California P, 2004. [First published 1961.]

Laws, G. Malcolm. *American Balladry from British Broadsides*. American Folklore Society, 1957.

Leitch, Roger, editor. *The Book of Sandy Stewart*. Scottish Academic Press, 1988.

Leitch, Roger, and Christopher Smith. "Archaeology and Ethnohistory of Cave Dwelling in Scotland." *Scottish Studies*, vol. 31, 1992–1993, pp. 101–8.

Lindahl, Carl, editor. *American Folktales from the Collections of the Library of Congress*. 2 vols. M. E. Sharpe, 2004.

Macaulay, Cathlin. "Dipping into the Well: Scottish Oral Tradition Online." *Oral Tradition*, vol. 27, no. 1, 2012, pp. 171–86.

MacColl, Ewan, and Peggy Seeger. *Till Doomsday in the Afternoon: The Folklore of a Family of Scots Travellers, the Stewarts of Blairgowrie*. Manchester UP, 1986.

MacColl, Ewan, and Peggy Seeger. *Travellers' Songs from England and Scotland*. Routledge, 1977.

MacDougall, James. *Highland Fairy Legends*, introduction by Alan Bruford. D. S. Brewer, 1978. [First published 1910.]

MacLean, Ishbel. "The Pearl Fishers." *Odyssey: Voices from Scotland's Recent Past, The Second Collection*, edited by Billy Kay, Polygon, 1982, pp. 57–63.

MacLellan, Lauchie. *Brigh an Òrain = A Story in Every Song*, translated and edited by John Shaw, MacGill/Queen's UP, 2000.

MacNeil, Joe Neil. *Tales until Dawn: The World of a Cape Breton Gaelic Storyteller*, translated and edited by John Shaw. MaGill/Queen's UP, 1987.

McCarthy, William Bernard, editor. *Jack in Two Worlds: Contemporary North American Tales and Their Tellers*. North Carolina UP, 1994.

McCormick, Andrew. *The Tinkler-Gypsies*. 2nd ed. John Menzies, 1907.

McKean, Thomas A. *Hebridean Song-Maker: Iain MacNeacail of the Isle of Skye*. Polygon, 1997.

McNaughtan, Adam, editor. "Hamish Henderson." *Tocher*, vol. 7, no. 43, 1991, pp. 1–11.

McNaughtan, Adam. "The Folk Revival in Scotland." *The People's Past: Scottish Folk, Scottish History*, edited by Edward J. Cowan, Polygon, 1980, pp. 191–205.

Meek, Donald E. "Gaelic Language and Literature in Argyll." *The Argyll Book*, edited by Donald Omand, Birlinn, 2006, pp. 232–42. [First published 2004.]

Munro, Ailie. *The Folk Music Revival in Scotland*. Kahn & Averill, 1984. [With an accompanying cassette, *Songs from The Folk Music Revival in Scotland*. Glasgow: Scotsoun SSC 076;

rev edition published as *The Democratic Muse: Folk Music Revival in Scotland*. Kahn & Averill, 1996.]

Munro, Ailie. "Lizzie Higgins, and the Oral Transmission of Ten Child Ballads." *Scottish Studies*, vol. 14, part 2, 1970, pp. 155–88.

Neat, Timothy. "Duncan Williamson, Argyllshire Traveller." *The Voice of the Bard: Living Poets and Ancient Tradition in the Highlands and Islands of Scotland*, by Timothy Neat with John MacInnes, Canongate, 1999, pp. 237–67.

Neat, Timothy. *Hamish Henderson: A Biography*. 2 vols. Polygon, 2007–2009.

Neat, Timothy. *The Summer Walkers*. Canongate, 1996.

Niles, John D. "Context and Loss in Scottish Ballad Tradition." *Western Folklore*, vol. 45, no. 2, 1986, pp. 83–106.

Niles, John D., editor. "From Word to Print—and Beyond." Special issue of *Western Folklore*, vol. 72, no. 3, 2013.

Niles, John D. *Homo Narrans: The Poetics and Anthropology of Oral Literature*. U of Pennsylvania P, 1999.

Niles, John D. "Orality." *The Cambridge Companion to Textual Scholarship*, edited by Neil Fraistat and Julia Flanders, Cambridge UP, 2013, pp. 205–23.

Niles, John D. "Orality." *The Oxford Encyclopedia of Literary Theory*, Oxford UP, 2019, https://oxfordre.com/literature/page/literary-theory/the-oxford-encyclopedia-of-literary-theory.

Okely, Judith. *The Traveller-Gypsies*. Cambridge UP, 1983.

Olson, Ian A. "Bothy Ballads and Song." Beech et al., pp. 322–59.

Olson, Ian A. "Scottish Contemporary Traditional Music and Song." Beech et al., pp. 379–404.

Omand, Donald, editor. *The Argyll Book*. Birlinn, 2006. [First published 2004.]

Opie, Iona and Peter. *The Oxford Dictionary of Nursery Rhymes*. Clarendon, 1951.

Ord, John. *The Bothy Songs and Ballads of Aberdeen, Banff and Moray, Angus, and the Mearns*. A. Gardner, 1930. [Reprinted as *Ord's Bothy Songs and Ballads*, introduction by Alexander Fenton, John Donald, 1995.]

Philip, Neil. *The Penguin Book of English Folktales*. Penguin, 1992.

Porter, James. "The Turriff Family of Fetterangus: Society, Learning, Creation and Recreation of Traditional Song." *Folk Life*, vol. 16, no. 1, 1978, pp. 5–26.

Porter, James, and Herschel Gower. *Jeannie Robertson: Emergent Singer, Transformative Voice*. U of Tennessee P, 1995.

Powell, Bob. "Scotland's Open-Air Museums." *An Introduction to Scottish Ethnology*, edited by Alexander Fenton and Margaret A. Mackay, John Donald, 2013, pp. 126–39.

Rehfisch, F., and A. Rehfisch. "Scottish Travellers or Tinkers." *Gypsies, Tinkers and Other Travellers*, Academic Press, 1975, pp. 271–83.

Robertson, Stanley. *Exodus to Alford*. Balnain Books, 1988.

Robertson, Stanley. *Reek Roon a Camp Fire: A Collection of Ancient Tales*. Birlinn, 2009.

Robinson, Mairi, editor. *The Concise Scots Dictionary*. Aberdeen UP, 1987. [First published 1985.]

Ross, Anne. *The Folklore of the Scottish Highlands*. Rowman and Littlefield, 1976.

Schutz, Alfred. "The Stranger: An Essay in Social Psychology." *Collected Papers*, vol. 2: *Studies in Social Theory*, Nijhoff, 1967, pp. 91–105.

Scott, Walter. *Minstrelsy of the Scottish Border*. 3 vols. Kelso, Scotland: James Ballantyne, 1802–1803.

Scottish Voices. An online publication of the University of Wisconsin Digital Collections Center, https://digital.library.wisc.edu/1711.dl/ScottishVoices.

Shaw, John. "Oral Traditions/Folklore of Argyll." *The Argyll Book*, edited by Donald Omond, Birlinn, 2006, pp. 213–22.

Shaw, John. "Storytellers in Scotland: Context and Function." Beech et al., pp. 28–48.

Shuldham-Shaw, Patrick, and Emily B. Lyle, editors. *The Greig-Duncan Folk Song Collection.* 8 vols. Aberdeen UP, 1981–2002.

Smith, Donald. *Storytelling Scotland: A Nation in Narrative.* Polygon, 2001.

Smith, Jess. *Jessie's Journey: Autobiography of a Traveller Girl.* Mercat Press, 2002. [Reprinted by Birlinn, 2008.]

Smith, Jess. *Tales from the Tent: Jessie's Journey Continues.* Birlinn, 2008.

Smith, Jess. *Tears for a Tinker: Jessie's Journey Concludes.* Birlinn, 2009.

Stewart, Elizabeth. *Up Yon Wild and Lonely Glen: Travellers' Songs, Stories, and Tunes of the Fetterangus Stewarts,* compiled and edited by Alison McMorland, UP of Mississippi, 2012.

Stewart, Katharine. *Crofts and Crofting.* William Blackwood, 1980.

Stewart, Sheila. *Pilgrims of the Mist: The Stories of Scotland's Travelling People.* Birlinn, 2008.

Stewart, Sheila. *Queen amang the Heather: The Life of Belle Stewart.* Birlinn, 2006.

Stewart, Sheila. *A Traveller's Life.* Birlinn, 2011.

Szwed, John F. *Alan Lomax: The Man Who Recorded the World.* New York: Viking Penguin, 2010.

Thompson, Francis. *Crofting Years.* Luath Press, 1984.

Uther, Hans-Jörg. *The Types of International Folktales: A Classification and Bibliography, Based on the System of Antti Aarne and Stith Thompson.* 3 vols. Academia Scientiarum Fennica, 2004.

West, Gary. *Voicing Scotland: Folk, Culture, Nation.* Luath, 2012.

Whyte, Betsy. *Red Rowans and Wild Honey.* Corgi Books, 1991. [First published by Canongate, 1990; 2nd ed. published by Birlinn, 2000.]

Whyte, Betsy. *The Yellow on the Broom: The Early Days of a Traveller Woman.* Chambers, 1979. [Reprinted by Birlinn, 2001.]

Williamson, Duncan. *The Broonie, Silkies and Fairies: Travellers' Tales.* Canongate, 1985; Harmony Books, 1987.

Williamson, Duncan. *Don't Look Back, Jack! Scottish Traveller Tales.* Canongate, 1990.

Williamson, Duncan. *Fireside Tales of the Traveller Children.* Canongate, 1983. [2nd ed. 1985; expanded 3rd ed. published by Birlinn, edited by Linda Williamson, 2009.]

Williamson, Duncan. *The Horsieman: Memories of a Traveller 1928–1958.* Canongate, 1994. [2nd ed. published by Birlinn, 2008.]

Williamson, Duncan. *The King and the Lamp: Scottish Traveller Tales.* Canongate, 2000.

Williamson, Duncan. *Land of the Seal People,* edited by Linda Williamson. Birlinn, 2010.

Williamson, Duncan. *May the Devil Walk behind Ye! Scottish Traveller Tales.* Rev. ed., Canongate, 1990. [First published 1989.]

Williamson, Duncan. *Tales of the Seal People.* Canongate, 1992.

Williamson, Duncan. *Tell Me a Story for Christmas: Traveller Tales by Duncan Williamson.* Canongate, 1987.

Williamson, Duncan, and Linda Williamson. *The Genie and the Fisherman and Other Tales from the Travelling People.* Cambridge UP, 1991.

Williamson, Duncan, and Linda Williamson. *The King and the Lamp: Scottish Traveller Tales.* Canongate, 2000.

Williamson, Duncan, and Linda Williamson. *A Thorn in the King's Foot: Folktales of the Scottish Travelling People.* Penguin, 1987.

Williamson, Linda. "Narrative Singing among the Scots Travellers: A Study of Strophic Variation in Ballad Performance." Unpublished PhD thesis, University of Edinburgh, 1985.

Williamson, Linda. "What Storytelling Means to a Traveller." *ARV: Scandinavian Yearbook of Folklore*, vol. 37, 1981, pp. 69–76.

Yates, Mike, editor. *Traveller's Joy: Songs of English and Scottish Travellers and Gypsies 1965–2005.* English Folk Dance and Song Society, 2006. [With accompanying CD.]

ARTICLES IN THE JOURNAL *TOCHER* FEATURING INDIVIDUAL
SCOTTISH TRAVELLERS

"Jeannie Robertson as a Storyteller." *Tocher*, vol. 1, no. 6, 1972, pp. 169–78.

"Jimmy McBeath." *Tocher*, vol. 2, no. 12, 1973, pp. 141–58.

"Davie Stewart." *Tocher*, vol. 2, no. 15, 1974, pp. 262–80.

"The Stewarts of Blair." *Tocher*, vol. 3, no. 21, 1976, pp. 165–88.

"Bessie Whyte." *Tocher*, vol. 3, no. 23, 1976, pp. 249–76.

"Duncan Williamson." *Tocher*, vol. 5, no. 33, 1979, pp. 141–87.

"Stanley Robertson." *Tocher*, vol. 6, no. 40, 1986, pp. 170–224.

"Willie MacPhee." *Tocher*, vol. 7, no. 44, 1992, pp. 78–90.

"Jimmy Williamson." *Tocher*, vol. 8, no. 56, 2000, pp. 371–87.

SELECTED DISCOGRAPHY

Barry, Margaret. *I Sang through the Fairs.* CD. Rounder Records 11661-1774-2. The Alan Lomax Collection, 1998. [Based on field recordings dating from the 1950s.]

Bothy Ballads: Music from the Northeast. CD. Scottish Tradition Series, vol. 1, 1971. [Reissued on CD as Greentrax Recordings CDTRAX 9001, 1993.]

Chokit on a Tattie: Children's Songs and Rhymes. CD. Scottish Tradition Series, vol. 22. Greentrax Recordings CDTRAX9022, 2006.

Duncan, Jock. *Ye Shine Whaur Ye Stand!* CD. Springthyme Records SPRCD 1039, 1996.

Festival at Blairgowrie. LP. Topic 12T181, 1967.

Folksongs and Music from the Berryfields of Blair. LP. Prestige/International INT 25016, 1962.

Henderson, Hamish. *Hamish Henderson Collects.* CD. 2 vols. Kyloe Records, 2005–2006.

Higgins, Lizzie. *In Memory of Lizzie Higgins 1929–1993.* Double CD. Musical Traditions MTCD337-8, 2006.

MacBeath, Jimmy. *Wild Rover No More.* LP. Topic Records 12T173, 1967.

McNaughtan, Adam. *Words, Words, Words.* LP, 1993. [Reissued as part of the double CD *The Words That I Used to Know.* Cocklenzie, East Lothian: Greentrax Recordings CDTRAX 195D, 2000.]

The Muckle Sangs: Classic Scots Ballads. Double LP. Tangent Records TNGM 119/D. Scottish Tradition Series, vol. 5, 1975. [Reissued on CD as Greentrax Recordings CDTRAX 9005, 2000.]

Reid, Jim. *I Saw the Wild Geese Flee.* Cassette, 1984. [Reissued as CD. Springthyme Records SPRCD 1015, 1996.]

Robertson, Jeannie. *The Queen among the Heather.* CD. Rounder Records. 11661-1720-2, The Alan Lomax Collection, 1998.

Robertson, Jeannie. *Scottish Ballads and Folk Songs by Jeannie Robertson, "World's Greatest Folk Singer."* LP. Prestige/International INT 13006. No date.

Robertson, Stanley. *The College Boy: Family Gems and Jewels from the Traveller Tradition,* edited by Ian Russell and Thomas A. McKean. Double CD. Elphinstone Institute EICD 004, 2009.

Robertson, Stanley. *Rum, Scum, Scoosh! Songs and Stories of an Aberdeen Childhood.* Double CD. Elphinstone Institute EICD 003, 2006.

Songs and Ballads from Perthshire: Field Recordings of the 1950s, edited by Maurice Fleming. CD. Scottish Tradition Series, vol. 24. Greentrax CDTRAX 9024, 2011.

Stewart, Belle. *Belle Stewart, Queen Among the Heather.* LP Topic Records 12TS307, 1976. [Reissued on CD by Greentrax Recordings as CDTRAX 114, 1998.]

Stewart, Elizabeth. *Binnorie: Songs, Ballads, and Tunes.* Double CD. Elphinstone Institute EICD 002, 2004.

Stewart, Lucy. *Lucy Stewart: Traditional Singer from Aberdeenshire, Scotland,* edited by Kenneth Goldstein. LP. Folkways album FW 03519, 1961. [Available as a custom CD.]

Stewart, Sheila. *From the Heart of the Tradition.* CD. Topic Records TSCD515, 2000.

The Stewarts of Blair: Traditional Ballads, Songs and Pipe Music by One of Scotland's Great Singing Families. LP. Topic Records 12T13, 1965. [Reissued on CD as Ossian OSS CD 96. No date.]

Strachan, John. *Songs from Aberdeenshire.* CD. Rounder Records 82161-1835-2. The Alan Lomax Collection, 1998. [Based on field recordings dating from 1957.]

The Travelling Stewarts. LP. Topic Records 12T179, 1969.

Turriff, Jane. *Singin' Is Ma Life.* CD. Springthyme Records SPRCD 1038, 1996.

Williamson, Duncan. *Mary and the Seal and Other Folktales: Traditional Storytelling by Duncan Williamson.* Cassette. Springthyme Records SPRC 1019, 1987.

Williamson, Duncan. *Put Another Log on the Fire: Songs and Tunes from a Scots Traveller.* Cassette. Veteran Tapes VT128, 1994. [Also available digitally as VT128CDR.]

Yates, Mike, editor. *Travellers' Tales: Songs, Stories and Ballads from Scottish Travellers.* CD. 2 vols. Kyloe Records 100 & 101, 2002.

See also the books with an accompanying CD or cassette; these are listed in section 1 of the Bibliography under Bruford and MacDonald; Munro; and Yates.

INDEX

References to illustrations appear in **bold**.

American Folklife Center, 312

animals, 142–44, **146**, **147**, 220, 221–22; as means of education, 145–46; as pets, 141–42, 146–48. *See also* animal tales; horses

animal tales, 217, 220, 221–22, 260

Argyll, 269–70. *See also* coastline of Argyll

Auchindrain township and museum, 287

Azadovskii, Mark, 307

"Bag o Salt, A" (story), 223, 304

bagpipes, 50–52, 56, 206–7, **206**, 243–45, **243**, **244**, 302; as treasured possession, 283

"Ball of Kirriemuir, The" (song), 291–92

"Banks of Red Roses" (song), 132–33, 294

basketmaking, 87–90, **90**, 91–95, **94**, 265, 288, 289; making a slipe, 89; peeling willows, 288, 289

Bennett, Margaret, 286

"Berryfields of Blair, The" (song), 302

"Big Jimmy Drummond" (song), 194–97, 300

bird song (imitated), 203–5, **203**, **204**, 302

Blairgowrie, Perthshire, as major meeting place, 99–100, 289–90. *See also* "Berryfields of Blair, The" (song)

"Bogie's Bonnie Belle" (song), 109–11, 292

Boguki, Peter, 6

"Bonnie One" (song), 35–37

bothy ballads, 107, 109–11, 291

bothy lifeways, 107–8, 109–11, 112–14, 291, 292–93. *See also* farms and farm life

"Boy and the Horn Spoon, The" (story), 152–54

Braid, Donald, 9, 10n4, 152n23, 298

broadside ballads, 189–91, 294, 297, 299, 309

Bruford, Alan, 22, 218, 315n3

burker tales, 305

Campbell, David, 9–10, 270, 281, 287, 290, 293, 294, 297, 303

Campbell, Thomas (poet), 264, 308

Campbell of Airds, Alastair, 279

cant (Scottish Travellers'), 15, 91, 137–38, 139, 194–95, 295, 316, 323

cantefables, 199–203, 301–2

caves, used as shelters or dwellings, 29, 31, **32**, 33, 279

ceilidh, 132, 177, 178, 179, 180, 199, 251, 260, 276–77; ceilidh house, 277

changelings, 295–96

childbirth, 27, 31–32, 279; death of mother in, 283

childhood, 143–44, 158, 211–13, 214, 217, 284; corporal punishment of children, 284; hanseling children, 286. *See also* children; children's songs and games; schooling

children, 141–42, 142–54, 163, **178**, **216**, **237**, **240**, **241**, **243**, **246**, **247**, **248**; adopted, 150–54; with disabilities, 148–49; and sex education, 145–46; taken away by authorities, 144–45. *See also* childhood;

ABOUT THE AUTHOR

John D. Niles is the author of *Homo Narrans: The Poetics and Anthropology of Oral Literature* (1999) and a number of other books relating to early medieval literature and the theory and practice of oral narrative. Before his retirement in 2011, he taught at Brandeis University, the University of California, Berkeley, and the University of Wisconsin–Madison, where he was the Frederic G. Cassidy Professor of Humanities.

Printed in Great Britain
by Amazon

46459479R00205